A Reader in

HISTORICAL
AND COMPARATIVE
LINGUISTICS

A Reader in
HISTORICAL
AND COMPARATIVE
LINGUISTICS

ALLAN R. KEILER
University of Michigan

HOLT, RINEHART AND WINSTON, INC.
New York   Chicago   San Francisco   Atlanta
Dallas   Montreal   Toronto   London   Sydney

PREFACE

This reader is offered as a survey of the most important areas of research in comparative and historical linguistics. In point of view it goes back no further than the contributions inspired and made possible by the neogrammarians of the last decades of the nineteenth century. Important examples of the work that has developed as a part of generative or transformational theory of the last several decades are included. This chronological segment of historical and comparative linguistics is less arbitrary and disparate than it might appear. Many of the same questions and, indeed, results, if one considers only the theoretical and speculative basis of the latter, are common to the earliest and latest segments of this sequence. They were interrupted mainly by the preoccupation of American linguists during the period from 1940 to 1960 with the logic and methodology of procedures of reconstruction, to a large extent part of the general syndrome during this time of the search for effective discovery procedures. To take one example, Vendryès' early discussion of sound change has the same end as Kiparsky's paper included here and written some forty years later. The central problem of both is the nonarbitrariness and universally restricted character of sound change. Vendryès' account seems more speculative than theoretically motivated today, but it is part of the same line of research as some current investigations into the nature of sound change.

I have divided this summary into five sections, with the articles in each section following one another chronologically. The first two sections, Linguistic Reconstruction and Theory of Sound Change, might be taken as the principal and interrelated subjects of historical linguistics. The last two parts, Dialectology and Universals and Typology, are the central areas of comparative linguistics. There are, to be sure, common themes and interrelated problems. To take another example, and to paraphrase Jakobson, one's knowledge of linguistic universals, both synchronic and diachronic, must be taken as a guide to the judiciousness of alternative reconstructions. Work in

v

language reconstruction, therefore, must be considered in the light of Jakobson's paper on typology.

I have also tried to preserve some balance between theoretical discussions and detailed linguistic analyses. In most cases the articles included here, in various degrees, strike this kind of balance. In other cases, healthy juxtapositions with this end in mind are possible. Whatmough's dissection of some of the methodological weaknesses inherent in the comparative method can be read with particular profit when put beside Hall's exploitation of comparative methodology in the area of Romance reconstruction. Juxtapositions that provide alternative points of view have been included, when meaningful, in each section. Saporta's approach to dialectology is an important partner to the common assumptions of Weinreich and Labov in this area. In short, I have tried to include here the kind of flexibility and adaptability that the more rigid framework of a book with a single point of view often lacks.

My appreciation to the authors and publishers represented in this reader is expressed with each selection. I must here indicate my gratitude to Holt, Rinehart and Winston, and especially to Jane Ross, Lester Sheinis, Wyatt James, and Elaine Romano for their patient and careful attention to a difficult manuscript in all of its phases. I am also grateful to Judy Rosenberg, who urged me to produce such a reader and who encouraged and counseled me as it was being done.

Madison, Wisconsin   A.R.K.
August 1971

CONTENTS

A Reader in
HISTORICAL
AND COMPARATIVE
LINGUISTICS

Part I
LINGUISTIC RECONSTRUCTION

1

GENETIC RELATIONSHIP AMONG LANGUAGES*[1]

H. A. Gleason, Jr.

That certain pairs of languages show relationships has long been known. Comparative linguistics arose to explain and exploit these relationships. It has developed methods of some power and achieved some important results. However, comparative linguistics has been characterized in recent years by rather scant discussion of theoretical and methodological questions. In the meantime demand for its results is increasing rapidly (e.g. by anthropologists) and the possibility of new departures in method has arisen. I propose to formulate a part of its basic theory in such a way that it can be tied in intimately with certain developing methods which may fall within the purview of this symposium.

1. We can assume that resemblances between languages can be of at least four origins: 1. They may be reflections of certain *language universals*. Thus it is commonly assumed that the rather frequent occurrence of items like [mama] for 'mother' may be conditioned in some way by some general feature of the process of language learning. 2. They may be *analytic artifacts*. That both Latin and English are considered to have a present tense may be due to the fact that Latin provided the model for English grammar. The English "present tense" was established on a scant basis under the strong stimulus of the model. Field linguists aim at describing a language in terms of its own structure. They never quite succeed, and occasionally they fail miserably. Similarities in their results can be mere reflections of their methods or their prejudices. 3. Resemblances may be the result of mere *chance*. 4. Similarities may result from *historic connections* between the languages. Linguists commonly distinguish, sometimes rather too sharply, between two

*Reprinted with the permission of the author and of the publisher, The American Mathematical Society, from the *Proceedings of Symposia in Applied Mathematics*, Copyright © 1961, Volume 12, pp. 179–189.

[1]This work is supported in part by the National Science Foundation.

subtypes: inheritance and borrowing. Thus the similarity between English *father* and Latin *pater* is an inheritance similarity, since both are assumed to have a direct and continuous descent from a generally similar word in the ancient language (proto-Indo-European) from which English and Latin both descend. *Paternity* and *paternitas* show a borrowing similarity, since we know that the English word is derived directly from the Latin.

The interest and usefulness of these four classes of resemblances are quite different, and the first task of the comparativist must be to distinguish them as clearly as possible and assign observed resemblances to the proper type. Resemblances rooted in language universals are of great interest in developing a general theory of language, but of little specific historical significance. Analytic artifacts are of little or no linguistic interest, but their control is of crucial importance in any careful comparative work. This can be accomplished by critique of sources, which, though commonly neglected and seldom discussed, is one of the essential techniques of comparative linguistics. Chance resemblances are of no interest, except as the linguist wishes to learn better how to recognize them and to exclude them from further consideration. Since they may bulk large, statistical techniques may be of considerable importance. Similarities due to historic connection are of great interest, since they can yield evidence from which historical reconstructions can be made. In practice, comparative linguistics restricts itself largely to attempting to identify and interpret similarities due to historic connection. It therefore marches closely on historical linguistics, and these commonly become almost indistinguishable.

2. Comparative linguistic work normally starts with vocabulary. This is most simply done by matching word lists on the basis of glosses for the several items in some third language. Thus we might compare Lamba[2] *iŋgoma* with Ganda *eŋŋoma* on the basis that they occur in the word lists opposite the English gloss 'drum'. In any pair of word lists some word-pairs may be resemblant, as that just cited. But there will also always be nonresemblant pairs as Lamba *inyati*, Ganda *embogo* 'buffalo'. Comparative linguistics, in the preliminary stages, concerns itself only with those word-pairs that are in some sense resemblant.

Linguists have commonly been uneasy about relying on vocabulary. They consider vocabulary to be the least significant part of a language. It may be very unstable and vary widely from speaker to speaker and situation to situation. Phonology and grammar are more central. Yet there are certain crucial advantages of vocabulary over other sectors of language for compara-

---

[2]Lamba and Ganda forms are from : C. M. Doke, *English-Lamba Vocabulary*, 1933; E. O. Ashton, E. M. K. Mulira, E. G. M. Ndawula, and A. N. Tucker, *A LuGanda Grammar*, 1954.

tive work. 1. Vocabulary items are relatively easily found and easily stated. 2. There can readily be obtained a sizeable sample of word-pairs (or glosses that will produce word-pairs) which come close to being independent of each other. This is possible because the vocabulary of a language is only partially structured. It is rather easy to avoid items likely to be structurally connected, or to detect and discard them when they do appear. Other sectors of language are more tightly structured, and the connections are sometimes less easily seen, so that statistically usable samples are very much harder to obtain. This either immensely complicates statistical reasoning or renders it impossible. Hence it is difficult to detect chance resemblances in other more central sectors of language. 3. Gloss lists can be selected in such a way as to bias our results in certain desirable ways. For example, word resemblances due to language universals are particularly common in a few specific meanings (e.g. child words for parents) and apparently negligible elsewhere. By eliminating such glosses, this source of resemblances can be minimized to the point of insignificance, and hence be safely overlooked in preliminary comparative work. Or again, the balance in frequency between similarities due to inheritance and those due to borrowing can be quite different in different sectors of the vocabulary. A list of glosses likely to produce a maximum proportion of inheritance similarities and a minimum of borrowing similarities is known as the "basic vocabulary." This is the result of no mystic property of any otherwise definable set of items, but merely a statement of cumulated past experience. Using such a gloss list, the finding of pairs similar by inheritance is greatly facilitated. Using a strongly "non-basic vocabulary," the other type may emerge more clearly. Using the two contrastively may differentiate the two types quite sharply.[3]

   3. Starting with a set of word-pairs drawn largely from the "basic vocabulary," the linguist attempts to sort out word-pairs that seem likely to be resemblant because of inheritance. He does this by attempting to find a set of criteria of similarity which is of the appropriate kind and so tight that it will pass relatively few word-pairs showing merely chance similarity, but which will, nevertheless, pass a considerable number of word-pairs. If this can be found it is said to define the word-pairs as *cognates*. The criteria themselves are stateable in terms of a set of equations known as *correspondences*. A correspondence is a statement that in a certain environment a given phoneme in one language will correspond—if the words are cognate—to a stated phoneme in another language. Thus Lamba *o* corresponds under most conditions to Ganda *o*. Lamba *g* corresponds to Ganda ŋ when and only when it follows ŋ and precedes some nasal (e.g. *m*) later in the same

   [3]An excellent discussion of a closely related problem can be found in: I. Dyen, *The Ngaju-Dayak 'Old Speech Stratum'*, Lg. 32: 83–87, 1956.

word. Lamba *iŋgoma* is said to be cognate with Ganda *eŋgoma* because every phoneme in each matches a phoneme in the other by some such rule, the order being preserved. (In other instances the order may be deformed in some regular and stateable manner.) Lamba *inyati* and Ganda *embogo* are not cognate because for most of the phonemes no such correspondences can be established.

The first step in comparative linguistics, then, after a sample of word-pairs has been obtained is to find in it a set of cognates and a set of correspondences, each characterizing and defining the other. Traditionally this has been done by inspection and re-inspection, guess and check, by a competent and experienced linguist. The work may be tedious and exacting.

4. Operational criteria used in discovering correspondences and cognates are manifold, but most fall into two general types. The first of these may be called *phonetic plausibility*. In some cases this means nothing more than merely sounding alike. For example, anyone who knows both English and German is inevitably aware of certain word-pairs which sound much alike. Such are possible cognates, and on further investigation some, but not all, pairs will prove actually to be cognates. On a more sophisticated level, phonetic plausibility may also serve to identify certain pairs of sounds as possible correspondences which are not phonetically similar. There are many known cases of *k (i.e., k in some proto-language) becoming by regular change $č$, $š$, s or g, or remaining k. Any two of these resultant sounds might, as a matter of phonetic plausibility, be considered as a possible correspondence since they might be derivable from *k. Occasionally, cases that an experienced linguist would call phonetically plausible seem to the layman quite unlikely. Thus Nyoro[4] -*gita* and Sotho -*fura* 'fat, oil', I would judge to be phonetically plausible, however unlike they may seem to the average observer.

In any but the most superficial type, phonetic plausibility may be a very complex matter. It is in essence a distillation of the linguist's experience, personal and second hand, with a wide variety of languages. In the case just cited, it includes a certain amount of knowledge not only of language in general, but also of Bantu languages in particular: that *f* may correspond to velar stops, that *i* and *u* may interchange in the situations in which *f* does so correspond, that in some languages voice is historically of no significance where the next syllable has *t*, and that *t* and *r* may correspond. It follows that any precise formulation of phonetic plausibility may be quite difficult,

---

[4]Nyoro and Sotho forms are from: M. B. Davis, *A luNyoro-luNyankole-English and English-luNyoro-luNyankole Dictionary*, 1952, A. Mabille and H. Dieterlen, *Southern Sotho-English Dictionary*, rev. ed., 1950.

though certain gross features may be so stated. The fullest use of the criteria of phonetic plausibility must, for some time, remain the function of a trained, experienced, and imaginative linguist.

5. The second general type of criterion is that of *recurrence.* Traditionally this has not been handled particularly well. The usual procedure is to go through a pair of word-lists and select all those word-pairs which look interesting. These are selected in part on the basis of phonetic plausibility, and in part on the basis of recurrence of phoneme-pairs. After this subjectively selected sample has been gathered, it is then examined carefully for recurrences, and those which are found are considered as tentative correspondences. These are checked by another, more complex type of recurrence which can be designated as *co-occurrence.* If such tentative correspondences are found together in the same word-pairs in such a way that they account for all or nearly all of the phonemes of the words, they are considered established. This is a rather stringent requirement, and only this stringency saves much traditional comparative work from being seriously misled.

Both types of recurrence can be used in a more satisfactory way. But this will require the examination of samples of word-pairs which are statistically acceptable. This means, at least, that they must not be selected on the basis of what phoneme-pairs they contain. Criteria of recurrence should, therefore, be applied *before* rather than *after* criteria of phonetic plausibility. Since this application is basically a matter of counting within a sample and some rather elementary calculation, the criteria of recurrence can be applied by machine. There is thus the possibility that at least a major segment of the work of finding the cognates and correspondences can be programmed onto computers. To do so may expedite the work. But more important, such programming may make better use of certain criteria and thus actually improve the reliability of the procedures. In any case it will render parts, at least, of the work easily checkable.

6. In 1954 I found myself maneuvered into arguing that comparative reconstruction could be done by machine. This was a bit against my better judgment, but nevertheless it led me to make some tentative experiments. The first of these was rather elaborately designed and involved a great deal of statistical calculation. It worked, but chiefly it indicated that a much simpler procedure would suffice. After five experiments, the first report was given before the Yale Linguistics Club in 1955.[5] Since that time the method has been applied to a number of other pairs of languages. Certain complications have been found, and some of them successfully met, and the technique has

[5]H. A. Gleason, Jr., *A Procedural Technique for Comparative Reconstruction.* This paper has recently been duplicated and is available for limited distribution.

been improved in a number of details. These experiments were not restricted to one group of languages, but have involved, so far, Mayan, Bantu, Dravidian, Indic, and Romance languages.

All of the experiments have been done by hand-sorting. But throughout, the aim has been to design a procedure which can be fully programmed in advance, and which will, therefore, meet at least one requirement for a machine. Actual machine programming is probably now feasible, and presumably will soon be attempted.

As it now stands, the procedure does not do reconstruction, but it does do a major part of the work of finding cognates and correspondences. The input is a number (preferably over 500) of word-pairs matched by having similar glosses. The process sorts these word-pairs into three sets. One of these consists of word-pairs with extremely high probability of being cognates and establishing a set of correspondences of similar very high probability. Typically, this set is defined by having *every* phoneme in *every* word-pair accounted for in terms of one of the correspondences, and *every* correspondence recurring at least three times in the set. This is an extremely strong condition. As a result the set can be considered so thoroughly established that it requires no further attention until a very much later stage of the comparison. Even then the expectation is that very little emendation will be required. A second set consists of word-pairs showing so little prospect of being historically connected as to warrant no expenditure of effort until a very much later stage in the comparison. Even then it is highly unlikely that more than a very few pairs will ever be of any historical interest. The third set consists of word-pairs which show some evidence of being interesting, but which fall short of being established as cognates by the very stringent criteria through which the first set was selected. (Most match in part by the same correspondences as define the first set, but do not match throughout.) These need and warrant the attention of an experienced linguist. He will ordinarily be able to justify treating many of them as cognates with little trouble, since he can apply to them additional criteria not easily built into the machine program. Of those which cannot immediately be shown to be cognates, many will present problems of potentially great interest.

One experiment[6] will serve as an example. This started with 329 word-pairs in Jacaltec and Tzutuhil, two Mayan languages of Guatemala. The procedure divided this sample into three sets: 1. 59 word-pairs, each of which matched throughout in terms of 25 correspondences. Each correspondence was found in at least 3 word-pairs in the 59. One of these was *ṣanab šaxap'* 'sandal'. The correspondence *s š* occurs in 5 word-pairs in the set; *a a*

---

[6]This is the experiment reported on at the Yale Linguistics Club. The languages are quite closely related; otherwise, a starting sample of only 329 word-pairs might not have been adequate.

in 32; *n x* in 5; *b p'* in 6. These cognates and correspondences form a core of firmly established items for any further work. 2. A set of word-pairs which largely match by these established correspondences, but not entirely. Among them was *q'ab q'a*ᵓ 'arm', included because *q' q'* and *a a* were both firmly established by recurrence in the first set (in 10 and 32 word-pairs respectively), but *b* ᵓ was found in only two otherwise acceptable word-pairs. This, and many others, the linguist will feel adequately justified in accepting as cognates, even though they fall outside the definitions set up for the mechanical procedures. It also includes some word-pairs like *ṣil šilšil* 'cricket', in which *ṣil šil* would be totally matched. The linguist will have to judge whether the process of reduplication can appropriately be inserted into the rules relating cognates in these two languages. 3. A set of word-pairs approximately two-thirds of the original sample, in which none of these established correspondences are found, or where only one or two are found, and which accordingly show very little prospect of being cognate. Included are items such as *ṣoç t' ot'* 'snail' and *xolom wa*ᵓ 'head'.

What the mechanical procedure accomplishes, then, is to organize the raw data into such a form as to allow maximum efficiency in the utilization of trained linguistic manpower. It is not wasted by being applied to pairs which can be firmly established without it, or which show no prospects of being established by it, but can be concentrated on those only which show the sort of problems which require its special abilities.

7. The procedure operates by tabulating phoneme pairs at some position (usually initial) from the whole sample of word-pairs in a contingency table. Those phoneme-pairs in which observed frequency exceeds expected frequency are taken to indicate the possible presence of cognates, and all word-pairs showing them are selected. The process is repeated within this smaller sample using the phoneme-pairs in some other position (say post-initial). After a number of such selections (three seems in most cases the most feasible), all pairs in the selected sample are checked, and the rejected part of the sample is gone through for word-pairs that partially match. The correspondences are thus set up by recurrence in the same word-pairs.

An example[7] will show the effect of this. A set of word-pairs from Tamil and Kannada was put through the process. Afterwards every word-pair was checked by a Dravidian specialist who gave a judgment on each. He labeled 27% as cognates without complications, 12% as cognate with complications, 10% as loans (mostly from Sanskrit), 50% as unrelated, and 1% as unassignable. In the experiment the disposition of each pair at each

[7]This experiment was reported on in full before the Linguistic Summer School at Dehra Dun, India, in 1957. I am indebted to Dr. Bh. Krishnamurti of Andhra University for the classification of the word-pairs.

step had been noted. This permitted an analysis of the effect of each selection:

	Number in sample	Simple cognates	Unrelated
Original	714	27%	50%
After 1st sorting	360	50	17
After 2nd sorting	263	57	6
After 3rd sorting	143	79	0
After checking	100	95	0

Each step raised the percentage of simple cognates and lowered that of unrelated words. When the final selection was reached, all unrelated words had been excluded, but five non-cognates remained. These were common loans from Sanskrit which had been borrowed so early as to have undergone all applicable phonologic changes in the two languages. They, therefore, showed exactly the same relationship to their matches as inherited native words. For this reason they could be identified as loans only by certain additional information not provided to the machine (i.e., a knowledge of Sanskrit), and the machine would, therefore, be entirely correct in accepting them as cognates. We may consider the experiment a success. The remaining simple cognates (48% of those in the original sample), the complicated cognates, and the remaining loans, were mostly in the set selected to receive the linguist's attention. The finally rejected set consisted almost wholly of unrelated word-pairs.

8. The traditional approach starts with a more or less random searching for interesting-looking word-pairs. An experienced linguist can make effective use of any sort of dictionary, or any sort of word-list, matching a French gloss in one with a German gloss in another, or matching more or less synonymous but different glosses. He can detect similarities of part of one word with part of another, leaving the justification of this to a later step. The mechanical procedure starts by matching two word-lists. This is efficient only when there is a considerable amount of standardization in the glosses and their arrangement. In many languages, it is of utmost importance that affixes have been removed, and the forms of entry standardized. Much of the raw material usable under traditional procedures cannot be used in the mechanical technique except after rather laborious preparation. This is at the present time a very serious bottle-neck.

The second difficulty is that the procedure will not, at present, operate in all the situations in which it might be desirable. Since the program I have been using makes no use of phonetic plausibility, and since it applies the criteria of recurrence more strictly than traditional procedures, it is not surprising that it will not handle languages very remote from one another—languages where the evidence of relationship is rather scant and unobvious. Some will consider this a serious defect, but to do so is to be too severe. There is a tremendous quantity of such low-level work which needs to be done, and any small increase in efficiency may be decidedly worthwhile. This is particularly true in larger language families, since the labor of list preparation increases arithmetically with the number of languages, but the labor of comparison geometrically. Moreover, the present limitations of the method are not necessarily permanent. Certain types of phonetic plausibility could be built in—particularly those dealing with simple phonetic similarities, or with symmetries. Some more complex matching procedures can be developed.

9. Each cognate and each correspondence can be assumed to be of some evidential value for past language conditions in the group. Some at least of these features will contribute to the reconstruction of certain parts of a proto-language from which all the languages of the group may be assumed to have been descended. This immediately transforms the nature of the investigation from a synchronic comparison of languages to a diachronic reconstruction of history. Such reconstruction is generally the first objective beyond the mere finding of cognates and correspondences. However, another operation, usually left implicit, must intervene before successful reconstruction can proceed.

10. Reconstruction implies some framework within which to operate. Two models of language development are commonly contrasted. One, the *Wave hypothesis*, envisions any period in the history of a language family in terms of an array of contiguous speech forms subject to various mutual influences by which innovations anywhere in the whole area may diffuse, but only in stateable ways. The reconstruction of history would then be the reconstruction of one or more of these earlier stages and, from examination of the results of diffusion, the analysis of the relationships between the speech forms that controlled those processes. Such a model seems to have a very considerable similarity to empiric reality. But it provides us with no very clear operating procedures for the initial stages of reconstruction. The factors are too many and too complex. It seems very nearly impossible to derive results which are not, in most instances, highly ambiguous, and inaccessible to procedural checks.

11. A second model, the *Stammbaum hypothesis*, envisions the history of a language family as involving a number of splits. These are generally dichotomous, and have the effect of replacing one language by two, each of which is a continuation of the one replaced, and each of which thereafter proceeds to develop independently. This is certainly the less obvious of the

two models. Sharp separations are rarely observed, and total independence of adjacent languages seems almost inconceivable. But in spite of these difficulties, it is this model which provides operational procedures for the initial stages of reconstruction that prove workable and productive. Perhaps this paradox stems from the fact that in the preliminary stages of historical reconstruction we deal only with selected segments of language—precisely those segments which do work most nearly in the Stammbaum way—though on general examination of any language situation we are impressed most easily by the segments of languages which operate most nearly in the Wave hypothesis way. In any case, it does not seem that the two hypotheses are ultimately contradictory, since in actual practice each seems inevitably to require correction by the other.

12. The Stammbaum hypothesis is, then, the best basis—possibly the only workable basis—for the earliest stage of historical reconstruction. It provides a clear basis for my statement above that *some* cognate pairs may be of evidential value in reconstructing a proto-language behind any language group. The Stammbaum model sets up a language family in terms of a series of branchings, preferably dichotomous. Just beneath each branching is a proto-language. This proto-language is accessible to the linguist in two ways: By comparison of languages in each of the two branches above it, and by comparison of a language above it with a language (necessarily a proto-language) below it. Every cognate pair in the ultimate languages is evidence for some proto-language, but direct evidence for only one, i.e., that at the convergence point of the two branches. Only certain ones are therefore of evidential value for the deepest proto-language. False reconstruction can only be avoided by assigning each pair of cognates to the correct proto-language. This can in turn be done if a workable Stammbaum is found, and the processes of finding that Stammbaum and making the assignments are practically synonymous.

It follows that the reconstruction of a proto-language is not, as it is commonly formulated to be, the next step after finding cognates. Rather the next step must be the finding of a most probable genetic tree. Comparative linguistics needs procedures for this task. It is interesting to note that there has probably been less publication on this subject and less discussion in textbooks or linguistics courses of this process that any of the other steps in reconstruction. This has been the most poorly understood and least adequately handled stage in the work.

13. The evidence for selecting a suitable Stammbaum might reasonably be looked for in the same place that the evidence for over-all relationship is found: in comparable word-lists. The requirements are the same as mentioned above. In particular, we want an appreciable sample, the individual

items of which show considerable statistical independence. Much of the work has, in fact, traditionally been done with vocabulary, often by superficial inspection. It can be made more precise by counting and some elementary calculation. All such methods—there are several of them—can be designated as *lexicostatistical*.

The simplest, of course, is simply to count similarities and differences. The assumption seems natural that the common proto-language will be later for two languages with more similarities than for two languages with less. In some instances this may suffice to draw a Stammbaum. Recently the assumption has been advanced that with a certain section of the "basic vocabulary" there is a reasonable constant and empirically determinable change rate. This is the method of *glottochronology*.[8] It merely adds an approximate temporal dimensioning to the Stammbaum. The method was suggested by an analogy to C_{14} dating. But this analogy is not correct. The decay rate for each C_{14} atom may be considered identical with the average for all such atoms. But the decay rates of different items in the basic vocabulary vary widely.[9] The rate for the whole is an arithmetic average. It cannot be handled simply in an exponential equation. Glottochronologic dates tend to heavy errors (underestimations) when the time is appreciably greater than that (about a millenium) for which the device was calibrated. But this can presumably be corrected. The technique needs a great deal more careful testing,[10] and particularly a better theoretic undergirding than it has had. It seems, however, certainly to have sufficient merit to warrant this work.

14. In a recent paper[11] I suggested two additional lexicostatistical methods. One of these may be nothing more than a convenient rule of thumb procedure. The other, however, is of some interest. It consists of counting, for any pair of languages, those instances where a word-pair is not cognate but where each has a cognate outside the pair. A minimum is taken to indicate immediate relationship (i.e., connection through one tri-junction only). Given four languages, it does not distinguish between the following five genetic trees:

[8]Glottochronology was first developed by Morris Swadesh on the basis of suggestions going back to Edward Sapir. The history and theory are now conveniently summarized, with a full bibliography, in: D. H. Hymes, "Lexicostatistics So Far," *Current Anthropology* 1: 5–44, 1960.

[9]M. Swadesh, "Towards Greater Accuracy in Lexicostatistical Dating," *IJAL* 21: 121–137, 1955.

[10]D. D. Thomas, "Basic Vocabulary in Some Mon-Khmer Languages," *Anthropological Linguistics* 2(3): 7–11, 1960. This represents the first attempt to broaden the basis of calibration beyond the limited number of cases where an ancestral language is available. More of this sort of work is urgently required.

[11]H. A. Gleason, Jr., "Counting and Calculating for Historical Reconstruction," *Anthropological Linguistics* 1 (2): 22–32, 1959.

On examination it is found that these are topologically equivalent, and collectively represent one of three ways to connect four labeled end-points through tri-junctions:

There are $1 \cdot 3 \cdot 5 \cdots (2n - 5)$ such distinct ways of connecting any n languages, and the technique selects one of these. Each represents $2n - 3$ genetic trees in the more familiar sense. The genetic trees in each such set differ only in the point at which the proto-language connects. From a linguistic point of view, this may be a crucial difference, of course. But generally speaking other methods will suffice to make this distinction clearly.

That this method should produce a totally non-metric result suggests a re-examination of the assumptions on which it operates. It turns out that not only is there no assumption about rate, but there is none about time in any form. The widespread criticism of glottochronology has centered about the assumption of a constant rate of change. With this criticism in the background it is interesting to note that rate assumptions are not at all universal in lexicostatistics. Those methods other than glottochronology which do have some assumption of rate of change have generally rather weak assumptions. It follows lexicostatistics as a whole will not fall if glottochronology should prove to be untenable.

In actual practice it is comparatively simple to tabulate for all the pairs in a moderate-sized language family the information from which these several types of lexicostatistical calculations can be made. With a suitable machine it would be entirely feasible even for large language families. Actual experiments have been rather limited so far, but it does seem that all three lexicostatistical methods are of value. They have not been found to give contradictory results. Under certain circumstances one will give a clear answer where the others are ambiguous.

15. In the sequence of procedures running from an input of suitable word-lists to an output of reasonably firm first reconstruction, two important steps can be programmed onto computers. There remain steps which must be handled in more traditional ways, but even these are greatly expedited by better organization of the material. There is a possibility that the programmable portions of total procedure may be expanded somewhat, and that they may be made more powerful. It seems, now, in principle possible to greatly increase the production of certain kinds of historical linguistic results. Various details of the operation remain to be designed or improved but this seems clearly possible. If the challenge of making available sufficient data of suitable quality and form can be met, we may have a greatly improved tool for the uncovering of history.

2

THE DEVELOPMENT OF THE INDO-EUROPEAN LABIOVELARS WITH SPECIAL REFERENCE TO THE DIALECTS OF ANCIENT ITALY*

Joshua Whatmough

It is a fact, not to be denied, that a textual critic is for ever working in a circle. His rules of grammar are established and tested by induction from and comparison with the evidence of manuscripts; but manuscripts themselves often break the rules, and then the critic faces about and asserts that the rules, based upon the manuscripts, convict the manuscripts of error. But, as great critics have seen, the task of a critic is precisely this, to tread his circle "deftly and warily." Now the fact that textual criticism always involves circular argument in this way is well known. It is not so well known, but it is no less a fact, that a comparative philologist, when he deals with Indo-European speech-sounds and their history, is also involved in circular argumentation, in assuming that which is to be proved as the basis of the argument, a not uncommon if more complex variety of *petitio principii*.

Where the factors involved are few and simple, the fallacy of reasoning is easily detected. Thus, the assumption of a distinction between consonantal $i̯$ and a spirant j (y) has been made for Indo-European. Why? Solely to account for Greek ζ- initially in certain words. But such a distinction explains nothing. The phonetician, knowing that two different results are found initially in Greek (*spiritus asper* and ζ) corresponding to a single result y in Sanskrit or i in Latin, says that an I.Eu. spirant j must be sharply distinguished from a consonantal $i̯$; then the comparativist proceeds to explain the observed different results in Greek by the phonetic distinction set up expressly for that purpose, and the explanation is a complete *non constat*. Yet this fallacy still passes current as established doctrine in many textbooks!

It is much more difficult to detect such a fallacy when the factors are both far more numerous and far more complex. Such a case is that notorious *pons* (I might almost say *circulus*) *asinorum*, the I.Eu. gutturals, as they are loosely called.

*From *Acta Jutlandica*, 9. 45–56 (1937).

Ideally the phonemic system of a language, even of Indo-European (of which we have no direct written record) should not be constructed on the basis of its phonological history; for then it will mislead, since it is expressly designed to explain that which requires explanation, and must necessarily tend to make certain distinctions from the very knowledge that exactly those distinctions require to be made. But *in practice* this is not possible except in the case of spoken languages; or, in the case of languages no longer spoken, in the very limited domain in which appeal may be made to the science of phonetics. That domain is limited for Indo-European precisely because our knowledge of the I.Eu. speech itself is obtained solely from the comparison of derivative languages of the most diverse histories and of widely different epochs. For the rest the appeal to phonetics is purely theoretical. The difficulty is one which lies in the nature of the case, and is inevitable; and the only way to combat it, is just to be open-minded, and never to allow dominant theory in a disputed matter to be taken as final. Even dominant views are sometimes much younger than young students suspect.

In the case, then, of the three series of I.Eu. gutturals of traditional doctrine, phonetic distinctions have been set up, notably that between the so-called "pure velars" and the palatals on the one hand, and between the "pure velars" and the labiovelars on the other, solely in order to assume, as the basis of argument, that which has to be proved. Not only that: the argument itself has now come the full circle, and the assumption of two guttural series only, as in the days of Ascoli and Fick, is once more in favour. Naturally the recent theories and the late nineteenth century theories differ widely in detail; indeed the recent theories differ widely from one another. But, as I said before, we have to deal, like the textual critic, with a paradoxical state of affairs that is in the nature of the case inevitable, and from which immunity is no more claimed for the views set forth here than it is granted to the current theory. What makes progress possible is the constant succession of theory and observation.

In fact there is some common ground in all current views which may be taken for granted, in that the assumption of labio-velar consonants may be considered both necessary and valid so far as regards the *centum* languages; and they are the languages with which this paper is concerned. Without exception, all current theories require the assumption that such sounds existed at some stage in the prehistory of the *centum* languages. Where the divergences come in is in regard to (1) the period at which the labiovelars came into existence; (2) the conditions under which they came into existence; and, in much smaller degree, (3) their precise phonetic character.

The most recent discussion, that by Kuryłowicz (*Études indoeuropéennes* I, 1935, ch. I), appears to me to have stated accurately the conditions under which labialized velars occurred in the prehistory of the *centum* languages. That is a matter susceptible of proof, and the arguments of Kuryłowicz seem to be cogent. It is not as clear that the labialized velars arose independently in the *centum* languages so late as Kuryłowicz maintains. As to their character, his views do not differ essentially from the orthodox theory of velar consonants accompanied by lip-rounding. The suggestions which are advanced in this paper are based upon facts which are generally accessible, but which have not been sufficiently emphasized; and hence their implications have not been clearly realized.

Now it is sometimes said that Keltic falls into labializing and non-labializing dialects. Thus Hirt (*Idg. Gram.* I, 1927, p. 24): "Sie [i.e. die alten keltischen Mundarten] zerfallen in zwei Abarten, einen *k*- und einen *p*-Dialekt, d.h. ein Teil der keltischen Sprachen wandelt die idg. Labiovelare (k^w, g^w, gh^w) in Labiale, ein anderer tut das nicht." But this division holds good only for the treatment of the breathed labiovelar plosive q^u (with which $\hat{k}u$, the palatal followed by consonantal u, was identified in Keltic),

Ir. *cia*, W. *pwy*, like Ir. *ech*, W. *ebol*.

On the other hand, the voiced labiovelar plosive g^u became *b* both in Irish and in Welsh,

Ir. *bo*, W. *biw*,

and here again $\hat{g}u$ must be distinguished,

Ir. *tiug*, W. *tew* 'thick', from *$te\hat{g}uos$;

whereas from the so-called "voiced aspirate" g^uh, and perhaps also from $\hat{g}hu$, we have *g* initially in both Welsh and Irish, *gw* in Welsh and *f(v)* medially:

Ir. *gonim* 'wound', W. *gwan* 'stab'.

Ir. *snigid* 'rain, sleet', W. *nyf* 'snow'.

Ir. *gorim* 'warm', W. *gori* 'incubate'.

The evidence for $\hat{g}hu$ is slight and uncertain, but there appears to be no objection on phonological grounds to the etymology of

Ir. *geilt*, W. *gwyllt* 'wild'

which would derive these words from the base *$\hat{g}huel$- postulated by Skt. *hvárate* 'go crooked', *hválati* 'stumble', cf. Gr. ἀπο-φώλιος (an epithet of the Minotaur *ap.* Eurip.), Walde-Pokorny I. 644.

The striking feature here is the greater degree of labialization, indeed the complete labialization, of the voiced plosive in both branches of Keltic, as contrasted with either the breathed plosive or the "voiced aspirate." And Keltic is not alone in this phenomenon. It has long been observed that Greek, outside the Aeolic dialects, shows β for g^u before ε and ι, where, on the analogy of the breathed plosive, δ would have been expected, and this β is, almost without exception, described as "irregular" or "unexplained" in the hand-books. Certainly the attempts to account for words like βίος and ὄφις (if the latter contains g^uh and not $\hat{g}hu$. Walde-Pokorny I. 65) either as non-

Attic or by means of special "phonetic laws" cannot be said to have succeeded. Moreover we have β before ϵ in contract verbs like $\alpha\lambda\,\varphi\epsilon\hat{\iota}\nu$ (Skt. *árhati*), $\tau\alpha\rho\beta\epsilon\,\hat{\iota}\nu$, where the *e* in the first syllable of the formant -*ei̯/o*- does not alternate with *o*, and in *es*-stems like $\check{\epsilon}\rho\epsilon\beta\sigma\varsigma$, $\tau\acute{\alpha}\rho\beta\sigma\varsigma$, or φ before consonants as in $\check{\sigma}\varphi\alpha\tau\alpha$, $\check{\sigma}\varphi\nu\,\iota\varsigma$ (both in Hesychius), in none of which is the appeal to analogy in order to explain the labial convincing. Analogy may not be used as a mere scape-goat; the conditions under which it operates are, in matters of phonology at any rate, strictly limited—namely to restore intelligibility where phonetic change has impaired it. As Kuryłowicz has pointed out (p. 13): "Il s'agirait donc en fin de compte d'exemples très archaïques d'introduction de labiovélaire (labiale) devant consonne, mais d'exemples datant de l'époque grecque, celtique etc. et non pas de l'époque indoeuropéenne." He adds further examples from Germanic, after Reichelt, in which again the voiced plosive and the "voiced aspirate" (g^u and g^uh) are concerned: "M. Reichelt a eu raison d'expliquer de cette manière les formes germaniques v.-h.-a. *nioro*, got. *siuns*, m.-h.-a. *zounen*, anglosaxon *éanian* contenant, en apparence, les labiovélaires g^uh, g^u suivies de consonnes." The greater degree of labialization in β from g^u and φ from g^uh in Greek, as compared with π from q^u, is, in short, so well known as to need no further emphasis.

In Latin also the development of g^u and g^uh is far less simple than that of q^u, but the greater complexity consists precisely in this, that the breathed plosive gives rise to either *c* or *qu*, with but a slight degree of labialization, whereas from the voiced plosive and the "voiced aspirate," under conditions that are well known and need not therefore be repeated here, we have the bilabial fricative $u̯$, as in

   uenio, toruos, nudus from an older **nou̯odos, niuem, uoueo*;
the labiodental fricative *f*, as in

   formus, -fendo;
and even the labial plosive in Lanuvian

   nebrundines
which is probably also good Latin.

Similarly in Germanic the breathed plosive q^u never gives complete labialization until quite recent stages of the Germanic languages, but always retains some part of its velar utterance (*hw*), save where by the operation of special accentual conditions (Verner's Law) it had first become voiced in character, as

   O.E. pret. pl. (W. S.) *sawon*, p. ptc. *gesewen*,

   O.E. *hwēol, hweowol* from *$\chi u̯e\mathfrak{z}u̯ló$-, cf. Skt. *cakrá*-
—the only exception to this general statement, indeed, appears in words in which partial or complete assimilation to a preceding labial has occurred, e. g., Goth. *wulfs, fimf*, and in passing we may remind ourselves that the Gothic

m in *fimf* bears witness to the bilabial character of the following *f*. But from the "voiced aspirate" $g^{\underline{u}}h$ we have *w*, as in Gothic

  warms, snáiws;

and, it would seem, even *b* as in *banja* (Hirt, *Idg. Gram.* I. 304), for the base **bhen-* set up by Walde-Pokorny (II. 149) is badly attested, and the solitary alleged Avestic cognates widely dissimilar in meaning. It must moreover be observed that the I.Eu. voiced plosive (labiovelar) $g^{\underline{u}}$ passed no further toward labialization than the labiovelar stage, Gothic

  qius, qens, naqaps,

unless by assimilation (*waírpan, wōpjan?*—both etymologies are disputed). This result, however, came about exactly because the sound had ceased to be voiced; in pro-ethnic Germanic not only was it no longer voiced, it also never passed through the fricative or spirant stages through which the I.Eu. breathed plosive or "voiced aspirate" passed in the course of their history in pro-ethnic Germanic.

     Even Hittite tells the same story. From $q^{\underline{u}}$ we have *ku* or *kw*, as in *ku-iš* [*kwis*], *ša-a-ku-wa* [*sakwa*] 'eyes'; but from $g^{\underline{u}}$ and $g^{\underline{u}}h$ we have the bilabial fricative *w* as in

  wa-al-aḫ-zi [*walh-*] 'strike' (cf. Gr. $\beta\acute{\alpha}\lambda\lambda\omega$),

and in

  wa-ra-a-ni [*warani*] 'is burnt' (cf. $\theta\epsilon\rho\mu\acute{o}s$).

     The ancient dialects of Italy, to which I now turn, offer evidence that does not conflict with what we have observed hitherto. The Lepontic inscriptions seem to indicate that $g^{\underline{u}}$ became *b*. At least so I interpret forms like *piuonei, piuotialui, piuotiui*, beside forms like Ligurian *fundus Biuelius* (Tab. Vel.), *Biuuo, Biuonia*—unless it be argued that the whole series of names is borrowed from some Keltic dialect, which seems improbable. So too *pruiam*, which I interpret as a noun, acc. sg. fem., meaning 'maiestatem' or the like, cf. Welsh *bryw*, Gr. $\beta\alpha\rho\acute{v}s$, Lat. *grauis*, Skt. *gurú-š*. Hence the interpretation of Lepontic *uenia* as 'wife' (Skt. *jánī*, Gr. $\gamma v v \acute{\eta}$, O.Ir. *ben*), which would require us to assume *ṵ-* initially from $g^{\underline{u}}$, appears extremely unlikely in the inscription (*P. I. D.* 321)

  metelui · maešilalui · uenia · metelikna · asmina · krasanikna.

It is improbable also on the ground that if the wife of Metellus was also a daughter of Metellus (*Metello Maesilalo . . . Metellifilia Asmina Crassanigena*), there is revealed a social relationship which is most unusual for Italy in the second or third century B.C. Hence *uenia* is best taken as a proper name 'Venia' (cf. *C. I. L.* v. 7700). But whether we assume *b-* or *ṵ-* from initial $g^{\underline{u}}$ in Lepontic, we have in either case a labial, either a plosive (*b*) or a spirant (*ṵ*), from the voiced labiovelar plosive $g^{\underline{u}}$. For $g^{\underline{u}}h$, the corresponding "aspirate," Lepontic so far has no direct evidence, but Ligurian has, as we shall see presently. And Lepontic, like Brythonic Keltic, seems to have labialized q^u completely (*-pe* 'and'; cf. Lat. *-que*, Gr. τε, Sk. *ca*), and this treatment of q^u, common to Lepontic and Brythonic Keltic, and partially also to Greek (π), we shall have to return to consider below. But Lepontic differs from Welsh in that $\hat{k}u$ survives in the form *kualui*, just as it does in Italic (Umb. *ekvine*)[1], which also has *p* for q^u (Umb. *panta*) as well as *b* for g^u (Umb. *benurent*) and *f* for g^uh (Umb. *vufetes* 'uotiuis', cf. Gr. εὔχομαι, Skt. *vāghát*-).

Ligurian, however, offers evidence confirmatory of the view that labialization is more thoroughgoing in the voiced plosive and in the "voiced aspirate" than in the breathed labiovelar plosive. Thus contrasted with *Stonicelius* (*-cel-*: Lat. *colo*, I.Eu. *q^uel-*; for *Stoni-* cf. the Ligurian local names Στόναι, *Stoeni*, Στουῖνοι), and with *Quiamelius* (i.e. *quia-* as in Greek τείω, τιμή, *-mel-* as in Lat. *molo*, Ir. *melim*, and hence 'precious stone', like *Goldstein, Goldberg*; cf. Lig. *Blustiemelus*), we find the *Biuelius* etc. already cited (g^u); and with g^uh we have *Bormiae*, which must be cognate with Latin *formus*, not with Latin *ferueo*. The widely distributed names meaning 'warm springs' (*Formiae*, Volsc. *Hormiae*, Sic. θερμαὶ Ἱμεραῖαι, and above all the Phrygian Γέρμη, Germ. *Würm*, *Wirmine*) prove this connexion. The perverse etymology that would compare O.E. *beorma* would never have been proposed save to bolster up the tottering and totally discredited hypothesis that Ligurian is not Indo-European, or if Indo-European must be Keltic. As a matter of fact *Aquae Bormiae, Bormo, Bormanus*, like *Porcobera*, shows the independent position of Ligurian; for being neither Keltic (which has *g* for g^uh and looses *p* altogether) nor Italic (which has *f-* for g^uh; moreover *Porcifera* is the Latin form of *Porcobera*), these words cannot have been borrowed. So too *Roudelius* (cf. *ruber, rufus*), and *Bodincus* (cf. *fundus*) cannot have been borrowed from Italic, nor *Berigiema* (cf. *fero, hiems*); again the Lepontic (i. e., I believe, Kelto-liguric) *pala* (cf. *se-pelio*, Umb. *pelsa-*, but O.Ir. *all* 'rock, cliff'), in the idiom in which Keltic shows *lokan* or *artuaš*, cannot possibly, with its initial *p-*, be Keltic.

From this survey of the evidence showing the development of the labiovelars in the *centum* languages, it appears to me that some new conclusions may be drawn. As I said at the outset, any such conclusion must be regarded as in the nature of a "working hypothesis." But it is at least clear that in all the *centum* dialects which show labialization at all, the phenomenon seems to be more completely carried out and more thoroughly established, if not to have begun, in the voiced plosive g^u. That is notably the case in Keltic, and in Italic, Latin included. But the so-called "voiced

---

[1]Compare Osc. *aíkdafed*, Umb. *eikvasese, eitipens* (?), Sabine *tesca, tescua* (Gloss. Lat. IV, 1930, p. 446) which contains ku like Lat. *pascua*, and the ethnicon *Aequi, Aequiculi*.

aspirate" follows closely; while the breathed plosive lags behind everywhere except in Brythonic Keltic and in Osco-Umbrian, for the labialization is far less complete in Greek.

It is of little moment for my present purpose whether Indo-European possessed labiovelars, or whether, as Kuryłowicz holds, velars first became labialized in the prehistory of the several *centum* languages. In either event I should offer the same explanation, namely that in the labiovelars we have to do with speech-sounds in which there was closure at both the front and at the back of the mouth, rather than at the back only with mere lip-rounding at the front. Such sounds are by no means impossible; they can be demonstrated experimentally as Panconcelli-Calzia[2] has shown, as true plosives with simultaneous double closure, that is labial and velar. Not only that; such sounds have been discovered to exist in certain Sudanese, Kamerun, and Togo-land dialects. These Panconcelli-Calzia writes as $\dot{p}$ and $\dot{b}$, and describes as formed by the tongue in the position of k and g, and by the lips, at the same time, in the position of p and b. Thus the conditions demanded by the Indo-European labiovelars as single, not complex sounds is fulfilled. This distinction, especially as between q^u and q plus u has long been emphasized, and it has always been insisted, even on the theory of velar plus lip-rounding, that the result was not a double consonant, on the ground that single consonants appear in the derived languages, like the Latin *qu* and the Greek π, neither of which "makes position" (*sequor*, $\overset{\prime}{\epsilon}\pi o\mu\alpha\iota$). It is important to observe, however, that the distinction is by no means so clear in regard to g^u and g^uh. But the labiovelar of the Brugmann tradition, as Sköld has very properly maintained, is something of an abstraction, and highly theoretical, not found in any spoken language.

On the other hand, labiovelars such as Sköld has postulated for Indo-European, are known to exist. They might be written φ and ϕ. At first sight they may seem improbable because we are not familiar with them; in English *backpart*, *backpiece*, there is no true equivalent, since there are two consonants involved in two different syllables in those words; so in *Egbert*. Besides, even these approximations do not occur initially; and in Germ. *Kapelle* there is a faint vocalic transition, a partially unvoiced vowel, between the k and the p. But modern English has a corresponding voiced fricative w; so had Gothic (w); so had classical Latin ($\underset{\circ}{u}$)—in all of these there is narrowing at the back of the mouth as well as rounding at the lips.

It is reasonable to suppose, however, that I.Eu. φ and ϕ would necessarily be unstable consonants. It is further, I think, significant, that Latin $\underset{\circ}{u}$ and Germanic w derive in part from the I.Eu voiced and "voiced aspirated"

[2]*Zeitschrift für Kolonialsprachen*, 9, 1918—19, 23 ff.; cf. Sköld in *Kuhns Zeitschrift*, 52, 1924, 147 ff., 59, 1932, 205 ff., and Meriggi, *Idg. Forsch.* 44, 1927, 1.

labiovelar plosives; and it is equally significant that the Germanic *qu* (Gothic *q*), from the I.Eu voiced plosive, no less than the Latin *qu* from the I.Eu. breathed plosive, are conspicuous as labiovelar *plosives*, not *labial* plosives, nor labiovelar *fricatives*, in that they are breathed. In the case of the breathed I.Eu plosive, the instability of the labiovelar consonant led to the result that the release, as distinguished from the closure, did produce a back plosive (*k*) or at most a plosive (*q*) with labial narrowing (*u̯*). But in the case of the sonorous voiced plosive *b̔*, which even to us whose native tongues possess no such sound, appears a priori easier to produce and to sustain than *φ*, the labial release more readily prevailed, especially where the plosive broke down into a fricative; hence Irish *b*, Ligurian *b*, Latin *u̯*, Germanic *w* (from *b̔* and, under Verner's Law, with voicing, from *φ*), and the "irregular" Greek *β* (before *ε* and *ι* even in non-Aeolic dialects). Indeed, it might be argued that we have to deal with *gƀ* (cf. Sköld, p. 149), if not also with *kf*, rather than with *φ* and *b̔*, at least at some point in the history of some of the *centum* dialects and under certain conditions (i. e. whenever *u̯* results), but not, I think, at the earliest stage of the history of the labiovelar breathed and voiced consonants, which, in order to account for the actual results in the *centum* languages, must have been plosives.

But as for the so-called "voiced aspirates" of traditional Indo-European phonology, it is impossible, I should maintain, after the convincing attacks made upon them by Walde and Prokosch (see Hirt, *Idg. Gram.* I, 219), for anyone to justify their existence in pro-ethnic Indo-European. The assumption of some variety of fricative fits the facts infinitely better. But if we have, then, to do not with *gᵘh* (or *b̔h*), but with *χᵘ* or *ȝᵘ* (write *χf* or *ȝƀ*), it is easy to account for the labialization in Latin and Umbrian *f* (*of-fendo, vufetes*), Germanic *w* and Latin *u̯*, Ligurian *b* (*Bormiae*), Hittite *w*, Greek *φ* and the rest. Indeed here we must bear in mind as a factor of first importance, the fricative stage that was either reached or passed through by these consonants at least in Germanic, Italic, and in Keltic, even if we do not admit it for pro-ethnic Indo-European.

The labial *p* of Osco-Umbrian, of Brythonic Keltic, Lepontic, and in part of Greek, is more difficult to account for. It is in any event secondary and not an astonishing issue from a breathed labiovelar of the type that we have postulated. As for Greek *κ*, *γ*, *χ*, where they occur (namely in association with *υ*), it is well known that a labiovelar is not maintained before *u* (Lat. *secutus, gula*), and it has been held that it never occurred at any time, even in pro-ethnic I.Eu., in that position. Greek *τ*, *δ*, *θ* are definitely peculiar: do they represent a compromise or mid-way position between the simultaneous front and back closure of the true labiovelar as dictated by accompanying front vowels? Or are we to think of *φ* giving rise to *t/p* consonants such as are said to occur in Gascony (Cuny, *Litteris*, 7, 1930, 150 n. 2)?

To recapitulate, briefly my theory is that there is at least in Irish *b*, Greek *β*, and Ligurian *b*, a greater degree of labialization in the voiced sounds than in the breathed sound, and that it was maintained with those sounds, even if it did not start with them, because in the true but unstable labiovelar, the labial element prevailed more readily with the additional sonority that voicing gives; in other words, whereas in the breathed sound the velar element was more commonly sustained, thanks to tension in the larynx, which supported closure at the velum, in the voiced sounds it was the labial element that was sustained, laxness in the larynx leading to openness at the velum, so that the labial element was acoustically more prominent, and therefore more commonly survived.

It is interesting to observe something like a reverse change in Italian in the substitution of *g* for Latin *u* in certain words, implying I think an intermediate labiovelar stage (*ɸ*?), e. g. *rigolo* (*rivulum*), Sienese *diagolo* (Tusc. *diavolo*), *ugola* (from *uvula*), *nugolo* (*nuvolo*), *pargolo* beside *parvolo*: so we have occasionally *c* substituted for *p* in vulgar Latin inscriptions, e. g. *commanuculus* in *C. I. L.* VI. 3079 and X. 1775. The very extensive labialization of Roumanian has often been compared with that which appears in the earlier I.Eu. *centum* languages, and again it may imply true labiovelars in the late Latin of Dacia. But the situation in a language that shows also extensive palatalization (like the I.Eu. *sat ə m* languages), as Roumanian does, combining the features both of labialization and of palatalization, is not strictly parallel. The Sudanese dialects really present a closer parallel, at least to the Greek developments, since in them we have dentals as well as labial and palatal consonants, just as in Greek, in alternation.

And if the course of the I.Eu. labiovelars is still a circular tour, at least it is a tour with some new and interesting sights.

TABLE

To show Incidence of Labialization.

	$\hat{k}\underset{\smile}{u}$	*φ*	*ɸ*	*ɸh*
Irish			*b*	
Welsh	*p*	*p*	*b*	*-f-*
Greek, before ε and ι	*π* (*π*)		*β* (*ð*)	*φ* (*θ*)
Latin	voiced (-ȝ^{w′}-), *w*		*u*	*f-, -u-, -b-* ?
Germanic				*w, b* ?
Hittite			*w*	*w*
Lepontic		*p*	*b, u*	
Ligurian			*b*	*b*
Osco-Umbrian		*p*	*b*	*-f-*
Totals:	2	3 (+1)	9 (−1)	7

3

THE RECONSTRUCTION
OF PROTO-ROMANCE[*][†]

Robert A. Hall, Jr.

1. Comparative Reconstruction: Desirability and Possibility

Leonard Bloomfield, in his book *Language*,[1] makes the statement:

> Students of the Romance languages reconstruct a Primitive Romance ("Vulgar Latin") form before they turn to the written records of Latin, and they interpret these records in the light of the reconstructed form.

Two later writers, discussing the reconstruction of earlier stages of related languages, have made relevant statements in this connection. Bruno Migliorini says:[2]

> Ci manca e ci mancherà sempre il metodo di ricostruire ciò che è il carattere fondamentale di una lingua: la sua consistenza in sistema, in un dato tempo e in un dato luogo.

George L. Trager, on the other hand, makes the programmatic declaration:[3]

> It seems to me that historical linguists must now restate their tasks much more precisely. When we have really good descriptive grammars of all existing French dialects, we can reconstruct Proto-Francian, Proto-

*From *Language* 26. 6–27 (1950). Reprinted in M. Joos, ed., *Readings in Historical Linguistics*, American Council of Learned Societies, 1957. Reprinted with the permission of the author and the Linguistic Society of America.

†Parts of this paper were read before meetings of the Linguistic Society at Rochester in 1946, the Cornell Linguistic Club in 1948, and the Modern Language Association at New York in 1948. I am indebted for suggestions to many colleagues and critics, including Professors F. B. Agard, C. F. Hockett, Y. Malkiel, W. G. Moulton, L. Pumpelly, and L. Spitzer—not all of whom agree with my fundamental thesis and none of whom are responsible for any errors the paper may contain in its present form.

[1]*Language* 302 (New York, 1933).
[2]*Linguistica* 104 (Firenze, 1946). On this point, cf. also the reviews by T. A. Sebeok (*American Speech* 22.137–8 [1947]) and the present writer (*Lang.* 22.259–61 [1946]).
[3]*Studies in Philology* 43.463 (1946).

Burgundian, Proto-Norman-Picard, etc. Then we can reconstruct Proto-French; then, with a similarly acquired statement of Proto-Provençal, we can formulate Proto-Gallo-Romanic; next, with similar accurately developed reconstructions of Proto-Ibero-Romanic, Proto-Italian, etc., we can work out Proto-Romanic as a whole.

These three statements stand in a historical relation to each other. Bloomfield's represents the aim of comparative reconstruction held by many Romance scholars of the epoch of Meyer-Lübke; Migliorini's, the disillusionment of post-Meyer-Lübkean scholars with that aim; and Trager's, the goal of some present-day workers, to return to comparative reconstruction and to revivify it with an infusion of descriptive (synchronic) analysis. Meyer-Lübke and his immediate followers attempted to apply the comparative method, as developed in the 19th century and particularly by the Junggrammatiker[4] of the 1870's, to the reconstruction of the common ancestral form of the Romance languages. This method, which requires the scholar to work backward in time, proved difficult of application and exposition, and even Meyer-Lübke, in such finished products as the *Grammatik der romanischen Sprachen*,[5] or his historical grammars of individual languages,[6] resorted to the procedure of presenting his material as developing forward in time, from Latin and "Vulgar Latin" to the Romance languages. Later and lesser comparatists in the Romance field tended toward the errors which often resulted from a misunderstanding of Neo-Grammarian procedure: abuse of "starred" forms and neglect of historical factors other than those of phonetic change, analogical new-formation, and learned borrowing. The comparative method and the Neo-Grammarian hypothesis of regular sound change came to be identified—in the Romance field especially through the influence of Croce, Vossler, and their "idealistic" followers[7]—with a positivistic approach which was no longer the mode. Modern Romance scholars, with few exceptions, have abandoned even the effort to reconstruct Proto-Romance,[8] and present work in the Romance field follows, in general, the technique of Hugo

[4] I use this term to refer specifically to Brugmann, Leskien, and the other Indo-Europeanists of the 1870's, 80's, and 90's who first developed the explicit formulation of the principles of comparative reconstruction. For that group of scholars—far more extensive in number and in time—who have accepted the basic postulate of regular sound-change, I would suggest using the term "regularist"; my "Terminological Notes," *Studies in Linguistics* 7.60–2 (1949).

[5] Leipzig, 1890–1900.

[6] E. g. *Italienische Grammatick* (Leipzig, 1890); *Historische Grammatik der französischen Sprache* (Heidelberg, 1908–21).

[7] Cf. the present writer's discussions of the "idealistic" approach and its effects on linguistics, in *Italica* 20.239–43 (1938); *Lang.* 17.263–9 (1941); *Italica* 23.30–4 (1946); *Lang.* 22.273–83 (1946); and *SIL* 6.27–35 (1948).

[8] Cf. such criticisms of the comparative method as those of Bàrtoli, *Introduzione alla Neolinguistica* (Genève, 1925; Biblioteca dell'Archivum Romanicum II.12); B. A. Terracini, *¿Qué es la Lingüistica?* (Tucumán, 1942).

Schuchardt (who, as is well known, stood aside from the Neo-Grammarian movement and made little use of comparative reconstruction): detailed examination of Classical and Late Latin material and of modern Romance material, bridging the gap between them with as few assumptions as possible concerning intermediate stages. Most present-day Romanists distrust hypothetical reconstructions attained by working backwards from later-attested material, as exemplified in Migliorini's remark.[9] Only a few scholars at present—in general, with training in both historical and descriptive technique—envisage, as does Trager in the passage cited, the reconstruction of Proto-Romance as a worthy goal, and not only for Proto-Romance alone, but also for all the intermediate stages between Proto-Romance and the present time.

Yet, even though current fashions in Romance linguistics are unfavorable to it, such an integral re-application of the comparative method as Trager proposes—of course, accompanied by as thorough as possible a synchronic analysis and description of each stage—is very much needed at present. Its use is not only possible but highly desirable, to correct certain serious misconceptions now widespread, concerning the relation of Romance and Latin, and the relation of the Romance languages to each other. One of these misconceptions is even reflected in Bloomfield's statement, where "Vulgar Latin" is equated with Proto-Romance. This terminological identification is a result of the customary conception of Romance linguistic history as having been unilinear in its development: Old Latin > Classical Latin > Vulgar (Imperial) Latin > the first stages of differentiation among the Romance dialects > the later languages. The normal procedure of manuals of historical grammar[10] is to trace Romance sounds and forms over a portion of this assumed development, usually from Classical Latin to the earliest attested stage of the language concerned. This works well enough for the languages usually studied: Italian, French and Provençal, and the Iberian languages, since "Vulgar Latin" as usually set up is essentially equivalent to the ancestral form of these languages, i. e. the intermediate stage of Proto-Italo-Western Romance. But it will not work for Eastern (Balkan) Romance or for South-

---

It must be emphasized that our reconstruction does not lead us to set up a completely "unified" or "unitary" Proto-Romance, as is often assumed (cf. most recently Y. Malkiel, StP 46.512 [1949]). We do not have to suppose absolute uniformity for protolanguages, any more than for any actually observed language (cf. B. Bloch, Lang. 24.194 fn. 1 [1948]). Our Proto-Romance was undoubtedly a composite of several dialects of the Latin spoken at the end of the Republican period.

[9]Cf. also Y. Malkiel, Lang. 21.149 (1945).

[10]E. g. Meyer-Lübke's *Grammatik der romanischen Sprachen*; Bourciez's *Eléments de linguistique romane*[4] (Paris, 1946); Grandgent's *Introduction to Vulgar Latin* (Boston, 1907); and the historical grammars of individual languages, e. g., for Italian: Meyer-Lübke's *Italienische Grammatik* and its various Italian reworkings; Grandgent's *From Latin to Italian* (Cambridge, 1927); and Pei's *The Italian Language* (New York, 1941).

ern Romance (Sardinian, Sicilian, Calabrian, Lucanian), which are in general conveniently neglected, or passed over with the remark that they show divergent developments from "Vulgar Latin." Departures from this customary procedure, such as efforts to trace Romance developments to features found in Old Latin but not in Classical Latin (thus skipping one or more of the traditional stages), often provoke irate tertiary responses, as in d'Ovidio's use of the term "rancido" for Old Latin when he was arguing[11] against Förster's suggestion of OLat. -nunt as an ancestor for the Italian 3 pl. verbal ending -no.[12] We can avoid this type of confusion only by re-applying the comparative method and seeing what it has to tell us about the relation of the Romance languages.

2. Procedure: Reconstruction of Intermediate and Ultimate Stages

A thoroughgoing and complete application of the comparative method to the Romance languages would have to follow essentially the steps that Trager proposes. A first approximation thereto would involve the comparison of the earliest attested stages of each language, with consideration of relevant modern dialectal material where the latter would shed light on aspects of the reconstructed ancestral language not evident from consideration of the earliest attested dialects;[13] the end results of the two procedures would, I believe, be approximately equivalent.

The reconstruction must be done by working backward and reconstructing the immediate ancestral forms of those languages which are most closely related (e. g. Portuguese, Spanish, Catalan, and Mozarabic; North and South French; etc.). It would be unjustified, for instance, to start off by comparing less closely related dialects in preference to more closely related ones, whenever the latter were available; although the picture of the ultimate ancestral language would perforce be the same, the intermediate stages of development would be seriously misrepresented by such a procedure. "Close relation," in this connection, means of course "sharing linguistic features" or "bounded by the same isoglosses," not only or mainly "juxtaposed geographically," since dialects going back to different intermediate stages can be found

[11]ZRPh. 23.313–20 (1898).

[12]ZRPh. 22.521–5 (1898).

[13]For instance, the evidence afforded by Upper Aragonese dialects for preservation of intervocalic unvoiced stops, or by Asturian (Cabranes) dialect for preservation of the distinction between final -u and -o (cf. Y. Malkiel, *Lang.* 23.63 [1947], reviewing Josefa María Canellada, *El bable de Cabranes* [Madrid, 1944; RFE Anejo 31]); the similar evidence afforded by Upper Bearnese for preservation of intervocalic unvoiced stops (cf. the discussion in Part 2 of this article) and their ascription to Proto-Gallo-Romance; or the evidence afforded by Central and South Italian dialects (in the so-called "metafonesi centro-meridionale") for the distinction between final -u and -o, which we must, therefore, likewise ascribe to Proto-Italo-Romance.

in close proximity to each other, as are, say, Neopolitan-Campanian, Lucanian, and the area which Lausberg calls the "outpost" (Vorposten) of Eastern Romance in Lucania.[14]

A concrete example of how this type of intermediate reconstruction can be done and what it gives us can be seen in the phonological system of Proto-Gallo-Romance. We shall set this up first on the basis of a comparison between Old South French (Provençal) and Old North French, later modifying our reconstruction of PGRom. on the basis of (1) internal re-analysis and (2) the evidence of other dialects. For the vowels, there are twelve basic sets of correspondences, given here with a provisional symbol assigned to each:[15]

	PGRom.	OSFr.	ONFr.	
1.	i	i	i	OSFr. vída vida 'life': ONFr. vĭðə viḍe
2.	E	e	éi	OSFr. téla tela 'cloth': ONFr. téilə teile
3.	e	e	e	OSFr. éntre entre 'between': ONFr. éntrə entre
4.	ɛ	ɛ	iɛ́	OSFr. kɛ́ra quera 'that he seek': ONFr. kiɛ́rəθ quiereț
5.	ɛ	ɛ	ɛ	OSFr. tɛ́rra terra 'earth': ONFr. tɛ́rə tere
6.	A	a	æ[16]	OSFr. ála ala 'wing': ONFr. ǽlə ele
7.	a	a	a	OSFr. kánta canta 'he sings': ONFr. čántəθ chanteț
8.	ɔ	ɔ	ɔ	OSFr., ONFr. mɔ́rt mort 'death'
9.	ɔ	ɔ	uɔ́ > uɛ́	OSFr. bɔ́na bona 'good': ONFr. buɔ́na buona > buɛ́nə buene
10.	o	o	o	OSFr., ONFr. fórn forn 'oven'
11.	O	o	óu	OSFr. góla gola 'throat': ONFr. góulə goule
12.	u	u	u	OSFr. núza nuza 'naked': ONFr. núðə nude

[14]*Die Mundarten Südlukaniens* (Halle, 1939; ZRPh. Beiheft 90), especially pp. 84–6.

[15]Examples are given first in phonemic transcription (easily identifiable as such by the phonemic stress mark in each form: see example 48), then in the conventional orthography of the language, with English glosses enclosed in quotes. The ONFr. conventional orthography is the normalized style used, for instance, by Schwan-Behrens-Bloch (*Grammaire de l'ancien français*[4] [Leipzig, 1932]) and by Jenkins in his edition of the *Chanson de Roland* (revised ed., Boston, 1929). The transcription is based on that of the IPA, except that c stands for [t^s], ʒ for [d^z], and a prime after a consonant letter indicates palatalization.

[16]The symbol suggested by me (StP 43.579 [1947]) for the phonemic entity in ONFr. which normally corresponds to /á/ of OSFr. and the other Romance languages, which assonated only with itself in the earliest stage of literary Old French (including the earlier stratum of the Roland), and which was later merged with /ɛ/ and spelled e. The exact phonetic nature of this phoneme is irrelevant, whether it was [æ] (as seems to me most likely, at least for the first stage of its development), [ɛ·], [e·], or what not.

All other correspondences between vowel phonemes can be stated in terms of these twelve, as divergent developments conditioned by phonetic surroundings or as developments of combinations of these twelve elements, e. g.:

| 12a. | e | e | ə | after certain consonants or clusters; e. g. OSFr. ǧúǧe jutge 'judge': ONFr. ǧúǧə [juge |
| 12b. | au̯ | au̯ | ɔ | OSFr. áur aur 'gold' : ONFr. ɔ́r or |

Similarly for the consonant phonemes, we find that there are thirty-five further correspondences, which at first we would set up as follows:

13.	p	p	p	OSFr. pέire peire 'stone' : ONFr. piέðrə pieɖre
14.	t	t	t	OSFr., ONFr. tánt tant 'so much'; OSFr. méta meta 'that he put' : ONFr. métəθ metet̞
15.	k	k	k	OSFr., ONFr. kórt cort 'short'; ONFr., OSFr. sék sec 'dry'
16.	b	b	b	OSFr. bátre batre 'to beat' : ONFr. bátrə batre; OSFr. ábas abas 'abbot' (nom. sg.) : ONFr. ábəs abes
17.	d	d	d	OSFr., ONFr. dúr dur 'hard'; OSFr. fréida freida 'cold' : ONFr. fréidə freide
18.	g	g	g	OSFr. góta gota 'drop' : ONFr. gótə gote
19.	f	f	f	OSFr. fáire faire 'to do' : ONFr. fáirə faire
20.	v	v	v	OSFr. víva viva 'alive' : ONFr. vívə vive
21.	s	s	s	OSFr. séda seda 'silk' : ONFr. séiðə seiɖe; OSFr. fɔ́sa fosa 'ditch' : ONFr. fɔ́sə fose
22.	c	c	c	OSFr., ONFr. cínk cinc 'five'; OSFr. fáca faza 'that he do' : ONFr. fácəθ facet̞
23.	ž	ž	ž	OSFr. dóže doze 'twelve' : ONFr. dóžə doze
24.	ǧ	ǧ	ǧ	OSFr. ǧúǧe jutge 'judge' : ONFr. ǧúǧə juge
25.	m	m	m	OSFr. amár amar 'love' : ONFr. amǽr amer
26.	n	n	n	OSFr. nɔ́č, nučč noch, nuech 'night' : ONFr. núit nuit; OSFr. menár menar 'to lead' : ONFr. mənǽr mener
27.	l	l	l	OSFr. lavár lavar 'to wash' : ONFr.

lavǽr laver; OSFr. ála ala 'wing' : ONFr. ǽlə ele; OSFr. fɔ́la fola 'mad' : ONFr. fɔ́lə fole

28.	r	r	r	OSFr. rábia rabia 'rage' : ONFr. rắgə rage; OSFr. árdre ardre 'to burn' : ONFr. árdrə ardre
29.	h	—	h	OSFr. ápča apcha 'axe' : ONFr. háčə hache
30.	w	g	gu̯	OSFr. gardár g(u)ardar 'to guard' : ONFr. guardǽr guarder
31.	p′	pč	č	OSFr. sápča sapcha 'that he know' : ONFr. sáčəθ sachet; cf. also example 29
32.	t′	č	i̯t	OSFr. fáč fach 'done' : ONFr. fáit fait
33.	b′	bi̯	ǧ	OSFr. kambiár cambiar 'to change' : ONFr. čanǧiǽr changier
34.	v′	vi̯	ǧ	OSFr. abreviár abreuiar 'to shorten' : ONFr. abreǧiǽr abregier
35.	s′	š, i̯s[17]	i̯s	OSFr. bašár baisár baissar 'to lower' : ONFr. baisiǽr baissier
36.	z′	ž, i̯z[17]	i̯z	OSFr. bažár baizár baisar 'to kiss' : ONFr. baiziǽr baisier
37.	c′	c	i̯s	OSFr. palác palatz 'palace' : ONFr. paláis palais
38.	ʒ′	z, i̯z[17]	i̯z	OSFr. po(i)zón po(i)zon 'poison' : ONFr. poizón poison; OSFr. plazér 'to please' : ONFr. plaizír plaisir
39.	m′	mi̯, mǧ[17]	nǧ	OSFr. komiát komǧát comjat 'leave' : ONFr. konǧiǽθ congict
40.	n′	n′	n′	OSFr., ONFr. bán′ banh, bain 'bath'; OSFr. sen′ór senhor 'lord' : ONFr. sen′óur seignour
41.	l′	l′	l′	OSFr. fíl′a filha 'daughter' : ONFr. fíl′ə fille; OSFr. trabál′ trabalh 'work' : ONFr. travál′ travail
42.	r′	i̯r, r[18]	i̯r	OSFr. váira vaira 'many-colored, bright' : ONFr. váirə vaire; OSFr. kuér cuer 'leather' : ONFr. kúir cuir

In addition to those listed above, there are five other correspondences of consonants occurring only intervocalically, which must, at first, be assigned separate symbols:

[17]Dialectal differentiation within OSFr.

[18]With /r/ occurring in word-final position and involving diphthongization of a preceding /ɛ/ or /ɔ/.

43.	ß	b	v	OSFr. kobrír cobrir 'to cover' : ONFr. kovrír covrir
44.	ð	d	ð	OSFr. -áda -ada ending of past part. (f. sg.) : ONFr. -ǽðə -ede
45.	ð	z	ð	OSFr. lauzár lauzar 'to praise' : ONFr. lɔðǽr loder
46.	z	z	z	OSFr. pauzár pauzar 'to put' : ONFr. pozǽr poser
47.	γ	g	i̯	OSFr. pagán pagan 'pagan' : ONFr. paii̯ǽn paiien

Other correspondences between consonants can all be interpreted as conditioned developments of one of the PGRom. phonemes tentatively assumed above, or as resulting from clusters of two or more consonants:

| 47a. | k (bef. a) | k | č | OSFr. kantár cantar 'to sing' : ONFr. čantǽr chanter |
| 47b. | ðr | i̯r | ðr | OSFr. páire paire 'father' : ONFr. pǽðrə pedre |

We must further assume at least one phoneme of stress:

| 48. | ´ | ´ | ´ | OSFr. kánta canta 'he sings' : ONFr. čántəθ chantet; OSFr. kantác cantatz 'you sing' : ONFr. čantǽc chantez |

Thus far we have set up twelve basic correspondences in vowels, thirty-five in consonants, and one in stress. Now these might conceivably represent the same number of phonemes in the parent language: forty-seven segmental phonemes is not an excessive number to posit for a language without transcending the limits of realism. But our task is not ended with the setting up of these forty-eight correspondences; after all, what we have obtained here is only a first approximation, and we must now proceed to examine our stock of "phonemes," just as we would our initial results in studying a language at first hand, and re-analyze and re-phonemicize, seeking to observe the distribution of elements within the parent language and, if possible, to reduce the number of unit phonemes that we posit.[19]

When we look over the material we have assembled, we notice, first of all, a marked limitation on the occurrence of those vowel correspondences which we have symbolized with capital letters (i. e. nos. 2, 4, 6, 8, 11; henceforth referred to, for brevity's sake, as "capital-letter vowels"). They occur only under stress; and they occur in both free and checked syllables, but the checked syllables in which they occur are almost exclusively limited to word-final position. That is, we find a great many correspondences of the

[19]For further discussion of this procedure of reanalysis and rephonemicization, cf. Zellig S. Harris, *Methods in Structural Linguistics* §9 (Chicago 1951).

type OSFr. ála ala 'wing': ONFr. ǽlǝ ele < PGRom. Ála, and also of the type OSFr. tál tal 'such': ONFr. tǽl tel < PGRom. tÁl, but almost none of the type which we may represent by a hypothetical OSFr. *másta: ONFr. *mǽstǝ, for which we would have to set up a PGRom. *mÁsta. The corresponding "small-letter vowels" (nos. 3, 5, 7, 9, 10) and the high vowels /i u/ (nos. 1 and 12) are much freer in their occurrence; we find them in both. stressed and unstressed, both free and checked syllables, but quite freely in non-word-final position, as in OSFr. kánta canta "he sings": ONFr. čántǝθ chantet, and OSFr. kantár cantar "to sing": ONFr. čantǽr chanter.

This limitation on occurrence suggests that the capital-letter vowels which we first set up for PGRom. may at one time have been positional variants of the corresponding small-letter vowels, whose occurrence was conditioned by certain factors which were later lost.[20] Let us assume, provisionally, that the capital-letter vowels were at first limited to free stressed syllables, and that the checked syllables in which they would seem to occur according to the evidence of ONFr. and OSFr. were, in PGRom. times, not checked but free, because of some vowel which earlier followed the final consonant but which was later reduced to zero. This following vowel we may provisionally symbolize by the cover-symbol /ǝ/, simply meaning "some as yet unidentified following vowel," without prejudice to any later reinterpretation we may make of it. Our previous reconstruction of PGRom. Ála 'wing' we now replace by ála; of tÁl 'such', by tálǝ; and, if we had need of reconstructing a PGRom. *mÁsta, we would replace it by *másǝta. By this device we reduce our inventory of PGRom. vowel phonemes from twelve to eight or possibly seven; five of the basic correspondences are now seen to be reflexes, very possibly, not of independent vowel phonemes in PGRom., but of conditioned developments of other vowels when stressed and in a free syllable.

But this new theory immediately comes into conflict with a further fact: that the small-letter vowels occur in free syllables in ONFr. and OSFr., as in OSFr. bátre batre 'to beat': ONFr. bátrǝ batre < PGRom. bátre; OSFr. kápa 'cape': ONFr. čápǝ chape < PGRom. kápa. How can we square this fact with our new theory? When we look further and observe the other instances of small-letter vowels occurring in free syllables in ONFr. and OSFr., we notice that we find them only before certain consonants that are intervocalic or that stand between vowel and /r/ + vowel (as in the examples

---

[20]For the significance of such limitations on occurrence and their implications for earlier stages of the language, cf. H. M. Hoenigswald, "Internal Reconstruction," *SIL* 2.78–87 (1944), and "Sound Change and Linguistic Structure," *Lang.* 22.138–43 (1946) ([139]); and for a discussion of the relation between phonemic change and the loss of factors which condition positional variants, cf. most recently W. F. Twaddell, *Lang.* 24.151 (1948) ([296–7]).

given). We could obviate our difficulty if we assumed that these consonants had some characteristic that caused them, though intervocalic, to check the preceding syllable—e. g. that they were ambisyllabic in PGRom. This means that there would have been a contrast in PGRom. between ambisyllabic and non-ambisyllabic intervocalic consonants, which phonetically would most probably have been a contrast between long and short, double and single.[21] Hence, if we set up PGRom. báttre instead of our earlier bátre, or káppa instead of kápa, and, similarly, a double consonant phoneme after each instance of a small-letter vowel in an apparently free syllable in PGRom., we find our difficulty removed. Nor is this a wholly abstract or unrealistic procedure, so far as our OSFr. and ONFr. evidence is concerned, for we must set up a PGRom. double consonant anyhow at least in the case of /rr/, as in the correspondence OSFr. térra terra 'earth': ONFr. térə tere < PGRom. térra.

Once we have set up double consonants for PGRom., we find that certain consonant correspondences which we set up originally, noting that they occur only between vowels or between a vowel and /r/ + vowel (nos. 43–7), now appear to be in complementary distribution with single consonants elsewhere: /β/ with /b/, /z/ with /s/, /ɣ/ with /g/. Hence we are justified in replacing such a first approximation as PGRom. koβrír 'to cover' with kobrír, since our first approximation of PGRom. ábas 'abbot' (cf. no. 6) is now reinterpreted as ábbas. But we are still in a quandary as to what we originally set up as /ð/ and /δ/, since both are in complementary distribution with /d/ elsewhere. On the evidence of OSFr. and ONFr. alone, we simply cannot decide the problem, and must leave it unsolved; according to the evidence with which we have been working so far, there were too many allophones in partial complementary distribution in PGRom., and we cannot tell what their earlier status was. Was their occurrence determined by some other factors now lost and not recoverable by deduction? Do they represent a dialectal differentiation within PGRom.? Or do they represent two phonemes which were earlier quite distinct?

Here the modern dialects give us an answer. In Béarn, in the upper mountain valleys, there are dialects which clearly indicate that, not only for the dental series, but also for the labials and gutturals, there were single unvoiced stop consonants as well as voiced stop consonants in PGRom.[22] Consider the following tables of correspondences, the first set showing PGRom. /p t k/ and the second set showing PGRom. /b d g/:

[21]Cf. M. Swadesh, "The Phonemic Interpretation of Long Consonants," *Lang.* 13.1–10(1937).

[22]Cf. the materials gathered by W. D. Elcock, *De quelques affinités phonétiques entre béarnais et l'aragonais* (Paris, 1938), especially the sections entitled *Versant béarnais* in Chapters 1–3 and the Conclusion in Chapter 4. The examples given here are from Elcock and the ALF.

Bearnese	OSFr.	ONFr.	PGRom.
sápo 'sap'	sába	sǽvə	sápa
espáto 'sword-like	espáda	espǽðə	espáta
part of plow'	'sword'	'sword'	
pleká 'to fold'	plegár	pleiiǽr	plekárə
hábo 'bean'	fába	fǽvə	fába
sudá 'to sweat'	suzár	suðǽr	sudárə
ligá 'to bind'	ligár	liiǽr	ligárə

These correspondences survive only scatteringly in Bearnese, and in a very restricted region; but they are sufficient, and the evidence (including absence of false reconstructions, i. e. hyper-urbanisms) is enough to show that they are relics of an earlier state of affairs, not later developments.[23] The evidence of Bearnese thus helps to remove a further doubt, and to assign PGRom. [ð] to the /t/ phoneme and [ð] to the /d/ phoneme, and also to distinguish between single intervocalic /p/ and /b/, /k/ and /g/ for PGRom.

Furthermore, it is obvious that for PGRom. we may retain the symbols used for correspondences nos. 31–42, but must interpret them phonemically as consisting of consonants plus a phonemic feature of palatalization, similar to the situation in modern Russian,[24] Marshallese,[25] and other languages. We are thus enabled to reduce our stock of PGRom. phonemes to the following:

Vowels			*Consonants*		
i		u	p	t	k
e		o	b	d	g
ε	(ə)	ɔ	f	s	
	a		v		
			c		
			ʒ		ǧ
		m	n		
			l		
		w	r		h

plus phonemes of palatalization and stress. Further reduction might be possible: we might suspect, for instance, that /ǧ/ was in complementary distribution with /i/ in hiatus, and thus eliminate one further phoneme.

The modern dialects are also of help in giving evidence for the occurrence in PGRom. of a greater variety of final vowels than we might deduce from the OSFr. and ONFr. evidence alone; cf. the final /i/ attested by such forms as otri, autri 'others' in the departments of Haute-Loire and Puy-de-Dôme (ALF map 76), and final /o/ or /u/ for, say, the types kútu kúto

[23]Cf. Elcock, op. cit. 121–2.
[24]Cf. G. L. Trager, "The Phonemes of Russian," *Lang.* 10.334–44 (1934).
[25]Cf. Denzel R. Carr, "Notes on Marshallese Consonant Phonemes," *Lang.* 21.268–9 (1945).

'elbow' and pénsu pénso 'I think' in SE France and Switzerland (ALF maps 330, 996).

Now if we were limited to the evidence of ONFr., OSFr., and the present-day dialects of Gallo-Romance, without benefit of the other Romance languages or of Latin, our reconstruction as first made and later amended and simplified would probably still be the occasion for fierce debates. There might be a disagreement among scholars as to the validity of the identification of capital-letter vowels with small-letter vowels, of our postulation of double intervocalic consonants, or of a separate series of single unvoiced intervocalic stops /p t k/ for PGRom., similar to the disagreement now existing over the so-called "laryngeals" of Hittite and the Indo-European languages.[26] Critics of the reconstructed Proto-Gallo-Romance might condemn it in the name of one special doctrine or another, or of some a-priori consideration.[27]

Fortunately, we are not in this position. Our next step, once having reconstructed PGRom., is to examine it in the light of the related Romance languages, when we have followed the same procedure and have reconstructed Proto-Ibero-Romance, Proto-Italo-Romance, Proto-Eastern (Balkan) Romance, and Proto-Southern Romance. What we find usually confirms our reconstruction of PGRom., and enables us to proceed farther back in our reconstruction to a still earlier stage. We need not go here into such detail for these intermediate stages as we have for PGRom.; suffice it to say that when we have reconstructions for these other groups as we already have for PGRom., we are able to reconstruct the further preceding intermediate stages and to arrive eventually at a reconstruction of PGRom. itself. Naturally, at each stage, we apply the procedures of descriptive linguistics to our results, examining them, reanalyzing and reinterpreting them. In this way, we establish Proto-Western Romance by comparison of Proto-Gallo-Romance and Proto-Ibero-Romance, affording light especially on the earlier status of vowels (definite elimination of our cover symbol /ə/, occurrence of final vowels) and of consonant clusters such as /kt/ and /ks/, which developed in PGRom. to /t'/ and /s'/, but in PIbRom. to /xt/ and /xs/. The inclusion of Proto-Italo-Romance again deepens our time perspective and enables us to set up Proto-Italo-Western Romance, approximately equivalent to the conventional "Vulgar Latin." PItRom. furnishes conclusive proof of the correctness of the consonant system (with unvoiced and voiced stops, double and single consonants) which we assumed for PGRom. and must also assume for PIbRom., and gives evidence for further distinctions in the consonant

---

[26]Cf. E. H. Sturtevant, *The Indo-Hittite Laryngeals* (Baltimore, 1942), and *An Introduction to Linguistic Science* 158–63 (New Haven, 1947) and references given in fn. 7, p. 160, particularly the criticisms of Pedersen and Bonfante.

[27]Cf. the present writer's discussion of such objections in *Lang.* 22.273–83 (1946).

system, e. g. /č/ vs. /c/, as in PItWRom. bráččiu 'arm' > PItRom. bráččiu: PWRom. bráccu, but PItWRom. póccu 'well' > PItRom. and PWRom. póccu. On the other hand, the extensive system of palatalized consonants which we had to set up for PGRom. is seen to have developed from earlier clusters of /i̯/ + cons. or cons. + /i̯/, merged with other combinations such as /k/ + cons. or cons. + /k/.

A still further deepening of perspective comes when we bring Eastern Romance (Balkan and the "outpost" in Lucania) into the picture, giving us Proto-Continental Romance, in which we find evidence for new consonant clusters (e. g. /p/ + cons., as in PBRom. sépte 'seven': PItWRom. sétte < PContRom. sépte) and a distinction among back vowels which we did not hitherto suspect, between two types of high vowels (cf. the table below). Finally the inclusion of Southern Romance (Sardinian, Lucanian, Sicilian) shows us an analogous distinction among front vowels. Thus, we eventually arrive at nine sets of basic vowel correspondences, for which we at first postulate nine vowel phonemes in the parent (Proto-Romance) language:[28]

PRom. phoneme	PSRom.	PERom.	PItWRom.
u ˆ	kúlu 'arse'	kúlu	kúlu
u ˇ	gútta 'drop'	gútta	gótta
o ˆ	nódu 'knot'	nódu	nódu
o ˇ	mórte 'death'	mórte	mórte
a	kárru 'cart'	kárru	kárru
e ˇ	térra 'earth'	térra	térra
e ˆ	éska 'bait'	éska	éska
i ˇ	píske 'fish'	péske	pésče
i ˆ	víta 'life'	víta	víta

Furthermore, we are justified in making a deduction concerning the phonetic character of the new phonemes for which we have here set up the symbols /u ˇ/ and /i ˇ/. Inasmuch as they gave /u i/ in some languages and /o e/ in others, we may consider that their phonetic character must have been intermediate between [u i] and [o e], i. e. lax [ʊ ɪ]. Theoretical considerations of phonetic patterning strengthen this assumption, in that the lax [ʊ ɪ] stand to the tense [u i] in exactly the same relation as do the lax [ɔ ɛ] to the tense [o e].

Then a further analysis of the vowel system thus obtained shows that it can be reduced from nine separate vowels to five vowels plus a phonemic feature which—so far as our Romance material shows—consists of the

---

[28]In this table and in following discussions of PRom. vowel phonemes, the symbol ˆ indicates relatively high and tense tongue position, and ˇ indicates relatively low and lax position; a raised dot · following a vowel symbol indicates length.

contrast between close and open, and which applies to four out of the five vowels of Proto-Romance. We can extract this feature and, if we choose, can symbolize it by /ˆ/ written after the close vowel, leaving the open vowel unmarked.[29] Further internal reconstruction might then lead us to suspect that the same contrast applied at one time to all five vowels; and careful consideration of its relation to stress in free and checked syllables might also lead us to suspect (though we might not be able to prove it in detail) that stress was at one time correlated in some way with syllable length, and that our feature symbolized by /ˆ/ was perhaps earlier one of length rather than closeness of vowel.

Similarly, among the consonants the occurrence of /k/ in Sardinian and Vegliote corresponding to /č/ in Italo-Western Romance—as in PRom. déke 'ten' > PSRom. déke (> OSard. déke > Mod. Sard. dége), PBRom. déke (> Alb., Vegl. dík), but PItWRom. déče—would give us a clue to the earlier status of that /č/ as an allophone of /k/ before front vowels, including /i̯/. The passage of [č] to independent phonemic status took place when a following [i̯] before a back vowel became merged with it and the resultant [č] thus came to contrast with [k] before back vowels, as in PItWRom. bráčču 'arm' from an earlier brákki̯u, contrasting in PItWRom. with (say) kúlu 'arse.' Similar considerations hold for PItWRom. /i̯/, which turns out to have come from a merger of PRom. /g/ before front vowel, with PRom. (initial or intervocalic) /i̯/; and for PItWRom. /c/ and /ʒ/, resulting from fusion of earlier /ti̯/ and /di̯/ respectively, as in PItWRom. póccu 'well' < PRom. púti̯u, and PItWRom. ɔ́rʒu 'barley' < PRom. ɔ́rdi̯u.

A further point is in order here. What should be done in the case of such correspondences as that shown in no. 29 under the Proto-Gallo-Romance consonant system, in which we find ONFr. /h/ corresponding to zero in OSFr., and, on further examination, in other Romance languages as well? We might, of course, carry our reconstruction of /h/ all the way back to PRom., but, as comparatists have long since realized, we should be wary of assigning to the parent speech a phoneme or other feature attested only in a single language. In this instance, almost all the words in which /h/ occurs are limited to the Italo-Western Romance group. We might be justified in carrying it back at least to that intermediate stage; but, with almost all these words absent from Eastern and from Southern Romance, we have doubts about its validity for Proto-Romance. If we use our knowledge of the neighboring Germanic languages, we immediately observe cognate words in

---

[29]We could, of course, operating on an abstract plane, equally well decide to extract lowness of tongue position as a separate phonemic feature and symbolize it by /ˇ/, leaving the high vowels unmarked. Our decision to extract height of tongue position and leave low vowels unmarked is admittedly determined by ulterior considerations, namely the ease of equating PRom. /ˆ/ with Latin /·/.

Germanic, and the obvious thing is to assume borrowing not earlier than the "Vulgar Latin" (PItWRom.) stage. Even if we did not have such knowledge, we would still have our doubts, and might suspect that these words showing initial /h/ had been borrowed into PItWRom. from some language having that phoneme, and that the phoneme had been lost everywhere except in ONFr. Similar considerations would keep us from assigning the phoneme /w/ of Germanic loan-words (as we know them to be) to PRom.

The phonemic system we finally set up for Proto-Romance is, therefore:

Vowels			*Consonants*		
i		u	p	t	k
e		o	b	d	g
	a		f	s	
			m	n	
i̯		u̯	l		
			r		

plus the phonemic features of vowel height /ˆ/ and stress, and the occurrence of double consonants.

The same technique, applied to the morphological system and the syntax (phrase and clause structure) of the Romance languages, would give us a good picture of the essentials of Proto-Romance as a linguistic system. We would see a system of nominal inflection with at least two numbers, two genders, and five cases (nominative, accusative, genitive, dative, and vocative), and verbal inflection with three persons, two numbers, two stems, and at least three tenses and various non-finite forms built on each stem. A large number of the formant elements of Romance derivation can be similarly reconstructed, including prefixes, suffixes, and compound types. Comparative syntax would show us a PRom. system of endocentric and exocentric phrase-types and the existence of the major clause having a verb or equivalent phrase as its essential element, accompanied or not by a subject. This system as reconstructed and outlined here is of course nothing novel to Romance scholars; the all important point is that we would arrive at it by methods of purely comparative reconstruction.

When we now turn to our records of Latin, we find our inferences—inverted predictions, backwards rather than forwards in time, as to what we may expect to discover concerning the past—largely corroborated. We find our reconstruction of phonemics very close to the facts as we know them for Latin; Classical Latin gives us evidence for certain further phonemic features (such as the existence of a phoneme /h/—not connected with the /h/ occurring in Germanic loan-words—and the occurrence of /m/ in word-final position) which we could not infer from any of the Romance material, and gives us a basis for a better understanding of some Romance phenomena such as the relation of vowel quality, quantity, and stress, and the loss of phonemic contrast between /a/ and /a·/. Yet Classical Latin differs in various respects from Proto-Romance, and is clearly not its direct ancestor. Thus, Romance shows a use of the relative kú⁀iu -a 'whose' as an adjective which was not accepted as a normal feature of Classical Latin, where cuius was an invariable; and we hage to go back to Plautine Latin to find cuius -a -um normally inflected as an adjective. Clearly, Romance is here continuing an Old Latin feature which was lost in Classical Latin. Similarly, Classical Latin gave to the word báro baró⁀ne 'strong man', which in Romance has meliorative meaning, a pejorative turn in the sense of 'lout, oaf', which has continued only in the Italian words báro and baróne 'knave, rascal'; Classical Latin baro·n- cannot be considered as the direct ancestor of the Romance words built on this stem and meaning 'man, husband, nobleman'.[30] From these and similar instances, we must conclude that Classical Latin and Proto-Romance were not "mother" and "daughter", but rather "sister" languages (very closely related and easily mutually intelligible), by comparison of which we are enabled to reconstruct a slightly earlier stage which we may label simply Latin.

It is perfectly true that if we had no knowledge of Latin, we should be unable to place Proto-Romance in space or in time, as Migliorini says in the passage quoted in our first paragraph. As it is, by comparison of what we know—other than by inference based on Romance sources—of Latin, we can place Proto-Romance reasonably well in time. We must place it far enough forward in time to include the simplification of /ei/ to /i·/ (ca. 150 B.C.), of /ae/ to /e/ (1st cent. A.D.) and of /n/ before /s/ to (at least) nasalization (1st cent. B.C.), and the loss of /h/ (ca. Catullus' time or earlier). On the other hand, we must place it far enough back in time to precede the merger of /e·/ and /i/, /o·/ and /u/ (1st–2nd cent. A.D.) and the establishment of a new series of palatal phonemes through merger of the palatal allophones of /k g/ before front vowels with the developments of /ki̯/ and /i̯/ respectively. On the whole, the period of the late Republic and the early Empire (Augustan era) is indicated as the best time at which to set Proto-Romance. Certain possible survivals of features attested in earlier Latin (e. g. Plautine cuius -a -um 'whose' as an adjective in Ibero-Romance; Plautine -nunt 3 pl. of verbs in Italian ⁀no) would indicate that the beginning of our period should perhaps be put as far back as 250–200 B.C.; this is confirmed by considerations of settlement history, earlier emphasized by Gröber and recently revived by Bonfante.[31]

[30]Cf. the present writer's discussion of this word, *SIL* 5.65–8 (1947).
[31]"L'origine des langues romanes," *Renaissance* 1.573–88 (1943).

3. Methodological Considerations

There are some who think that the procedure we have advocated here, the comparative reconstruction of Proto-Romance, is useless or even harmful:[32]

> For what concerns Vulgar Latin, the application of the comparative method has proved not merely largely unnecessary, but partly harmful. There is an unbroken stream of Latin-Romance written material that permits us to observe the changes that took place without having to reconstruct them by the comparative method, which was the only one applicable in the case of the other groups mentioned [Indo-European, Germanic, Celtic, Slavic]. Eyewitnesses are far more cogent than circumstantial evidence, in linguistics as at law.

We suggest, on the contrary, that comparative reconstruction, as applied to Proto-Romance, is useful and beneficial, both for Romance linguistics and for linguistics in general. We shall discuss, in the following paragraphs, certain methodological considerations relating (a) to the comparative method as such; (b) to the relationships of the Romance languages; and (c) to future work in Romance linguistics.

A. The Comparative Method. The comparative method, as developed in Indo-European and Finno-Ugric linguistics in the 19th century, and later applied to other fields such as Malayo-Polynesian, Algonquian, Athabaskan, Uto-Aztecan, Bantu, etc., is a means whereby we are enabled to reconstruct the essential traits of a linguistic system from which divergent languages have developed by later differentiation. The comparative method rests, indeed, on two basic assumptions: one, that phonetic change is regular;[33] the other, that where we find obviously related but different forms, they are to be considered as having developed from an earlier common source unless evidence to the contrary can be adduced.[34] Both of these are assumptions, not exceptionless iron "laws": there are many exceptions, but wherever exceptions are found, our assumptions are productive in that they lead to further examination and re-formulation of the facts.[35]

Romance occupies a crucial position in this respect, in that it offers one of the few instances in which we have quite full material for the "daughter" languages, and also very full data for a language which, though not exactly

---

[32] M. A. Pei, *Symposium* 1:3.118 (1947).

[33] Cf. the discussion in Bloomfield's *Language*, Chapter 20.

[34] Cf. Bloomfield, *Language* §18.2.

[35] Cf. the penetrating and illuminating discussion of the comparative method and of the assumption of regular phonetic change by C. F. Hockett, "Implications of Bloomfield's Algonquian Studies," *Lang.* 24.117–31 (1948), especially 125–7 ([286–7]).

the parent language, was extremely close to it. On the other hand, we do not have adequate data on the actual parent language itself (Proto-Romance) nor for the intermediate stages between Proto-Romance and the earliest documents in specifically Romance speech. Such written material as is available from the Late Latin period is so confused and untrustworthy that it would be unrealistic to interpret it literalistically and consider it a faithful reflection of popular speech.[36] These gaps must be filled in by reconstruction. Now when we reconstruct such Proto-Romance forms as u̯í ˄ ta 'life', béne 'well', dormí re 'to sleep', etc., we find that they correspond point for point to well-attested Latin words such as vīta, bene, dormīre and so on; the instances of such correspondences can be numbered in the thousands. Hence we are justified in concluding that the method which we have followed in the reconstruction of Proto-Romance is accurate, and that we have a right to go further and extrapolate from known Romance data to the establishment of hypothetical Proto-Romance forms. For instance—to keep to elementary, well-known material—Romance gives us no basis at all for assuming a cluster /ns/,[36a] or final /m/ in polysyllables, or initial /h/ in any words except those borrowed from Germanic (cf. above). We must reconstruct PRom. ómine 'man', píske 'fish', mé ˄ sa 'table' and the like, even where Classical Latin wrote (and at one time spoke) hominem, piscem, mēnsam. We must reconstruct PRom. méle 'honey', féle 'gall', sále 'salt', even where Classical Latin offers us only mel, fel, sal; and we must take the word of our reconstruction as being basically more correct for PRom. than the Classical Latin. Sometimes we find direct confirmation of our reconstructions (positive or negative), as in Latin graphs like cosul for consul, or in Late Latin salem for sal. More often, the confirmation is indirect, as in Catullus' poem on Arrius

---

[36]H. F. Muller, *The Chronology of Vulgar Latin* (Halle, 1929; ZRPh. Beiheft 78); H. F. Muller and P. Taylor, *A Chrestomathy of Vulgar Latin* (New York, 1932); H. F. Muller, *L'Epoque mérovingienne* (New York, 1945), and cf. the review of the latter book by A. H. Krappe, *Philological Quarterly* 26.92–5 (1947).

[36a] In this connection, the Romance words belonging to the family of It. pensare, Fr. penser, Sp. pensar 'to think' seem at first to contradict this statement, and to give evidence for a cluster /ns/. The answer is that the evidence thus afforded is valid only for Italo-Western Romance. In Roumanian and Sardinian, only forms without /n/, meaning 'weigh' or 'press, worry', are present; cf. Meyer-Lübke, *REW*[3]§6391. For Proto-Romance, therefore, we have the right to set up only /pe sáre/ 'to weigh, press down'; the learnèd word /pe ˄ nsáre/ is to be ascribed only to the PItWRom. stage. Naturally, as soon as /pe ˄ nsáre/was introduced from Classical Latin, it brought the cluster /ns/ back again, but evidently only into that part of Romance speech which was continued in Italy and the West. A similar argument applies in the case of the Greek loan-word kámptein 'bend, turn, double around, bow down' > Lat. campsāre > It. cansare 'set aside, avoid' and Sp. cansar 'weary', and other Romance words showing the cluster /ns/. (Cf. *Lang.* 14.205–6 and 19.154–6.) Late Latin spellings such as thensaurus for thesaurus show simply that there was a dialectal difference at the time, and do not necessarily prove that we must assume the cluster /ns/ for PRom.

and his misplaced aitches, or in classical prosody (which elides final syllables ending in m); and in the same category of indirect confirmation come the fluctuations in spelling and grammar which we find in inscriptions and other documents which reflect popular speech to a certain extent. If, for instance, we find in an inscription[37] sepulchrum istu 'this tomb' in one line, and sepulchru istum in the next, we do not assume that each vagary of spelling represents directly a corresponding vagary of speech (which is unrealistic in the light of all we know of human spelling behavior); instead, we draw on our knowledge of the Romance languages and of reconstructed Proto-Romance, to interpret both of these spellings as standing for /sepúlkru ístu/ (or perhaps /sepólkro ésto/), and istu(m) as meaning 'this'.

But there are certain qualifications we must make immediately. One is that comparative reconstruction is of course limited to the available material and the deductions we can make therefrom. For this reason, every scrap of reliable evidence which we can find is of value, and even unreliable evidence needs to be taken into account and sifted for its bearing on the problem in hand.[38] The existing Romance languages and dialects give no evidence for a contrast between /a/ and /a˄/ in Proto-Romance, although we might suspect on grounds of internal evidence that such a contrast had been present earlier; but if we had trustworthy material from some now lost Romance dialect which showed this contrast or developments thereof, we would be enabled to push our reconstruction still further back and to set up with certainty a pre-Proto-Romance contrast of /a/ vs /a˄/ or /a·/. To a large extent, of course, Classical Latin fulfills this function, and enables us to state as certainties what would otherwise remain plausible but not absolutely certain hypotheses.

It also goes without saying that comparative reconstruction must be accompanied by descriptive reanalysis at every stage. If this is not done, we run the risk of needlessly multiplying the non-essential and non-significant

---

[37] In an inscription of the Christian era from Rome, reprinted in Muller and Taylor, *A Chrestomathy of Vulgar Latin* 108, without further indication of source.

[38] For this reason, old documents and relic forms in modern speech acquire a value, in this connection, seemingly quite disproportionate to their usefulness in other connections (literary or esthetic, or even in characterizing modern dialects). The scholar reconstructing a proto-language must, of necessity, be something of an anticuario verbal (as one Aragonese termed Elcock; cf. Elcock, op. cit. 19). Opponents of the comparative method have made a reproach of this fact, and have characterized comparatists and Neo-Grammarians as "seekers after dead fossils" and the like; cf. M. G. Bàrtoli, *Introduzione alla Neolinguistica*; B. A. Terracini, *¿Qué es la Lingüística?* 34; G. Bonfante, *Lang.* 23.360, 367 (1947). There is, of course, as much justification for "fossil-seeking" in this connection as there is in any other historical study, such as geology or comparative anatomy. Far from being out of touch with the process of growth and change in biological or social life, the good "fossil-seeker" derives an understanding of life from his work.

features we set up for each stage of our reconstruction; when this potential of error is raised to several powers in successive stages of comparison, we may obtain an extremely over-complicated picture. Occasionally, scholars have made such unrealistic suggestions as setting up a special phoneme to cover one individual discrepant etymological correspondence, as Bovet did in hypothesizing a phoneme which he labeled /Δ/ and an etymon symbolized by /ambΔáre/ for Fr. aller, It. andare, etc.[39] It is only to this type of exaggeration that we may legitimately apply such strictures as the following:[40]

> ... the traditional neogrammatical procedure of piling up everything in the reconstructed mother tongue, which becomes a sort of monstrous accumulation of all possible words, forms, sounds, and declensions of every kind ...

But we can see from the foregoing discussion that this description is not applicable to intelligent reconstruction, practiced with all the resources of descriptive analysis and with all care given to eliminating the effects of possible borrowings, analogical reshapings and other interfering factors. When thus performed, the example of Proto-Romance shows us that comparative reconstruction comes close enough to the "real thing" to be regarded as quite trustworthy.

Taken in this way, and with full realization of all the factors involved, our procedure with Proto-Romance proves also the validity of the "family-tree" type of reconstruction. Many recent writers have questioned the "family-tree" principle in historical linguistics, and have declared it incompatible with the fact that linguistic changes spread.[41] Actually, however, there is no contradiction between "Stammbaumtheorie" and "Wellentheorie":[42] the "family tree" is a schematic description of the *occurrence* of changes, the "wave theory" covers the description of their *spread*. There are, of course, continual splittings-off of new dialects in any language, which often become overlaid again (wholly or partially) by the introduction of features from other dialects, or which themselves spread and overlay other dialectal developments. Our family-tree must be as detailed as we can make it, to give us as close a picture as possible, by successive approximations, of the ever-

[39]Cf. E. Bovet, *Ancora il problem* andare, *in Scritti varî di filologia* (A Ernesto Monaci) 243–62 (Roma, 1901); and the criticisms of his procedure by E. Gorra, *Rassegna bibliografica della letteratura italiana* 10.103 (1902), and by C. Salvioni, *Archivio glottologico italiano* 16.209–10.

[40]G. Bonfante, *Lang.* 23.374 (1947).

[41]E. g. Bàrtoli, Terracini, Bonfante.

[42]As pointed out most recently by A. Goetze, *Lang.* 17.168 (1941); cf. also the well-balanced discussion of the relation between comparative method and linguistic geography by Bloomfield, *Language*, Chapters 18–20.

changing reality, the differentiation of a language into multifarious dialects and of their later relationships (replacement, merger).

The method of comparative reconstruction and its schematic representation in the "family tree" gives us a statement of linguistic relationships as such, by their main dividing isoglosses and in the order of their origin. In connection with these relationships, the geographical position of the languages concerned is a matter which it is often useful to know, but never essential. Sardinian, for instance, would be a valuable witness to certain features of Proto-Romance (distinction between /i/ and /e˄/, "hard" /k/ and /g/ before front vowels), whether its speakers lived in Sardinia, South America, or Timbuctoo.[43]

B. The Relationship of the Romance Languages. It is customary to represent the Romance languages as developing in a unilinear fashion, from Old Latin through Classical Latin to "Vulgar Latin", and then differentiating into the various branches, as shown in Figure A. But when we apply the comparative method, we get a decidedly different picture of the relationship of these languages to each other, as shown in Figure B. For each of the later stages of dialectal differentiation, marked on Figure B as "Roumanian dlcts"

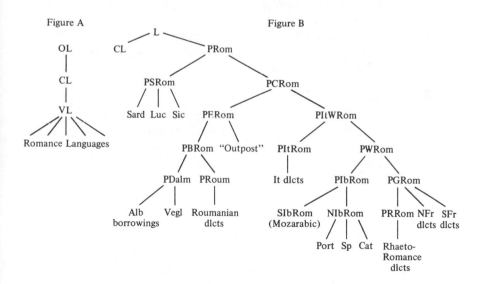

---

[43]It is through exaggeration of the factors of geographical position that M. G. Bàrtoli and his followers have been led into setting up ad-hoc rules (norme) by which all the evidence is judged. Cf. Bàrtoli's unsuccessful attempts to explain important exceptions to his rules, such as the conservative character of Sardinian (*Introduzione alla Neolinguistica*) or of Italian in the center of the Romance-speaking territory (*Per la storia della lingua d'Italia*, AG1B 21.72–94 [1927]).

(i. e. dialects), "It dialects," etc., further branches would have to be set up for which there is not room here.

We must recognize that, as suggested in Part 2 of this paper, the time of Proto-Romance unity must be pushed back far enough to include the features (nine-vowel system = five vowels plus contrast between tense and lax; "hard" /k/ and /g/ before front vowels) for which Eastern and Southern Romance (especially Sardinian) give evidence. The earliest group to split off, through not sharing in the merger of /i˅/ and /e̩/, involved Sardinian, Lucanian, and Sicilian;[44] the next to split off, through not sharing in the parallel merger of /u̩/ and /o̩/, was Eastern, particularly Balkan, Romance. For the intermediate stage that was the parent of both Balkan Romance and the other Romance languages of the European continent we may provisionally adopt the name Proto-Continental Romance; and for the intermediate stage that was the parent of the Romance languages not included in the Southern or the Eastern groups, the term Proto-Italo-Western Romance. In this stage we find the merger of /ki̯/ with /k/ before front vowels into /č/, of /i̯/ with /g/ before front vowels into /ǧ/, and the seven-vowel system /i e ɛ a ɔ o u/ customarily ascribed to Vulgar Latin. (It is not surprising that such a vowel system is customarily set up for VL, since the latter is usually established on the basis of Italo-, Gallo-, and Ibero-Romance.) If we wish to keep and use the term "Vulgar Latin," it would be well to restrict it to the sense of Proto-Italo-Western Romance as here defined.[45] Proto-Italo-Romance was then differentiated from Proto-Western Romance (the ancestral form of Gallo- and Ibero-Romance) by the assimilation of certain consonant clusters in PItRom. (/pt ps kt ks/ etc.) and by the development of a series of palatalized consonants in PWRom. (cf. Part 2 above). Later differentiations took place within each group, such as the sonorization of intervocalic unvoiced consonants in certain dialects of Gallo-Romance and of Ibero-Romance (later spreading to almost the entire Western Romance territory), the diphthongization or raising of vowels in stressed free syllable in Francian and Tuscan, etc., giving rise to the sub-varieties of each major division.

Even this proposed reorganization of the scheme of relationships among the Romance languages is sketchy, and will do only for a tentative grouping. Some dialectal divisions that undoubtedly once existed in the time

[44]Cf. H. Lausberg, *Die Mundarten Südlukaniens*; and M. L. Wagner's works on Sardinian, especially his *Historische Lautlehre des Sardischen* (Halle, 1941; ZRPh. Beiheft 93) and *Flessione nominale e verbale del sardo antico e moderno, Italia Dialettale* 14.93–170 (1938) and 15.1–29 (1939).

[45]Certainly it is not conducive to clarity to use the term "Vulgar Latin" to apply indiscriminately to all material written in Latin since Classical times, since the degree to which popular speech is reflected in such documents varies greatly and is anything but trustworthy. "Late Latin" is a much better term for this type of material, since it implies no judgment as to the accuracy with which the writing reflects everyday usage.

of the Empire must have been lost in later centuries, and it is perhaps to the effects of such lost dialectal divisions that we should ascribe a number of apparently inexplicable divergent developments in modern Romance, such as the anomalous l- of Italian luglio 'July' < PRom. ḭú~liu, and the equally anomalous initial /ǧ/ of Italian giglio 'lily' < PRom. lí~liu.[46] In any case, our picture of the intermediate stages of dialectal differentiation in Romance should be made as detailed as possible, with all the means at our disposal.

C. Future Work in Romance Linguistics. Future work in Romance Linguistics should represent a carrying forward of all the constructive traditions established in the last century since the time of Diez, without exclusion of any type of approach on a-priori grounds. It should include, therefore, the synchronic analysis of as many modern and medieval Romance linguistic systems as possible; the comparative reconstruction of Proto-Romance and intermediate stages of Romance dialectal development; and the interpretation of historical and geographical data in the light of the results thus obtained—with, of course, resultant further illumination of our previous analyses and reconstructions.

We must emphasize especially that synchronic analysis, comparative reconstruction, and the direct study of historical data such as documents and texts are by no means mutually exclusive. They are but different angles from which the same material—human speech and its history—can be approached, and all are equally essential.[47] To emphasize any one of these approaches at the expense of any other is harmful, in that it gives a false perspective. The latter half of the 19th century may have erred in over-emphasizing comparative reconstruction at the expense of other aspects of research; but the first half of the 20th century has erred far more in its almost complete neglect of comparative work in Romance. It must be the task of the second half of our century to restore a proper balance between comparativism and philology, to heal the unfortunate breach that has arisen between them, and to integrate into Romance linguistics the more recently developed techniques of structural analysis.

[46]That is to say, we might assume that in a certain dialect of PRom., initial /l/ and /ĭ/ were merged, either in /l/ or in /ĭ/ or in a third development (such as /l'/), so that PRom. lí~-lḭu and ḭû~lḭu came to be identical in their initial sound. Then at a later stage, these two forms were subjected to "false regression", with *ḭí~liu and *lú~liu arising as overcorrected forms and surviving in Italian. Cf. J. Babad, ZRPh. 19.270 (1895); also C. H. Grandgent, *From Latin to Italian* 70; Meyer-Lübke (tr. Bàrtoli and Braun), *Grammatica storica della lingua italiana e dei dialetti toscani* 91–2 (Torino, 1931); Pei, *The Italian Language* 50–1 (New York, 1941)—all of which either leave the problem unsolved or assume some kind of dissimilatory process.

[47]Cf. the discussion of the relation between philology, field method, and reconstruction, by C. F. Hockett, *Lang.* 24.118 ff. (1948) ([282 f.]).

Furthermore, workers in Romance linguistics are especially favored, as we have pointed out, in having material available at both ends of the period they study. For this reason, scholars in other fields often look to them for methodological guidance; Romance should be the ideal proving ground for linguistic method, and especially for testing the principles and procedures of comparative reconstruction, which is so essential in other fields where the parent speech is completely undocumented. But workers in Romance have all too often felt that the availability of material at both ends of their period frees them from the necessity of comparative reconstruction, and have turned their attention elsewhere. Hence a gap has developed between Romance and other fields of linguistics, to the regret of thoughtful scholars.[48] It is incumbent on Romance scholars to analyze and interpret their exceptionally full stock of linguistic material, using all the methods of study at their disposal, working both backward and forward in time. Only thus will Romance linguistics be enabled to do what others expect of it: to serve not only as an end in itself but as a model and a training-ground for workers in all fields of historical linguistics.

[48]Cf., for instance, L. H. Gray, *Foundations of Language* 460 (New York, 1939).

4

COMPARATIVE METHOD[*]

Henry M. Hoenigswald

When different changes, including different sound changes, affect different parts of one speech community (language split), we are faced with one earlier stage (ANCESTOR or PROTO- language) and two or more later stages (DAUGHTER languages, or, with regard to each other, SISTER languages). The procedure whereby morphs of two or more sister languages are matched in order to reconstruct the ancestor language is known as the COMPARATIVE METHOD.[1]

12.1. Sets of Correspondences

In the figures which follow, the phonemes of the ancestor language are entered, as heretofore, on the horizontal axis. The vertical axis, upward and downward, respectively, contains the phonemes for each one of two daughter languages.

If a phoneme a of the ancestor language in a given environment class (1) appears as m in one daughter language and as t in the other daughter language, corresponding morphs in the two sister languages will be matched in such a way that m in one answers t in the other. Such a pair of phonemes, one in the first language and one in the second, is a SET OF CORRESPONDENCES, written t/m (see Fig. 110).

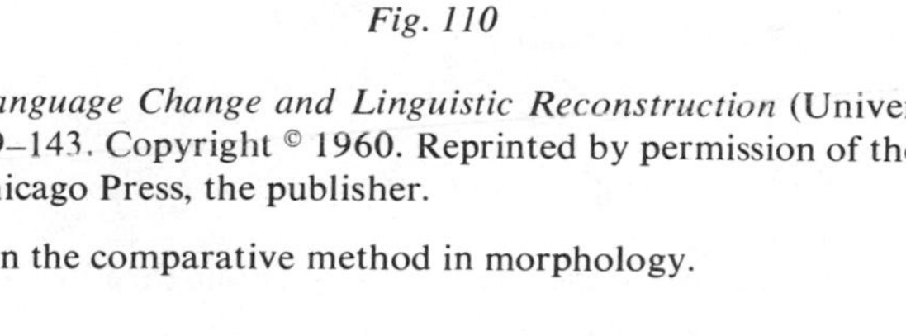

1			t	1	
			DAUGHTER LANGUAGE I		
a	1	PROTO-LANGUAGE			
			DAUGHTER LANGUAGE II		
1			m	1	

Fig. 110

*From *Language Change and Linguistic Reconstruction* (University of Chicago Press, 1960), 119–143. Copyright © 1960. Reprinted by permission of the author and the University of Chicago Press, the publisher.

[1]See 7.2 on the comparative method in morphology.

A given phoneme in a sister language may appear in more than one set; in addition to *t/m*, there may be *u/m* and *t/n*.

These three sets will arise, for instance, from three proto-phonemes and two mergers, one each in each daughter language (see Fig. 111).

The three sets *t/m*, *u/m*, and *t/n* all occur in the same environment, "1/1", hence they are in contrast with one another.[2] In the following sections sets and their distributions as they arise from sound change in sister languages will be examined. First we shall deal with a limiting case (12.2), then with cases in which one daughter language remains unchanged (12.3–6), and then with change in both daughter languages (12.7).[3]

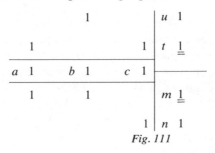

Fig. 111

12.2 Correspondence Sets in Phonemically Unchanged Daughter Languages

In the minimal instance neither language changes phonemically (see Fig. 112).

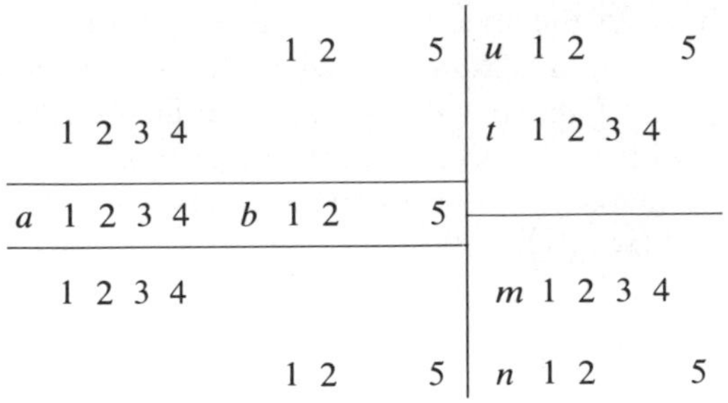

<pre>
                  1 2   5 │ u 1 2   5
        1 2 3 4   │ t 1 2 3 4
 ───────────────────────────┼──────────────
 a 1 2 3 4 b 1 2   5   │
        1 2 3 4   │ m 1 2 3 4
                  1 2   5 │ n 1 2   5
</pre>

Fig. 112

As a result these sets exist:

t / m in environment 1/1 2/2 3/3 4/4
u / n in environment 1/1 2/2   5/5.

---

[2]One numeral ("1") is used to denote corresponding environment classes in three languages (see n. 1 of chap. 9).

[3]"Unchanged" in respect to the segments in question. (See 13.1.1.)

Clearly, each set in each subenvironment represents a phone or an aggregate of phones of the proto-language. If the environments are assumed to be stable (9.1), hence distinct (as "1", "2", "3", "4", "5") in the proto-language, there were at least two contrasting phones in 1,2 and only one in 3,4,5. The phone represented by *t/m* may then be rewritten *$*a$; that represented by *u/n*, as *$*b$ even in the environments 3,4 and 5, respectively. Since *t*-in-3,4 is assigned to the phoneme *t*, and *m*-in-3,4 to the phoneme *m*, presumably on phonetic grounds, it is simplest to infer that the antecedent of *t/m* in 3/3,4/4 was more "similar" to *$*a$ than to *$*b$. Conversely, *u/n* is to be assigned as a descendant of *$*b$ rather than *$*a$.

12.3. Correspondence Sets from Sound Change in One Daughter Language

Reassignment without merger (see 9.1.2) in one daughter language (II)

		1	2		5	*u*	1	2			5		
	1	2	3	4		*t*	1	2	3	4			
a 1 2 3 4	*b* 1 2	5											
	1	2	3			*m*	1	2	3				
		4		1 2	5	*n*	1	2		4	5		

Fig. 113

(Fig. 113) produces these sets:

> *t / m* in 1/1 2/2 3/3
> *t / n* in   4/4
> *u / n* in 1/1 2/2   5/5

Again, in 1,2, *$*a$ and *$*b$ may be reconstructed by observing *t/m* and *u/n* in contrast and by extending the reconstruction to *a* in 3 and *b* in 5 on the same grounds as before. There is, however, a third set, *t/n*, in a non-contrasting position (viz., 4). The proto-phone which it represents was, then, distributed complementarily with the phones already assigned to *$*a$ as well as with those assigned to *$*b$. The sister languages give no clue as to which of the two it resembled more.

12.4. Unconditional Merger in One Daughter Language

If language II goes through an unconditional merger (see 9.1.3.1) (Fig. 114) we obtain:

> *t / m* in 1/1 2/2 3/3 4/4
> *u / m* in 1/1 2/2   5/5

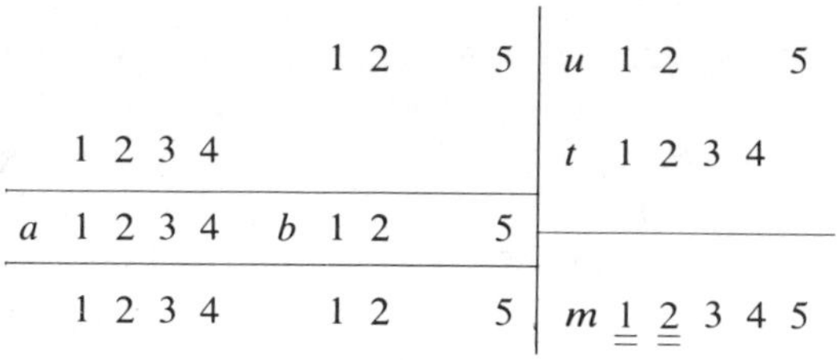

```
                    1 2        5 │ u  1 2        5
        1  2  3  4               │ t  1  2  3  4
    ─────────────────────────    │───────────────
  a  1  2  3  4   b  1  2    5    │
    ─────────────────────────    │───────────────
        1  2  3  4      1  2  5   │ m  1̲  2̲  3  4  5
```

Fig. 114

or two PARTIALLY LIKE sets (as *t/n* was partially like the other two sets in the last example) in normally contrasting and non-contrasting environments. Each set may be taken as continuing one proto-phoneme, *a* and *b*. Specifically, the merger of *a* and *b* in environment 1,2 has been retrieved.

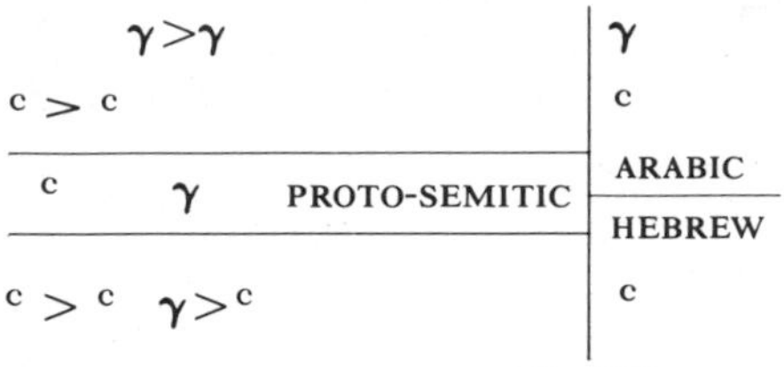

```
            γ>γ                        │  γ
     c  >  c                           │  c
    ─────────────────────────────      │────── ARABIC
        c      γ      PROTO-SEMITIC     │
    ─────────────────────────────      │────── HEBREW
     c  >  c    γ>c                     │  c
```

Fig. 115

Thus sound change in Hebrew (see 9.1.3.1) (Fig. 115) produces these set of correspondences between (unchanged) Arabic and Hebrew

c/c in most positions
γ/c in most positions

and hence allows us to reconstruct proto-Semitic *c and *γ.

12.5. Sets Resulting from Conditional Merger with Primary Split in One Daughter Language

This is the most general instance of phonemic merger (see 9.1.4.1) (Fig. 116).

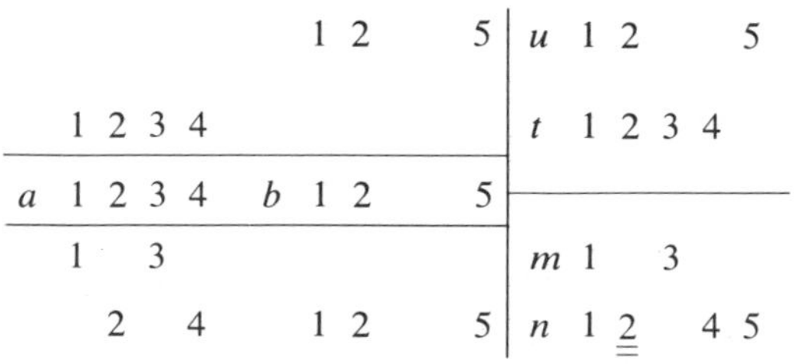

```
                    1 2        5 │ u  1 2        5
        1  2  3  4               │ t  1  2  3  4
    ─────────────────────────    │───────────────
  a  1  2  3  4   b  1  2    5    │
    ─────────────────────────    │───────────────
        1     3                   │ m  1     3
           2     4      1  2  5   │ n  1  2̲     4  5
```

Fig. 116

The resulting sets are:

$t \,/\, m$ in 1/1   3/3
$t \,/\, n$ in   2/2   4/4
$u \,/\, n$ in 1/1 2/2   5/5

The sets t/m and t/n are complementary; in addition, they are partially alike, which means that they may be taken as continuations from a proto-*a with split in language II. The set u/n contrasts with both t/m (in 1/1) and t/n (in 2/2) and hence represents a proto-*b: contrasting phones, even if "similar," are assigned to different phonemes. This is not binding for t/n in 4/4; this phone could be reconstructed equally well as belonging to *a or to *b.

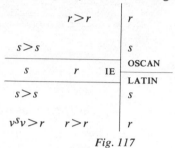

Fig. 117

Thus, in Oscan and Latin, IE (or proto-Italic) s and r have developed, as illustrated in Figure 117. These sets obtain:

s/s not between vowels   ——
s/r ——   between vowels[4]
r/r in all positions

for example, Oscan *pis*, Lat. *quis* 'who'; Oscan *aasa*, Lat. *āra* 'altar'; Oscan -*r*, Lat. -*r* (mediopassive ending).

12.6. Sets Resulting from Secondary Split in One Daughter Language

In secondary split (see 9.2) environments are merged as shown in

	1	2		3	4	*t*	1 2 3 4		
a	1	2		3	4				
	1	2>5				*m*	1		5
				3	4>5	*n*		3	5

Fig. 118

[4]This also includes position after semivowels and after vowel length; compare Figs. 81 and 90.

Figure 118. These sets ensue:

t / m in 1/1 2/5
t / n in   3/3 4/5

The two sets are complementary and partially alike and are therefore to be reconstructed as erstwhile allophones of one *a. Thus, from the secondary split of IE k^w into Indo-Iranian $č$, k, we have Figure 119. Correspondence

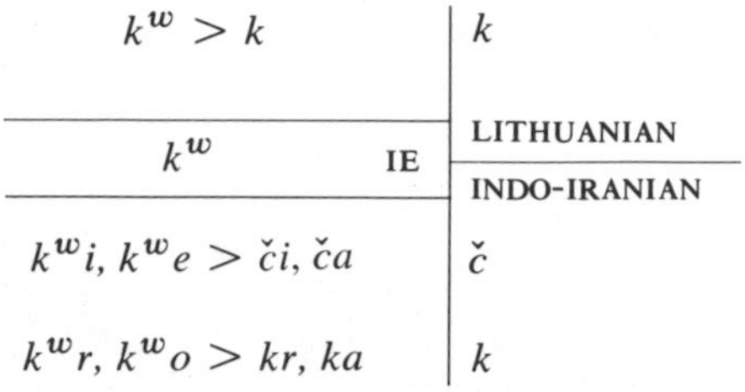

$k^w > k$	k
k^w — IE	LITHUANIAN
	INDO-IRANIAN
$k^w i, k^w e > či, ča$	$č$
$k^w r, k^w o > kr, ka$	k

Fig. 119

sets arise between Lithuanian and Indo-Iranian as follows:

	before i/i	before r/r	before e/a	before a/a
$k/č$	x		x	
k/k		x		x

Their distribution is, in other words, complementary, and one phoneme ("k^w") may be reconstructed.

12.7. Correspondence Sets from Sound Change in Both Daughter Languages

The preceding discussion suggests that allophones survive as complementary and partially like correspondence sets if one daughter language stays unchanged. Sound change occurring in both languages may jeopardize our chances to reconstruct.

12.7.1. Merger in Each Daughter Language; Different Sets Resulting

As Figure 111 shows, merger in each language need not, however, interfere with reconstruction. The problem summarized there has great importance in comparative work: it involves two phonemes in two sister languages forming three contrasting sets, leading to the reconstruction of a proto-language with three rather than two contrasts, or with a more elaborate phonemic structure than either daughter language (insofar as that particular sector of the phonemic system is concerned). Thus, if proto-Semitic were reconstructed from any two Semitic languages other than South Arabic, there would be sets of correspondences between sibilants, up to three in each language, for example, Akkadian š, s, North Arabic θ, s, š, and Hebrew š, ś, s.

If certain pairs of daughter languages are chosen, there are altogether four sets, for example, North Arabic/Akkadian: θ/š, š/š, s/š, s/s. In South Arabic there actually exist all four contrasting sibilants which represent the otherwise reconstructable proto-Semitic phonemes.[5] Similarly, Arapaho confirms, with its own θ:t:l:n, the reconstruction of proto-Algonquian *θ:*t:*l:*n, which could have been arrived at from such sets as Fox/Cree n/t, t/t, n/y, n/n.[6]

12.7.2. Multiple Origin for One Set

The same set may arise from more than one source. Here two rather different contingencies must be considered. The former (12.7.2.1) is less favorable to reconstruction: the latter (12.7.2.2), a more complicated process, leaves open certain possibilities. Under (12.7.2.3) both are confronted within one framework.

12.7.2.1. Duplicate Merger

The environments in which the same set arises overlap: two originally contrasting proto-phones merge (Fig. 120). (Note that here, and under

$$
\begin{array}{ccc|c}
4\ 5 & 4\ 6 & & t\ \ 4\ \ 5\ \ 6 \\
\hline
a\ 4\ 5 & b\ 4\ 6 & & \\
\hline
4\ 5 & 4\ 6 & & n\ \ 4\ \ 5\ \ 6 \\
\end{array}
$$

Fig. 120

12.7.2.2, index numbers and phoneme symbols are chosen so as to make the examples fit into the more general formulation below.) There is no trace of the twofold origin of the set t/n (or Slavic d / Iranian d) (Fig. 121). It might in

$$
\begin{array}{ccc|c}
d > d & dh > d & & d \\
\hline
d & dh & \text{IE} & \text{SLAVIC} \\
 & & & \text{IRANIAN} \\
\hline
d > d & dh > d & & d \\
\end{array}
$$

Fig. 121

fact be inferred that the common source of daughter languages I and II (of Slavic and Iranian) had only one, not two, phonemes.

Of course the merger of a and b into t and n, respectively, need not be unconditional. If the total picture were as shown in Figure 122, it would still be true that t/n is found to occur in 4,9,5,6, with no possibility to distinguish a (4,5) from b (4,9,6) or to establish complementary distribution of t/o with that part of t/n which comes from a.

[5]Bergsträsser, *Einführung* 4.
[6]Bloomfield, *Linguistic Structures* §6; Gleason, *Introduction* 341.

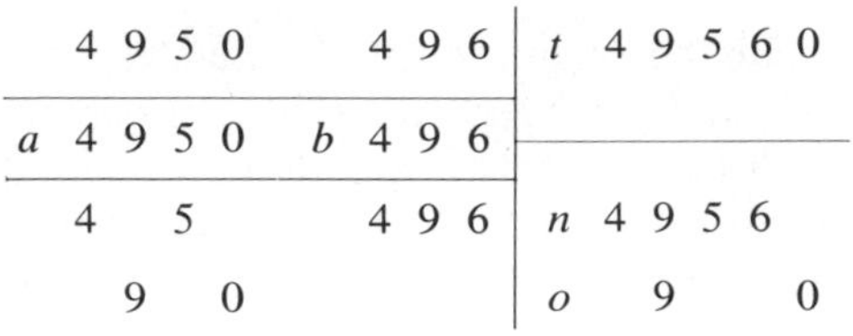

```
  4 9 5 0        4 9 6 | t  4 9 5 6 0
  ─────────────────────
a 4 9 5 0    b 4 9 6 ───────────────
  4     5        4 9 6 | n  4 9 5 6
  9     0              | o     9     0
```

Fig. 122

12.7.2.2. Composite Sets

The environments in which a set arises from one proto-phoneme are different from those in which the same set arises from another proto-phoneme (two originally complementary proto-phones are reassigned [see 12.8]), as shown in Figure 123. In this figure t/n-in-3 comes from a; t/n-in-2, from b.

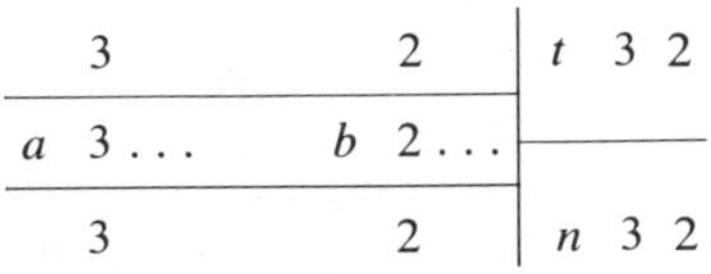

```
      3          2  | t  3 2
  ─────────────────────
a 3 . . .    b 2 . . . ────────
      3          2  | n  3 2
```

Fig. 123

For fuller discussion we single out the example in Figure 124; the conditioning of the mergers which provides the background for the comple-

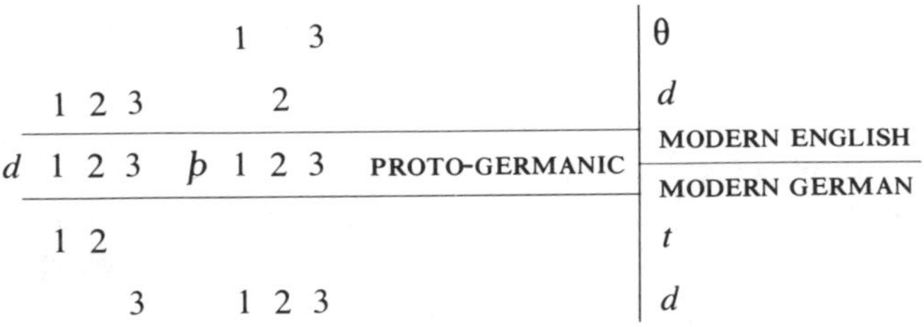

```
        1     3              | θ
  ─────────────────────────────
  1 2 3       2              | d
  ─────────────────────      MODERN ENGLISH
d 1 2 3   þ 1 2 3  PROTO-GERMANIC ──────────
                             MODERN GERMAN
  1 2                        | t
        3     1 2 3          | d
```

Fig. 124.—1 = many environments (e.g., after $*r > r/r$); 2 = after $*l > l/l$; 3 = after $*n > \emptyset/n, n/n$.

mentarity of the two parts of the set is also represented. The set d/d arises twice: from $*l\þ > $ E ld and from $*nd > $ G nd.

The observable sets are:

	"1"	"2"	"3"
d/t:	after r/r, etc.	after l/l	——
$θ/d$:	after r/r, etc.	——	after ϕ/n
d/d:	——	after l/l	after n/n

Examples are: E *sword*/G *Schwert-*, *hold*/*halten*; *hearth*/*Herd-*, *mouth*/*Mund-*; *gold*/*Gold-*, *bind*/*binden*.

This array contains indications of its historical origin. First, in no environment are there more than two contrasting sets. This suggests that there were never more than two phonemes involved. In analogy to synchronic procedure, it may be asked if one set cannot be treated as an "overlapping" phone and be divided into two parts: one part complementary with one remaining set, the other part complementary with the other remaining set. Now, clearly, the third set, *d/d*, which is partially alike with both the first (same English component) and the second (same German component) sets, is the most promising candidate for such a division. Hence *d/d* after *l/l* may be assigned with θ/d; *d/d* after *n/n*, with *d/t*. This amounts to reconstructing two proto-phonemes: *$\not b$* ($>$ E θ, but after *l*, $>$ E *d*; $>$ G *d*) and *d* ($>$ E *d*; $>$ G *t*, but after *n*, $>$ G *d*), and that, as we know, is the correct solution. In fact, the older German texts write "nt" in words like *bintan* 'bind'; the records change to *binden* in Middle High German times.

12.7.2.3. General Formula

An extension constructed upon the last example will furnish a more general formulation. If there had been further environment classes—for example, one ("4") in which both *d* and *$\not b$* had occurred originally and had both yielded *d/d*, or one each ("5", "6") in which only *$\not b$* or only *d* had occurred and yielded *d/d*—the first observation (with regard to there never being more than two sets contrasting) still holds. But as *d/d*-in-4,5,6 is complementary with both *d/t* and θ/d, its prehistory is indeterminate, except for the possibilities offered by internal reconstruction.

$$
\begin{array}{llllllllll}
 & & & & 1 & \ \ 3 & & 8 & | & u \\
 & 1\ 2\ 3\ 4\ 5\ 7 & & & & 2 & \ \ 4\ 6 & & | & t \\
\hline
a & 1\ 2\ 3\ 4\ 5\ 7 & b & 1\ 2\ 3\ 4\ 6\ 8 & & & & & | & \\
\hline
a & 1\ 2 & \ \ \ \ 7 & & & & & & | & m \\
 & 3\ 4\ 5 & & & 1\ 2\ 3\ 4\ 6\ 8 & & & & | & n \\
\end{array}
$$

Fig. 125

In Figure 125 we consider two proto-phonemes, *a* and *b* (taking the place of Germanic *d* and *$\not b$* in the last example). They contrast in the environment classes 1,2,3,4; only *a* occurs in 5,7; only *b* occurs in 6,8.

The following sets ensue:

t / m in environments 1/1 2/2   7/7
u / n in environments 1/1   3/3   8/8
t / n in environments   2/2 3/3 4/4 5/5 6/6

The three sets are nowhere in full contrast. Therefore, one set may be broken up and divided between the two proto-phonemes needed; t/n, which is partially like each of the other two, is selected for that role (see above).[7] Thus t/n-in-2/2 is grouped with u/n ("*b", split in daughter language I); t/n-in-3/3 is grouped with t/m ("*a", split in daughter language II). The origin of t/n-in-4/4, 5/5, 6/6 remains undetermined.

12.7.3. Split in Both Daughter Languages

If two daughter languages let the same phoneme split up, the feature of partial likeness between resulting sets is endangered.

12.7.3.1. Split with Intersecting Conditioning

Consider the following: In Indo-Iranian, IE *s* > *s* (after *e* . .) and > *ṣ* (after *u* (*/w/) . .); *r* generally > *r* (Fig. 126). Altogether there are four relevant environments for IE *s*: after *e*, before consonant ("1"); after *u*,

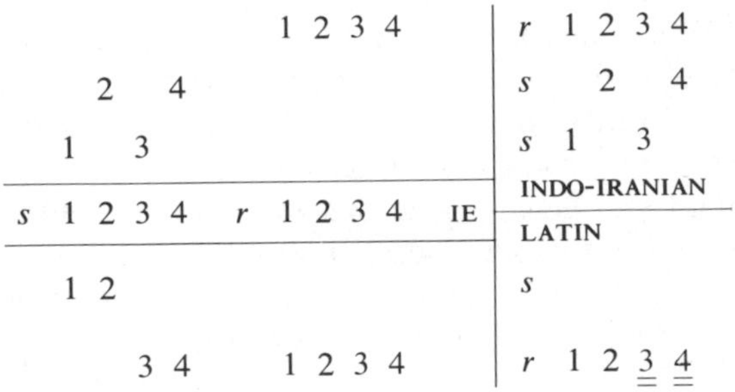

```
                  1 2 3 4      │  r  1 2 3 4

          2     4              │  s     2     4

          1     3              │  s  1        3
                               │ ─────────────────
   ─────────────────────────── │  INDO-IRANIAN
    s  1 2 3 4   r  1 2 3 4  IE │  LATIN
   ───────────────────────────
          1 2                  │  s

              3 4      1 2 3 4  │  r  1  2  3  4
```

Fig. 126

before consonant ("2"); after *e*, before vowel ("3"); and after *u*, before vowel ("4") (Fig. 126). As a result, Indo-Iranian and Latin correspond thus:[8]

s/s in 1/1 ("asp/esp")
ṣ/s in   2/2 ("usp/usp")
s/r in   3/3 ("asu/eru")
ṣ/r in   4/4 ("uṣu/uru")
r/r in 1/1 2/2 3/3 4/4

The first four sets are still neatly complementary with regard to the surrounding sets. Each, however, is partially like only two out of the other three complementary sets (thus s/s is partially like ṣ/s and also partially like

---

[7]Compare the breaking up of *o* in Fig. 64.

[8]It is, of course, an impressive physical fact that the environments which stay together share phonetic features: 1 and 2 = non-intervocalic, 3 and 4 = intervocalic; 1 and 3 are *e* . . , 2 and 4 after *u* . . . In other words, the conditioning is phonetically "simple" in both languages. (See 8.1.2.)

s/r but unlike *ș/r*). The fifth set, *r/r* (added for fuller background), contrasts, of course, with the first four. As a result, IE **s* (from the first four) and IE **r* may still be reconstructed as contrasting proto-phonemes.

12.7.3.2. Duplicate Split

The chainlike relation between the first four sets obtains if the conditions for the split in each language are independent and therefore intersecting (in Indo-Iranian: after *u*, etc.; in Latin: between any two vowels). But if the same allophonic division which has been made distinctive in one daughter language also operates, wholly or in part, in the other, sets without partial

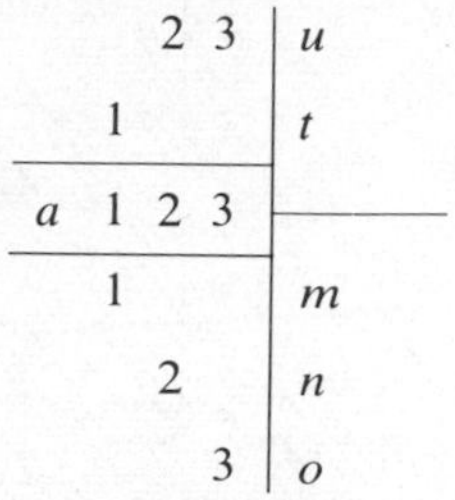

```
        2  3  │ u
           1  │ t
   a  1  2  3 ├──────
           1  │ m
           2  │ n
           3  │ o
```

Fig. 127

likeness will result. For instance, Figure 127 (with an allophonic difference between 1 and 2,3 leading to duplicate split) implies these sets:

t / m in 1/1
u / n in   2/2
u / o in   3/3

that is, three complementarily distributed sets of which one (*t/m*) is totally different from the other two. So long as the split-off phones do not MERGE in duplicate fashion as well (12.7.2.1), their distribution remains indicative of

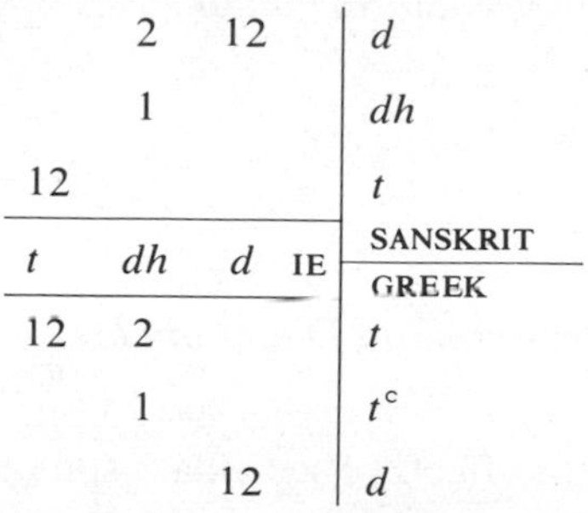

```
      2      12  │ d
          1      │ dh
   12            │ t
                 │ SANSKRIT
   t    dh   d  IE├────────
                 │ GREEK
   12    2        │ t
          1       │ tᶜ
             12   │ d
```

Fig. 128.—2 = before a following syllable beginning with an aspirate; 1 = otherwise. IE **dh* splits along the same lines in Sanskrit and in Greek, but in Sanskrit it splits by merging with IE **d*; in Greek, by merging with IE **t*. **t* in 2 was rare.

their origin. Figure 128 (with legend) is an illustration. The sets from *dh*, viz., *d/t* before, say, *h/k^c* in the next syllable and *dh/t^c* before, say, *j/g* in the next syllable, are unlike (owing to duplicate split) but complementarily distributed (owing to mergers in different directions and hence to continuing recognizability of the conditioning environments).

12.7.3.3. Primary Split Based on Duplicate Merger

If the process of merger which at the same time constitutes a ("primary") split in each daughter language is duplicated from one daughter language to the other, the split itself is lost (i.e., it can be reconstructed only

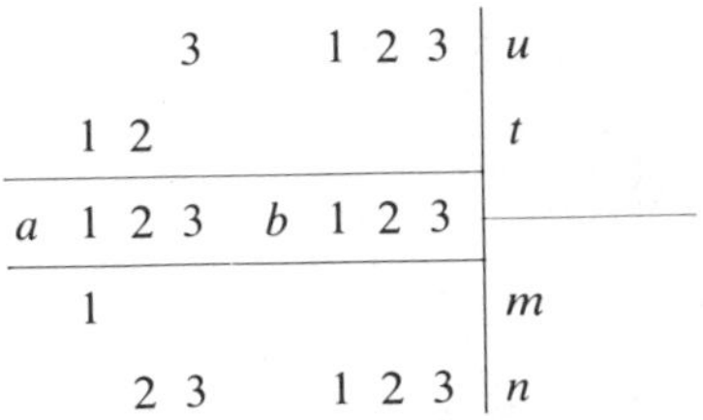

$$
\begin{array}{ccc}
& 3 \qquad 1\ 2\ 3 & u \\
1\ 2 & & t \\
\hline
a\ \ 1\ 2\ 3 \quad b\ 1\ 2\ 3 & & \\
\hline
1 & & m \\
& 2\ 3 \qquad 1\ 2\ 3 & n
\end{array}
$$

Fig. 129

as having taken place before the dialect division). If the changes are like those shown in Figure 129, with *a*-in-3 and *b*-in-3 merging in each language, the sets are:

$t\ /\ m$ in environment 1/1
$t\ /\ n$ 2/2
$u\ /\ n$ 1/1 2/2 3/3.

There is no indication (outside of morphophonemics) that u/n-in-3/3 contains a proto-phone which had split off from *a*. The split itself in this example is non-duplicate (12.7.3.1). If there is duplicate split (12.7.3.2; i.e., if there is no relevant environment class 2), we obtain

$t\ /\ m$ in 1/1
$u\ /\ n$ in 1/1   3/3;

that is, the sets are unlike.

12.7.3.4. Secondary Split Based on Duplicate Merger in Environment

Next we consider the effects of secondary split, that is, of merger in the environment such that former allophones come to stand in contrast (see 9.2). As the discussion in 12.6 shows, this is not fatal so long as it takes place in one daughter language only; it simply leads to what are in effect partially like (but still different) environment sets (2/5 and 4/5 in Fig. 118) as settings for partially like sets of phonemes (*t/m* and *t/n*). Evidently, once the same environmental distinctions which are obscured in daughter language II are partly or wholly obscured in daughter language I as well, the merger, along with the secondary split associated with it, can no longer be retrieved without the help of internal reconstruction. A proto-*a* may split as shown in Figure 130. The two daughter languages agree in (1) assigning *a*-in-1,2 and *a*-in-3,4,6 to different phonemes and in (2) merging 2 and 4 themselves. In addition, 6 is merged with 2 and 4 in daughter language I (the resulting

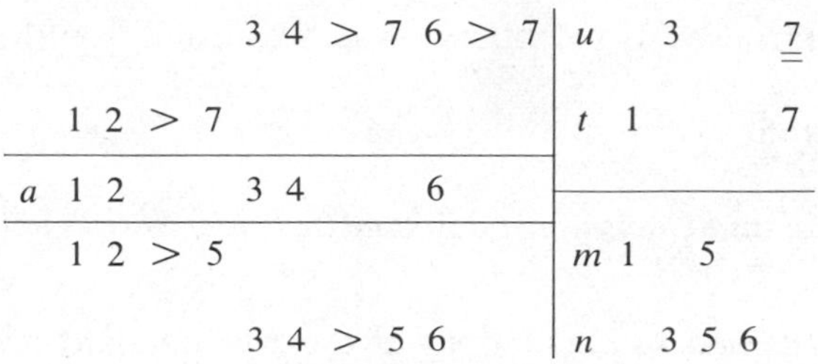

$$3\ 4 > 7\ 6 > 7 \ \Big|\ u \quad 3 \qquad \underline{\underline{7}}$$

$$1\ 2 > 7 \qquad\qquad\qquad t \quad 1 \qquad\quad 7$$

$$a \quad 1\ 2 \qquad 3\ 4 \qquad 6$$

$$1\ 2 > 5 \qquad\qquad\qquad m\ 1 \quad 5$$

$$3\ 4 > 5\ 6 \qquad\qquad n \quad\ \ 3\ 5\ 6$$

Fig. 130

environment class is labeled "7"), while it remains distinct in II (although, of course, simply as part of the environment—3,6—in which *n* does not contrast with *m*). The daughter languages correspond thus:

t / *m* occurs in 1/1 7/5
u / *n* occurs in   7/5 3/3 7/6.

To the extent that the environments have undergone duplicate merger (2 with 4 into 5 and the same 2 and 4 into 7), the two resulting sets contrast. In the present example the sets are unlike because the split itself was duplicate (12.7.3.2); if this had not been so, a chain of like sets would have arisen (12.7.3.1).

Umlaut, that is, a conditioned sound change turning fronted allophones of rounded vowels into phonemes due to merger in following syllables, occurs in various Germanic languages after their separation. The precise conditioning is not quite uniform. We compare (somewhat schematically) one daughter dialect (I) in which umlaut has been carried out in fewer

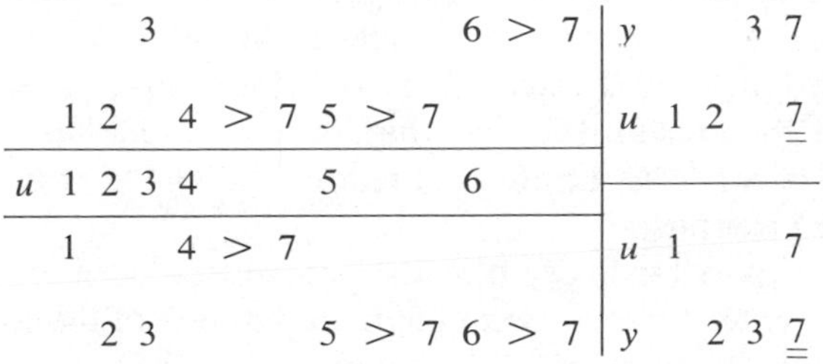

$$3 \qquad\qquad\qquad\qquad 6 > 7 \ \Big|\ y \qquad 3\ 7$$

$$1\ 2 \quad 4 > 7\ 5 > 7 \qquad\qquad u\ 1\ 2 \quad \underline{\underline{7}}$$

$$u \quad 1\ 2\ 3\ 4 \qquad 5 \qquad 6$$

$$1 \qquad 4 > 7 \qquad\qquad\qquad u\ 1 \qquad 7$$

$$2\ 3 \qquad\qquad 5 > 7\ 6 > 7 \ \Big|\ y \qquad 2\ 3\ \underline{\underline{7}}$$

Fig. 131

environments (3, 6) with another (II) where it has occurred in more environments (2, 5 in addition to 3, 6); moreover, environments 4, 5, and 6 are merged, duplicate fashion, into "7" in both daughter languages (Fig. 131).

As a result, we obtain

u / u in environment 1/1   7/7
u / y 2/2   7/7
y / y 3/3 7/7,

and we might erroneously reconstruct three phonemes, contrasting in 7/7.

12.8. Conclusion

12.8.1. *Internal and Comparative Reconstruction: Merits and Limits*

The merits and the limitations of the two standard methods for the reconstruction of the phonemic shape of morphs and for the reconstruction of sound change might be summarized as follows.

Internal reconstruction is based on the principle that phonemes which alternate represent, wholly or in part, former co-allophones. Internal reconstruction can recover processes of split, provided that morph boundaries occurred between the phone in question and the phone(s) making up the conditioning environment. It recovers processes of merger insofar as they are incidental to processes of split. The chances for successful internal reconstruction diminish as morpheme loss, analogic innovation, and further sound change overlay the effects of the split.

The comparative method is based on the principle that sets of recurring phoneme correspondences between two related languages continue blocks of positional allophones from the mother language; therefore, if such sets are subjected to the treatment accorded to phones in synchronic phonemics, a reconstruction is obtained. If split affects the same proto-phoneme in each daughter language, the partial likeness between the sets of correspondences is impaired, but their distribution remains intact. If merger affects the same proto-phoneme in each daughter language, it must not be duplicate merger, that is, the same set must not arise twice in the same environment, or the original contrast is beyond retrieval. It is evident that the strength of the comparative method rests on the fact that, once a merger has taken place, no subsequent event can have the effect of reconstituting the original distinction between merged morphs.

It would be possible to combine the procedures for internal reconstruction of each daughter language with the manipulation of the correspondence sets. For instance, in comparing Oscan and Latin (12.5), we might write our sets, instead of simply

OSCAN	*s*	*s*	*r*
	—	—	—
LATIN	*s*	*r*	ɾ

in this fashion:

OSCAN	*s*	*s*	*r*
	—	—	—
LATIN	*s* ~ *r*		*r*

thus indicating that the particular instances of Lat. *r* which are matched by an Oscan *r* are either alternating or indeterminate (10.1.1).

The combination of internal and comparative reconstruction is particularly enlightening in the recognition of composite sets. Our example above (12.7.2.3) probably contains only indeterminate occurrences of proto-(*l*)þ and (*n*)*d*, owing to the absence in sufficient strength of morpheme boundaries preceding the dentals. The following example, however, will serve: in Greek, IE **t* yields *t*; in Germanic, it yields þ initially and after accented vowel, but *d* after unaccented vowel. However, IE **dh* > Gk. *t*ᶜ, except > Gk. *t* if the next syllable begins with another aspirate; *dh* goes to *d* generally in Germanic. Thus some instances of Gk. *t*/Germanic ("Gmc.") *d* are from IE **t*; others are from IE **dh*. Moreover, Gk. *t* < **dh* is typically initial and does not seem to occur in environments in which IE **t* becomes Gmc. *d*. Not only is it true, therefore, that the environment range of *t*/*d* falls into two parts—one in which *t*/*d* is complementary with *t*/þ, the other in which it is complementary with *t*ᶜ/*d*—but there are also, among the *d*'s of the first-named range, near-instances of alternation with þ (e.g., *patér*/Gothic *fadar* 'father', *p*ᶜ*rátēr* 'member or a brotherhood'/*broþar* 'brother'), and corresponding instances of alternation of the Gk. *t* of the last-named range with *t*ᶜ (e.g., *trép*ᶜ*ō* 'I thicken', *t*ᶜ*répsō* 'I shall thicken'/Gothic *drobjan* 'trouble').

The presence of alternation may decide questions in which mere complementary distribution admits more than one solution; what in synchronic phonemics can serve only purposes of elegance without being necessarily relevant is here an overriding factor, since alternations are normally the outcome of a split. This becomes strikingly clear where φ is in some way part of the picture (9.1.3.2).

According to one plausible interpretation of the data, Figure 132 summarizes the antecedents of parts of the Greek and the Celtic vowel system;[9] where 1 and 2 are certain interconsonantal environments, 1 includes *VC——CV*, 2 includes *#C——CC*. Clearly, if φ were an ordinary phoneme, it would be said to have undergone duplicate split associated with non-duplicate merger. The result is as may be expected:

[9]Hoenigswald, *Lg*. 35.419.

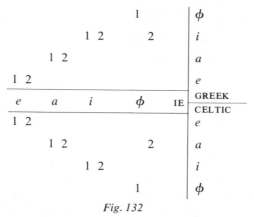

Fig. 132

in other words, Gk. *i*, where it corresponds to Celtic *a* (as in *pítnāmi* 'I spread'), occurs only between consonants and consonant groups that do not themselves, in that environment, cluster with each other. The fact that ϕ in any language and the set ϕ/ϕ in any two sister languages have an enormous distribution is not really an obstacle to recognizing its complementariness with other phonemes or other sets, since the occurrence of ϕ or ϕ/ϕ can always be stated negatively. However, in this case alternation serves to throw the mutual exclusivity of ϕ/ϕ and *i/a* into relief, since the paradigm of Gk. *pítnāmi* (with *i* in environment 2) contains such forms as perfect middle *péptamai* (with "ϕ in environment 1"). Physically, the Indo-European source of the set *i/a* may be pictured as a non-phonemic vowel-like segment occurring in certain consonantal environments. It is traditionally represented by "*ъ̄*" ("shwa secundum").[10]

12.8.2. *The Reality of Reconstructions*

In a literal sense reconstruction procedures serve only to identify the number of contrasting entities in the proto-language. But actually they do much more: they furnish presumptions about the location of these contrasts in the sequence (i.e., about the order in which the reconstructed segments follow each other), and they give us information on the physical nature of the proto-phones and proto-phonemes. These indications depend to some extent on the physical consensus between the daughter languages (as distinct from

[10]This amounts to reconstructing an allophone of ø (an automatic anaptyctic vowel). There is no compelling theoretical reason against the setting-up of such an entity. (See also 4.2.3.) The view of shwa secundum here represented is reported by Edgerton, *Lg.* 10.264 and more fully explained by Hoenigswald, *Lg.* 29. Celtic is named here because shwa secundum is plentifully attested in Celtic and Italic. Actually, evidence in a case like this must be pieced together from all over the Indo-European family.

recurrence of correlations in sets) and on certain considerations of phonetic and typological plausibility.[11]

Where there is consensus, that is, where the phones making up the phonemic correspondence set are phonetically similar, the proto-language may be thought, as a first approximation, to have had an equally similar phone. If the period of unity is relatively recent, the morphs of the daughter languages may be expected to resemble each other phonetically as well as to correspond to each other phonemically. But our examples in the previous chapters, with their implied or express phonetic comment, show that a great deal of phonetic similarity may persist, at least for some phonemes, for a very long time. The first step in recognizing common descent is usually the recognition of phonetic similarity (as in the early days of Indo-European studies the similarity of such etymologies as Skt. *mātr-*, Lat. *māter*, Old High German *muotar* 'mother', etc.). Later the more remote regularities are discovered, and in the event of conflicting correspondences, one of which involves relatively similar phones whereas the other does not, the search for doublets (5.2) may turn up proof which makes it certain that the two rival sets do not represent original contrast but contact under two separate sets of circumstances, or analogical new creation. Thus consensus, or similarity, is not only not needed for proof of relationship; where it cannot be expected considering the presumable time depth since separation, its appearance is suspect rather than welcome.

Even if true consensus exists, however, this does not necessarily mean that the ancestor language was identical with the daughter languages. Just as the comparative method sometimes leads to reconstructions (12.7.1) which are phonemically quite unlike either daughter language, and just as we know that some such developments are hidden from us because of duplicate merger, so there is no reason to suppose that consensus cannot be the result of duplicate development. If a typological change overtakes both daughter languages (8.4), the result may well be that they resemble each other, phonetically as well as in other ways, more than each resembles the mother language. Like duplicate merger, this may not be reconstructable. If more than two daughter languages are known, and if they may be treated as witnesses for the same reconstructed stage (chap. 13), there is often near-consensus on phonetic matters. The Indo-European stops show great similarity in Italic, Greek, Indic, Baltic, Slavic, and Celtic, with Germanic far apart (although the phonemic correspondences are extremely simple); this great majority alone, unless overridden by weightier areal or phonetic considerations, militates in favor of regarding the Germanic phones as secondary. Here the phonetic considerations, too, may be said to confirm the conclu-

[11]See Bonfante, *Word* 1;2.

sions: much of the phonetic alteration which takes place in German, like the replacement of stops by spirants, is of a rather widespread type, familiar at least to observers of the better-known European languages.

If there is neither complete nor even majority consensus, the phonetic and typological probabilities provide the only support. For conditioned sound change valuable phonetic clues may be obtained from the surrounding segments, using the fact that conditioned sound change is largely assimilatory (8.1). Scholars have attempted to determine the phonetic nature of the laryngeals in older Indo-European by making inferences from the secondary split in the surrounding segments which accompanied the disappearance of the laryngeals from the consonant system. Thus the laryngeal labeled ∂_3 (or γ) has been said to show "o-color" (if it is true that $\partial_3 e > o$, $e\partial_3 t > o{:}t$) and voicing (if $p\partial_3 > b$).[12] Similarly, there have been efforts to reconcile (in a chronological sequence) the somewhat contradictory evidence which Germanic, on the one hand, and Greek and Vedic Sanskrit, on the other, contribute toward the determination of the nature of the Indo-European word-accent phoneme on whose phonemic presence or absence the three languages agree: the effects in Germanic (voicing of spirants after an unaccented syllable) and the complete absence of any such effects in Sanskrit and Greek combined with the consensus of these languages tell two conflicting stories: the former evidence points to stress, the latter to pitch, as the phonetic characteristic.

In judging the concreteness of a reconstructed stage, we should not forget that, quite aside from phonetic detail, duplicate merger is lost in the comparative method and that unconditioned merger is lost in internal reconstruction (12.8.1). It is therefore always possible that we have missed a contrast which actually existed. The indications that this is so, if any, are in some sense typological. Reconstruction of the Romance languages apparently results in the setting-up of nine vowels. It is probable that eight of these (four front and four back) may be paired as long and short on the basis of the occurrence of the word accent in penultimate syllables. But this dichotomy is marred by the presence of a lone ninth-vowel correspondence (by consensus low unrounded) which acts in some forms like a long vowel, in others like a short one, while many forms, with the ninth vowel elsewhere than in the crucial type of penult, are indeterminate. The indications are, then, that the low vowel did at one time also occur either with or without following length and that a and $\bar{a}$ later merged unconditionally. The metrical evidence from recorded Latin (2.2) and the reconstructed earlier history of Latin itself both make it certain that a and $\bar{a}$ were in contrast; but, when dealing with material where we are not so fortunate as to possess these further controls, we cannot be sure. If it were true that language structure universally requires more than one vowel in a phonemic system, the fact that older Indo-European seems to

[12]See 12.8.3.2.

reconstruct with only one vowel would be highly suspicious (the different character of the known Indo-European vowel systems from those in the later languages should, of course, not be used as an argument [8.4]).[13] If one shares the suspicion, one should seek indications of an early merger of different vowel qualities into the one reconstructable vowel—the unusual nature of the phonemic system would then have only been temporary. If the merger was truly unconditional, no indications of that sort may be hoped for.

The few instances in which reconstructions may be checked against recorded texts in the proto-language or a very close relative thereof (13.1) have shown, on the whole, that they are rather effective. This is more definitely true, at the present juncture, of phonological and morphophonemic structure than it is of the lexicon, and particularly of syntax.

12.8.3.1. Sample Reconstruction (I)

In conclusion, we offer two sample reconstructions. The first concerns a sector of Indo-European consonant phonemics from two daughter languages, Vedic Sanskrit and Germanic. It is understood that analogical disturbances and pseudo-sets resulting from borrowing (e.g., in Germanic by borrowing from another Indo-European language) have been previously eliminated.[14]

The sets are (Sanskrit/Germanic):

I	II	III	IV	V	VI	VII	VIII	IX	X	XI	XII
t/t	*t/d*	*t/þ*	*d/d*	*d/t*	*dh/d*	*p/p*	*p/b*	*p/f*	*b/b*	*b/p*	*bh/b*

In each language three dental and three labial phonemes are involved. In Sanskrit all are stops: *t* and *p* have voiceless unaspirated phones, *d* and *b* voiced unaspirated, and *dh* and *bh* voiced aspirated. In Germanic the main allophones are: voiceless stops for *t* and *p* (perhaps lenis after *s* and other spirants [?]), voiceless spirants for *þ* (interdental) and *f* (bilabial), and voiced stops and spirants for *d* and *b*. The phoneme inventory is thus somewhat similar in the two languages. If fuller data were given, this similarity would probably appear more pronounced.

Examples: I *ásti:ist* 'is';[15] II *pitár-:fadar* 'father'; III *bhrätar-:broþar* 'brother'; IV *dehí-* 'wall':*d(e)igan* 'knead'; V *védu:walt*

---

[13]Jakobson, *Eighth Congress* 9; but there are Caucasic languages with one vowel phoneme and a consequently large allophonic spread (Allen, *Eighth Congress*, Discussion). Furthermore, the term "vowel" is not well defined: is a language which has syllabic (nuclear) allophones for certain of its phonemes, as Indo-European does for /y,w .../, typologically a "one-vowel" language?

[14]With permission from the editor of *Language* and from the American Council of Learned Societies, this section is based on the contents of an article published in *Lg.* 26 = *Readings in Linguistics* 298. The sample has been simplified by means of a few omissions.

[15]The Germanic examples are mostly Gothic.

'I know'; VI *mádhya-:midjis* 'middle'; VII *spás-* 'watcher': OHG *spehon* 'look out'; VIII *lip-* (stick,) smear':*bi-leiban* '(stick,)stay'; IX (*see* II); X *bódhati* 'awakes, is attentive':*ana-biudan* 'charge with, bid'; XI *rámbate* 'hangs down':MG *lampen* 'droop'; XII (*see* III).

The following sets are partially alike:

I	II	III								share Skt. *t*
			IV	V						share Skt. *d*
					VII	VIII	IX			share Skt. *p*
								X	XI	share Skt. *b*
	II		IV		VI					share Gmc. *d*
						VIII		X	XII	share Gmc. *b*
I				V						share Gmc. *t*
					VII			XI		share Gmc. *p*

Sets IV and X occur when the next syllable begins with Skt. *h*/Gmc. *g*, Skt. *dh*/Gmc. *d*, or a few other sets; sets VI and XII do not occur in these environments. Sets II and VIII occur only after Skt. unaccented vowel/Gmc. vowel with or without certain consonants intervening; sets VI and XII occur in this environment also, as well as in others. Sets I and VII are found after sets whose Germanic component is a spirant (e.g., after Skt. *s*/Gmc. *s*, or after *p/f*).

Possible applications of our procedure may, however, be in conflict. Let us examine the entire table of partially like sets (given above) for the distribution of the sets in various environments. Sets IV and V, as well as X and XI, are in contrast; for, in the few surroundings where IV and X are found, V and XI occur also. The same is true, as has been shown, for sets II and VI, and equally for sets VIII and XII, whose distribution is parallel to that of II and VI. No contrast can be established between any other two partially like sets: they are all more or less obviously in complementary distribution. This leaves the following choices. Set I may be grouped together with III (and possibly II [see the next statement]), which would amount to reconstructing a single source for all occurrences of Skt. *t*; but also with V, which is one of the sources of Gmc. *t*. Set II may be grouped with I and III (all sharing Skt. *t*), but also with IV, though not with VI (both Skt. *d*). Set III is grouped with I and perhaps II (see above). Set IV cannot, as we have seen, be grouped with V (Skt. *d*); hence it can be grouped only with VI or perhaps II (Gmc. *d*). Set V can belong only with I (Gmc. *t*), provided I is not rather linked with III (and II), in which case V would stand alone. Set VI goes with IV but not with II. The relationships among sets VII and XII are parallel to those among sets I and VI; in what follows sets VII and XII will not be specially noted.

Examining the possibilities for economy, we find that two different choices will each result in three reconstructed phonemes for sets I and VI (and three more for VII and XII); no choice will yield fewer than three, and several others will yield more. The two possibilities of grouping sets as reflexes of only three phonemes in the proto-language are these: either I and V, II and III, and IV and VI or else V by itself, I and II and III, and IV and VI. In other words, the only question still unsolved is whether set I (*t/t*) should be derived from the common source of II (*t/d*) and III (*t/þ*), or from the source of V (*d/t*), that is, from **t* or from **d*. We note that set I occurs only after *s/s*, *p/f*, etc. (set VII probably only after *s/s*).

It may sometimes be irrelevant to decide the status of such a set as I. In some instances of ambiguity, both possible reconstructions may be equally effective. However, for set I (though not for VII) we can go a step farther. It is true that I (*t/t*) nowhere contrasts with II and III, or with V, since II, III, and V do not occur in the same environments as I (say, after *s/s*). But it is also true that V (*d/t*) occurs in at least one environment where II and III do not: after *y/s*, as in Skt. *meda-* 'fat':Modern German *Mast* 'fattening'. (Here Skt. *y* is seen in the second element in long *e*.) Upon further examination the set *y/s* is, in turn, found to occur only in positions from which *s/s* is barred; there is an equation *st = st* (*ásti:ist*) and an equation *yd/st* (*meda-:Mast*), but there is no *sd/st* and no *yt/st*. Consequently, the choice between the two possible assignments of set I (*t/t*) will affect also the status of the set *y/s*. As soon as set I is grouped with V (i.e., derived from **d*), the sets *s/s* and *y/s* must be said to contrast with each other before **d* of the proto-language, and we must reconstruct something like **sd* for *ásti:ist* and **zd* for *meda-:Mast*. But if set I is grouped with II and III (i.e., derived from **t*), we need to reconstruct only **st* and **sd*. The former grouping requires the reconstruction of a new Indo-European phoneme **z*, of very limited distribution; the latter grouping requires only such Indo-European phonemes as have been reconstructed already on the basis of other evidence and at the same time gives them a more complete distribution (both **t* and **d* now occur after **s*).

Thus considerations of economy have again decided the dilemma. On the strength of the general parallelism between the dentals and the labials, set VII (*p/p*) will now be grouped with VIII and IX rather than with XI.

To sum up, we have obtained the following reconstructions and sound laws: IE **t* for sets I, II, and III; IE **dh* for sets IV and VI; IE **d* for set V; IE **p* for sets VII, VIII, and IX; IE **bh* for sets X and XII; IE **b* for set XI; "Verner's law" for sets II and VIII; "Grassmann's law" for sets IV and X; and the treatment of **t* and **p* after a Germanic spirant for sets I and VII. Incidentally, we have also decided against the reconstruction of IE **z*.

If we arrange the six labial sets in three columns, each representing one of the three reconstructed phonemes, we obtain the familiar-looking graphic expression of Figure 133,[16] and similarly for the three Indo-European

[16] $\breve{V}$ = unaccented vowel.

COLUMN 1	COLUMN 2	COLUMN 3	
		$bh > bh$	bh
	$b > b$	$bh .. (h) > b .. (h)$	b
$p > p$			p
$*p$	$*b$	$*bh$ IE	SANSKRIT
			GERMANIC
$(s)p > (s)p$	$b > p$		p
$(\breve{V})p > (V)b$		$bh > b$	b
other $p > f$			f

Fig. 133

dentals. It should be noted that the split of *bh in Sanskrit is a primary one (the new b and the old b merge). The "Verner" split of *p into f and b in Germanic is ultimately both primary (p after unaccented vowel merges with *bh after unaccented vowel) and secondary (since unaccented vowels and accented vowels merge, or /'/ merges with ϕ, *$\breve{V}p$ yields Vb, while *$\acute{V}p$ yields Vf, thus placing Gmc. b and f in contrast irrespective of the $b < $ *bh). The "change" *$sp > sp$ is merely a reassignment (see Fig. 53), although it follows from what was said above that the case of the parallel dental phoneme *t is different, since *st and *sd [zd] were in contrast, while there was no occurrence of *sb.

Finally, internal reconstruction confirms the splits. The past-participle morpheme alternates between d and t in Gothic: *salbod-* 'anointed' (after vowel):*hafts* 'fettered' (after Germanic spirant); since the split was primary, the alternation is automatic. The preterit singular had its accent on the stem syllable, and the preterit plural on the ending, hence Gothic *þarf* 'I need':*þaurbum* 'we need'; the split, partly secondary, left an irregular alternation.[17] In Sanskrit, reduplication, which generally consists of a prefix beginning with the first consonant of the stem (*pa-pat ..*, *da-da ..*), has b, d for stems beginning with $bh ..$, $dh ..$ (*da-dh ..* etc.), still a near-automatic alternation in historical Sanskrit.

12.8.3.2. Sample Reconstruction (II)

The following is a summary of one of the phases of the so-called laryngeal theory for Indo-European. From the daughter languages (say, from Sanskrit, Greek, and Latin, in this order) these sets may be formed:

---

[17]Note that the comparative reconstruction does not get rid of the allomorphic variation. The stem morphemes are now reconstructed with variable accent rather than with variable stops. In other words, the proto-language had morphophonemes $\acute{V} \sim \breve{V}$.

After Vowel[18] *before Consonant*	*Between Consonants*
y[19]/i/i	i/i/i
n/n/n	a/a/en

so that the first row yields a proto-phoneme *y, the second a proto-phoneme *n, occurring in such sequences as *teyp pyt* (presumably [pit]) k^w*ent pnt*. There is, moreover, a widespread alternation $\phi \sim e$, with the result that morphemes have allomorphs such as *teyp $\sim$ typ, pent $\sim$ pnt*.

In the first position (V———C) there is also

:/:/: (vowel length) ("*:")

complementary with these four sets (in C———C)

i/e/a ("*∂_1")
i/a/a ("*∂_2")
a/e/e ("*e")
a/a/a ("*a").

Vowel length, however, "alternates" only with ∂_1 and with ∂_2 (and not with e or a). Hence allomorphs *pe:t $\sim$ p∂_1t* and *pa:t $\sim$ p∂_2t* parallel our earlier *pent $\sim$ pnt*. At this point we arbitrarily and provisionally rewrite *:* as an allophone of ∂_1 (rather than of ∂_2). This will transform *pe:t $\sim$ p∂_1t* into a simply alternating *pe∂_1t $\sim$ p∂_1t* (compare *pent $\sim$ pnt*), while *pa:t $\sim$ p∂_2t* becomes an automatically alternating *pa∂_1t $\sim$ p∂_2t*. By internal reconstruction we might conclude, however, that the alternation is a product of an earlier merger and that *pa∂_1t* was at one time *pa∂_2t*.

Renewed examination of the etymologies reveals the fact that at the stage now reached ∂_1 occurs never after a, and ∂_2 never after e.[20] The two items ∂_1 and ∂_2 do contrast, however, between consonants. On the other hand, how generally do a and e themselves contrast with each other? The question is worth asking because of a notable restriction in the occurrence of a; the vowel a is found freely only before ∂_2 and after $\#$ (i.e., initially). If it can be shown that initial ∂_2 is lost, then a was at one time entirely conditioned by a neighboring (preceding or following) ∂_2. Now, in the environment $\#$———e none of the sets :/:/:, i/e/a, i/a/a exist. But there is evidence for an alternation between ∂_1 and ∂_2 (represented by their vowel length allophones), on the one hand, and initial ϕ (which, of course, does "occur" between $\#$ and vowel), on the other: root morphemes of the type *ep$\sim$p, ap $\sim$ p*

---

[18]That is, *e* or *a* (see below). The vowel *o* is left out of account (see n. 21).

[19]A phonemic expression of the second component of the Sanskrit "diphthong" *e*.

[20]This is merely an explicit, digit-by-digit expression of the fact that *e:* alternates with ∂_1 and *a:* alternates with ∂_2.

(on a par with *pent* ~ *pnt* above) will appear, in a construction which calls for a prefix (or reduplication) ending in *e* and the lesser ("zero grade") allomorph of the root (. . . *e-pnt*), as follows: . . *e-ə₁p* . . *a-ə₂p* (i.e., . . *e:p* . . *a:p*). From this it may be inferred that both *ə₁* and *ə₂* were lost initially before a vowel, that the contrast between *e* and *a* was a matter of secondary split, and that the one vowel in existence before the conditioned loss of *ə₁* and *ə₂* had an *a*-like allophone in the neighborhood of *ə₂* and an *e*-like allophone elsewhere (including near *ə₁*). It may then be labeled *e*, with the explanation that *ə₁e* > *e*; *ə₂e* > *a*; *eə₁C* > *e:*; *eə₂C* > *a:*—in terms of the most recent stage of proto-Indo-European.

To return to the older stages, *ə₁* and *ə₂* are now seen to have once had a distribution very much like that of *y* and *n* (and other phonemes like them), in that all of them occur not only in *V——C* and in *C——C* but also in *#——e* (words begin with *ye* . . , *ne* . .). There is a fourth type of environment which is of some interest: after vowel plus voiceless stop and before vowel (*et——e*). Here most consonants occur freely (*etye*, *etne*, etc.). In at least some cases where *ə₂* comes to stand in the crucial environment, Indo-Iranian presents an otherwise unexplained correspondence. Thus if Lat. *rota* (older *rotā*) 'wheel' continues an IE *roteə₂*, the Sanskrit word for '(wheeled) chariot', *ratha-* should represent *rotə₂-o-*, with a well-known adjective-forming suffix and the alternation *e* ~ *φ* noted above.

The discovery of the previously unknown Hittite brought partial confirmation of the hypothesis of which the foregoing is a small and schematic sample.[21] Roughly, it developed that, in about one-half the etymologies in which *ə₂* would have to be reconstructed (and for which Hittite has a representative), the Hittite form shows a consonant ("laryngeal") phoneme (*ḥ* or *ḥḥ*), next to which the vowel *a* occurs, while *e* does not. In the remainder of the cases (again insofar as there is Hittite evidence at all), Hittite has *φ*, but the same vocalic effect. Since the difference is in no way conditioned, it is necessary to recognize two "*a*-colored laryngeals": one which has survived as a Hittite consonant, and another which has the same history in Hittite as in the other languages and which therefore remains recoverable only in indirect fashion.

---

[21]See also 13.4. It goes without saying that this is not a full résumé of the laryngeal hypothesis; for such a résumé see, for instance, Polomé, *Revue belge* 30. It is important to realize, however, that the contribution of Hittite to the whole reconstruction is often exaggerated. See also Lehmann, *Proto-Indoeuropean Phonology*, 85–98.

5

INTERNAL RECONSTRUCTION OF PHONEMIC SPLIT*

James W. Marchand

[*The paper evolves a set of premises for the internal reconstruction of phonemic split, outlines a practical procedure for application to concrete problems, and supplies examples to illustrate the procedure.*[1]]

The technique of IR,[2] first elaborated by the latter-day neo-grammarian Eduard Hermann, has received much attention in recent scholarly publications.[3] Its exponents have alleged two values for IR: (1) it affords us a check on traditional reconstruction in language groups whose history is well known, such as Indo-European, and (2) it affords us a means of reconstructing proto-languages for languages or language families with little or no known history.[4] It must be admitted that, owing to the pioneering nature of previous work, IR has been applied exclusively to the first of these. In discussions so far, as is natural, only well-known examples have been used, and no attempt has been made to use the technique for little-known languages. The changes have been typed, and the sort of thing one must look for has been indicated, but no discussion has yet given us a practical method for operating on a single language, without using other languages. So far,

*From *Language* 32.245–253 (1956). Reprinted by permission of the author and the Linguistic Society of America.

[1] I am indebted to H. M. Hoenigswald and K. L. Pike for valuable suggestions.
[2] Following the practice of H. M. Hoenigswald, I use the abbreviation IR for internal reconstruction.
[3] E. Hermann, Über das Rekonstruieren, *KZ* 41.1–69 (1911); H. M. Hoenigswald, Internal reconstruction, *SIL* 2.78–87 (1944); id., Sound change and linguistic structure, *Lg.* 22.138–143 (1946); J. H. Bonfante, On reconstruction and the linguistic method, *Word* 5.83–91, 132 ff. (1947); R. A. Fowkes, Synchronic method and Welsh consonantism, *Word* 9.142–5 (1950); Carl H. Borgström, Internal reconstruction of Pre-Indo-European word-forms, *Word* 10.257–88 (1954).
[4] Hoenigswald, *Lg.* 22.142.

discussion has been in the most general terms. This may be sufficient for the IE linguist, who knows to a great extent what the end result must be before he begins reconstructing; but if IR is to be useful for the linguist in the American Indian field, for example, there must be a rigorous methodology which can be applied in all analogous cases in the same manner. Our methodology must tell us what to look for and how to find it. It must afford us a means of reconstructing from the language at hand, without outside sources. This article is an attempt to provide such a methodology for a restricted problem: the reconstruction of phonemic split.

The techniques of IR are merely refinements and extensions of the techniques of reconstruction practiced by traditional Indo-European linguists.[5] IR suffers from the same defects as normal reconstruction and is subject to the same reservations. Like normal reconstruction, IR depends on the discovery of cognate morphemes. In normal reconstruction, this discovery of cognates is a heuristic process, the course of which no one has thus far been successful in describing. Its results are testable in terms of phonetic laws and semantic likeness. In IR, neither of these criteria can be used. The basic problem in IR is to find a means of discovering cognate morphs, and a means of testing the findings. In IR, the problem of the discovery of cognate morphs is solved for us by a synchronic description of the morphemics. It may be said that all the allomorphs of a morpheme are cognate with one another, unless suppletion has occurred. If we can find a technique which will allow us to discover or discard cases of suppletion, we will have a method of discovering internal cognates. As to testing our results, a certain amount of unreality is doubtless attached to any reconstruction: we have no guarantee that the units we reconstruct existed in the form in which we reconstruct them. There are only two tests which can be applied to determine the "correctness" of a reconstruction: (1) methodological rigor and correctness, (2) the number and value of forms (especially anomalies) which are explained by it.[6] Both of these tests should be applied to any reconstruction, especially to IR.

In the following, an attempt is made to set down the premises which allow us to reconstruct phonemic split. Then a practical technique of operating on a corpus is outlined step by step. Some examples illustrate the application of the technique.

---

[5]Bonfante 83 f.; Hoenigswald, *Lg.* 22.142; Borgström 276.

[6]Cf. Eugene Nida, *Morphology*[2] (Ann Arbor, 1949): "The test of such a reconstruction is in the number and significance of the correlations which may be discovered." Cf. further A. Meillet, *Introduction à l'étude comparative des langues indo-européennes*[3] 32 (Paris, 1938): "La preuve la meilleure qu'une langue appartient à une famille donnée consiste à montrer que cette langue conserve, à titre d'anomalies, des formes qui, dans la période de communauté initiale, ont été normales."

Premises

1. All the allomorphs of a morpheme are cognate, or else suppletion has taken place. This premise is of course tautological, since it is derived from the definition of suppletion.[7] It should be noted that this is true both of morphophonemic variants (where the choice of the allomorph is conditioned by the phonemic environment, e.g. the plural morpheme /z ~ s ~ ɪz/ in English /dɔgz/ *dogs*, /hæts/ *hats*, /hawzɪz/ *houses*) and of morpheme alternants (where the choice of the allomorph is conditioned by the morphemic environment, e.g. the plural morpheme /rən/ in the English /tʃɪldrən/ *children*).

2. If one or more phonemes regularly alternate, under any conditions whatsoever, with one or more other phonemes in the same morpheme, these phonemes must have derived from the same phoneme or group of phonemes, or else suppletion has taken place. This is a simple corollary of the first premise; if two allomorphs are cognate, they must stem from one and the same morpheme of a previous stage of the language, existing in one phonemic shape. In such a case, we say that phonemic split has taken place.[8] In order to guard against using cases of suppletion to prove split, we take the following precaution: the variant forms must have the same phonemes in as many positions as they have different ones, and these phonemes must be in the same order.[9] That is, given an allomorph with the phoneme sequence *abcd*, we should accept an allomorph of the same morpheme with a phoneme sequence *abef* as cognate and proving phonemic split (i.e. that *cd* and *ef* derive from the same phonemes), but a form *aghi* regularly alternating with *abcd* would be under suspicion of suppletion and could not be used. A further precaution is necessary if we do not wish to base far-reaching conclusions on insufficient evidence: isolated paradigms and hapax legomena cannot be used. We will use an alternation as proof of split only if the alternation occurs under the same conditions in combination with at least three morphemes, or if the morphophoneme in question occurs in at least two morphemes. For example, given the Lithuanian masculine paradigm:[9a]

> nom. sg. /l,ésas/ 'thin'
> dat. sg. /l,ɛsám/

[7]Bloomfield, *Language* 215: "If the language does not show parallel cases which warrant our describing the deviant form in terms of phonetic modification, an alternant of this sort is said to be suppletive . . ."

[8]Roman Jakobson, Prinzipien der historischen Phonologie, *TCLP* 4.252 (1931).

[9]Cf. van Ginneken's remark in *TCLP* 4.297 (1931): "M. van Ginncken se demande si on peut parler de l'identité d'un morphème dans les cas où la plupart des phonèmes qui le composent alternent."

[9a]Commas in the transcription denote palatalization.

nom. pl. /l,ɛs,ì/
dat. pl. /l,ɛs,émz/,

we must assume that /s/ and /s,/, at least in this paradigm, were members of the same phoneme in Pre-Lithuanian, since the alternation /s/ ~ /s,/ occurs also in other morphemes. The choice of /s/ or /s,/ is not, as might appear from the paradigm given, phonemically conditioned.

3. If two phonemes of a later stage of a language correspond to one phoneme of an earlier stage of that language, each must correspond to a different conditioned variant (allophone) of that phoneme, as it is impossible to think of another possibility.[10] Since different phonemes must be phonetically different throughout at least part of their distribution, it follows that a phonetic difference is necessary in order that split may take place.

4. Excluding outside influence (borrowing etc.), there are only two ways in which a split can occur: either (a) one of the allophones of one phoneme falls together with an allophone of another phoneme, or (b) the factor conditioning the allophonic variation becomes lost.[11] Where (a) has occurred, the previous structure is recoverable by the methodology used for the reconstruction of phonemic merger, since such a split is also a merger. For example, in OHG every /a/ occurring before *i*-sounds developed an allophone [e].[12] Normally /ɛ/ did not occur before *i*-sounds; in those rare instances where it did occur before *i*-sounds (as *gëstirn* 'yesterday', *fëlis* 'rock') /ɛ/ also developed an allophone [e]. Since [e] was phonetically more similar to /ɛ/ than to /a/, it became a member of the /ɛ/-phoneme.[13] Such pairs as /gast/:/gɛsti/ (*gast* 'guest' nom. sg., *gesti* nom. pl.) reveal the fact that /a/ and /ɛ/ had merged, as well as the fact that /a/ had split, since /a/ and /ɛ/ contrast in all positions except before *i*-sounds.

An example of a split of type (b) (split through the loss of a conditioning factor) can also be seen in OHG. In "classical" OHG, the phoneme /o/ had two basic allophones, [ö], occurring only before *i*-sounds, and [o], which never occurred before *i*-sounds. Thus we have the pair /mohti/ [möhti] (*mohti* 3d sg. pret. subj. of *mugan* 'to be able', Tatian132.19) and /mohta/ [mohta] (*mohta* 3d sg. pret ind., Tatian 67.13). When, during the course of

---

[10]Jakobson (252–3) cites Polivanov and van Ginneken to this effect. He himself is somewhat more cautious; he says: "Tatsächlich ist das Identitätsverhältnis zwischen A und B anscheinend ausgeschlossen. . . . Meistens sind A und B kombinatorische Varianten." He does not qualify his statement.

[11]Jakobson 251–3.

[12]Cf. H. Penzl, Umlaut and secondary umlaut in Old High German, *Lg*. 25.223–39 (1949), especially 224 on the use of the term *i*-sound.

[13]W. F. Twaddell, A note on Old High German umlaut, *Monatshefte* 30.180–1 (1938).

the 11th century, unaccented *a*- and *i*-sounds fell together in the sound [ə] (spelled "e"), [ö] and [o] split into /ö/ and /o/, since they now occurred in contrast in identical environments: /möhtə/ (*möhte* 3d sg. pret. subj.) and /mohtə/ (*mohte* 3d sg. pret. ind.).[14]

5. In order to recover the structure previous to a split of type (b), we must discover the conditioning factor which has been lost, and this must appear in our reconstruction. The statement of distributions for the earlier stage (the reconstructed language) must be such that the two phonemes of the later stage are interpreted as allophones of one phoneme in the earlier stage. This is a corollary of the rule of Polivanov and Jakobson that every split presupposes a merger, either with zero or with another phoneme.[15] It may be remarked that every recoverable merger presupposes a split; complete merger is not recoverable.

(*a*) If a phoneme has merged in some positions with zero or with another phoneme, this will leave traces in its distribution, unless other factors have caused it to be reintroduced into these positions.

(*b*) The loss (merger) of a conditioning factor will cause us to interpret the former allophones as phonemes because of contrast in some positions alone, whereas most of the phonemes of the language will contrast more or less freely. In the Lithuanian example cited above (Premise 2), /s/ and /s,/ contrast only before back vowels; /s/ never occurs before front vowels. It is thus natural to assume that a front vowel has been lost wherever we find /s,/ occurring before back vowels, and this is demonstrated by other criteria (see below, Procedures 4 and 5).

(*c*) If, in a paradigmatic set, the only overt formal signal of a paradigmatic morpheme consists of a component of the base morpheme, or of the replacement of a phoneme in the base morpheme, it is assumed that the phonemes in question are the result of a split, and that the conditioning factor was once contained in the paradigmatic morpheme, the split now bearing the load of differentiation. Thus, the only overt formal signal of the preterit subjunctive in the MHG form /möhtə/, as compared to the 3d sg. pret. ind. /mohtə/, is the replacement /ö ← o/. /ö/ and /o/ must derive from the same phoneme, as demonstrated above (Premise 4). The replacement now bears the load of differentiation formerly borne by the suffixes /i/ and /a/.

(*d*) If, in a paradigmatic set, one feature of a paradigmatic morpheme

---

[14]Ibid.; Penzl 224–5.

[15]Jakobson 26 (*citation from Polivanov*): "*in einer ungeheuren Masse der Fälle wird die Divergenz (Phonologisierung) von der einen oder andern Konvergenz (Entphonologisierung) begleitet und wird dabei von ihr diktiert.*" Jakobson comments: "*Hier ist die Phonologisierung kombinatorischer Varianten gemeint und in Anwendung auf diese ist das Gesetz ausnahmslos richtig.*"

consists of the subtraction of a phoneme of the base morpheme (for some but not all phonemes), it is assumed that this phoneme originally occurred in this position and has, for some phonological reason, become lost. In the Greek 3d declension we find, for example:

	nom. sg.	*gen. sg.*
	/pʰúlaks/ 'guard'	/pʰúlakos/
	/gúps/ 'vulture'	/gu:pós/
	/tʰɛ:s/ 'serf'	/tʰɛ:tos/
	/elpís/ 'hope'	/elpídos/.

Since one feature of the paradigmatic nom. sg. morpheme /s/ consists of the subtraction of a phoneme of the base morpheme in the case of the apicals, but not in the case of the labials and velars, it is assumed that the phonemes in question (the apicals) originally occurred in this position and were lost.[16]

Procedures

The following steps are used to recover the previous structure:

1. Split is assumed to have occurred if two or more phonemes alternate in the same morpheme, subject to the reservations set down in Premise 2 above. Split is assumed to have occurred if the conditions set down in Premise 5c or Premise 5d are fulfilled. This step is necessary in order that we may know which phonemes to direct our attention to. Thus, given the alternation /s ~ s,/ in the Lithuanian example cited in Premise 2, we state that /s/ and /s,/ were members of the same phoneme in Pre-Lithuanian, and concentrate our attention upon these two phonemes.

2. Statement of the total distribution of the phonemes in question is necessary in order that the following steps may be performed. In Lithuanian, /s/ occurs only before back vowels and nonpalatal consonants, /s,/ occurs before front vowels, back vowels, and palatal consonants.

3. If possible, all positions where contrast occurs must be excluded. Since it is our purpose to discover what conditioning factor was lost, causing former allophones to come into contrast, a position in which they contrast is not of interest at this stage. In our Lithuanian problem, we exclude the position before back vowels.

4. From these distributions a hypothesis is formed. If we have excluded all positions in which they contrast, the phonemes will now be in complementary distribution. It should normally be possible at this point to define the phonemic environments of each phoneme and thus to discover the

[16]Cf. Nida, *Morphology* 26 ff.

factors conditioning the original allophonic variation. These factors are added in our reconstruction. The hypothesis should interpret the phonemes in question as having been members of a single phoneme in an earlier stage of the language (in the reconstructed language). If more than one hypothesis is possible, all must be stated, to be tested later.

Having excluded the position before back vowels in our Lithuanian problem, we find /s/ and /s,/ in complementary distribution, with /s/ occurring only before nonpalatal consonants and /s,/ occurring before front vowels and palatal consonants. We assume the loss of a front vowel or a palatal consonant after every /s,/ occurring before a back vowel. Thus, we state the following for Pre-Lithuanian: there was a phoneme */s/ (or */s,/) with allophones *[s] before back vowels and nonpalatal consonants and *[s,] before front vowels and palatal consonants.

5. If Procedure 4 is impossible, i.e. if the merger which caused the split has been with zero (if the feature causing the allophonic variation has disappeared from the language), we cannot do more than set up hypotheses. Such hypotheses are always suspect. Since the only overt formal signal of the past tense of the English verb /sɪŋ/, for example, is the replacement of a phoneme of the base morpheme /æ ← ɪ/, /ɪ/ and /æ/ must derive from the same phoneme. Since the factor causing the original allophonic variation (usually assumed to have been the IE pitch accent) has disappeared from the language, we can only set up hypotheses. Without outside sources, we can never determine the factor causing the original allophonic variation.

6. All our reconstructions must be tested according to the number and value of the forms (especially anomalies) which they explain. If our assumed reconstruction does not help to clear up some troublesome forms, it is suspect, and at any rate is valueless. In this case, the split is probably bound to certain morphemes and is actually a merger. If a choice between two possible solutions is necessary, we should choose that solution which explains the larger number of anomalies or which is intrinsically the more probable.[17]

Returning to the Lithuanian problem, the assumption of a lost front vowel or palatal consonant after /s,/, when this occurs before a back vowel, helps clear up a number of anomalies. The definite adjective is demonstrated to be in origin a combination of the indefinite adjective with the pronoun of the 3d person (cf. Latin *beātus ille*). If we compare, for example, the nom. pl. fem. indefinite /g,ēros/ 'good' with nom. pl. fem. definite /g,ēros,os/, the acc. pl. fem. indefinite /g,ɛràs/ with acc. pl. fem. definite /g,ɛrás,as/, we will reconstruct, according to what has been said previously, for the definite forms */g,ērosjos/, */g,ɛrásjas/, since /j/ does not occur after /s/ before a back vowel. The

---

[17]Cf. Bonfante, passim.

resemblance of the reconstructed endings */jos/ and */jas/ to the pronoun of the 3d person (nom. pl. fem. /jõs/, acc. pl. fem. /jás/) is obvious. In this manner we can explain that both the morpheme indicating the definite adjective declension and the morpheme preceding this are inflected.

Examples

The following examples will serve to clarify the procedures and to demonstrate their value in practical operations:

Example 1. Note the following Gothic paradigm:

nom. sg. -/triu/ (*triu* 'tree' J 15.1)
dat. sg. -/triwa/ (*triwa* J 15.4)
dat. pl. -/triwam/ (*triwam* L 14.43)
acc. pl. -/triwa/ (*triwa* K 9.7).

Procedure 1: Since /u/ and /w/ alternate regularly in this and similar morphemes, they must derive from the same phoneme(s) of Pre-Gothic.

Procedure 2: /w/ and /u/ are in contrast only in final syllables, in the positions C( )C and C( )0.[18] Otherwise /w/ occurs only before a vowel or before /l/ or /r/ plus vowel, and /u/ occurs only before a consonant or before /l/ or /r/ plus consonant.

Procedure 3: We exclude final syllables from consideration.

Procedure 4: /w/ and /u/ are now in complementary distribution, with /w/ occurring only before vowel or /l, r/ plus vowel, and /u/ never occurring in that position. Our hypothesis should be that there was one phoneme */u/ (or */w/) in Pre-Gothic, which had both syllabic and nonsyllabic allophones, the nonsyllabic occurring before vowel and before */l/ or */r/ plus vowel, and the syllabic occurring elsewhere. If we apply this rule to our reconstruction, adding a vowel after every final /w/ and after every /w/ preceded and followed by a consonant in final syllables, we can say that the reflex of /w/ and the reflex of /u/ were members of the same phoneme in Pre-Gothic.

Procedure 5: Although the assumption that the reflex of /w/ and the reflex of /u/ were members of the same phoneme in Pre-Gothic does not clear up any anomalies by itself, the assumption of a lost vowel after every final /w/ and after every /w/ before consonant in a final syllable, provides a point of entry for the reconstruction of the Pre-Gothic nominal and verbal endings. It brings out the essential similarity between the *a*-, *i*-, and *u*-stems. Thus, if we reconstruct a Pre-Gothic */snaiuas/ for /snɛws/ and a Pre-Gothic */saiuis/ for /sɛws/, the similarity with /manwus/ < */manuus/ is evident. If we reconstruct

---

[18]Cf. W. G. Moulton, The phonemes of Gothic, *Lg.* 24.82 (1948). In this and the following statements, some simplification has been made; the material has not been essentially altered.

the nom. sg. as */saiuis/, then the present gen. sg. /sɛwis/ must be the reflex of a Pre-Gothic */saiuis/ plus some other feature, and so forth. Using such reasoning, we are able, from the assumption of the loss of a vowel after final /w/ and after /w/ between consonants in final syllables, to reconstruct most of the Proto-Germanic endings known from other criteria. Of course, our knowledge of Proto-Germanic should not be called upon in performing the internal reconstruction.

Example 2: Note the following Old Irish paradigm:

nom. sg. /fir^a/ *fer* 'man'
gen. sg. /fir^i/ *fir*
dat. sg. /fir^u/ *fiur*.[19]

Procedure 1: Since the only overt formal signal of the paradigmatic morphemes in this and similar paradigms consists of the replacement of a phoneme in the base morpheme, or, in one type of analysis, of a component of the base morpheme, /r^a/, /r^i/, and /r^u/ were members of the same phoneme in Pre-Irish.

Procedure 2: /r^a/, /r^i/, and /r^u/ contrast only in word-final position; in all other positions, we find the following distributions: /r^a/ occurs before /a/, /a:/, /o/, /o:/ and *a*-colored consonants; /r^i/ occurs before /i/, /i:/, /e/, /e:/ and *i*-colored consonants; /r^u/ occurs before /u/, /u:/, and *u*-colored consonants.[20]

Procedure 3: We exclude final position.

Procedure 4: /r^a/, /r^i/, and /r^u/ are now in complementary distribution. It is clear that we must assume the loss of vowels or consonants in order to account for the split. We must assume an original mid-back or low-central vowel following /r^a/, a high- or mid-front vowel following /r^i/, and a high-back vowel following /r^u/, or else an *a*-colored consonant following /r^a/, an *i*-colored consonant following /r^i/, and a *u*-colored consonant following /r^u/.

Procedure 5: The reconstruction of lost vowels allows us to reconstruct a great many of the endings of Pre-Irish, and places us on a better footing for comparison with the other Indo-European languages. It allows us to connect the Ogam inscriptions to Old Irish, and clears up many of the connections to Gaulish. Within Irish itself, it clears up many anomalies, such as the connection between the acc. sg. *ā*-stem *thuaith* and such forms as *bein*, between the declension of *beo* and that of *fer*:

[19] /r^a/ represents a normal trilled *r*-sound, /r^i/ a palatalized trilled *r*-sound, /ru/ a trilled *r*-sound with simultaneous lip-rounding; cf. R. Thurneysen, *Handbuch des Altirischen* 1.96 ff. (Heidelberg, 1909).

[20] Thurneysen 93 ff.; H. Lewis and H. Pedersen, *A concise comparative Celtic grammar* 96 ff. (Göttingen, 1937).

nom. sg. *beo*   nom. sg. */fir/ + /a/, /a:/, /o/, or /o:/
gen. sg. *bii*   gen. sg. */fir/ + /i/, /i:/, /e/, or /e:/
dat. sg. *biu*   dat. sg. */fir/ + /u/ or /u:/

Since the assumption of lost consonants does not help to clear up anomalies, the assumption of lost vowels is considered to be correct.

Example 3: Note the following Lithuanian paradigm:

nom. sg. /ʒõd,is/ 'word'
gen. sg. /ʒõdʒo/
dat. sg. /ʒõdʒui/
acc. sg. /ʒõd,i/

Procedure 1: Since /d,/ and /dʒ/ alternate in this and other paradigms, they must derive from the same phoneme of Pre-Lithuanian.

Procedure 2: The palatalized stop /d,/ occurs only before front vowels and palatal consonants, the affricate /dʒ/ occurs only before back and front vowels, never before consonants.

Procedure 3: We exclude the position before front vowels.

Procedure 4: /d,/ and /dʒ/ are now in complementary distribution, with /d,/ occurring only before palatal consonants and /dʒ/ occurring only before back vowels. Note that palatalized /d,/ and plain /d/ are shown to have been members of the same phoneme in Pre-Lithuanian by such pairs as /edu/ 'I eat' and /ed,i/ 'you eat'. We cannot then assume that an original */d,/ + a back vowel yielded */dʒ/, a process which in itself seems unlikely, since before back vowels we find /d/. The fact that /dʒ/ does not occur before consonants, and that /d,/ does not occur before back vowels, whereas most palatal consonants occur before both front and back vowels, suggests a lost front vowel or consonant after /dʒ/. The logical assumption is /j/, since this phoneme does not occur between consonant and vowel, and since /dʒ/ occurs before every other vowel (only rarely before /i/, however). We then set up the following hypothesis, to be tested in Procedure 6: that there was a phoneme */d,/ (or */dʒ/) in Pre-Lithuanian, with the allophones * [d,] before front vowels and palatal consonants, and * [dʒ] before */j/.

Procedure 5: The assumption that */d,/ + */j/ yielded */dʒ/ is confirmed by the fact that /d,/ + /j/ in compounds (but not across open juncture) results in /dʒ/, cf. /m,ɛdʒóju/ 'to hunt', compounded of /m,ɛd,/ (cf. the word /m,ẽd,is/ 'woods') plus /jóju/ 'to ride'. The connection between the *jo*-stems ending in a /d,/ or /t,/ and those ending in other consonants is cleared up:

nom. sg. /ʒõd,is/   < */ʒõdıs/   /ɛ́l,n,is/   < */ɛ́lnis/ 'stag'
gen. sg. /ʒõdʒo/   < */ʒõdjo/   /ɛ́l,n,o/   < */ɛ́lnjo/
dat. sg. /ʒõdʒui/   < */ʒõdjui/   /ɛ́l,n,ui/   < */ɛ́lnjui/
acc. sg. /ʒõd,i/   < */ʒõdi/   /ɛ́l,n,i/   < */ɛ́lni/

The examples will demonstrate that a great deal of reconstruction can be done and tested without appealing to outside sources, i.e. without using comparative material. It is hoped that the technique outlined in this article may be of use in both comparative and historical work. One distinct advantage of the present approach to the internal reconstruction of phonemic split is that it permits the reconstruction not only of the split, but also of the merger underlying the split, which cannot be recovered by the techniques proposed for the reconstruction of phonemic merger. This approach should therefore prove valuable in operating with languages which have undergone weakening and loss of final syllables, like those treated here. One advantage that IR has over normal reconstruction is that the language reconstructed is nondialectal in the spatial sense; the language arrived at by IR admits of dialectal variation only in time.

6

INTERNAL RECONSTRUCTION IN SENECA*

Wallace L. Chafe

1. This paper has a threefold purpose. It aims first to call attention to shortcomings in the existing theory of internal reconstruction. Second, it makes suggestions for a revised theory. And finally, it illustrates and amplifies these suggestions by applying them to the reconstruction of pre-Seneca from the synchronic data available in my *Seneca morphology*.[1]

The Existing Theory

2. Only three papers concerned primarily with the theory of internal reconstruction have appeared in this country in relatively recent years;[2] two of these were earlier and later treatments of the same subject by the same author. A few additional papers have dealt with the internal reconstruction of specific features in specific languages, on a more or less ad hoc theoretical basis.[3] I shall comment only on certain aspects of the papers by Hoenigswald (1946) and Marchand.

3. Hoenigswald's paper demonstrates various characteristic effects of sound change upon phoneme distribution and morphophonemic alternation. He states that the resulting patterns may be "so typical as to make it possible to recover from them the process to which they owe their existence." It is

*From *Language* 35.477–495 (1959). Reprinted by permission of the author and the Linguistic Society of America.

[1]Yale University dissertation (1958, unpublished). Part of an earlier draft of this paper was read to the departmental seminar of the Columbia University linguistics department in November 1958, and thanks are due for suggestions offered at that meeting. My Seneca field work during the summers of 1956–8 was sponsored by the New York State Museum and Science Service, William N. Fenton director. Any work that I do in the Iroquois field is built upon the solid foundation provided by Floyd G. Lounsbury.

[2]H. M. Hoenigswald, Internal reconstruction, *SIL* 2.78–87 (1944); id., Sound change and linguistic structure, *Lg.* 22.138–43 (1946); J. W. Marchand, Internal reconstruction of phonemic split, *Lg.* 32.245–53 (1956).

[3]See references in Marchand, fn. 3.

instructive, however; to consider two different morph alternations which Hoenigswald cites in different places in his article. One is the alternation *-t-/-þ-* 'past participle' in Gothic (*hafts* 'restrained' / *salbōþs* 'anointed'). *-t-* occurs after *f*, *h*, and *s*, while *-þ-* occurs in all other environments. The other alternation is *bunt-/bund-* 'alliance' in German.[4] *bunt-* occurs in syllable-final position, *bund-* in all other environments. The most economical inferences based on these data are that in Gothic either (a) *þ* > *t* after *f*, *h*, and *s*, or (b) *t* > *þ* everywhere except after *f*, *h*, and *s*; and that in German either (a) *d* > *t* in syllable-final position, or (b) *t* > *d* everywhere except in syllable-final position. Hoenigswald chooses inference (b) for Gothic, inference (a) for German. The completely parallel data provide no basis for these opposite choices, much less for the conclusion that the Gothic situation "allows us to reconstruct one original morpheme *-to-*".

4. Marchand's paper contains a number of such arbitrary choices and unwarranted conclusions. Several are involved in his discussion of the phonemes *s* and *s'* in Lithuanian (247–50).[5] From the fact that *s* occurs before nonpalatal consonants and back vowels while *s'* occurs before palatal consonants and all vowels, Marchand hypothesizes "the loss of a front vowel or a palatal consonant after every *s'* occurring before a back vowel." Another plausible hypothesis would be the loss of a nonpalatal consonant after every *s* occurring before a back vowel; i.e. that *s* once occurred only before nonpalatal consonants. Marchand, however, accepts the hypothesis quoted without considering alternative possibilities, and then for no apparent reason decides that the lost phoneme was **j*. This enables him to reconstruct definite adjective forms ending in **-jos* and **-jas*, whose resemblance to the third person pronouns *jōs* and *jás* is "obvious." Thus "the definite adjective is demonstrated to be in origin a combination of the indefinite adjective with the pronoun of the third person." The demonstration, based as it is upon a series of apparently unjustified inferences, seems to me not convincing.

5. I hope that these examples, which can fairly be said to represent the last word in internal reconstruction, will suffice to show that there is need for further theoretical discussion, and that at the moment it is even possible to doubt whether rigorous internal reconstruction is possible at all.

Suggestions for a Revised Theory

6. Internal reconstruction is a procedure for inferring part of the history of a language from material available for a synchronic description of the language, and from that alone. If highly probable historical inferences

---

[4]Written phonemically.

[5]The prime indicates palatalization. In Marchand's original article, palatalization is denoted by a comma.

can indeed be made from such data, the procedure is of crucial importance in three situations: (1) when we are confronted with a language with no known relatives and no written history, (2) when we wish to reconstruct recent details of language history which are not accessible through derivation from a proto-language even when a proto-language is available, and (3) when we wish to reconstruct the prehistory of a proto-language. In other situations internal reconstruction can be a useful supplement to and confirmation of the comparative method and other historical procedures.

7. Most of historical linguistics is fundamentally dependent upon the technique of comparing cognate forms. These forms may be from different languages, as in the comparative method proper, or from different stages of the same language, as in the use of written records; but with the possible exception of some aspects of dialect geography there is no generally recognized historical technique that does not involve the comparison of cognates.[6] Such comparison seems to me to be the only conceivable basis for internal reconstruction.

8. The forms which are available for comparison in internal reconstruction are cognate morphs. To some extent this is also true in the comparative method, where, for example, we can compare only the initial morphs of Sanskrit *ákṣi* and Latin *oculus* 'eye'. But while it is often possible in the comparative method to compare whole words that are cognate, for example Skt. *ásti* with Lat. *est* '(he, she, it) is', entirely cognate words that differ in form and are thus productive for reconstruction are available internally in two specialized guises only: sandhi forms, i.e. word variants conditioned by the syntactic environment, and stylistic variants, i.e. a pair of alternative forms between which the only semantic difference is the same as between another such pair, while the morphemic content of the first pair has nothing in common with that of the other.[7] The differences between the variants in either of these two categories can usually or always be reduced to differences between morphs. More important in probably most languages, because of the greater range and diversity of their occurrences, are the cognate morphs which do not fall into either of these categories. Although the statement is

---

[6]Cf. G. Bonfante, On reconstruction and linguistic method, *Word* 1.144 (1945). Bonfante was referring only to the comparison of separate languages or dialects when he excluded comparison from the "chronology of the texts" and described it as optional for certain others among his ten historical methods.

[7]Although not discussed in precisely these terms, an extensive illustration of stylistic variants is provided by C. T. Hodge, Some aspects of Persian style, *Lg.* 33.355–69 (1957). Others prefer to regard such alternative forms as containing morphs in free variation; see for example P. L. Garvin, On the relative tractability of morphological data, *Word* 13.17 f. (1957).

obviously not completely true, and will have to be modified below, let us assume for the moment that all the allomorphs of any morpheme are cognate.

9. Supplied in this way with cognate forms, we are in a position to reconstruct the pre-language by following, essentially, the familiar comparative method, modified as necessary to accommodate the purely internal data. At this point reference can be made to the formulation of the comparative method offered by Hoenigswald.[8] The first step is the discovery of recurrent phoneme correspondences. Hoenigswald speaks of SETS of correspondences, meaning by set a class of recurrent, phonemically identical correspondences. In the rest of this paper I shall speak simply of correspondences, with the understanding that only recurrent correspondences are usable for any kind of reconstruction. A correspondence *t/d*, for example, is extractable from German *bunt-/bund-* 'alliance', *runt-/rund-* 'round', etc. Whenever it is useful to do so, correspondences between identical phonemes can be established when the phonemes occur within the same morpheme in different environments. For example a correspondence *t/t* can be set up on the basis of *laut-/laut-* 'loud' (*laut* 'loud' / *lauter* 'louder'), *bunt-/bunt-* 'motley' (*bunt* 'motley' / *bunter* 'more motley'), etc. The usefulness of such a procedure will become clear in what follows.

10. Correspondences which have one member in common can be called SIMILAR (Hoenigswald's PARTIALLY ALIKE). Thus the correspondences *t/d* and *t/t* of the previous paragraph are similar. It is also necessary to consider the distribution of correspondences relative to their environments. The environment of a correspondence is expressed in terms of neighboring correspondences, but it is often convenient to group together the pertinent neighboring correspondences into a generalization. Thus we can say that the German correspondence *t/d* occurs in the environments BEFORE SYLLABLE ONSET OR PAUSE/ELSEWHERE.[9]

11. We can now group together similar correspondences that are in complementary distribution and assign them to the same reconstructed phoneme. If there is a choice, we follow the principle of economy and reconstruct phonemes that have the widest possible distribution in the pre-language. Two environments A/B and C/D are in complementary distribution if (a) they have nothing in common, or (b) A and C have something in common but B and D do not (or vice versa). Otherwise the environments contrast. The *t*'s of Germ. *laut-*, *bunt-*, etc. occur both before syllable onset or

---

[8]The principal step in comparative grammar, *Lg.* 26.357–64 (1950).

[9]This way of indicating the pertinent environments of a correspondence, often with the aid of abbreviations for phoneme categories (as V for vowel) will be followed throughout the paper. Thus, to write that the correspondence *a/b* occurs in the environments V-V/-x, y-means that *a* occurs intervocalically while *b* occurs before *x* and after *y*.

pause and elsewhere, and thus we can regard them as forming a correspondence *t/t* that contrasts with *t/d*. These two correspondences must therefore be assigned to different reconstructed phonemes. On the other hand there is no correspondence *d/d* which occurs in these environments, so that *t/d* and *d/d* can both be assigned to a phoneme **d*.

12. Up to this point we have followed quite analogously the procedure formulated by Hoenigswald as "the principal step in comparative grammar." We are faced with certain complications, however, that modify the picture so far presented, and that serve in part to distinguish the situation of internal reconstruction from that which confronts the comparative method. The complicating factors are basically two: the sequential nature of the phonemic changes which provide the data for internal reconstruction and which the latter aims to reconstruct, and the occurrence of irregular changes, notably analogy and suppletion. Suppletion is like analogy, except that semantic rather than formal identities are involved.[10]

13. Irregular changes are a complication in the comparative method as well. Since they are by definition restricted to specific grammatical environments, it is usually possible to isolate them from the regular phonemic changes. For example, in Wulfila's Gothic the correspondence *t/þ*, occurring in the environments *f-*, *h-*, *s-*/elsewhere (§3), contrasts with the correspondence *t/t* because of words like *aftiuhan* 'to draw away'. Following the procedure so far outlined, we could not, therefore, assign *t/þ* to **t*. The change which resulted in the occurrence of *t* after *f* was, however, restricted to certain morphemically definable environments, and this circumstance provides a clue to its isolation in the internal reconstruction of Gothic. It may be noted that analogically introduced allomorphs, while still cognate with the other allomorphs of a morpheme, will only accidentally yield recurrent correspondences. It is the occurrence of suppletion that forces a modification of the assumption made in §8 that all the allomorphs of a morpheme are cognate. As stated by Marchand (246), "all the allomorphs of a morpheme are cognate, or else suppletion has taken place." There is little likelihood of suppletion yielding recurrent correspondences, so that there seems to be no need for defending ourselves against it with such arbitrary procedural restrictions as those suggested by Marchand (246 f.).

14. The complications which arise from the sequential nature of the changes clearly distinguish internal reconstruction from the comparative method. For while the latter yields inferences regarding a single proto-

---

[10]The term "analogy" could of course be used in a wider sense to include both processes.

language assumed to exist at the particular time when the compared languages diverged,[11] our experience with the history of languages shows us that the morphophonemic alternations in a language do not result from simultaneous sound changes, but from a series of independent changes, both regular and irregular, any of which may modify and obscure the results of previous changes. Internal reconstruction thus yields inferences concerning not one but several different historical stages of a language: the term "pre-Seneca" does not refer to a single stage in the history of Seneca, but to a series of stages. It is therefore of importance to consider whether there is any means of reconstructing the chronological order of the changes leading to the synchronic morphophonemic picture, of being able to say that at any particular stage of the language such and such changes had or had not occurred and to describe the phoneme distribution at that stage.

15. It is here that the distinction between automatic and nonautomatic[12] morphophonemic alternations is productive. The way in which this distinction is useful for internal reconstruction has never been made entirely clear; it is not relevant for the reconstruction of phonemic changes as such, but for the reconstruction of a relative chronology of the changes. Automatic alternations—those that are wholly predictable in phonological terms applying throughout the language, not just in a particular grammatical environment—can be inferred to be the results of the most recent sound changes, since they have not been made unpredictable by subsequent changes. Hence, the phoneme correspondences extracted from automatic alternations can be used directly as the basis for reconstruction as described above, with no danger that the distributions have been disturbed by subsequent changes. Since the *bunt-/bund-* alternation is automatic, the reconstruction of **d* as described in §11 is immediately possible. The forms reconstructed from automatic alternations can be regarded as one stage historically removed from the attested language.

16. Now at this first reconstructed stage it usually happens that certain alternations not automatic in the attested language were still automatic. On the basis of these alternations it is possible to reconstruct forms two stages removed from the attested language, and, barring other complications, the procedure can be continued in this way from each historical stage to one that preceded it. There was, for example, a stage of Greek at which the phoneme correspondence Ø/s in the environments V–V/elsewhere was extractable from alternations like *gene-/genes-* 'generation' (*géneos* gen. sg./*génessi* dat.

---

[11]Although of course the picture is often complicated by gradual rather than sudden and complete divergence.

[12]Hoenigswald (1946) uses the terms "compulsory" and "noncompulsory."

pl.). But such alternations were not automatic because of the existence of *s* between vowels in words like *ambrosíā* 'ambrosia'.[13]

17. A digression is necessary here, for there are two possible interpretations of the concept of automaticity. One is that alternations are automatic so long as they can be generalized in terms that apply AT MORPHEME BOUNDARIES to all BASIC ALTERNATES containing a certain feature. A basic alternate is either an actually occurrent allomorph or a morphophonemic construct to which general rules can be applied to yield the various alternates that occur. Under this interpretation the existence of intervocalic *s* in *ambrosíā* does not demonstrate the nonautomaticity of the *gene-/genes-* alternation, since a morphophonemic rule that *s* > Ø between vowels would be irrelevant to the morphology of *ambrosíā*. The other interpretation of automaticity is that alternations are automatic only if they can be regarded as conditioned by the total pattern of phoneme distribution in the language. Under this interpretation the *gene-/genes-* alternation would be automatic only if *s* never occurred intervocalically, and words like *ambrosíā* are sufficient to demonstrate that it does so occur. It is the latter interpretation that is implied by Hoenigswald's use of the term "compulsory" and will be followed here, since it is more useful in the procedure outlined. Note that the Greek alternation Ø/*s* would be automatic even if in some morphemes there were *s*'s which alternated with other phonemes in the environment V–V (presumably as the result of earlier changes). It is only necessary that *s* should not occur in this environment.

18. Returning to our example, let us assume that at this particular stage of Greek the alternation exemplified by *-bros-/brot-* 'mortal' (*ambrosíā* above/*ámbrotos* 'immortal') was automatic. For the correspondence *s*/*t* we can reconstruct a **t*,[14] and infer that **ti* > *si*; **ambrotíā* > *ambrosíā*. We now find that at the stage which we have reconstructed there are no *s*'s between vowels, so that the alternation exhibited by *gene-/genes-* is automatic. For the correspondence Ø/*s* we can reconstruct **s*,[15] and infer both that **s* > Ø between vowels and that this change preceded the change **ti* > *si*.

19. The nonsimultaneity of changes in the pre-language does not

[13]Cf. Hoenigswald 1946, §5.

[14]*s*/*t* is in contrastive distribution with Ø/*s*, so that the reconstruction of an **s* is precluded. See fn. 15.

[15]Zero is an acceptable reconstruction only if epenthesis is plausible as a historical explanation. Epenthesis is plausible whenever the environments in which it might have taken place are definable in strictly phonological terms. That is not the case here, so that we are led to assign Ø/*s* to **s*.

always obscure the distribution of phoneme correspondences. In the example above from Greek, *s/t* and *Ø/s* could be assigned to **t* and **s* respectively without regard for the chronology involved. But even if its reconstruction is not always essential to the reconstruction of phonemes, the chronology is itself a part of the history of a language. Automaticity is the principal criterion for its reconstruction, but other clues are often present in particular situations; see for example §31 and §46 below.

20. Internal reconstruction has both synchronic and historical limitations. The amount of such reconstruction possible in a particular language is, on the one hand, a function of the nature and extent of the morphophonemic alternations in that language. On the other hand, as we progress further back in time it inevitably becomes more and more difficult to arrive at satisfactory reconstructions. The obscuring of language history by the various types of language change is cumulative, and may vary greatly in effect both from language to language and within different environments in the same language, so that it is impossible to set well defined historical limits to the applicability of internal reconstruction. Indeed, some kind of change occurring at some time during the history of a language is inferable from any morphophonemic alternation.[16] My major concern in this paper, however, is with changes that are widely and systematically reflected in the attested language.

21. This section has suggested in broad terms procedures for the reconstruction of phonemic changes and their relative chronology. The following discussion of internal reconstruction in Seneca provides an elaboration of what has been said, and suggests ways of handling some of the detailed problems that arise in a more extensive treatment of an individual language.

Application to Seneca

22. Seneca was the language spoken by the westernmost of the Five Nations of the Iroquois.[17] It is still in use today on reservations in New York State and Ontario. Its phonemes include:

---

[16]Cf. F. G. Lounsbury, *Oneida verb morphology* 14 f. (New Haven, 1953). Note that with chronologically and environmentally isolated changes it is sometimes impossible to distinguish phonemic from analogic change.

[17]Published descriptions of Seneca have been C. F. Voegelin and W. D. Preston, Seneca I, *IJAL* 15.23–44 (1949); and N. Holmer, Seneca II, *IJAL* 18.217–22 (1952), Seneca III, *IJAL* 19.281–9 (1953), and *The Seneca language, a study in Iroquoian* (Upsala and Copenhagen, 1954). These works were based on very little contact with the language and are at best preliminary sketches.

vowels (V)[18]
  oral vowels (V$_a$) *a, æ, e, i, o*
  nasalized vowels (V$_\varepsilon$) ɛ, ɔ
resonants (R) *n, w, y*
obstruents (O)
  oral obstruents (O$_t$) *j, k, t, s*
  laryngeal obstruents (O$_h$) *h,* ˀ
vowel length, written *:*
accent, written with the acute accent mark[19]

k and *t* are voiced before a vowel or resonant, voiceless elsewhere. *j* is a voiced affricate [dz].

23. Seneca is a fusional, polysynthetic language.[20] A language of this type provides considerable raw material for internal reconstruction. Not all of the possibilities offered by the data will be examined here, but enough of them will be taken up to illustrate points in the application of the suggested theory. The order in which topics are discussed is dictated solely by convenience of presentation:

    (a)   the history of *tn* and *kn* (§§24–31)
    (b)   *t* and *k* in clusters of oral obstruents (§32)
    (c)   the loss of resonants before laryngeal obstruents (§33)
    (d)   the history of *h* (§§34–6)
    (e)   the reconstruction of a fourth resonant (§§37–42)
    (f)   VV > V: (§43)
    (g)   the history of *a* (§§44–8)
    (h)   the sources of vowel length (§§49–53)
    (i)   the loss of length in vowel clusters (§§54–9)
    (j)   the accent (§§60–1).

24. The history of *tn* and *kn*. Certain changes centered around the history of reconstructed *t* and *k* before *n* will be taken up first. The development of an epenthetic *h* and of a stylistic distinction will be included as relevant here.

25. The sequence *tn* occurs in modern Seneca, to my knowledge, only in the word ˀ*óætnɛ*ˀ*ta*ˀ 'fern'. If this one word is disregarded, the following

---

[18]The indicated symbols for phoneme categories will be used below to abbreviate the descriptions of environments.

[19]Additional prosodic phonemes, including other accents as well as pitches and junctures, are not involved in the discussion in this paper.

[20]I.e. it has a relatively small proportion of agglutinative morpheme junctures and a relatively large number of morphemes per word. See J. H. Greenberg, A quantitative approach to the morphological typology of language, *Method and perspective in anthropology* 192–220 (R. F. Spencer, ed.; Minneapolis, 1954).

alternation becomes automatic: when a morpheme which elsewhere ends in *t* is followed by a morpheme with initial *n*, it occurs with *h* in place of the *t*. Thus the inclusive person morpheme exhibits the correspondence *h*/*t* in (for example) *hninʒes* 'we (incl. du.) like it'/*twanʒeˀs* 'we (incl. pl.) like it'. The reciprocal morpheme, *-atat-* in most environments, has the shape *-atah-* in *te:yatahnʒeˀs* 'they (masc. du.) like each other'. The correspondence *h*/*t*, then, occurs in the environments *-n*/elsewhere. As will be seen in §35, there are widely distributed correspondences containing *h* which contrast with *h*/*t* and speak against the assignment of the latter to *h. Assigning it to *t, on the other hand, conflicts with no other correspondences and widens the distribution of *t in the pre-language. Thus we can infer that *tn > *hn*; *tninʒeˀs > *hninʒeˀs*, *teyatatnʒeˀs > *teyatahnʒeˀs*. The anomalous form *ˀóætnɛˀtaˀ* can only be explained as the result of some recent historical development other than regular sound change.

26. The factors involved in the change *tn > *hn* are clarified through consideration of the history of the sequence *kn. The two oral stops, *t* and *k*, are distributed in nearly the same way in Seneca phonological structure, so that a comparison of the history of *k* with that of *t* suggests itself.

27. There is in Seneca an *h* that always occurs between a morpheme which elsewhere ends in *k* and a morpheme which elsewhere begins with *n*: for example, between *-k-* 'first person' and *-noˀsɛ-* 'to be uncle to' in *hakhnóˀsɛh* 'he's my uncle', and between *k-* 'third person nonmasculine' and *-ni-* 'dual' in *khninʒeˀs* 'they (nonmasc. du.) like it'. The sequence *kn is nonexistent. This *h* is thus an empty morph,[21] its presence determined solely by the phonological environment. An empty morph can be thought of as alternating with zero in all other environments, so that in this case we have the phoneme correspondence *h*/Ø occurring in the environments *k–n*/elsewhere. *h and Ø are both possible antecedents. Now the *h* in the sequence *khn* is not always an empty morph, since it is sometimes clearly assignable to the morpheme containing the *n*. In the word *ˀakhnyéˀstaˀ* 'my chestnut', for example, the morpheme meaning 'chestnut' is *-hnyeˀsta-*. This segmentation is based on the alternation of this form with *-:nyeˀsta-* after a vowel; cf. *ˀo:nyéˀstaˀ* 'the chestnut', but *honóˀsɛh* 'he's his/her uncle' with no : before the *n*. The alternation *hn*/ *:n* is parallel to *hw*/ *:w* in (for example) *ˀakhwístaˀ* 'my money', *ˀo:wístaˀ* 'the money', where there is no question of the *h* being an empty morph since *kw* also occurs. This alternation of *h* with : will be taken up in §§34 ff. Of significance here is the fact that a more widely distributed *h* can be set up on the basis of correspondences other than and contrasting with the *h*/Ø correspondence provided by the empty morph.

[21]C. F. Hockett, Problems of morphemic analysis, *Lg.* 23.333 (1947).

28. If we reject *$*h$*, we are left with the possibility of Ø as the antecedent of the h/Ø correspondence under consideration. Since it is possible here to define phonologically the environments in which epenthesis might have taken place,[22] zero is an acceptable reconstruction and we can infer that *kn > khn; *haknóʔsɛh > hakhnóʔsɛh, *kninɉeʔs > khninɉeʔs. Reconsidering the history of *tn, and assuming a parallel development for *t* and *k*, we can infer that *tn > *thn, and that there was then a second change in which *thn > hn. This hypothesis is supported by the fact that *thn does not occur in modern Seneca.

29. Every form that contains the sequence *khni* has a stylistic variant (§8) containing *ki* instead. Similarly, every form that contains the sequence *hni* in which the *h* is in morphophonemic alternation with *t* has a stylistic variant containing *ti* instead. Without committing ourselves as to the semantic difference between the two styles, let us assign *khni* and *hni* to style A and *ki* and *ti* to style B. Examples of style A are *khninɉeʔs* (§27) and *hninɉeʔs* (§25). The contrasting forms in style B are *kinɉeʔs* and *tinɉeʔs*. As discussed above, the sequences involved in style A can be traced to *kni and *tni. Because of the lack of *h* in the forms of style B, it is most economical to infer that the origin of the stylistic differentiation preceded the development of the epenthetic *h* between *k* or *t* and *n*. Thus there was evidently at one time a stylistic or dialectal alternation between *kni and *ki*, and between *tni and *ti*. The sequences *kni and *tni then underwent the developments indicated, while *ki* and *ti* remained unchanged.

30. Other parallel alternations, which will simply be mentioned here, are those of style A *khny* and *hny* with style B *ky* and *ty* respectively. Furthermore, when style A has forms containing initial *hni* and *hny* in which the *h* belongs to the masculine morpheme (and thus is not in morphophonemic alternation with *t*), there are style B alternates with *hi* and *y* respectively, implying that initial *hy > y. The noninitial development of these forms with the masculine morpheme is more complicated, since it involves the history of postvocalic *h (§§34 ff.).

31. To summarize, we have so far reconstructed the following sequence of changes. First to occur was the development of the distinction between styles A and B, perhaps originally found in two separate dialects. This development amounted to the loss, in style B, of *n* between *k*, *t*, or *h* and *i* or *y*. Second came the appearance of an epenthetic *h* between *t* or *k* and *n*. Finally, *t* was lost before *hn*. In reconstructing the relative chronology of these changes it was not necessary to make use of the automaticity criterion, but only to assume a parallel development for *t* and *k*, and to follow the principle of economy in placing the origin of style B. The fact that the

[22]Cf. fn. 15.

correspondences *h/t* and *h/Ø* both derive from automatic (or virtually automatic) alternations, however, helps to show their lateness relative to changes involving **h* discussed below.

32. *t and *k in clusters of oral obstruents. Before we leave *t* and *k* we may note that there are automatic alternations which make it possible to reconstruct the history of these two phonemes in clusters of oral obstruents. The correspondence *Ø/t* occurs in the environments *–sO, –s#, k–#, s–#/* elsewhere, where *#* indicates a word boundary.[23] Examples are *-the^{ʔ}-/ -the^{ʔ}t-* 'to pound corn' (*^{ʔ}othé^{ʔ}shæ^{ʔ}* 'flour, meal'/*kothé^{ʔ}tɔh* 'she has pounded the corn'), *-ɔto:wæ-/-ɔtowæ:t-*[24] 'to hunt' (*hɛnɔto:wæ:s* 'they hunt'/*honɔtowæ:tɔh* 'they have hunted'), *-o^{ʔ}k-/-o^{ʔ}kt** 'to come to the end' (*^{ʔ}o:to^{ʔ}k* 'it's at the end'/*^{ʔ}o^{ʔ}ko^{ʔ}ktɛ^{ʔ}* 'I came to the end'), *-s-/-st-* 'causative' (*^{ʔ}o^{ʔ}kto:kɛs* 'I straightened it'/*kotókɛstɔh* 'she has straightened it'). In a parallel fashion, *Ø/k* occurs in the environments *–sO, –s#, t–#, s–#/*elsewhere. To reconstruct zero as the antecedent of these correspondences would imply that *t* and *k* developed epenthetically in an unpredictable way in a wide range of improbable environments; hence zero is not acceptable here. To reconstruct **t* and **k*, however, for *Ø/t* and *Ø/k* respectively presents no distributional difficulties and yields pre-language phonemes with fewer distributional restrictions. We can infer that **t* and **k* were lost before an **s* that was followed by an obstruent or a word boundary, and that they were also lost in word-final position after an oral obstruent.[25]

33. The loss of resonants before laryngeal obstruents. In modern Seneca the resonants (*n, w,* and *y*) occur only before vowels, with the exception of *n* in the cluster *ny*. They alternate automatically with zero before the laryngeal obstruents (*h* and ^{ʔ}). From these alternations we can extract the correspondences *n/Ø, w/Ø,* and *y/Ø* in the environments *–V/–O*h; *n/Ø* also occurring in the environments *–y/–O*h. Examples are *-kowan-/-kowa-* 'to be big' (*kakowanɛh* 'it's big'/*^{ʔ}okowahé^{ʔ}ɔh* 'it's gotten big'), *-sin-/-si-* 'leg' (*hotsínya^{ʔ}kɔh* 'his leg is cut off'/*^{ʔ}atsíhashæ^{ʔ}* 'garter'), *-ahsaw-/-ɔhsa-*[26] 'to begin' (*ɛtwáhsawɛ^{ʔ}* 'we (incl. pl.) will begin'/*hɛnɔhsaha^{ʔ}* 'they begin'), *-iey-/-ie-* 'to die' (*wa^{ʔ}áie^{ʔ}* 'she died'/*yáieyɔs* 'she's dying'). Zero is again not an acceptable reconstruction, and we are led to reconstruct **n, *w,* and **y* as the antecedents of *n/Ø, w/Ø,* and *y/Ø* respectively. The historical inference is of course that **n, *w,* and **y* were lost before the laryngeal obstruents.

---

[23]At which there is always a potentiality of juncture, although the juncture is not always present. We may infer that the prejunctural forms have been generalized.

[24]The correspondence *Ø/:* after the *æ*'s is discussed in §52.

[25]*k, t,* or *s.j* does not occur in this position.

[26]The correspondence *a/ɔ* at the beginning of these forms is discussed in §47.

34. The history of *h. It is profitable at this point to examine the distribution of the resonants reconstructed in §33, for a suggestive gap is evident. *n, *w, and *y all occur before both vowels and obstruents, but they occur before the latter—and here we are interested specifically in h—only across morph boundaries. Furthermore, the only intervocalic h's at this first reconstructed stage occur within morphs—never at morph boundaries. Since the morphophonemic alternations on which we have based our reconstructions have yielded phoneme correspondences at morph boundaries only, providing no data for the reconstruction of changes within morphs, the pattern described clearly implies that all presently intervocalic h's were formerly preceded by resonants. Since such resonants occurring within morphs had no overt reflexes, there is no way that we can know whether a particular one was *n, *w, or *y. The symbol R can be used to indicate simply some resonant. Thus the modern Seneca root -ɔhe- 'to be alive' can be reconstructed as *-ɔRhe-. We have now reconstructed a stage of the language at which h alternates automatically with either vowel length or zero, according to the environment. This gives us the correspondences h/:/Ø, on the basis of which we can reconstruct an *h that is two stages removed from the modern language.

35. The correspondences h/:/Ø occur in the environments O–V, O–R, V–O-/V–R/V–OO, V–O#, V–V. This is a formidable set of symbols. It means that morphemes having h between an obstruent and a vowel or resonant, or between a vowel and a single obstruent that is not word-final, occur with : instead of h between a vowel and a resonant, and that they occur with Ø instead of h between a vowel and two obstruents or a single word-final obstruent, as well as between two vowels. Examples are -hwaji:yæ-/-waji:yæ- 'family' (khwaji:yæ ^{ʔ} 'my family'/ha:waji:yæ ^{ʔ} 'his family'), -hyatɔ-/-yatɔ- 'to write' (khyatɔ́ɔ ^{ʔ} 'I write'/ha:yátɔ: ^{ʔ} 'he writes'), -ha ^{ʔ}-/-a ^{ʔ}- 'iterative' (^{ʔ}ote:kha ^{ʔ} 'it burns'/tá:snyea ^{ʔ} 'he takes care of it'), -his-/-ist-[27] 'to shove' (^{ʔ}o ^{ʔ}khis 'I shoved it'/hóistɔh 'he's shoved it'), -a ^{ʔ}swaht-/-a ^{ʔ}swat- 'to put out a fire' (^{ʔ}aká ^{ʔ}swahtɔh 'I've put out the fire'/ha ^{ʔ}swátha ^{ʔ} 'he's putting out the fire', sa ^{ʔ}swat 'put out the fire!').

36. These correspondences are in complementary distribution with any h/h set up on the basis of morphemes that retain an h in various environments. We are thus justified in assigning them to *h and inferring that *h > : between a vowel and a resonant; that *h > Ø between vowels, as well as between a vowel and two obstruents or a single word-final obstruent. We can also infer that these changes preceded the changes involving resonants described in §33. It must also have preceded the loss of t before hn described

[27]The correspondence Ø/t at the end of these forms was discussed in §32.

in §28, since sequences of V*hn* resulting from the latter change did not become V:*n*.

37. The reconstruction of a fourth resonant. We are now in a position to discuss the reconstruction of a fourth resonant phoneme that no longer exists in Seneca. In some environments it became one of the other resonant phonemes, while in others it simply dropped out, sometimes leaving traces in the surrounding phonemes. There are many bits of evidence in the language that point to the earlier presence of such a phoneme, and the way in which it is reconstructed below is perhaps only one of several ways leading to the same result. The alternations from which the correspondences cited below can be extracted are nonautomatic in modern Seneca, but are automatic at the stage just reconstructed, i.e. before the changes involving **h*. The loss of the fourth resonant, at least in the environments cited in §§38–40, must then have preceded the loss or change to : of postvocalic **h*.

38. In addition to, and in contrastive distribution with the correspondence *n*/Ø referred to in §33—i.e. reconstructed **n*—there is another correspondence *n*/Ø which occurs in the environments --*y*/elsewhere.[28] Examples are -*kan*-/-*ka*- 'story' (*wa:kanya$^{\backprime}$k* 'he broke off the story'/*hoka:ot* 'he's telling stories'), -*hsɔhkan*-/-*hsɔhka*- 'lips' (*hotehsɔhkánya$^{\backprime}$kɔh* 'his lips are broken off' [referring to a false-face]/*hahsɔ́hkaes* 'his lips are long').

39. Bearing the same relation to reconstructed **w*, there is a correspondence *w*/Ø which occurs in the environments *o*(:)–V$_a$/elsewhere. Examples are -*wæ:n*-/-*æ:n*- 'sugar' (*$^{\backprime}$owæ:nɔ$^{\backprime}$* 'the sugar'/*$^{\backprime}$akæ:nɔ$^{\backprime}$* 'my sugar'), -*wi*-/-*i*- 'to be done, cooked' (*$^{\backprime}$o:wi:h* 'it's done'/*$^{\backprime}$ɛka:ih* 'it will get done').

40. Similarly, contrasting with **y* is a correspondence *y*/Ø which occurs in the environments *i*(:)–V$_a$, O$_t$–*o*, O$_t$–*ɔ*/elsewhere. Examples are -*hwajiy*-/-*hwaji*- 'family' (*khwajiyæyɛ$^{\backprime}$* 'I have a family'/*kathwáji:ne$^{\backprime}$* 'I'm walking along with my family'), -*nesty*-/-*nest*- 'board' (*kanéstyo:tɔ$^{\backprime}$* 'boards are standing' [a personal name]/*kanéstæ$^{\backprime}$es* 'it hits the board'), -*yɔt*-/-*ɔt*- 'post' (*$^{\backprime}$o$^{\backprime}$kyɔto:tɛ$^{\backprime}$* 'I set up a post'/*tkɛɔto:t* 'there's a post standing there' [name of Brant, N. Y.]).

41. These three correspondences are in complementary distribution with each other, so that we are led to ask whether the common feature of zero is enough to establish similarity. On the face of it, it would seem that zero ought to count neither for nor against similarity. Similarity, however, does not dictate but merely permits assignment to the same reconstructed pho-

---

[28]"Elsewhere" here and in §§39 and 40 does not include all other environments; specifically, it does not include the limited environments described in the other two of these three paragraphs.

neme, and anything that does not count against it in effect counts for it. The validity of all reconstructions is strengthened by independent supporting evidence. When similarity based on zeros is involved, supporting evidence is particularly desired. In the present case there are factors which leave no room for doubt as to the advisability of relating these three correspondences. One such factor is that the overt members of the correspondences are members of the same distributional class, the class of resonants. More telling is the fact that other correspondences, not yet cited, are overtly similar to two of the above three, and overlap their environments.[29] Examples are the correspondence *n/y* in *-wi:n-/-wi:y-* 'offspring' (*yɔtwi:nyaʔs* 'she cuts off her offspring' [a reference to sterilization]/*yewi:yæʔ* 'her offspring'), and the correspondence *w/y* in *-hyo:wi-/-hyony-*[30] 'to tell' (*ʔakáthyo:wi:h* 'I've told about it'/*ʔɛkathyonyá:nɔ:ʔ* 'I'm going to tell about things').

42. Various types of evidence, then, point to the assignment of these correspondences to the same reconstructed phoneme, but this phoneme cannot be **n*, **w*, or **y*. That it was a resonant seems probable from its distribution, and from the fact that all its overt reflexes are resonants. I reconstruct it as **r*, for three independent and more or less trivial reasons: *r* is the first letter of the word resonant, it is phonetically plausible as a resonant, and the cognate phoneme in several related languages is, by a happy coincidence, *r*.[31] We can infer the changes (a) **r > n* before *y*; (b) **r > w* between *o(:)* and an oral vowel; (c) **r > y* between *i(:)* and an oral vowel, as well as between an oral obstruent and *o* or *ɔ*; and (d) **r* was lost everywhere else. The automaticity criterion, supported by the evidence presented below in §46, shows that these changes involving **r* took place before the loss or change to *:* of postvocalic **h*. Further considerations, however, indicate that this dating applies only to **r* before a vowel or, in the case of **ry*, before a resonant. We have already established that the changes involving **h* themselves preceded the loss of resonants before laryngeal obstruents (§33). It can now be seen that the resonants lost in this position included not only **n*, **w*, and **y*, but also **r*; e.g. *-tha-* < **-thar-* 'to talk' in *hatíthahaʔ* 'they talk'. Thus **r* before a laryngeal obstruent was not lost at the same time as **r* before a vowel, but survived until all four resonants were lost in this position. The reconstruction of **r* is confirmed by a large amount of interlocking evidence in modern Seneca, some of which will come to light in connection with the reconstructions to be discussed in the remainder of this paper.

[29]Because of the nature of the environments, a three-way correspondence *n/w/y* would be impossible.

[30]For the correspondence *:/Ø* after the *o*'s, see §50.

[31]Note that **r* is one specific phoneme, while **R* in reconstructions indicates either **n*, **w*, **y*, or (see below) **r*.

43. *VV > V:*. It is necessary here to note that when **h* and **r* were lost between two identical vowels, the second of these vowels became *:*; e.g. **ʔɛtwáhashɛːʔ* > *ʔɛtwáːshɛːʔ* 'we (incl. pl.) will hold a council', **hotiriyóʔteʔ* > *hotiːyóʔteʔ* 'they're working'. This statement is of course dependent upon the phonemicization of vowel length as a separate phoneme *:*, rather than as vowel gemination. Such a phonemicization was dictated by the phonological impossibility of assigning the *:* segment in such a sequence as *-óːɛ-* in *ʔɔkwaʔnikóllːɛʔ* 'our minds' to any vowel phoneme, since, while it has the length of a single vowel, its first half is most similar to *ó* and its last half to *ɛ*.

44. *The history of *a.* The correspondence *æ/a* can be assigned to a reconstructed phoneme **a*. It is found in alternations that are automatic at the stage at which the alternations leading to the reconstruction of **r* are automatic, i.e. prior to the changes involving **h*. If we use **r* to represent all correspondences reconstructable as **r*, it is possible to say that *æ/a* occurs in the environments **r–/*elsewhere, with some further distributional limitations to be noted below. An example is *-æti-/-ati-* 'to be on the other side of' (*skáɔshætih* 'on the other side of the box' [**-hɔshr-* 'box']/*skanɔtatih* 'on the other side of the town'). As a further example, Seneca noun roots occur in certain environments, such as before the noun suffix *-ʔ*, in what I have called their combining allomorphs, which consist of the noncombining allomorph plus a supplementary final vowel which is most often *a*; e.g. *-ʔwasta-* 'stick' in *-kaʔwástaʔ* 'a stick' (cf. *-ʔwast-* in *kaʔwástowaːnɛh* 'a big stick'). After **r*, however, this supplementary phoneme is *æ*; e.g. *-neːstæ-* 'board' (< **-neːstr-æ/a-*) in *kaneːstæʔ* 'a board'. Since *æ/a* is in complementary distribution with any *a/a* set up on the basis of morphemes that retain an *a* in varied environments, we can assign it to **a* and infer that **ra > æ*, subject to the limitations discussed in the following paragraph. This change can only have been simultaneous with the loss of **r*.

45. It appears that we can establish a double correspondence *æ-:(< *æ-æ/a-a*, with the indicated phonemes occurring on either side of the environments **–r–/**–:r–*. Examples are *-kæ:-* (< **-kæræ-*)/*-kaːa-* (< **-kaːra-*) 'story' (*teʔkakæːʔ* 'not a story'/*kakaːaʔ* 'a story'), *-hsikwæ:-/-hsikwaːa-* 'fork' (*kahsikwæːʔ* 'a fork'/*hotíhsikwaːaʔ* 'their fork'). The inference is that **ara > æ:*, while **aːra > aːa*. It seems also that **ahra > *aha*; e.g., *ʔoʔkálːt < ^*ʔoʔkáhaht < *ʔoʔkáhraht* 'it passed by' (cf. *ʔoʔkhæt < *ʔoʔkhraht* 'I passed by'). By the procedure followed above we can also infer that **arɔ > ɛɔ*, while **aːrɔ > aːɔ* (*ʔohsikwɛɔt* 'it has a fork on it, rattlesnake'/*hotíhsikwaːɔt* 'they've attached a fork to it'); and that **aro > eo*, while **aːro > aːo* (*sekeotɛh* 'tell a story!'/*hokaːot* 'he's telling stories').

46. It is now possible to present a confirmation of the chronology involved in the loss of the phoneme *r before vowels. A morpheme *-hraht- 'to pass by' is reconstructable as the antecedent of the morph -hæht- in ˀakhæhtɔh 'I've passed by' (see also ˀoˀkál:t and ˀoˀkhæt in the paragraph above). Another allomorph, -æht, occurs in ˀóæhtɔh 'it has passed by', reconstructable as *ˀohráhtɔh.³² Now if the *hr of this form had become *:r before the loss of the *r (§36), the resulting sequence *o:ra would have become o:wæ (§42), leaving us with *ˀo:wæhtɔh. The existing form, ˀóæhtɔh, can only have resulted if the loss of *r preceded any change involving h; thus, *ˀohráhtɔh > *ˀohæhtɔh > ˀóæhtɔh.

47. Unlike æ/a, the correspondence ɔ/a is found in alternations that are automatic in modern Seneca. Its environments are n– (except n–o), Vɛ–, Vɛˀ–, Vɛ(s)w–/elsewhere. Examples are -ɔ:w-/-a:w- 'to belong to' (honɔ:wɛh 'it belongs to them'/ˀaka:wɛh 'it belongs to me'), -ɔti-/-ati- 'to be on the other side of' (jawéɔtih 'on the other side of the flower' [a personal name]/skanɔtatih 'on the other side of the town)', -ɔ:w-/-a:w- 'objective' (nɔˀɔ:wɛh 'how it happened'/nɛya:wɛh 'how it will happen'), -ɔse-/-ase- 'to be new' (hoɔwɔse:ˀ 'his boat is new'/ˀoyéˀkwase:ˀ 'new tobacco'). This correspondence contrasts with *c reconstructed on the basis of morphemes which contain ɔ in all their allomorphs; e.g. -ɔhe- 'to be alive' (ˀakyɔ:heˀ 'we [excl. pl.] are alive', hɛnɔ:heˀ 'they [masc. pl.] are alive'). It is, however, in complementary distribution with any correspondences reconstructable as *a, and can thus be assigned to that phoneme. Thus *a > ɔ after n, after a nasalized vowel, and after a nasalized vowel plus ˀ, w, or sw.

48. Other correspondences imply that *æ > ɛ in the environments where *a > ɔ. Note the correspondence ɛ/æ in -ɛ:ˀse-/-æ:ˀse- 'to be cousins' (honé:ˀse:sheˀ 'they're in opposite moieties'/ˀɔkwæ:ˀse:sheˀ 'we're in opposite moieties'). That *æ > ɛ after a nasalized vowel is implied by the final vowel of the combining allomorphs in ˀoˀké:ɛˀ 'ashes' (containing a noun root whose noncombining allomorph is reconstructable as *-aˀkéhr-), kaˀníkɔɛˀ 'mind' (*-ˀnikɔhr-). We already know that the phoneme æ did not exist as anything more than an allophone of *a until *r was lost before vowels, but this does not necessarily mean that the change æ > ɛ came later than the loss of *r, since it is conceivable that it was the earlier sequence *ra which became ɛ. It seems impossible to relate chronologically the changes discussed in this and the preceding paragraphs to any of the other changes discussed in this paper. Their parallelism, however, suggests that these two changes themselves occurred simultaneously.³³

³²See §61 for the shift of accent.

³³The environments of these changes have been stated as if they were more recent than the loss of intervocalic *h, but can equally well be stated in terms appropriate to earlier stages; e.g. *Vɛh(r)- rather than Vɛ-.

49. The sources of vowel length. It has already been demonstrated that vowel length can be inferred in some cases to be a reflex of *h*; in others, of a vowel that was preceded in the pre-language by an identical vowel plus *h* or *r* (§36, §43). There remain, however, cases of vowel length which cannot be accounted for in either of these ways. If we assign these remaining cases to a phoneme *:* at the earliest stage of the pre-language that we have reconstructed, i.e. before the loss of prevocalic *r*, we find that it occurs only after the final or penultimate vowel of a word, and that it occurs after the penultimate vowel under different conditions depending on whether this vowel is even or odd, counting from the beginning of the word.

50. *:* occurs after an odd penultimate vowel, provided the vowel is not *a*, whenever there is a following single consonant other than a laryngeal obstruent; e.g. (*)ʔoʔkati:yoʔ 'I fought', (*)ʔɛkáhtɛ:tiʔ 'I'll go'; but *hatíhnyɔʔɔh* (> hatí:nyɔʔɔh) 'white men'. It occurs after *a* only when the latter is the first vowel of the word and the word is not an imperative form (does not end in the imperative morpheme); e.g. (*)ha:tɔh 'he says', but *srakoh* (> sækoh) 'take it out!'.

51. There is in modern Seneca a syntactically functioning accent pattern peculiar to imperative utterances, and we need only to assume its existence at our earliest reconstructed stage to infer that *:* after an odd penultimate vowel was automatic at that stage. Its (not quite complete) lack of occurrence after *a* is interesting, for there is both internal and comparative evidence to suggest that *a* originated as an epenthetic vowel, although prior to the differentiation of the Northern Iroquoian languages (cf. §44).

52. *:* occurs after an even penultimate vowel, as well as after any final vowel, so long as there is not a following laryngeal obstruent or sequence of two or more obstruents; e.g. (*)ʔaki:tɔh 'it means me', (*)kanɔ́hse:s 'long-house' (cf. *ʔoʔkhist* > ʔoʔkhis 'I shoved it'), (*)kani:yɔ:t 'it's hanging'. In some grammatically determined environments it also occurs before a laryngeal obstruent or sequence of two or more obstruents; e.g. *ʔoʔkɛ́hraʔɛ:ʔ* > ʔoʔkɛ́:ʔɛ:ʔ 'it's gray', *ʔoʔkɛ́hraʔɛ:ʔɔh* > ʔoʔkɛ́:ʔɛ:ʔɔh 'it's grayish', (*)twake:htɔh 'I've come from there', (*)ʔoʔkɔ:ta:ʔt 'I shook it'.

53. We can thus distinguish two classes of laryngeal obstruents and obstruent clusters: (a) those before which *:* does not occur after an even penultimate or final vowel, and (b) those before which it does. Those in class (a) belong to the majority of roots and nearly all suffixes, while those in class (b) belong to the remaining roots and a few allomorphs of aspect suffixes. In order to reconstruct a stage at which *:* was entirely conditioned by the phonology, it would be necessary to infer a phonological distinction of some sort between the two classes of morphemes thus defined, and no uniquely acceptable hypothesis suggests itself. Nevertheless, the near automaticity of the pattern indicates the likelihood of an earlier stage at which vowel length was nonphonemic.

54. *The loss of length in vowel clusters.* Certain complications in the history of vowel length have been ignored up to this point. In reconstructing its history, it has been necessary to overlook certain words in modern Seneca which do not exhibit the correspondences that have been described. In all of these words the discrepancies are found in the neighborhood of uninter- rupted vowel sequences that developed as a result of the loss of intervocalic **r* or **h*. It would have been possible to take these words into account whenever correspondences containing vowel length were introduced, but if this had been done the discussion at each point would have been greatly complicated, and at each point it would have been necessary to repeat essentially the same details. Consideration of these cases has, therefore, been postponed until all the sources of vowel length were dealt with. Since these cases were omitted in our reconstructions up to this point, the simplest way to approach them now is to start with morphemes as we have reconstructed them, to consider the forms that we would expect in modern Seneca as the result of the historical developments already inferred, and to compare these with the actually existent modern forms. The discrepancies yield readily to classification.

55. It appears that simultaneous with or following the loss of intervo- calic **r*, but before the loss of intervocalic **h* (§57), *:* was lost within or after any cluster of two or more vowels except between the penultimate and final vowels of a word; e.g. **ʔorɛːnɔʔ* > *ʔoɛnɔʔ* 'song', **ʔohsikwarɔːt* > *ʔohsikwɛɔt* 'rattlesnake'; but **kakaːraʔ* > *kakaːaʔ* 'story', **hokaːroːt* > *hokaːot* 'he's telling stories'.

56. The change *h* > *:* between a vowel and a resonant occurred only if the vowel was single. If the *h* was preceded by a vowel cluster it did not become *:* but was simply dropped; e.g. **ʔoríhwaʔ* > **ʔóihwaʔ* > *ʔóiwaʔ* 'thing, cause'.[34]

57. In accordance with what was said in §43, it must be added here that in sequences of the shape VV: the length metathesized, yielding V:V; e.g. **wahaːyɔʔ* > *waːayɔʔ* 'he arrived', **wɛnókahɛːthaʔ* > *wɛnóka:ɛthaʔ* 'they make holes'. The latter example shows that the change described in §55 occurred before the loss of intervocalic *h*, since *:* would otherwise have been lost.

58. Finally, *:* was lost within a vowel cluster whenever it was followed by more than two vowels in the same word; e.g. **waharihwáste:rist* >

---

[34]See §61 for the shift of accent.

wahaihwáste:is > *wa:iwáste:is* > *waiwáste:is* 'he noticed it'. If my notes are correct, there is some dialect divergence here; there are some speakers who say *wa:iwáste:is*.

59. There is in addition a colloquial or fast speech style in which : never occurs within a vowel cluster; e.g. *hokaot, waiwásteis* alongside the forms cited in §55 and §58.

60. *The accent.* In general, we can reconstruct words in which the reconstructed accent occurs on the antecedents of the accented vowels in modern Seneca. Exceptions to this statement, i.e. cases where certain factors point to the advisability of reconstructing an accent that occurs on the antecedent of an unaccented vowel in modern Seneca, are discussed in §61. Disregarding these exceptions for the moment, we can say that at the stage preceding the loss of provocalic *r the accent occurred on every even penultimate vowel that was not followed by *:; e.g. (*)ʔakyɛ́htɔh 'I've hit it', (*)ʔoká́ʔɔh 'it's good, pleasing'. If the penultimate vowel was either odd or followed by *:, the reconstructed accent occurred instead on the nearest preceding even vowel that was followed, either directly or with a single intervening odd vowel, by *h, *ʔ, or a cluster containing two obstruents or *s plus *n or *w; e.g. *ʔawɛ́hi:yo:h > ʔawɛ́:iyo:h 'beautiful flower', *wahɔwɔkɔ́taʔe:k > waɔwɔkɔ́taʔe:k 'they hit him on the nose', (*)wakáyɔstha ʔ 'it's getting old', *ʔakéswatɛ:shraʔ > ʔakéswatɛ:shæʔ 'my costume'. As in modern Seneca, there are many words in the reconstructed language that contain no accent. It can be seen that at this stage of the pre-language the occurrence of the accent was correlated with the occurrence of vowel length: given one, the other was predictable. The question whether this means that either vowel length or accent was nonphonemic at this stage will be left unanswered. If, as in the modern language, both accent and vowel length were syntactically as well as morphologically significant, their phonemic status cannot be determined on the basis of morphology alone. In any case, the two features became mutually unpredictable when the changes we have discussed disturbed the pattern of odd and even vowels. Modern Seneca has such contrasts as *waɛʔ* 'he said it', *wa:ɛʔ* 'he put it in it', and *wa:ɛʔ* 'he put it on it', from *wahɛʔ, *waha:rɛʔ, and *waháhrɛʔ respectively.

61. If we consistently reconstruct words in which the reconstructed accent occurs on the antecedents of the accented vowels in modern Seneca, we find that there are some words in which this accent does not conform to the distributional pattern just described. All such cases, however, turn out to involve accented vowels in modern Seneca which are immediately followed by other vowels. Furthermore, if the accent in the pre-language is recon-

structed to occur on the antecedents of these immediately following vowels, rather than of the accented vowels themselves, the pattern described in §60 applies without exception. We can thus infer that when two vowels, the second of which was accented in the pre-language, came to be adjacent to each other as a result of the loss of intervocalic *r or *h, the accent shifted to the first vowel. Examples are *hehóˀyaːks > héoˀyaːs 'he throws it there', *tɛyotiháˀheˀt > tɛyotíaˀheˀt 'it's going to become differentiated'.

62. Summary. The following chart summarizes the major changes that have been reconstructed in this section of the paper, with an indication of their relative chronology. (Numbers refer to paragraphs.) Changes not separated by horizontal lines have no reconstructable relative order. Note that all the changes open to the bottom of the chart are represented by automatic alternations in the modern language.

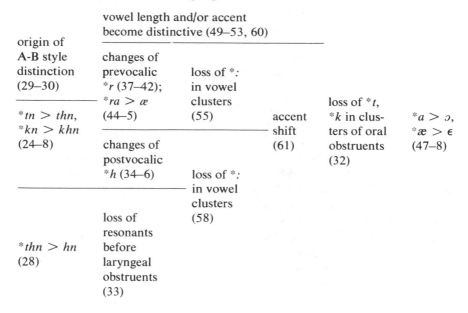

Conclusion

63. By virtue of the different materials upon which they operate, internal reconstruction and the comparative method are independent techniques; but, as I have tried to show, they are related methodologically. It would seem that a certain order of application is inherent in the relationship between the two; that internal reconstruction naturally precedes the comparative method, since the results of the former are implicit in the individual languages which are taken as starting points for the latter. Comparison of

Seneca with other Iroquoian languages, for example, is appreciably simplified if we can compare not modern Seneca, but reconstructed pre-Seneca
forms which contain postvocalic *h* before vowels and resonants, and the
other features discussed above. The only danger here, aside from unwarranted inferences in our reconstructions, is that the reconstructions may in
some cases antedate the divergence of the languages compared in the comparative method. Such cases ought always to be easily recognizable, so long
as we keep in mind the attested data and the chronology of the reconstructions. In general, because of the cumulative process of obscuration mentioned in §20, internally reconstructed features tend to be more recent than
those reconstructed by the comparative method.

64. Finally, it is worth noting that our reconstructed pre-language is
inevitably more regular in its morphophonemics than the language that we
take as our starting point. From alternations that are not phonologically
predictable we reconstruct alternations that are.[35] This is the only direction
in which internal reconstruction permits us to go; but the fact should not be
taken as evidence that languages regularly develop from the agglutinative to
the fusional type, as was thought by some nineteenth-century linguists.
Rather, it should be seen as a limitation of our method, which permits the
reconstruction of sound changes because we can assume that they occur
without exceptions, but does not permit, except indirectly in relation to the
sound changes, the reconstruction of regularizing but sporadic analogic
changes.

[35]On this point see C. H. Borgström, Internal reconstruction of Pre-Indo-European
word-forms, *Word* 10.276 (1954).

Part II
THEORY OF SOUND CHANGE

7

SOME THOUGHTS
ON SOUND LAWS*

J. Vendryès

After many years of harsh discussion, the existence of "sound laws" is today almost generally accepted. If there is someone who still does not believe in their existence, he has only to consult the excellent work of Weschssler, *Giebt es Lautgesetze?*, which is comprehensive enough to easily furnish whatever is necessary to remove any doubts and refute any objections he might have. But phoneticians have only arrived at establishing the legitimacy of their science by providing a more precise and even somewhat different meaning to the term "sound law." To believe in the existence of sound laws is simply to recognize that language change is governed by laws that are universally determined; that, in addition, every sound change has a natural cause; and that phonetic changes that appear to be exceptional are only disturbances brought about by equally natural causes within the regular play of phonetic phenomena. This conception, based on careful research, is the only scientific one. It does not force the linguist to accept blindly some arbitrary sound law that the superficial study of language might suggest. There is, in fact, nothing in common between the formulas set up by linguists and the imperative laws discovered by chemists and physicists. On the contrary, this conception imposes on the linguist a more severe caution and a more rigorous methodology. We will try in the following pages to analyze the notion of sound law and to draw some of the practical consequences of it.

"The regularity in the transmission of sounds," writes Meillet in the preface of his *Recherches sur l'emploi du génitif-accusatif en vieux-slave* (p. 6), "results from changes in the articulatory system and not the articulation of an isolated word" (compare *Indog. Forsch.*, X, p. 63). This implies that all the phonemes of a language are linked together very closely and are

*From *Mélanges linguistiques offerts à Antoine Meillet* (Paris, 1902), 115–131. Reprinted in the author's *Choix d'études linguistiques et celtiques* (Paris, 1952), 3–17. (Original title: "Réflexions sur les lois phonétiques," tr. by A. R. K.)

mutually conditioned. Hermann Paul has, in fact, already said just this: "There exists in all languages a certain harmony in phonological systems; one sees, therefore, that the direction in which a certain sound changes is dependent on the direction taken by all of the remaining sounds" (*Prinz. der Sprachg.*, 3d edition, p. 54).

The articulatory system is the same among individuals of the same generation belonging to the same social group, and it is in the passage from one generation to another that an articulatory system is ordinarily modified (Rousselot, *Les changements phonétiques*, p. 349 ff.). When, through a defect in articulatory coordination, one part of this system happens to break down, the harmony of the whole system is broken; and the axis is shifted and equilibrium reestablishes itself in a different articulatory position. A whole range of articulations then becomes impossible and is automatically replaced by another, until a new shifting of the articulatory apparatus determines a new range of changes.

Every sound change, therefore, involves not just a specific phoneme but a general type of articulation, and the change of one phoneme presupposes the concomitant change of many other phonemes. This principle of the coherence of sound systems has occasionally been disputed on the pretext that in certain languages there are isolated sound changes that seem to be outside the sound system of the language. But this pretext is illusory and results exclusively from a lack of information. When sound changes appear isolated, one must always look for the cause.

One of the most curious facts of this kind is without doubt the loss of *p* in the Celtic languages. This phenomenon, which is, moreover, attested not only in Celtic (it occurs in Armenian also) is entirely isolated, since the other voiceless stops *k* and *t* remain and the other bilabial stop *b* is not changed (at least at that period when *p* disappears). But a phoneme such as *p* can be modified insofar as it is a stop (and therefore *t*, *k*, *b*, *d*, *g* should also be modified), or as a voiceless stop (in which case *t* and *k* should also be modified), or finally as a bilabial voiceless stop (which explains its isolation).

It remains, therefore, to determine how a voiceless bilabial stop can be modified without the other voiceless stops undergoing the effects of the same change. The articulation of *p* at the extremity of the oral cavity, and its bilabial articulation, which is weaker than that of the dentals and velars, make it clear that *p* can change to *f* without *t* and *k* becoming *þ* or *ch*. Once the change of *p* to *f* is accomplished, one can easily understand that the language did not delay in eliminating a fricative that disturbed the harmony of the system, that is, was asymmetrical.

Another fact, less well-known than the loss of *p*, but just as characteristic, is provided by Britannic. It is known that when a word ended in a vowel, the initial consonant of the following word underwent a certain alteration, which manifested itself in the case of a voiced stop by a change to the corresponding fricative. This is the source in northern Welsh of the rule that, after a certain number of words, enumerated in the grammars, initial *d* becomes *t*; and initial *b, f* (*v* in French). One would say, then: *gofynais i'r dyn fwyta* (for *bwyta*) 'I asked the man to eat'; *gofynais i'r dyn ddyfod* (for *dyfod*) 'I asked the man to come'. But the velar consonants behave exceptionally; the same alteration is here implemented as the loss of the consonant. One says, therefore: *gofynais i'r dyn weled* 'I asked the man to see', from the verb *gweled*. This lack of parallelism will astonish only those who do not know the fleeting and unstable character of the voiced velar fricative which, like *yod*, with which it is closely related, frequently tends to disappear in intervocalic position. Once again, the special treatment of an isolated phoneme is not in contradiction with the system as a whole.

One can similarly explain the change of intervocalic *gh* > *h* in Latin, and the subsequent loss of *h*, while *bh* and *dh* become respectively *b* and *d* under the same conditions; and also the change of *g* and *b* to fricatives in the history of French, which coalesced with *y* and *v*, while *d* disappeared completely, since there was no homorganic fricative in the language (compare Meillet, *Revue internationale de sociologie* I, p. 315). One could bring forth other examples of the same kind. It is always possible to discover the reason for the isolated character of a sound change, provided, of course, that the change is phonological.

There are, in effect, changes that are not phonological. Although sound changes are in principle generalities and not individual particularities that are generalized, it can happen that sound changes emanate from a single individual; but the principle of the rigorous transmission of sounds cannot be affected by this fact.

The case of the famous Arrius is well-known, whom Catullus pokes fun at in his poem LXXX (compare Bréal, *Mém. S. L.*, X, p. 1). This person pronounced every *c* with aspiration. He said, for example, *chommoda* for *commoda*. In this, he only conformed, by way of snobism, to a fashion common enough in his time. When the Greek civilization burst upon Rome, bringing along its tastes, its habits, and its language, distinguished Romans tried to pronounce *x*. They found it elegant to preserve it in words that they borrowed from Greek and even to introduce it into their own vocabulary in words in which it had never occurred. Sempronius changes his agnomen from *Gracus* (geai) to *Gracchus* in order to make it rhyme with *Bacchus* (compare Cicero, *Orator*, 48, 160). One said *Orchus, pulcher, sepulchrum, choronae, chenturiones, praechones* (Quintilian, I, v, 20). In spite of their $k, \overset{,}{\alpha}\gamma \kappa \upsilon \rho \alpha, \, '\!A\lambda \kappa \mu \acute{\eta}\nu \eta$ became *anchora, Alchimena* (*Corp. Inscr. Lat.*, IX, 4296). Servius (*ad Aen.*, III, 224) relates that, in his time, the word *pulcher* still preserved the aspiration. Here we have the history of an individual and arbitrary pronunciation that does not conform to the spirit of the Latin language. This pronunciation could have become extended, or could have endured longer. It is only by chance that the Romance languages do not show any trace of it. But the influence of will upon pronunciation cannot be denied *a priori* (compare B. Delbrück, *Grundfragen der Sprachforschung*, 1901, p. 100 ff.). An individual can always take on any accent that he wishes, in the same way that he can disfigure himself or cut off some limb. But these facts do not compromise the principle of sound change any more than the willful mutilations of the Oceanic peoples compromise the principle of physiological evolution. It is precisely the role of the phonetician to unravel, in the history of a language, what is natural and what is due to human will. The phenomena that fall within the second category are always recognizable as asymmetrical. That is, they are not part of the system and it is not possible to make them conform to the system.

A sound law is valid only if it is in agreement with those principles that govern the articulatory system of a language at the moment when it operates. If there are no isolated sound changes, there are no isolated sound laws either; and it is by comparing contemporary sound changes that the linguist can appreciate the exactitude of a particular sound law.

This, however, is not enough. Everyone will realize easily enough to what degree the notion of sound law is incomplete if there is lacking the essential idea which must dominate all historical research, that is, the idea of time. Not only are sound changes, which are generally only formulas, conditioned by the whole articulatory system at the moment when they arise, but they are also determined by the earlier history of the same language. They depend on the physiological makeup of the brain and oral cavity; and if it is true that the physiological makeup of these organs is modified in every new generation, at least in the same social group, owing to heredity, they are modified only in a rigorously determined way. Every sound change can then be considered as the result of deep-seated and hidden forces, for which the term tendency is suitable enough. It is these tendencies that continually modify the structure of language; and the history of every language results, in the last analysis, from the perpetual play of tendencies. Thus there is great interest attached to introducing into the notion of sound law that of "phonological tendency," since sound laws are only the manifestations of sound changes and every sound change is only a particular fact within the history of a phonological tendency at a given moment.

Practically, the notion of phonological tendency has important advantages. By determining more precisely the origin of phonological phenomena, it allows us to understand with ease the more complex ones among them.

It can happen, for example, that a sound change is the result of an accidental competition of two different tendencies operating in the same direction.

The word for "five" in Irish has an unexpected vocalism. The Indo-European word was *penqe*, which, having become *qenqu* in the western dialects, should have given *céic* in Irish. The only attested form, however, is *cóic*. This is usually explained as a result of the influence of the preceding velar (compare Brugmann, *Grundriss*, I, 2nd edition, p. 125). But this cannot be the only influence because, in words like *cenn* (head) from *qennos* or *cerc* (rooster), from *qerqa* (Wh. Stokes, *Urkeltischer Sprachschatz*, pp. 59 and 61), the vowel *e* remained intact. In reality, the tendency that caused the velar to round the *e* of *cóic* was helped by another, namely the tendency toward differentiation.[1] Meillet has recently pointed out in what specific conditions the phenomenon of differentiation takes place (*M.S.L.*, XII, p. 14). Thus, one of the most common vocalic differentiations is the passage of the *ei* diphthong > *oi* (*M.S.L.*, XII, p. 31). This is precisely what took place in Irish. The tendency toward differentiation would probably not have sufficed to change *céic* to *cóic*, but the two tendencies combined resulted in the change in question, and thus the form *cóic* is explained only by the competition of two phonological tendencies operating in the same direction.

On the other hand, it can happen that two phonological tendencies conflict in the same language at a given moment. In such a case, either a kind of compromise will immediately be produced between the two tendencies, each one granting the other some influence; or the conflict will perpetuate itself for several centuries. In this way, with each tendency operating only to the degree permitted by the other, if the first should weaken, the second will gradually increase in importance and will annihilate the effects of its rival according to a rigorous progression. When the two tendencies in question are those that control the whole phonological system, the result of their conflict can be extremely serious. It is well-known that Latin owes to a large extent the inconsistencies of its morphology and the peculiarities of its phonology to the conflict of two strong tendencies, one of which induced it to give a rigorously fixed quantity to each syllable, and the other, to pronounce the first syllable of each word with a particular intensity.

Finally, it sometimes happens that a predominant phonological tendency, favored by special circumstances, can operate with all its vigor and precipitate in certain words a sound change that remains checked in others. There are in every language small words or groups of words, veritable mainsprings of conversation, whose phonological attrition is particularly appreciable. In the first place, this is the result of very frequent use; but above all, it is due to the fact that since they are understood even before they are spoken, the speaker can dispense with accurately pronouncing them and

---

[1]This explanation is confirmed by the word *coire* (cauldron), from *qeryo-* (cf. Strachan, *Bezzenberger's Berträge*, XX, 30).

ordinarily pronounces them in a reduced form. In French one says *wimsyoi,
wimmzel* for "oui, monsieur," "oui, mademoiselle"; in Spanish, *usted* for
"vestra merced"; in German, *gmoeñ*, for "guten Morgen," *ntax* for "guten
Tag," *pfiatdigot* for "Behüt, dich Gott," and *Kschamster Diener* for "Gehor-
samster Diener," and so forth. Such words are entirely irregular from the
point of view of sound laws, but the notion of phonological tendency permits one to interpret them in an exact way. One has often invoked, in order
to explain them, the famous theory of language tempo (Sprechtempo):
wimsyoe, gmoeñ would then be "allegro" forms; *oui, monsieur, guten
Morgen*, "lento" forms. But this conception rests on a serious error. It is
incorrect to believe that a word exists simultaneously in language in two
forms and that one or the other is used according to the rapidity of conversation. There is, in reality, a word *Morgen* that exists in thought and a word
moeñ which is pronounced by the speech organs. The second interests only
the phonetician, and it will appear perfectly regular if one realizes that it is
the result of the application of a phonological tendency carried to the extreme. It shows to what degree the action of some phonological tendency is
carried out if nothing succeeds in impeding it. Such groups, in which the
only syllable clearly perceptible is the stressed syllable, whereas the unstressed syllables become simple resonances in which the liquids and nasals
are simple humming sounds among the impact of the stops, give some indication of what a language would become if the stress accent acted freely.
The "allegro" form is, in reality, a borderline form.

One can see, from the forms that have just been given, to what degree
the notion of phonological tendency is theoretically more exact and practically more fruitful than that of sound law. It alone permits one to determine
with precision the cause of sound changes and to interpret scientifically those
very changes that seem to be most resistant to any scientific methodology. In
order to extract from the notion of phonological tendency all of the insight
that it entails, it is advisable now to attempt a classification of these
tendencies.

There exists, first of all, a series of phonological tendencies whose
special feature is to be general and external, that is, that belong to no special dialect, but are found in all, and seem accordingly to result from human
nature itself.

Such tendencies, moreover, do not exist only in phonology. Semantics
furnishes numerous examples of them. The French child who finds his cake
"more better" is guilty of a barbarism, which many before him were also
guilty of, from the time of the Vedic priests and authors of the *Mahabharata*,
who said *crésthatamah* 'the most beautiful' (R.V., I, 113, 12) or *garīhasta-
rah* 'heavier' (R.V., VII, 5324), to the Latin writers who concocted a
minerrimus (Paul. Best., 122, 17 Th.) or a *minimissimus* (Arnobius), sur-

passing the Greek poets who risked a αμεινότερος Mimnermus, XIII, 9). Compare also Avestan *sraēštot ǝma-* 'the most beautiful' or *draējištōt ǝma-* 'the poorest'. Breton even today obeys such a tendency, since their word *gwelloc'h* (better) contains the comparative suffix that does not exist in Welsh *gwell* (with the same meaning). The mind always tends to eliminate irregular forms in causing them somehow to fit the rule. The same happens in phonology. The Welsh peasant who says *skléža* for *stléža* (to creep) produces an assimilation determined by the constitution of the oral cavity, by the nature of the phonemes *k*, *t*, and *l*, and by their respective point of articulation. But in so doing he does not invent anything, because the tendency to change *tl* to *kl* is manifested in many other dialects, and in dialects as distantly related as Latin and Baltic (compare Latin *pōclum*, Lithuanian *ženklas*, both containing the same suffix *-tlo-*; compare *Annales de Bretagne*, t. XVI, p. 307).

General phonological tendencies, by penetrating into the sound system of a particular language, produce the most varied effects.

Some examples are those that govern the formation of onomatopoetic and expressive words, recently elucidated by Grammont (*Revue des langues romanes*, t. XLIV, 1901).

Other examples are those that cause dissimilation, metathesis, and differentiation.

When the same articulatory movement must be repeated twice in one word, one has the natural tendency to pronounce it only once, and a dissimilation is thus produced. The liquid *l* has replaced *r* in the following words under the influence of a neighboring *r*: Span. *arbol*, Port. *arvol*, Prov. *albre* from Latin *arborem*; French *flairer* from *fragrāre* (already *flagrāre* in Catullus, II, 101 Baehrens), *crible* from *cribrum*, *pèlerin* from *peregrinum*. All of the facts of this kind have been classified by Grammont in his excellent book on dissimilation.

When two parts of the same word differ in intensity under the influence of a stress accent or simply as a result of their respective position, they tend to exchange one of their elements, the stronger always claiming the most characteristic element. In this case metathesis takes place. Thus, in the following words, the less intense part has given up a sonorant element to the more intense: Port. *fresta* (window) from *festra*, *crasto* from *castro*[2]; Old Prov. *cranc*, Welsh *cranc*, Breton *krank* from *cancrum*; Breton *prenest* from *fenestra*; Breton (Douarnenez) *tribi* (to eat) from *degri*, Irish *cloice* (comrade) from *coicle* (from **co-cele*) and *stripach* (prostitute) derived from *stuprum*.

---

[2]Cf. Leste de Vasconcellos, *O Archeologo Portugues*, I, p. 3: "*castro*, or, according to popular pronunciation, *crasto*, means 'an old well-fortified town'."

When the articulation of two consecutive sounds requires the same articulatory position, it often happens that the speaker avoids this necessity and creates a difference between the two phonemes in shifting the articulation of one of them. It is this phenomenon that Meillet has recently studied under the name of differentiation. Thus, the diphthong *ei* will become *oi*, and instead of *rei* one will say *roi*; or a sequence of sibilant and fricative will become sibilant and stop: Anglo-Saxon *hilpestu* from *hilpespu*, Latin *hasta* from **ghaspā*, and so forth (*M.S.L.*, XII, p. 14).

The phenomena of dissimilation, metathesis and differentiation result from general tendencies that are independent of any particular language and are found, in a way, above and beyond languages (compare Grammont, *Dissimilation*, p. 15). These tendencies, although phonological, have a psychological basis originating in the brain. The intended word is not pronounced as it should be, either because one's attention is unevenly distributed or exaggerated: if the attention centers on one of the syllables in a word to the detriment of the others, an error of pronunciation becomes possible that the favored syllable benefits from (dissimilation or metathesis); if the attention is preoccupied inordinately in maintaining two consecutive phonemes that are easily assimilable because of their respective points of articulation, the equilibrium of the vocal organs may be lost, and they will tend to exaggerate their effort in the opposite direction.

Often the fear of some evil leads to a greater evil. It is the fear of assimilation that produces differentiation. In every case, it is a question of natural tendencies of the mind (psychological), whose effect is conditioned only by the speech organs and by articulatory movements.

To these tendencies, one can connect all of those that have as a result the elimination of a group of phonemes difficult to pronounce. When the speaker must pronounce in succession two phonemes whose respective places of articulation are distant from one another in the oral cavity, it happens frequently that one of the phonemes disappears and merges with the other, or a connecting phoneme is inserted between the two, or finally, that one of the phonemes changes its point of articulation, so that it is articulated closer to the other, without merging with it. A group such as *alda*, for example, will become *alla* or *alada*; a group *adla* will become *alla*, *adala* or *agla*. These phenomena of assimilation, epenthesis, and articulatory displacement involve a distinct character that allows them to be distinguished from the former. The tendency that produces them is still psychological, because they arise from a default of coordination between thought and the speech organs; but they depend more heavily on the latter, since they are predominantly physiological. In the former, the attention is badly distributed or exaggerated at some definite point, and the attention itself is responsible for the mistake. In the latter, the attention becomes diverted or has passed too quickly. The speech organs, then, profit from this absence and, in their laziness to execute an articulatory movement, do not completely carry out the impulse from the brain. Here the speech organs are the principal initiators of the committed error. Nevertheless, in both cases, phonological tendencies are involved, both of which are of an absolutely general scope and which are manifested in the most varied languages.

There exists a second series of phonological tendencies that one can call "particular" or "internal" and that are special to each language. They are distinguished from the preceding in that they are in no way psychological in nature. They are linked intimately to the physiological aspect of the speech organs and determine, consequently, in a perfectly natural way, the normal evolution of language, general tendencies intervening only to favor or impede the behavior of the others. From a certain point of view, one can say that there are as many particular tendencies as there are individuals. Each individual, actually, by the very fact that he differs from his contemporaries, carries the germ of new tendencies. But these completely relative differences between individuals of the same social group can be considered negligible if one compares the individuals of another social group. Within each group, a kind of mean is established, and the resemblance to the whole is sufficient, so that one can abstract the differences of detail. Nature itself thus strengthens the social link that maintains the identity of tendencies; and one can say that if the identity of tendencies is the cause of the homogeneity of dialects, inversely it is the difference of tendencies that creates the diversity among dialects.

A single example will suffice to demonstrate this. The semivowels *y* and *w* have undergone two absolutely different treatments within the two great insular Celtic dialects, Gaelic and Britannic; and comparing the results of these respective developments, one notices that their distinct evolution is due in reality to the initial difference of two phonological tendencies. Gaelic tends to weaken the articulation of *y* and *w*; and Britannic, on the contrary, to maintain it. From this results a distinct series that is very characteristic.

Y has its point of articulation in the front region of the palate. If the tongue rises insufficiently in the oral cavity, it allows too much air to pass through; and in place of *y*, one hears only a vague kind of *h*, which itself ends up often by disappearing. *W* is more complex than *y* because it entails two distinct elements, one articulation at the back region of the palate and another with the lips. If the tongue rises toward the palate with too much flabbiness, a simple *h* will result, just as in the above case. But a point of support will always remain at the lips, and the labial articulation will generate a fricative *v*, and even *f*, if the air column is sufficient to cause devoicing. On the other hand, if the speaker tends to maintain the articulation, he risks altering it by reinforcing it, in which case both *y* and *w* will become either fricatives with more limited aperture, or even simple stops.[3]

Thus, in Gaelic, the articulation of *y* weakened in most environments to the point of disappearing, but in Britannic it was regularly preserved. Initially, the Irish words *óc* (young), *aig* (ice), *eirin* (chicken) lost *y*, which remained in the corresponding Welsh words *ieuanc, ia, iar*. Sometimes in Irish, initial *y* combined with the following vowel under circumstances that it has still not been possible to determine with any certainty: *icc* (health), but Welsh *iach* (healthy); *íth* (boiled), but Cornish *iot*. This is also true for words borrowed from Latin very early: on the one hand Irish *enair* from **īēnārius* (for *iānuārius*); on the other hand, *Isu, Issu* (the only forms in the manuscript of Würzburg, except 19c 12) from *Iēsus*. In Britannic, on the contrary, initial *y* has been preserved until today, as the examples cited above show. In the Welsh of the *Mabinogion*, before initial consonantal *y*, the article often has the form *yr*, which is special to the preconsonantal position: *eisted a oruc yr iarll* (the count got up). Sometimes even the articulation of initial *y* has been reinforced in Britannic and replaced by the stop *g*. The name for 'hen' is dialectically *giar* in the south of Wales; in Breton one finds *geo* (yoke) for *ieo* (Welsh: *iau*); *avel quien* (cold wind), Grégoire de Rostrenen, and so forth.[4]

In a final syllable, the semivowel *y* was not preserved in Gaelic, but merged with the following vowel, whose preservation it thus favored. In Britannic, on the contrary, the articulation of *y*, reinforced and slightly shifted, produced the voiced alveolar fricative transcribed by *dd*. Hence the opposition of Irish *niie* (new), *céle* (comparison), *máile* (baldness), *caire* (blame), *firinne* (truth), and so forth; and Welsh *newydd, cilydd, moeledd, cerydd, griwionedd*, and so forth. Here as well, the distinct tendencies mentioned above are clearly manifested.

The treatment of the semivowel *w* is also characteristic. In Gaelic, in initial position, according to the process indicated above, *w* became *f*; but in Britannic, through a strengthening of the articulation, it became the voiced stop *gw*: Irish *fann* (weak), *fedb* (widow), *fern* (ell), *find* (white), *fiu* (worthy), *folt* (hair), and so forth; in Welsh *gwan, gweddw, gwern, gwyn, gwiw, gwallt*, and so forth. This happens even before a consonant: Irish *flaith* (power), *fracc* (woman), and so forth, Welsh *gwlad, gwrach*, and so forth. In Old Welsh, *gw* occurs even medially: *petguar* (four), *taquelquiliat* (silent observation) Loth, *Vocabulaire vieux breton*, p. 202 and 218, *nant y equic* (valley of the doe) *Liber Landauensis*. The two tendencies are equally distinguished in the case of the initial group *sw-*: in Gaelic, *w* disappeared

---

[3]Thus *w* became *g* in Persian and Armenian.

[4]Latin *iạnuạrius* in the same way became *genver* in Breton, where an initial stop might also be due to a neighboring sibilant in the phrase "mis genver" (cf. the name of the month of February: Henry, *Lexique étymologique breton*, p. 170, n. 2).

and a simple sibilant remains; in Britannic, the semivowel transformed the sibilant into a velar fricative, hence Irish *sant* (desire), *serb* (bitter), *siur* (sister), as opposed to Welsh *chwant, chwerw, chwaer*. The loss of *w* in Irish is, furthermore, in this instance relatively recent, since the softening of *s* is manifested practically by *f* (*-hw-*): thus, from *siur* one has *mo fiur* (my sister), from *sennid* (it resounds), the perfect *sefaind* through the stages **mo hwiur, *sehwaind*.

One could easily pursue this study and extend it to other special cases—the opposition of two tendencies would always manifest itself with the same rigour. Thus, all of the transformations that the Indo-European semivowels *y* and *w* have undergone in the Celtic languages result in the first place from the initial difference of two tendencies, and their lawful evolution could be formulated in a few words.

It is in the establishment of laws of this kind that linguists must always expend their effort. The observation of facts counts for little if one cannot provide an explanation for them. To say that, in some languages, at a given time, *p* becomes *b*, is not to formulate a law, but simply to set forth the validity of some fact. It is necessary to connect this fact with all the contemporary facts and to find the cause of it by putting it into the chronological series to which it belongs. To say that a medial *a* in Latin becomes *e* or *i* is not to give an explanation. It is necessary to state that at a certain period in the history of Latin, under the influence of the stressed initial syllable, short medial vowels tended to become close vowels. This formula, in its generality, is alone admissible, because it takes account of the phenomenon and explains at the same time the apparent exceptions that might be found.

The abundant phenomena in the Germanic languages summarized by Grimm's Law and Verner's Law, and that one calls upon readily to prove the rigour of sound laws, can in the same way be reduced to the three following formulas:

1. At a certain epoch in the history of the Germanic languages, the glottal vibration in the production of the voiced phonemes tended to be delayed.
2. At a period subsequent to the former, the puff of breath that accompanied the occlusion of aspirates tended to prevent a complete stoppage.
3. At a period subsequent to the two preceding ones, the vocal cords tended to vibrate during the emission of the intervocalic voiceless fricatives, except when they were prevented from this by the muscular relaxation following the articulation of the accent (compare Gauthiot, *M.S.L.*, XI, p. 192).

These three formulas appear more obscure and complicated than those that one normally gives. In reality, they are clearer and simpler, because they dispense with any commentary. They carry within themselves their explanation. They offer, in addition, the advantage that, in summarizing the evolution of a part of Germanic phonology for a certain period, it suffices to relate to these all of the formulas of contemporary facts in order to have the system in its entirety. In addition, they can serve as norms and allow one to verify the value of phonological formulas that one might discover subsequently.

One is thus led to envisage in the following way the role of the linguist in the establishment of sound laws. When a sound change is given, it is first necessary to analyze its physiological nature and then to determine the tendency that produced it. If the tendency in question is a general one, it suffices to relate the phenomenon to the possibilities furnished by experience, since general tendencies in language are, as a preliminary, once and for all classified and catalogued. If, on the contrary, it is a question of a particular tendency, the task will be somewhat different, but just as thorny. It will require a minute understanding of the articulatory system of the language in which the change occurred and will presuppose, in addition, that the linguist has determined in advance the evolution of this same system, so that he is capable, so to speak, of tracing its whole line of development. It will be necessary in effect to connect the new phenomena to all of the phenomena attested in the same language. But most often the two preceding facts will need to be combined, because there is hardly any change that does not result from the conjunction of two or more tendencies, sometimes in accord, sometimes in conflict.

In every case, the scope of sound laws will be broadened both in place and time. A sound law must be as general as possible and provide elucidations about the nature and cause of the phenomena that it is supposed to formulate. The linguist will become accustomed in this way to disengage the causes from the phenomena themselves and always to connect particular facts to general laws, which must be the object of every science and the preoccupation of every scholar.

8

PRINCIPLES OF
HISTORICAL PHONOLOGY*

Roman Jakobson

It is understandable that at first the attention of phonologists was concentrated principally on the primary concepts of the new discipline: on phonemes, their reciprocal relations and their distribution. But as soon as these basic questions have been settled, one will have to examine carefully phonological phenomena from the point of view of space (that is, phonological geography) and from the point of view of time (that is, historical phonology). Let us try to sketch, in a preliminary essay, the fundamentals of historical phonology.[1]

I

In traditional historical phonology, it was characteristic to treat phonetic changes in an isolated manner, without taking account of the whole system that undergoes these modifications. This kind of methodology went hand in hand with the world view that reigned at that time: the creeping empiricism of the neogrammarians, which viewed any system, and in particular the linguistic system, as a mechanical whole (*Und-Verbindung*) and not at all as a formal unity (*Gestalteinheit*), to use the terms of modern psychology.[2]

*First published in German in *TCLP*, IV (Copenhagen, 1931). A slightly different version appeared in the Appendices to N. S. Trubetzkoy, *Principes de phonologie* (Paris, 1949), tr. by J. Cantineau. Reprinted (in French) in Jakobson, *Selected Writings*, I (Mouton, 1962), 202–220. (Original title: "Principes de phonologie historique," tr. by A. R. K.)

[1]The way in which historical phonology was born will not be examined here.
[2]Compare, for example, K. Koffka, *Psychologie. Die Philosophie in ihren Einzelgebieten* (Berlin, 1925), pp. 531 ff: "The condition under which one can understand an identity, and in general a relation, is for two terms to be not simply juxtaposed, but entering as parties into a form. As they were formerly isolated with respect to each other, they are now tied to each other and can reciprocally influence each other."

Phonology opposes to the isolating method of the neogrammarians an integrating method. Every phonological fact is treated as a part of the whole, which is related to other parts of higher levels. Thus the first principle of historical phonology will be: *every modification must be treated as a function of the system of which it is a part.* A phonological change can be understood only by elucidating its role within the system of the language.

Once a phonological change has taken place, the following questions must be asked: What exactly has been modified within the phonological system? Have certain phonological differences been lost, and if so, which? Have new phonological differences been acquired, and which? Or finally, if the inventory of phonological oppositions remains unchanged, has the structure of individual oppositions been transformed? Or in other words, has the place of a specific opposition been changed, either in its reciprocal relations with other oppositions, or in its differentiating ability? Every phonological unit within a given system must be examined in its reciprocal relations with all other units of the system before and after the given phonological change:

(Ex. 1) In White Russian t' changes to c' and similarly d' to $ʒ'$. If we describe the change of t' to c', we must make clear first of all the relations of the phoneme t' with the other phonemes of the system to which it belonged, therefore with t, d, d', s, s', c, and so forth; and secondly, the relations of the phoneme c' with the other phonemes of the system in question, that is with the unchanged phonemes t, d, s, s', c, and so forth, and with the newly created phoneme $ʒ'$.[3]

II

A phonological change need not necessarily involve a change in function. It can simply augment the number and diversity of combinatory variants of a phoneme:

(Ex. 2) In many dialects of Russian ɛ changes to ẹ (close e) before a palatalized consonant.

(Ex. 3) The phoneme r is palatalized at the end of a word in certain Norwegian dialects.

Or on the contrary, one of the combinatory variants is generalized, two variants combining into a single one:

(Ex. 4) In many southern dialects of Russian the unaccented a phoneme occurs as a before narrow accented vowels and as a mid-vowel before

[3]In order to interpret phonologically a sound change, it is necessary to know in an exact way the phonological system of the given language and also its evolution. This is why I draw most of my examples from the history of the Slavic languages, because their phonological evolution is particularly well-known to me.

open accented vowels. In a part of these dialects, the variant *a* was generalized later. The contemporary phonetic forms *m'ilá*, *p'iták*, and so forth, attest to the fact that the phonetic form *vadá* preceded the phonetic form *vadá*: the mid-vowel that appeared after the palatalized consonant ended up by coalescing with the variant of the phoneme *i* in the same position. A phonological mutation, therefore, took place here: the unaccented α phoneme was replaced in the position indicated above by the unaccented *i* phoneme. Consequently, the subsequent unification of the variants of the phoneme *a* could not be extended to these cases.

(Ex. 5) In certain Slavic dialects, the voiced bilabial stop occurs before a vowel as a labiodental *v*, and in all other positions, as the bilabial *w*. But in the majority of Slavic dialects one of these two variants (most often *v*) is found generalized.

Finally, the fundamental variant of a phoneme can be modified phonetically, the system of phonemes remaining identical and the relations between the given phoneme and all of the other phonemes unchanged: one must therefore consider such a change as extraphonological as well:

(Ex. 6) There are dialects of Russian which have an accented vocalic system with seven vowel phonemes. Certain of these dialects have the following system of accented vowels:

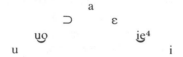

In the other dialects of the same type, instead of the close vowels *u̯o*, *i̯e*, one finds *ǫ*, *ę*, which seems a secondary phenomenon: *ǫ*, *ę* have, in this system, the same place as *u̯o*, *i̯e*. Consequently, the replacement of one of the pairs of vowels by the other does not alter the phonological system.

III

In the case where a phonetic change is manifested in the phonological system, it can be regarded as the vehicle of a *phonological mutation* or a bundle of phonological mutations. We will use the term *mutation* in order to stress that phonological changes occur in leaps:

(Ex. 7) In Southern Russian unaccented *o* coalesces with *a*. Perhaps intermediate degrees existed: *o* was changed to a very open *o* and then to an *a°* and finally into an *a* as it progressively lost its rounding. But from the phonological point of view, there are only two stages: 1. $o(o^{a}, a^{\circ})$ is distin-

[4]*u̯o* comes from *o* with rising pitch, *i̯e* from the Proto-Slavic dipthong *ě* ("jat").

guished from *a*; and these are two different phonemes; 2. the implementation of *o* is no longer distinguished from *a*: the two phonemes have coalesced into one. There is no third alternative.

The formula for the phonological mutation is:

$$A : B > A_1 : B_1$$

One must distinguish two principal categories of mutations: one of the two relations (A : B or $A_1 : B_1$) is phonological or both of them are: A : B as well as $A_1 : B_1$ are different varieties of the same phonological relation. The first category is divided into two types: *the suppression of a phonological distinction can be called "dephonologization" (or "phonological devalorization") and the formation of a phonological distinction, "phonologization" (or "phonological valorization").*[5]

IV

Dephonologization: A and B are opposed phonologically, whereas there is no phonological difference between A_1 and B_1.

In analyzing dephonologization, one must ask the following questions: What is the nature of the phonological opposition A : B? Is it a disjunction or a correlation? If it is a correlation, does its loss represent one particular case of a more general process (that is, the loss of a correlation entirely), or does the correlation still exist? What is the nature of the extraphonological relation $A_1 : B_1$? Is it a relationship of variants and of what kind: combinatory? stylistic? Or does it involve a phonetic identity (two exact realizations of one and the same phoneme)? If the relation $A_1 : B_1$ is a relationship of extraphonological variants, A_1 is phonetically similar to A, and B_1 phonetically similar to B, and only the conditions by which each appears are changed. But if A_1 is phonetically similar to B_1, then either $A_1 \neq A$ and $B_1 \neq B$, that is, A and B have coalesced into a certain sound C which is distinguished phonetically both from A and B; or $A_1 \neq A$, but $B_1 = B$, that is, A > B. The classification of types of dephonologization must take into ac-

---

[5] I find the terms "phonologization" and "dephonologization" more appropriate than the terms "divergence" and "convergence" that E. Polivanov used in his noteworthy studies on dephonologization ("Iz teorii fonetičnogo Instituta v čest' prof. A. E. Šmidta, Taškent, 1923, pp. 106–115, and "Faktory fonetičeskoj èvoljucii jazyka, kak trudovogo processa," *Učenye zapiski Instituta jazyka, literatury, III*, pp. 20–42), because in scientific language the latter are usually bound up with another meaning. Thus in biology, convergence is used to describe the acquisition of similar traits by different organisms, without bothering to find out whether it is a question of related or nonrelated organisms (cf. e.g., L. Berg, *Nomogenez*, Pb., 1922, chap. 18). Similarly in linguistics one designates by the term convergence similar phenomena in the independent development of different languages (cf. Meillet, "Convergence des développements linguistiques", *Linguistique historique et linguistique générale*, Paris, 1921, pp. 61 ff).

count the existing relationship between the phonemes before the mutation, of the relationship existing between the sounds as a result of the mutation, and the relationship that exists between each resulting sound and its proto-type. Let us consider examples of dephonologization:

A disjunction results in a relationship of combinatory variants:

(Ex. 8) In some Russian dialects, two disjunct phonemes, unaccented *e* and unaccented *a*, change into combinatory variants of one and the same phoneme: after palatalized consonants, this phoneme is represented by *e*, after nonpalatalized consonants, by *a*. This dephonologization was accomplished in the following way: *a* became *e* after palatalized consonants (*p'atak p'eták, p'at'i p'et'i*), *e* became *a* after nonpalatalized consonants (*žen'ix žan'ix*).

A disjunction results in a relationship of combinatory stylistic variants:

(Ex. 9) The phonemes ʒ and *z* coalesced in the majority of Japanese dialects into one and the same phoneme: in initial position, after a nasal, this phoneme is realized by ʒ; between vowels in a careless style, by *z*; and in a more careful kind of speech, by ʒ.[6]

A disjunction results in an identity (A > B):

(Ex. 10) Certain Polish dialects coalesced two series of consonants into a single series: (1) š, ž, č, ǯ; (2) *s, z, c,* ʒ: š > s, ž > z, č > c, ǯ > ʒ; therefore š:*s* > *s*:*s*, and so forth.

A disjunction results in identity (A > C, B > C):

(Ex. 11) In several northern and central Russian dialects, palatalized *s'* and *z'*, as well as š and ž, which had still not lost their palatalization, coalesced into intermediate consonants, particularly the palatalized dorsals ŝ, ẑ.

A correlation results in a relation of combinatory variants (the correlation is suspended):

(Ex. 12) The pair *b* : *p* and all of the other oppositions between voiced and voiceless stops lost n Chuvash their phonological character: between a voiced phoneme (that is, all the vowels and the voiced consonants) and a vowel, *b* and the other voiced consonants became generalized; in all other positions *p* and the other voiceless consonants were generalized.

A correlation results in an identity (the correlation is suspended: A > B):

(Ex. 13) In western Slovak, long *á* coalesces with short *a*, and all the other long vowels are similarly shortened: the correlation of vowel quantity was suspended.

(Ex. 14) In Common Slavic, aspirated consonants lose their aspiration and coalesce with the corresponding nonaspirate consonants.

[6]Polivanov, "Faktory. . . . ," p. 35.

A correlative pair results in an identity (the correlation is maintained: A > B):

(Ex. 15) In some White Russian and Ukrainian dialects, the palatalized consonant *r'* became nonpalatalized *r*. The other pairs of consonants that make up the correlation of palatalization remained unchanged.

It is characteristic that in the suppression of correlations, it is ordinarily the marked correlative term that is suspended (see N.S. Trubetzkoy, *Die phonologischen Systeme*, p. 97): in example 13 the length of vowels, in example 14 the aspiration of consonants, in example 15 palatalized *r'*.

V

Phonologization: Between A and B there is no phonological difference, but between A_1 and B_1 such a difference exists. In analyzing phonologization, one must ask the following questions: Do A_1 and B_1 represent a disjunction or a correlation? If it is a correlation, then is the mutation under question only an enlargement of an already existing correlation, or is it part of a more general phenomenon—the formation of a new correlation? As far as the relation between A_1 and B_1 is concerned, Polivanov and van Ginneken consider the existence of extraphonological variants as an indispensable condition for phonologization. In effect, a relationship of identity between A and B is apparently excluded. Consequently, from the phonetic point of view, $A_1 = A$, $B_1 = B$. Most often A and B are combinatory variants.

A combinatory variation results in a disjunction:

(Ex. 16) In Latvian *k*, *g* became *c*, *ʒ* before back vowels. The sounds *k* and *c* (or *g* and *ʒ*) were combinatory variants of one and the same phoneme. After the passage of the diphthong *ai* to *i* in final syllables, *k* became possible in the same position where *c* appeared, that is, *k* and *c* became disjunctive phonemes.[7]

A combinatory variation results in a correlation (a new correlation is formed):

(Ex. 17) In some Latvian dialects, dental consonants became palatalized before front vowels. These were combinatory variants of the dental phonemes, but since under certain conditions unaccented vowels disappeared, there was constituted a phonological opposition between the palatalized consonants that preceded them and the corresponding nonpalatalized consonants. Thus a correlation of consonantal palatalization was formed in these dialects.[8]

[7]See J. Endzelin, *Lettische Grammatik* (Heidelberg, 1923), p. 89.
[8]See Endzelin, p. 90.

A combinatory variation results in a pair of correlative phonemes (the correlation already existed):

(Ex. 18) In Old Polabian, the phoneme x was represented before certain vowels as a voiceless velar spirant x, and before other vowels as a voiceless palatal spirant $\hat{x}$. These were two combinatory variants: they changed into two autonomous phonemes when the weak mid and low vowels coalesced, and there occurred a differentiation of words such as feminine *saux̌a*—neuter *saux̂a*. The pair $x{:}x$ was incorporated into the correlation of palatalization that already existed in Polabian.[9]

There are also examples of phonologization in which the relation A : B is one of stylistic variants. These variants can gradually become lexicalized. In other words, the affective variant of the phoneme can be solidified by words that are most often pronounced with an emotive nuance. These words form a particular stylistic level in the vocabulary of the language in question. Next the affective character gradually disappears in some of these words: the corresponding variant of the phoneme loses its emotional basis and is felt to be a specific phoneme:

(Ex. 19) Meillet points out the characteristic introduction of an expressive phenomenon in Latin—the gemination of consonants. Geminative consonants, which were foreign to the intellectual vocabulary of Indo-European, represent a common phenomenon in words that carry an affective nuance. They were solidified by these words; and when they had lost their sentimental value and were neutralized, the geminative consonants were conserved as specific phonemes.[10]

Similar examples where an emotive variant of a phoneme is transformed into an independent phoneme are relatively rare, but another series of phenomena extensively utilized is related to it. When a language borrows foreign words, it accommodates them to some extent to its own system of phonemes, and partially retains the phonemes of the foreign language. Words containing such phonemes are still felt as foreign words, that is, belonging to a particular stylistic level. But these words occasionally begin to enter the general vocabulary, and the language thus becomes enriched with new phonemes whose foreign character is no longer felt. Foreign phonemes that the language appropriates for itself most easily are those that become incorporated into already existing correlations.

(Ex. 20) Russian, like the other Slavic languages, borrowed a considerable number of foreign words containing the phoneme f. In those cases where there was a tendency to completely Russify the borrowed word having an f, this phoneme was replaced by xv, x or p. F was an indication of the

[9] N. Trubetzkoy, *Polabische Studien* (Wien, 1929), pp. 91 ff., 38 ff., 123.

[10] *Esquisse d'une histoire de la langue latine* (Paris, 1928), pp. 166 ff.

foreign character of a word, and sometimes it was introduced into borrowed words where it had no place, for example, *kufárka* instead of *kuxárka* 'cook', and so forth. But gradually a portion of the words that retained *f* were assimilated to native Russian words (*fonár'*, *lif*, *f̌ilin*, *Fédja*, and so

forth), and the fundamental Russian archiphoneme $\boxed{\text{v, v}'}$ was enriched by

two new phonemes: $\boxed{\begin{array}{c} \text{v, v}' \\ \text{f, f}' \end{array}}$

VI

Alongside dephonologization and phonologization there exists still another group of phonological mutations, that is, rephonologization (or phonological revalorization): the transformation of a phonological distinction into a heterogeneous phonological distinction with a different relation to the phonological system from the first. A and B as well as A_1 and B_1 are opposed phonologically, but the phonological structure of these oppositions is different. In this reorganization of the phonological structure resides the principal difference between rephonologization and the cases cited above the extraphonological sound changes (Ex. 5, 6).

There are three types of rephonologization: (I) The transformation of a pair of correlative phonemes into a disjunctive pair; (II) the transformation of a disjunction into a correlation; and (III) the transformation of a pair belonging to a correlation into a pair belonging to another correlation. One must always consider whether it is a question of (*a*) the outcome of a single pair of correlative phonemes or (*b*) the correlation itself.

I a. A pair of correlative phonemes results in a disjunction (the correlation is maintained):

(Ex. 21) In Old Polish, palatalized *r'* became *ř*. The other pairs of the correlation of palatalization were conserved.

(Ex. 22) In the southern areas of the Slavic languages of the northwest and east, *g* became a spirant *γ* with the same point of articulation, and its relation with *k*, which was part of a correlation, became part of a disjunction.

I b. A pair of correlative phonemes results in a disjunction (the correlation is suspended):

(Ex. 23) In Italic, *bh* became *f*, and similarly each one of the other aspirated stops changed into a simple fricative, but all of these resulting phonemes coalesced to *f*, except *x*, which ended up as *h*.

(Ex. 24) In Old Czech, the correlation of consonantal palatalization was suspended. The palatalized sounds *s'*, *z'* lost their palatalization. The same thing happened in certain conditions to palatalized labials, which in other conditions were changed to the groups "nonpalatalized labial + j." The oppositions between the phonemes *t*, *d*, *n* and the corresponding palatalized phonemes were rephonologicized: these oppositions of correlative phonemes change into disjunctive localized differences between apical and palatal consonants (compare R. Jakobson, *Über die phonologischen Sprachbünde*, *TCLP*, IV).

II a. A disjunction results in a pair of correlative phonemes (the correlation already existed previously):

(Ex. 25) The Indo-European palatal *ĝ* ends up in Old Slavic as *z*, that is, it becomes the corresponding voiced sound of the phoneme *s*.

(Ex. 26) The change of *g* to γ, which is peculiar to a part of the Slavic languages (compare Ex. 22), furnished a voiced opposition for the phoneme *x*, which was disjunct with respect to *g*.

I know of no examples of the creation of a new correlation by a rephonologization of a disjunct pair (II *b*), nor of cases in which a pair of correlative phonemes becomes separated from an existing correlation and is joined to another correlation, that is, modifies its differentiating mark (III *a*).

III b. A correlation changes to another correlation. These kinds of mutations are of many different varieties.

(Ex. 27) According to the description of Meillet, a whole bundle of rephonologizations modified the consonantal correlations of Armenian.[11] The Indo-European opposition between voiced aspirated consonants and nonaspirated consonants ended up as an opposition between voiced and voiceless sounds, voiced aspirates ending up as simple voiced sounds and the old simple voiced sounds as voiceless ones. The Indo-European opposition between simple voiceless sounds and aspirated sounds was replaced by a distinction of tense and lax aspirated voiceless sounds: the tense aspirated voiceless sounds coming from aspirated voiceless ones, the lax aspirated voiceless sounds coming from simple voiceless sounds. It is characteristic that the marked series of the correlation of aspirated consonants has been replaced by a marked series of new correlations, (voiced and tense consonants).

(Ex. 28) Certain Polish dialects replace the opposition of the vowel *a*

[11]See A. Meillet, *Esquisse d'une grammaire comparée de l'arménien classique* (Vienna, 1903), pp. 7 ff., and *Les dialectes indo-européens* (Paris, 1922), chaps. X, XI, XIII.

and *á* by the opposition *ä* and *a*.[12] This modification of a single pair of correlative phonemes attests to a change in the differentiating particularity of an entire correlation: in the first case, there exists the correlation of rounded and unrounded vowels, in the second case a correlation of front and back vowels (compare R. Jakobson, *Über die phonologischen Bünde, TCLP,* IV). All the other oppositions of the correlation are capable of two interpretations: *e-o, ę-ǫ, i-u.* In these pairs one of the terms is opposed phonologically to the other as a nonrounded vowel to a rounded vowel, and at the same time as a front vowel to a back vowel.[13]

One must separate from the rephonologizations that we have just discussed cases of the fusion of two existing correlations, that is, cases where all of the existing pairs of a correlation end up by coinciding with the existing pairs of another correlation, which is a kind of dephonologization:

(Ex. 29) In Proto-Czech the opposition between long vowels with rising pitch and long vowels with falling pitch is transformed into an opposition between long and short vowels. Vowels with falling pitch have been identified with short vowels (dephonologization). It is characteristic that the unmarked series of the pitch correlation coincided with the equally unmarked series of the quantitative correlation.

VII

There are sound changes that modify not the inventory of phonemes of a language but only its inventory of groups of phonemes. As the phonological structure of a language is characterized not only by the repertory of phonemes, but also by the repertory of groups of phonemes, a phonetic change that modifies admissible groups of phonemes in a given language constitutes a phonological fact in the same way as modifications of the inventory of phonemes. There are two different kinds of these phonological mutations:

(Ex. 30) In several Russian dialects, the group "*é* + palatalized consonant" was transformed into the group "*i* + palatalized consonant." In this way, the relation between the above stated group and the old group "*i* + palatalized consonant" is dephonologized; the relation between the old group "*é* + palatalized consonant" and, for example, "*ó* + palatalized consonant" is rephonologized and the relation between the two combinatory variants of

---

[12]See K. Nitsch, "Dyalekty jezyka polskiego," *Encyklopedya Polska, III* Dzial III, Cześć II, p. 264.

[13]This example is equally instructive from another point of view, e.g., the pair *i-u* remained unchanged ($A_1 = A$, $B_1 = B$), and the conditions under which the two phonemes exist are not changed. Nevertheless, the replacement of the pair *á-a* by the pair *ä-a* suffices to bring about, because of the structural laws of the system, a rephonologization of all of the other pairs.

the phoneme *é* (a close vowel before palatalized consonants and an open vowel in other positions) is phonologized. The repertory of phonemes is not modified, but a combination of phonemes has been lost in the language.

If the mutations of groups of phonemes do not by themselves modify the system of phonemes, they become evident, on the other hand, in the functioning of phonemes. The frequency of use of different phonemes is changed and eventually also the degree of their functional load.

(Ex. 31) The mutation considered in Ex. 30 represents an increase in the frequency· of the phoneme *i* and a corresponding decrease in the frequency of the phoneme *é*. The functional load of the phonological difference *é-i* becomes less, because these phonemes could at one time be opposed to each other independently of what followed them. After this mutation, however, they can occur only when no palatalized consonant follows them. But *é* appears in this position very rarely: *é* has become *ó* before nonpalatalized consonants, whereas in final position *é* gave in some cases *o*, in some cases *á*; *é*, when not followed by a palatalized consonant, does not appear in these dialects except as the end result of the diphthong *ie* ("jat′ ").

It would be a dangerous simplification to overestimate the role of the statistical factor in language evolution, but we must not forget either that the dialectical law of the passage from quantity to quality is also important. The low frequency and the weak functional load of a phonological difference naturally favors its loss:

(Ex. 32) In the Serbian dialect reflected in the grammar of Brlić, the opposition of the two kinds of accent on a short syllable is only possible in an initial syllable after pause (compare R. Jakobson, *Die Betonung und ihre Rolle in der Wort- und Syntagmaphonologie, TCLP*, IV). The limited use of this opposition was undoubtedly partly responsible for its suppression. As soon as such a suppression took place, it served to set in motion a whole accentual evolution in many Serbian dialects.

VIII

All of the cases of phonological mutations that we have examined are characterized by a common factor: All the terms of these mutations are equal with respect to their phonological character. If A and B are phonemes, A_1 and B_1 are also; if A and B are groups of phonemes, A_1 and B_1 are groups of phonemes to the same extent. But it is not of the least importance from the point of view of historical phonology that there exist mutations in which the resultant A_1 is not similar, as far as its phonological character is concerned, to its prototype A.

I. *A phoneme splits into a group of phonemes.* Consequently the distinction between two phonemes changes into a distinction between a group of phonemes and a phoneme (rephonologization):

(Ex. 33) The long phoneme *i̯e* (= long "jat'") changes, in a part of the Serbo-Croatian dialects, into a dissyllabic group of two phonemes *i* + *e*. In the place of the disjunction *i̯e*—*i*, and so forth, there appears an opposition between the group of phonemes "*i* + *e*" and the phoneme *i*, and so forth.

(Ex. 34) In Ukrainian the palatalized labials change before *á* into the groups "labial + *j*"; *p'*:*p* (a pair of correlative phonemes) becomes *pj*:*p* (relation between a group of phonemes and a phoneme); *p'*:*j* (disjunction) becomes *pj*:*j*.

The difference between a phoneme and a group of phonemes can change into an identity of two groups of phonemes (dephonologization):

(Ex. 35) In Ukrainian the group *pj* which comes from *p'* (compare Ex. 34) coincided with the old group "*p* + *j*." One should compare, for example, *pjat'* (from *p'at'*) and *pjanyj* (with old *pj*).

A transformation can occur from a combinatory variation into a significant difference between a group of phonemes and a phoneme (phonologization):

(Ex. 36) *p'* before *i* and *p'* before *a* (compare Ex. 34) in Ukrainian were originally combinatory variants of one and the same phoneme *p'* (the degree of palatalization was different according to the following vowel). With the change of *p'* before *a* to *pj*, the relation between the two variants becomes phonological.

II. *A group of phonemes is transformed into a phoneme.* There are two possibilities:

a) The result of the transformation produces a phoneme that already existed in the system:

(Ex. 37) In the Slavic languages of the east and southwest, the group *dl* changed to *l*. This result is identical to one of the phonemes of the original group. On the one hand, there is here a dephonologization, that is, *dl*:*l* becomes *l*:*l*, and on the other hand a rephonologization, that is, *dl*:*n* becomes *l*:*n*, and so forth.

(Ex. 38) In Latin the group *dw* became *b* initially. The result is not identical to any of the phonemes of the original group. The relation of *dw* to *b* is dephonologized, and its relation with the other phonemes is rephonologized.

b) The result of the transformation constitutes a phoneme that was until then unknown in the system:

(Ex. 39) In Serbo-Croatian the groups *tj*, *dj* became *ć*, *đ* (palatal stops). This process characterizes a rephonologization of the relation between *tj*, *dj*, and all the other phonemes existing in the language.

(Ex. 40) In Kirghiz, after the merging of the old long and short vowels, new long vowels appeared as a result of a contraction of groups of phonemes: in *ēr* 'addle' (distinct from *er* 'man') compare Uzbek *egær* 'saddle'; or, for example, Kirghiz *tō* 'mountain' from *taw*, coming from *$t^a\mathrm{\aa}$.[14] These contractions produced in this case a new correlation of phonemes.

(Ex. 41) The transformation in French of the group of phonemes "vowel + *n*" into nasal vowels introduced a correlation of nasality for the vowels into the phonological system.

(Ex. 42) In certain Chinese dialects a transformation of the groups "vowel + stop" into vowels with glottal stop (according to the Chinese terminology: the fifth tone of the vowels) produced a new prosodic correlation.

The numerous mutations of the type *dl* becoming *l* (compare Ex. 37) represent a reduction of a group of phonemes to a single phoneme. The transformation of a phoneme to zero can be limited to specific groups of phonemes, but it can also be more general. This is a particular case of the same type of mutation.

(Ex. 43) Certain Serbo-Croatian dialects lose the laryngeal phoneme *h* (from Old Slavic *x*). It disappears in all positions. This is a particular case of the tendency that is manifested in these dialects to divide all of the fricatives into pairs of voiced and voiceless ones.

The inverse phenomenon evidently does not exist, that is, a phonetic zero cannot under any circumstances change into a phoneme.

IX

When one discovers the existence of a great many mutations that occurred at the same time, one must analyze the entire bundle of these mutations as a whole. The connection existing among these mutations is not due to chance: they are intimately tied together. The laws that preside among their reciprocal relations must be clarified. One of these laws, very fruitful for the elaboration of the principles of historical phonology, was established by Polivanov: phonologizations "never occur without being accompanied by another innovation"; "in an overwhelming number of cases a divergence (= phonologization) is accompanied by some conversion (= dephonologization) and is found to be dictated by it."[15] Here it is a question of the phonologization of combinatory variants, and in a sense the law is indeed without exception. Such a combination of phonologization and dephonologization must be considered, from the point of view of the mutations of groups of phonemes, as a rephonologization. A difference is replaced by another difference, and this complex of mutations is only distinguished from

[14]Polivanov, *Vvedenie v jazykoznanie* (Leningrad, 1928), p. 196.
[15]"Faktory . . .", p. 38.

rephonologization in a single way: in the rephonologization of phonemes, the implementations of the phonological opposition remain the representatives of the same phonemes that before the mutation were opposed phonologically. On the other hand, in the "rephonologization of groups of phonemes" the differentiating aspect of the groups of phonemes remain, but the differentiating function passes from certain phonemes to others, for example, to the neighboring phonemes of the same groups of phonemes:

(Ex. 44) In certain Chinese dialects, the voiced and voiceless consonants merge. The voicing correlation of consonants is replaced by a correlation of pitch of the following vowels: low tone of the vowel is substituted for the voiced feature of the preceding consonant; rising pitch corresponds on the contrary to the voiceless character of the consonant in question.[16] The difference in pitch, at first a combinatory variation, became a correlative property.

(Ex. 45) In the Ukrainian dialects of the northwest, from which is descended the dialect of the parish of Kornicy of the old government of Sedlec,[17] the phoneme á occurred after palatalized consonants as a diphthong *ia* (a combinatory variant). The subsequent palatalization of *r* rendered the opposition *ia-a* phonological after *r*, and consequently *ia* becomes an independent phoneme. The scheme of this mutation would be in phonological transcription:

$$r'á:rá > ri̯a:rá^{18}$$

X

Contrary to the phonologization of combinatory variants, the phonologization of stylistic variants is not tied to a dephonologization (see Exs. 19, 20). In other words, *there does not exist, in the framework of a system belonging to a single style of language, phonologizations that are not compensated for by dephonologizations*. The tendency to multiply phonological differences is foreign to a "specific functional dialect"; such an isolated phonologization is possible only as a result of the reciprocal reaction of two different functional dialects (of two styles of language). The phonologization of a phonemic difference is here compensated for by the loss of its stylistic value. A *permutation of functions* takes place in this case.

[16]See B. Karlgren, *Études sur la phonologie chinoise* (Stockholm, 1915), chaps. 14, 16.

[17]See N. Jančuk, "Kornickij govor b. Konstantinovskogo uezda Secleckoj gub.," *Trudy post. komissii po dialektologii russkogo jazyka*, IX, pp. 13 ff.

[18]See also examples 16–18, which are typical cases of the rephonologization of phonemes. It is thus that in example 16 the relation *i:ai* is dephonologized, in example 17 *ti: t # > t' # : t #*, etc. (# = phonological zero).

As far as I can see, dephonologization is also based on a permutation of functions, particularly in those cases where dephonologization is not tied to any other mutation. Dephonologization can be a generalization of a phenomenon that originally constituted a specific peculiarity of a style of a particular language, for example, careless and hasty discourse. A phenomenon that signals a specific style of language, an oratorical nuance that is particularly emotional, can then be transported into a style of speaking that does not include this nuance, and be thus transformed into a kind of linguistic norm:

(Ex. 46) As the Russian grammarians of the eighteenth century attest, the educated classes of Moscow still conserved in their speech the diphthong *ię* ("jat́ ") as a specific phoneme, but in careless and hurried discourse it was already becoming merged with *é*. Dialectologists observe a similar phenomenon: a removal of the differences between *ię* and *é*, *uǫ* and *ó* into "allegro" kinds of speech in the Russian dialects that conserve in principle the difference between these phonemes.[19] This is the first stage in the loss of a differentiation; the second stage would be the displacement of relations between the careless style and careful style of speech.

(Ex. 47) The confusion of unstressed *e* and unstressed *i*, which I was witness to in the dialect of Moscow, was realized at first only in deliberate and careless discourse. The difference between the two phonemes was still felt as normal, but the following generation generalized the "allegro" style of unaccented vocalism as a linguistic norm.[20]

If one puts aside reciprocal relations of different styles of language, one notices that the tendency not only of multiplication, but also of diminution of phonological differences, is foreign to languages. *Within the framework of an isolated functional dialect, one cannot speak either of an increase or a reduction of a phonological system, but only of a restructuring, that is, of its rephonologization.*

XI

We have already indicated that it is only by means of an "integrating method" that it is possible to describe a phonological change. One must investigate what the phonological differences are, which ones have undergone the modification, what differences remain unchanged, and in what manner the functional load and utilization of all of these phonemes were changed. In addition, one must consider the sound change in terms of relationships to the

---

[19]See N. Durnovo, *Dialektologičeskie razyskanija v oblasti velikorusskix govorov*, I, 2e liv. (1918), pp. 53 ff.

[20]In *Remarques sur l'évolution du russe* (Prague, 1929, pp. 48 ff.) I interpret the fall of the weak semivowels of Slavic as a generalization of the careless style of speech.

sound systems of different functions. But the description of mutations does not yet exhaust historical phonology. We still have the task of interpreting these mutations.

A description furnishes the data concerning two linguistic situations, the period before and after the change, and allows us to investigate the direction and meaning of this change. As soon as this question is posed, we pass from the terrain of diachrony to that of synchrony. A mutation can be the object of a synchronic investigation in the same way as invariable linguistic elements are. It would be a grave fault to consider static and synchrony as synonymous. The static viewpoint is a fiction: it is only a scientific procedure to help us; it is not a particular aspect of the way things are. We can consider the perception of a film not only diachronically, but also synchronically: the synchronic aspect of a film is not identical with an isolated image extracted from a filmstrip. The perception of movement is already present in the synchronic aspect. The same is true for language. The work of Ferd. de Saussure spares us from having to prove that a consideration of language from the point of view of synchrony is a teleological mode of understanding. *When we consider a linguistic mutation within the context of linguistic synchrony, we bring it into the sphere of teleological problems.* It follows necessarily that the problem of finality can be applied to a chain of successive mutations, that is, to diachronic linguistics. It is, in effect, the logical end result of the work of the neogrammarians, begun several decades ago, at least in the sense that they made the first effort to emancipate linguistics from the methodology of the natural sciences, which reigned at their time, and in particular from the quasi-Darwinistic clichés propagated by Schleicher and his disciples.

If a rupture in the equilibrium of a system precedes a given mutation, and if a suppression of disequilibrium results from this mutation, we have no trouble in discovering the function of this mutation: its task is to reestablish the equilibrium. However, when a mutation reestablishes the equilibrium in one point of the system, it can disturb the equilibrium at other points and consequently provoke the necessity for a new mutation. In this way, a whole series of stabilizing mutations is often produced:

(Ex. 48) The loss of the reduced vowels (weak "jers") in the Slavic languages brought about a correlation of palatalization for consonants. All of the Slavic languages have a tendency to disassociate the palatalization correlation of consonants from the pitch correlation of vowels by suppressing one of the two oppositions. The Slavic languages that have suppressed the pitch correlation (that is, the opposition of rising and falling pitch) in favor of a correlation of palatalization have been spared having to give up either the autonomous differences of vocalic quantity or a free accent, since these two correlations are ordinarily incompatible in a language that does not have a pitch correlation. Certain Slavic languages have taken the first alternative; others, the second.[21]

But it would be a mistake to limit the spirit of each phonological mutation to the reestablishment of equilibrium. If the phonological system of a learned language normally tends toward equilibrium, the rupture of the equilibrium, on the contrary, forms a constitutive element of the emotional and poetic language. This is why a static phonological description sins the least amount against reality in those cases where the object of this description is a system of learned language.

The expressive capacity of affective discourse is obtained by means of a great exploitation of extraphonological phonetic differences existing in the language in question, but for the highest degree of affectivity, discourse has need of more efficacious procedures and does not stop even before the deformation of the phonological structure: for example, different phonemes merge, phonemes whose articulation is modified with a view toward overcoming the automatism of indifferent discourse; or emphasis goes as far as a violation of existing prosodic correlations; or finally, certain phonemes are "swallowed up" because of the acceleration of tempo. This is all given favor by the fact that in affective language, information gives way to emotivity, and hence the phonological value of certain phonological differences becomes attenuated. Similarly, the poetic function forces the language to overcome the automatism and imperceptibility of the word—and this also goes as far as displacements in the phonological structure.

(Ex. 49) B. Miletić notes that in Štokavian, under the influence of emphasis, "falling" pitch of short vowels changes into a "rising" pitch.[22]

(Ex. 50) Sometimes the loss of phonological differences serves to satisfy aesthetic needs: for example, the Russian dialect of Kolyma is characterized by a tendency to replace the phonemes *r*, *l* and in particular palatalized *r'*, *l'* by the phoneme *j*. This pronunciation is designated there by the term *sladkoglasie* 'honeyed speech'; and according to one investigator, the majority of the population can easily articulate, without any difficulty, palatalized *r'*, *l'*, and so forth but think that such a pronunciation is ugly.[23]

The different functions of language are intimately bound up with each other, and the permutation of functions is permanent. The spirit of equilibrium and the simultaneous tendency toward its rupture constitute the indispensible properties of that whole that is language.

[21]I described this cycle of phenomena more thoroughly in *Remarques sur l'évolution phonologique du russe*, *TCPL*, II (Prague, 1929).

[22]*O srbo-chrvatských intonacich v nářeči štokavském* (Prague, 1926), pp. 13–14, 20.

[23]V. Bogorz, "Oblastonoj slovar' kolymskogo russkogo narečija," *Sb. otd. rus. jaz. slov.* IAN, XVIII, no. 4, p. 7.

The joining together of the static and the dynamic is one of the most fundamental dialectic paradoxes that determine the spirit of language. One cannot conceive of the dialectic of linguistic development without referring to this antinomy. Attempts to identify *synchrony*, *static*, and the domain of application of *teleology* on the one hand and, on the other, *diachrony*, *dynamic*, and the sphere of mechanical causality illegitimately narrow down the frame of synchrony, make of historical linguistics a conglomerate of disparate facts, and create the superficial and harmful illusion of an abyss between the problems of synchrony and diachrony.

9

FUNCTION, STRUCTURE, AND SOUND CHANGE*

André Martinet

I. Introduction

Today, just as twenty years ago, many linguists would be tempted to agree unreservedly with Leonard Bloomfield that "the causes of sound-change are unknown."[1] Not a few would infer from this statement that any research aimed at determining such causes is inevitably doomed to failure. Scholars who regard linguistics, primarily and even exclusively, as a descriptive discipline both on the synchronic plane and in evolutionary matters will most naturally be tempted to favor these views since they afford a justification for their reluctance to go beyond mere statements of directly observable facts, such as "English *p* and *b* are distinct phonemes" or "French *u* ([ü]) corresponds to Latin *ū*." The modern followers of the neogrammarians who are ready to reckon with mutual influence IN THE SPOKEN CHAIN, but who ignore and would deny the fact that the nature of a given phoneme depends on that of its neighbors IN THE PATTERN will find themselves in agreement with those phonemicists who conceive of "structure" as resulting from combinatory latitudes of distinctive units in the chain rather than as based upon the latter's partial phonic identities and differences. Whoever sees in a phonemic pattern nothing but a convenient way of summarizing the behavior of segments in the utterance is hardly prepared to conceive of it as a dynamic reality. The componential analysis of phonemes, which is the first step toward the setting up of a pattern based upon phonic identities and differences, is still often looked upon as an amusing but impractical refinement of more traditional methods, and its wide implications are rarely perceived. Yet it is felt by an increasing number of structurally minded linguists[2] that it paves the way toward a better understanding of phonetic evolution.

---

*From *Word* 8.1–32 (1952). Reprinted by permission of the author and The International Linguistic Association.

[1] *Language*, New York 1933, 385.
[2] A bibliography will be found in A. G. Haudricourt & A. G. Juilland, *Essai pour une histoire structurale du phonétisme français*, Paris 1949, 119–120; see, *ibid.*, ix–xiv and, 1–13. Later contributions will be cited in the course of this paper.

What would seem to prevent a general acceptance of diachronic phonemics as a legitimate discipline is not only the wide-spread feeling that linguistics would jeopardize its hard-won scientific character by venturing beyond the limits of pure description, but also an irrational conviction that there should be one and only one answer to the question: Why do sounds change? and that a principle of explanation which can be shown not to account *in toto* for any change chosen at random is *ipso facto* to be rejected as invalid. This conviction is so ingrained that, in the case of conditioned sound changes, some linguists would probably reject the view that well-known conditioning factors afford a partial answer to the question. In Old English, intervocalic *s* as in *céosan* is found to have been shifted to [z] whereas *s* has been preserved as [s] elsewhere. We know for sure that intervocalic position was instrumental in the change. But, of course, intervocalic position was not enough, since Old Icelandic has preserved a voiceless *s* in *kjósa*, and hundreds of easily accessible languages show no sign of voicing their intervocalic sibilants. The unknown reason, or reasons, which let Old English *s* become a prey to its vocalic environment are, in the opinion of some, the only elements of the case that deserve the name of "cause." And yet, can we not imagine that the voicing in question may have resulted from a concurrence of phonetic circumstances, one of which (intervocalic position) we know, and the others (nature of the accent or various other prosodic features) we are not well enough informed to recognize? All of these would be of a similar nature, and if we should have to distinguish among them, the distinctions would not be made because they are of intrinsically different nature, but exclusively on the basis of what we happen to know about the one or the others. It is methodologically unsound to assume anything about the importance or lack of importance of unidentified factors. Above all we have no right to postulate that these should all be of one and the same type, and that, short of the identification of some sort of ever present *deus ex machina*, any theory of the causes of sound change has to be resolutely brushed aside. Bloomfield's sweeping statement that the causes of sound change are unknown should be replaced by the one that some of the causes are still either unknown or difficult to identify or to verify. This could by no means be interpreted as an invitation to restrict linguistic activities to descriptive practices, but, on the contrary might incite the reader to investigate the possibilities of reducing the domain of the unknown.

So far external factors of sound change, among which interdialectal and interlinguistic influences stand in the foreground, have been the object of much theorizing but of little factual observation. Among internal factors only those that can be found in the spoken chain and account for allophonic differences, have been submitted by phoneticians to a more or less exhaustive examination. It remains to investigate to what extent the coexistence in the pattern of a number of phonemic units can account for their synchronic nature and diachronic comportment. We know that an [s], when placed IN A GIVEN CONTEXT in the utterance, may develop in a certain way. We have to determine what we can expect from /s/ when placed in the frame of A GIVEN PATTERN.

The problem of the causes of sound change would remain one of the central problems of linguistic science even if we should refuse to consider linguistics as an historical discipline, because we shall not fully know what language is and how it works before we have determined why languages change. No one would maintain that morphology, syntax, and lexicon change irrespective of the communicative needs of the speakers. It remains to be seen whether this is true or not of phonology. If it can be shown that phonetic evolution is not as "blind" as some of our predecessors meant it to be, we shall be able to discover not all but some of the so-far unknown factors of phonological evolution.

We shall, in what follows, center our attention on "regular" sound changes, the type whereby all the performances of a given phoneme, every-where or in a well defined context, are eventually affected. There are spo-radic sound changes of many kinds, some of which may be due to causes similar to those which may be adduced or supposed for "regular" changes. But it is felt that the consideration of sporadic changes would needlessly com-plicate our research. It should further be stressed once more that we are ultimately concerned here with the behavior of speakers keeping distinct or merging various phonemes of A PATTERN and not at all with what has normally been so far the practically exclusive preoccupation of historical phoneticians, namely the mutual influencing of successive phonemes in THE SPOKEN CHAIN. In phonemic terms, our predecessors were intent upon ac-counting for the appearance of combinatory variants or allophones. By now, it should be a well established fact that one and the same phoneme when appearing in different contexts may be submitted to divergent treatments, and this should need no further emphasizing. In the frame of the present exposition, it is completely immaterial whether a change affects a phoneme in all contexts or only in phonemically well defined ones, whether what is eventually merged or kept distinct is two phonemes or two combinatory variants of different phonemes. We know that combinatory factors of sound change play a considerable role, but if we want to be able to identify functional and structural factors, we have to concentrate upon them and keep the former out of our field of vision as far as this is practicable. In order to simplify the exposition, it is therefore advisable not to stress at every turn the existence of allophonic deviations, and to establish the following convention:

unless otherwise stated, what will be said of phonemes applies equally to those allophones whose phonic evolution happens to be deviating. In theoretical discussions, it will look as if we were always operating with phonemes whose unity is never endangered. But illustrations will show that allophones are also involved. Allophones will usually be presented in the form of a cluster of phonemes: the front allophones of a /k/ will appear as /ki/, /ke/, or both /ki/ and /ke/. In other words we no longer deal with a single phoneme /k/ but the phoneme clusters /ki/, /ke/. In view of the fact that phoneme clusters often coalesce into single phonemes in the course of phonological evolution and would seem frequently to exert an influence upon the pattern behavior of single phonemes, the use of clusters instead of allophones will actually result in a simplification. We can accordingly reword what we said above about our statements applying to allophones as well as to phonemes: unless otherwise stated, what we say about phonemes applies to larger phonemic units as well.

II. Function

It is an obvious fact that the pronunciation of a given phoneme in one and the same word by a given speaker varies from one utterance to another. The variation is normally imperceptible, but strictly speaking, no two pronunciations can be exactly alike. Under certain conditions the variation may be more considerable. In any case, we have to reckon with a range of possible dispersion even in the speech of one person and still more so probably if we consider all the speakers of a given community. The existence of such a range of dispersion is of course obvious if we consider a phoneme with important allophonic variations, i.e. a phonemic unit whose actual performances are largely dependent on the context as is the case for instance with English /k/ whose range of dispersion covers a large part of the palato-velar area, or with Russian /a/ which varies, depending on context, from [æ] to [a]. But what is stressed here is not the dispersion resulting from combinatory variation, but that which may affect a phoneme in a well characterized context.

Some scholars have been tempted to interpret de Saussure's statement that a linguistic "value" is everything that the other "values" of the same system are not[3] in the sense that this range of dispersion of every phoneme is limited only by those of other phonemes. This is certainly not universally true. It is probably meaningless to try to imagine whether [φeil] would, by English speakers, be interpreted as *pale* or as *fail*, because [φ] is a normal rendering of neither /p/ not /f/, and if, under most unusual circumstances, any one said [φeil], the interpretation as *pale*, *pail*, or *fail* would depend on the context. In the frame of a homogeneous speech community it is probable that the

---

[3]*Cours de linguistique générale*, Paris 1931, 162.

normal range of dispersion of every phoneme in a given context will not be contiguous to those of its neighbors, but that there will be a margin of security in the form of a sort of no man's land. We speak here of "normal" range because it is a well-known fact that, under unusual circumstances such as severe intoxication, neighboring phonemes of the pattern may be completely merged. It is then clear that the minor evil consisting in an impingement upon the margin of security must also occur in "abnormal" circumstances. Abnormal circumstances of the kind considered here are not likely to affect the articulation of a single phoneme only, but that of most, if not all, of the phonemes of the pattern, and this in itself will be a perceptible mark of their abnormality. Hearers will unconsciously make allowances for it, discount deviations, or rely more heavily on context and situation in their interpretation of what they hear. Among "abnormal" circumstances we might also include the cases where the language is spoken by a foreigner who has not achieved a complete mastery of the phonetics of the language. Here again allowances will be made.

For a full understanding of what will follow, one should remember that, on all occasions, it is far easier for man not to be than to be accurate; as Jespersen puts it[4] "it requires less effort to chip wood than to operate for cataract"; the main difficulty for children in learning to speak, or to write or draw, for that matter, is not to produce sounds, bars, or curves, but to hit upon the right sound, bar, or curve asked for at a given instant by the necessities of communication. This applies to adults' phonemes as well. For each one of them, in a given context at least, there must be an optimum which we might call the center of gravity of every range of dispersion, but actual performances will normally fall somewhat off the mark. In the normal practice of speech, some of them are even likely to fall very far off it. If too dangerously near the center of gravity of some other phoneme, they may be corrected, and, in any case, will not be imitated. If unusually aberrant, slightly beyond the normal range of dispersion, but not in a direction where misunderstanding might arise, they would in no way threaten to impair mutual understanding. If not, in themselves, imposing any strain on the organs, they might well end up as establishing a legitimate extension of the acceptable range.

We shall reckon with a sound shift as soon as the normal range of a phoneme (in a given context—from now on this shall be understood) is being ever so little displaced in one direction or another, whereby the margin of security which separates it from its neighbors increases or decreases. We do not choose to discuss at once the possible causes of such a shift, but rather try to determine how it may affect other phonemic units of the pattern. Let us

[4]*Language, Its Nature, Development, and Origin*, London 1922, 263.

call A the phoneme whose normal range is being displaced, B the one separated from A by an increasing margin, C the one separated from A by a decreasing margin. The dynamic situation will thus look as follows:

$$B \quad A\rightarrow \quad C$$

If, as the saying goes, "phonetic laws work blindly" i.e. irrespective of communicative needs, the outcome of this situation will necessarily be a merger of A and C unless, for some mysterious reason, the trend is stopped or reversed. If it is found that B and C begin to shift in the same direction as A, so that the situation becomes

$$B\rightarrow \quad A\rightarrow \quad C\rightarrow$$

it will be assumed that the same unknown reason is affecting the three units equally. As a rule, in such a case, it will be difficult to prove that A actually began to shift before B and C did, and, if this could be shown, one could probably argue that, for some unknown reason, A was more susceptible to being shifted and therefore yielded to the push before the two others. If one is not inclined to be economical, one could of course also assume three different causes for the different shifts.

The basic assumption of functionalists in such matters is that sound shifts do not proceed irrespective of communicative needs, and that one of the factors which may determine their direction and even their appearance is the basic necessity of securing mutual understanding through the preservation of useful phonemic oppositions. Lest we should give the impression that we are dealing with some sort of linguistic providence, we shall have to present a fairly detailed analysis of how we may conceive the working of the various observable phenomena.

Let us revert to the afore-mentioned situation where A is drifting toward C and away from B, and concentrate our attention first on the possible ensuing comportments of B: (1) the normal range of B may remain what it was before A began to shift, or it may happen to start drifting in any direction but toward A; in this case, we shall assume that the shift of A exerts no influence, or at least no direct influence, on the comportment of B; (2) the normal range of B will begin to shift in the direction of A: thus

$$B\rightarrow \quad A\rightarrow$$

If it can be shown that the shift of A actually preceeded that of B, and/or that the shifts of A and B can not be ascribed too well to the same general phonetic trend such as a general tendency toward aperture, closure, or other, so that the situation would more adequately be represented as

$$B\rightarrow \quad A\rightarrow$$

functionalists will assume that B has. as it were, "taken advantage" of the space left vacant by the drifting away of A. In fact, the chances are that B is environed by other phonemes and separated from them by margins of security which we may assume, for simplicity's sake, to have been just as wide as the one which originally separated B from A. At that time, any random deviation of B out of its normal range and in the direction of any one of its neighbors was not likely to be imitated since it would have tended to conflict with communicative needs. When however A started to shift away from B, chance deviations out of the normal range of B and in the direction of the receding A would no longer conflict with communicative needs; from that time on, B was contained on all sides except in the direction of A, and the center of gravity of its range naturally began to shift away from the sections of the field where it could not expand. What will often happen in such cases is that one of B's neighbors will in turn take advantage of the space left vacant by B so that a sort of chain reaction will be set in motion which may eventually affect an important section of the pattern.

At this stage of the exposition, it is not easy to present illustrations taken from actual languages, because every shift considered will involve the play of certain internal factors which have not so far been presented and discussed. Yet, in a few cases, such factors may be temporarily discounted without distorting the facts, although it will become clear at a later stage that the proof of the coherence of the shifts presented can only be administered if all factors are taken into consideration.

A comparison of the phonemic pattern of the Hauteville dialect[5] with those of vernaculars spoken in the same region shows that, at about the same time, the following shifts must have taken place: (1) /ẽ/, from Lat. ĪN, > /ẽ/ (lowering); (2) /ẽ/, chiefly from Lat. EN, = /ɛ/ (denasalization); (3) /ɛ/, from Lat. Ĭ, E, > /a/ (lowering and retraction); (4) /a/, chiefly from Lat. A in open syllables, > /ɔ/ (raising and rounding). Since there was previously no /ɔ/ in the pattern, none of these four shifts has resulted in any phonemic merger. Schematically the process can be represented as follows

$$\tilde{e} \rightarrow \quad \tilde{\epsilon} \rightarrow \quad \epsilon \rightarrow \quad a \rightarrow$$

There has been no wholesale lowering in the front series since /i/ and /e/ are intact, no wholesale raising in the back series since /u/ and /o/ have not moved, no wholesale denasalization since /ã/ and /ɔ̃/ remain by the side of the new /ẽ/. Therefore the whole shift can not be accounted for as resulting from one and the same general phonetic trend. Taken one by one, each of the first

[5]As presented in A. Martinet, Description phonologique du parler franco-provençal d'Hauteville (Savoie), *Revue de linguistique romane* 15.1–86; see, in particular, 2–3.

three shifts should have resulted in a merger. As a matter of fact, every one of the four phonemes involved has kept clear of the others. Since the margin of security between the old /a/ and /o/ was twice as wide as every one of the others in the vocalic pattern, it seems most likely that /a/ was the first to start moving. Today all margins of security have approximately the same width and no shift is in progress. It seems difficult to escape the conclusion that some necessity of preserving existing phonemic distinctions has been at work throughout the process.

Another illustration is afforded by the Portuguese dialect of São Miguel in the Azores.[6] A comparison with standard Portuguese shows that /u/ has been shifted to /ü/, /o/ has passed to /u/, /ɔ/ has been raised toward /o/ without always reaching it, /a/ has assumed a back value "tending toward open *ó*." This description of the shift is not exhaustive; some features of it, which would only assume full significance at a later stage of this study, have been left out. The powerful influence of standard Portuguese has obviously exerted some disturbing influence. It seems clear, however, that /u/ took the lead in its shift toward /ü/, /o/ soon followed, /ɔ/ began its shift with a certain delay, and /a/ was last to move. Schematically the process could be represented as follows:

The shift of /u/ to /ü/ raises a problem which we are not yet ready to tackle.[7] Let it suffice to say that it may have resulted from a pressure exerted upon /u/ by its partners of the back series. It should only be stressed here that if three of the particular shifts involved can be described as raisings, the /u/ > /ü/-shift is of a totally different phonetic nature, and yet a causal connection between the fronting and the raisings can hardly be denied.

Let us now direct our attention to the possible comportment of C, the phoneme toward which the range of dispersion of A is moving for reasons so far unknown. The range of C may well not move away from invading A, and a phonemic confusion will take place. The undeniable frequency of such mergers is sometimes held as a powerful argument against the assumption that the preservation of phonemic distinctions is a factor of phonological evolution. Since phonemes, by definition, serve to distinguish between words and forms, any phonemic merger will inescapably involve confusions detrimental to the normal functioning of the language, and yet mergers do take place.

In a number of cases it might be argued that C is, as it were, at the end

[6]Cf. F. M. Rogers, Insular Portuguese Pronunciation: Porto Santo and Eastern Azores, *Hispanic Review* 16.1–32, in particular 13.

[7]The problem is dealt with by Haudricourt-Juilland, *op. cit.*, 100–113.

of its tether, that its performance represents an extreme phonetic possibility as when it is an /i/ badly pressed by an invading /e/ with surrounding diphthongs which block all way of escape. An objection would be: how is it that these circumstances have not, from the start, prevented the range of /e/ from moving into the margin of security separating it from /i/? But of course the unknown reasons pushing /e/ upward may simply be more powerful than the functional factors working for conservation. This does not mean that the latter do not exist. It must be stressed over and over again that no one has ever pretended that internal phonemic factors are the only ones or even necessarily the most potent. What we have to show is not that these factors explain all features of phonological evolution, but that there are cases where no understanding can be reached unless they are duly taken into account.

It will be seen that both the articulatory and acoustic nature of the distinctive features involved may be a factor of some importance in the fate of an opposition. But, at this stage, the problem which shall detain us is whether the relative importance of the opposition in the satisfaction of communicative needs plays a role or not in its own elimination or preservation. The question to be answered is whether, everything else being equal, a phonemic opposition which serves to keep distinct hundreds of most frequent and useful words will not offer a more successful resistance to elimination than one which only serves a useful purpose in very few instances. What makes this answer particularly difficult is that we know, thus far, so little that is definite about other factors involved. The first step we have to take in order to bring some clarity into the affair is to investigate whether and how the distinctive importance of a phonemic opposition can be evaluated.

The functional importance of a phonemic opposition is often called its functional yield or burden (Fr. *rendement fonctionnel,* German *funktionelle Belastung*). There is no complete agreement as to what this term is meant to cover. In its simplest somewhat unsophisticated acceptation, it refers to the number of lexical pairs which would be complete hononyms if it were not that one word of the pair presents one member A of the opposition where the other shows the other member B: the pair *pack–back* is part of the functional yield of the /p/–/b/ opposition in English, and so are *repel–rebel, cap–cab* and hosts of others. The number of such /p/–/b/ pairs being considerable, it is said that the functional yield of the /p/–/b/ opposition is high. If we try to do the same with, say the English /θ/–/ð/ opposition, we shall find only a few pairs like *thigh–thy, mouth* n.–*mouth* v.; it will be said that the functional yield of this opposition is low. Provided we consider a given dictionary as fully representative of the lexicon of the language under consideration, it is possible to make exhaustive lists for every one of the phonemic oppositions, although in practice only those would be considered that involve phonemes which componential analysis has shown to be minimally distinct: In English

/s/–/š/ and /s/–/z/ would be included in the research, but not /s/–/ž/ or /š/–/z/. Thereby vague labelings like "high," "medium," "low" can be advantageously replaced by exact numerical ratings.

It is of course easy to point out the drawbacks of such a method as a tool for determining the actual number of cases where a given phonemically distinctive feature is by itself the sole element which prevents misunderstanding, as the degree of vocalic aperture would be if *give me a pen!* were uttered in a situation which did not give any clues as to whether a *pen* or a *pin* is wanted. In order to be fully valid, any rating of the functional yield of an opposition should be based upon a frequency rating of such linguistic situations as the one just mentioned. Since such a count is practically impossible, one might be content with a listing of those lexical pairs that could be conceived of as likely ever to give rise to such indeterminacy as illustrated above by *pen* and *pin*. But, in order to avoid subjective decisions, one would probably have to be satisfied with the exclusion of only such pairs as involve words belonging to different parts of speech and therefore not likely ever to appear in the same grammatical context. In that case, among the pairs cited above *pack–back*, *repel–rebel*, *cap–cab* would pass muster, but *thigh–thy* and *mouth* n.–*mouth* v. would be rejected. Yet, even then, some complications might arise: the minimally distinct Fr. pair *poignée–poignet* will never give rise to conflict as long as the two words are used in the singular since, in that case, the difference of gender will show up one way or another and would tell which is which even if the /e/–/ε/ opposition happened to be blurred; but in the plural (*les poignées–les poignets*) the vocalic opposition might have to bear all the distinctive burden. Furthermore this type of evaluation would completely disregard the essential factor of frequency and would give equal rating to *prig–brig* (Thorndike frequency levels 19 and 16 respectively) and *pack–back* (2 and 1). In view of all the difficulties involved, it is perhaps just as indicative in most cases and certainly incomparably simpler to determine the lexical frequency of every phoneme involved, assuming that the more frequent a phoneme is, the more likely it is that it will have to assume clearly distinctive functions. Lexical frequency is probably preferable to actual frequency in texts or utterance because it is not exceptional that a phoneme such as English /ð/, which enters into the minimally differentiated pair /θ/–/ð/ with a very low functional yield, appears very frequently in texts or utterances. There might however be cases where a lexically very frequent phoneme is less frequent in speech than some other one with lower lexical frequency, if for instance the former appears mostly in learned, the latter in everyday lexical items. In such a case, the conclusions derived from a lexical count would have to be tempered by reference to the actual situation in speech. Generally, the method would have to be adapted to the language under consideration.

From what precedes, it is clear that the functional yield of an opposition can only be evaluated with any degree of accuracy if we deal with linguistic stages for which fairly exhaustive word lists are available. This circumstance makes it practically impossible to check the validity of the functional assumption in the case of prehistoric sound shifts. It would seem, for instance, that the merger of *o, and *a in Slavic, Baltic, and Germanic is in some way connected with a relative rarity of *a (from *a or *$ə$) in these languages where *$ə$ is dropped in second medial syllables, and vocalic sonants universally develop high vowels. But since we do not know the lexicon of Slavic, Baltic, and Germanic at the time when they merged *o and *a, we can hardly go beyond vague assumptions. Even in the case of early Romance, our fairly exhaustive knowledge of Classical Latin vocabulary gives us an imperfect picture of the lexical resources of the vulgar language from which we would have to start. In the case of certain mergers taking place in modern cultural languages for which full data are available, the functional yield has been found to be extremely low: the Parisian French merger of /ɛ̃/ and /œ̃/ which is in full swing, practically never results in any homonymic conflict, and the lexical frequency of /œ̃/ is of the lowest.[8] The same could be said of the merger of /ñ/ and /nj/ which seems to be gaining ground,[9] and of the earlier confusion of /lʸ/ and /y/. In the same language, the old distinction between long and short /i/, /ü/, /u/, /e/ whose function was practically restricted to distinguishing between masculine and feminine words is now practically eliminated among Parisians.[10] Since gender in French is usually expressed in accompanying articles or pronouns, the actual yield of these oppositions was very low, and this circumstance may well have been instrumental in the merger. It is interesting to notice that, to this day, French speakers have not found a universally accepted solution for the irritating problem resulting from the homonymy of *l'amie, l'ami, mon amie, mon ami*.[11] If low functional yield is accepted as a factor of the merger, we shall have to conclude that even one very useful pair is not enough for preserving a phonemic opposition.

[8]Lip-rounding, which distinguishes /œ̃/ from /ɛ̃/, is an unstable feature in the case of such very open articulations. The same is true of course for /ɔ̃/ which we might expect to merge with /ã/ in forms of speech where /œ̃/ merges with /ɛ̃/ (actually [æ̃]). But the functional yield of the /ɔ̃/—/ã/ opposition is very high in French, and the merger is only attested in such northern Gallo-Romance dialects (and the corresponding local forms of Standard French) as have kept *en* phonemically distinct from *an* so that the frequency of /ã/ (= *an*) is much lower than in the standard language.

[9]Cf. A. Martinet, *La prononciation du français contemporain*, Paris, 1945, 170–173.

[10]*Ibid.*, 94–109.

[11]The language affords no easy solution by means of composition, such as exists in English: *boy friend, girl friend;* most French speakers will pronounce the *-e* of *amie*, which results in a phonemically exceptional combination, phonetically [a' mi' ə] or [a' mi' œ].

The actual importance of functional yield in the preservation of phonemic oppositions can not be assessed on the basis of the limited information
available to date. It will have to be tentatively considered as one of the
internal factors of phonological evolution, and the possible extent of its
influence will have to be evaluated wherever feasible. The problem will have
to be reconsidered when we possess a large body of relevant data. It should
however be pointed out immediately that (1) two neighboring phonemes will
not necessarily tend to merge simply because the functional yield of their
opposition is practically nil: /š/ and /ž/ in English are not found to approach
each other in spite of the exceptionally low yield of their opposition; (2)
semantic extension, word composition, and morphological reshuffling frequently afford easy solutions to the problems which may arise when a
functionally important opposition is being threatened by the drifting together
of two phonemes: as soon as the margin of security is invaded and danger of
misunderstanding arises, speakers will be induced to give preference to such
alternative words, phrases, or forms as will remove all ambiguity.

We now revert again to our theoretical example of a phoneme A
drifting in the direction of a phoneme C, but this time we shall assume that C,
instead of awaiting the impending merger, recedes before the invader preserving all the time a margin of security between A and itself. This type of
assumption conflicts of course with the traditional views concerning the
"blindness" of "phonetic laws." Yet it is not too difficult to understand how
a phoneme can yield under the pressure of one of its neighbors. As soon as
the margin of security separating A from C is invaded by the former, any
performance of C that falls too close to that margin will incur the danger of
being misinterpreted and will therefore be disfavored. Thereby the center of
gravity of the range of C will be displaced away from A. If may be that, in so
doing, C will exert upon one of its other neighbors the kind of pressure that A
is exerting upon it, and that neighbor will in its turn be shifted further, away
from invading C. We shall thus observe a chain of reactions similar to the
ones we have noticed in the case considered above of A and B.

In practice, it may often be difficult to tell whether we have to do with a
B→ A→ chain, or drag-chain, or an A→ C→ chain, or push-chain. Even in
the B→ A→ type, there is some amount of pressure from such neighbors of B
as are not included in the diagram. In order to simplify the exposition, we
have purposely refused to investigate factors acting upon A and determining
the drift of its range. But among them may, in the case of B→ A→, figure a
pressure exerted by B and its neighbors. We have, in the case of Hauteville,
suggested the existence of what amounts to a tendency toward equidistance
between the phonemes of the same pattern or, in other terms, toward
equalization of the mutual pressures. Hauteville's /a/ passing to /ɔ/ would
result from this equalizing tendency. São Miguel's /u/ > /ü/ would result

from a pressure exerted upon /u/ by the other three back phonemes of a series where margins of security are, by nature, narrower than in the corresponding front series. We thus probably have to reckon with pressure everywhere, so that the suggested distinction between drag and push would often be blurred. We may say that, in some cases, the move of the leading phoneme is one which our phonetic and phonemic experience would lead us to expect, and in others, that it is the move of the last phoneme which would seem to make more sense. What we have called A is the first phoneme in the former case and the last phoneme in the latter. Now A was the phoneme whose move we took for granted all the time, so that our final judgment in such matters will depend on our interpretation of such factors as we have not so far investigated, or as will ultimately remain out of the frame of this study.

The difficulty of deciding which unit is leading the shift may be illustrated by the following example: (1) Italian *qui* is derived from ECCV [M] HĪC and generally, in the traditional vocabulary, /kwí/ should result from Lat. dissyllabic /ku + í/ or /ko + í/; (2) *chi* /ki/ is from Lat. QVI, QVIS, and generally, /ki/ drives from Lat. /kwi/; (3) *ci-* /či/ as in *città* is from Lat. *ci-* /ki/ as in CĪVITĀTEM; three phonemic units have thus been kept distinct although the articulation of every one has changed. The whole shift can be schematized as follows:

$$\text{kuí} \rightarrow \quad \text{kwi} \rightarrow \quad \text{ki} \rightarrow \quad \text{či}$$

Since palatalization of dorsals before front vowels is a most frequent phenomenon, we might be tempted to call this a drag shift: /ki/ was first palatalized, then /kwi/ could be reduced to /ki/, and /kuí/ could become a monosyllabic /kwi/. But we could also start from /kuí/ and argue that since hiatuses in general were being widely reduced in Imperial Latin, /kuí/ would tend to pass to /kwi/ and thereby exert a pressure on former /kwi/'s. These in turn would press upon /ki/'s with the result that they would be articulated farther forward in the mouth and become palatalized. This whole shift can not have been general in the Romania: QVI must still have been something like /kwi/ pretty late in northern Gallo-Romance since the purely French palatalization, which is found to affect /ki/ in Germanic loans as in *échine* from *skīna*, leaves the dorsal intact in the reflex of QVI; only the palatalization in CI- must have spread out of its original domain to the provinces with the well known exceptions of Sardinia and Dalmatia. This latter account of the shift is highly satisfactory in as much as it ties up neatly with what is universally recognized to have been the fundamental trends of Vulgar Latin phonological evolution: the tendency to eliminate hiatuses obviously resulted from the development of stress accent; the resistance of individual phonemes or clusters must have been negligible in comparison with such a powerful irreversible trend; /kuí/ had to become /kwi/ and actually did everywhere.

But was the functional yield of the /kuí/–/kwi/ opposition so important that /kwi/ had to recede before the invader? Many Latin speakers in northern Gaul and elsewhere just let the two groups merge. Could we not think that if the merger did not take place in central Italy, it was because Latin speakers there had already palatalized CI and considerably weakened the /w/ of QVI thus making room for /kuí/? On the other hand, it can not be argued that a push shift is to be discounted here on the ground that there are so many known cases of palatalization of dorsals which certainly do not result from a pressure upon /ki/ exerted by /kwi/ and /kuí/. There is no valid reason for assuming that the ultimate cause of such a palatalization is necessarily the same in all cases. What is needed here, as elsewhere, is a large body of tentative functional and structural explanations for the most varied cases of the type of phenomenon under consideration, and a set purpose never to let one's self be deterred from causal research by the complexity of the problems.

III. Structure

We have, in what precedes, been generally considering the problem of sound change as if every phoneme were characterized by one specific articulatory feature, entirely different from that of every other phoneme of the language. In fact this would seem to be the exception rather than the rule. The articulation of the majority of consonants in most languages implies the combination of two or more characteristic features, every one of which is to be found in some other phoneme or phonemes of the language. These features may be defined in articulatory or acoustic terms. We shall here as a rule operate with articulatory data, since they are more readily available and better known. A feature is said to be characteristic in this connection if it is phonemically distinctive. In a language like English, the lungs play a role in the production of every single phoneme, and practically the same role; therefore the pulmonic articulation is never characteristic and never distinctive. On the contrary, the bilabial articulation characterizes three phonemes /p/, /b/, and /m/ and is distinctive since it keeps these phonemes apart from e.g. /t/, /d/, and /n/ respectively. The occlusive nature of these bilabials is not characteristic or distinctive since English bilabials are always articulated as stops. Instrumental research may show that the bilabial articulation is not quite the same for /p/, /b/, and /m/, nor is the apical articulation quite of the same type for /t/, /d/, and /n/, but whatever difference may be found could, in the case of English, easily be shown to result from such concomitant (glottal or nasal) articulations as distinguish /p/ from /b/ or from /m/, /t/ from /d/ or from /n/, and so forth. We have thus to do with an automatic deviation with no distinctive significance and comparable to the one which makes the /k/ of /ki/ different from that of /ka/. A number of consonantal phonemes characterized by one and the same articulation will be said to form a "series" if their other characteristic articulations can be located at different points along the air channel. Thus in English /p/, /t/, /č/, /k/, all characterized by the same glottal articulation but distinguished by the region where the stoppage takes place, will form a series, and so will /b/, /d/, /ǰ/, /g/.

A number of phonemes characterized by one and the same articulation at a given point of the air channel, but distinguished from one another by some other distinctive articulation will be said to form an "order." Thus in English /p/, /b/, /m/, will form a labial order, /t/, /d/, /n/ an apical order, and so forth. In regard to vowels, it seems more advantageous to label as "series" a number of phonemes characterized by the same type of resonance cavities, but distinguished by different degrees of oral aperture, and as "order" a number of phonemes characterized by the same degree of aperture but distinguished by different types of resonance cavities. In English, /i/, /e/, /æ/ form a front series; /i/, /u/ a high order. In such matters /y/ and /w/ are often advantageously grouped with the vowels and may form a special order if they are phonemically distinct from /i/ and /u/.

It should be pointed out that both series and orders are oppositional in nature just like any other phonemic entity. Just as a phoneme as such presupposes other phonemes, a series presupposes one or more other series, an order, one or more other orders. A language whose consonantal inventory was restricted to /p/, /t/, /ț/, /c/, /k/, /q/ would not present any consonantal series because its six phonemes would have no distinctive features in common. A language with /p/, /t/, /k/, /m/, /n/, /ŋ/ would present two series, one of non-nasals and one of nasals, and three orders, labial, apical, and dorsal. Series and orders presuppose a larger unit grouping them into a whole, namely, the "correlation," which includes two parallel series and a number of coupled phonemes belonging to the same orders. The six phonemes of our second theoretical example would form the following correlation:

$$\begin{array}{ccc} p & t & k \\ m & n & \eta \end{array}$$

Strictly speaking, a phoneme which phonetically would seem to belong to one series, is actually no member of that series and of the correlation to which that series belongs if it has no correspondent in the other series: if a language had only the five consonants /p/, /t/, /k/, /m/, /n/—and no /ŋ/—/k/, in the theory, would not belong to the non-nasal series comprising /p/ and /t/ since the absence of nasality is not distinctive in combination with dorsal articulation. In a language where there is only one lateral phoneme /l/ articulated with the tongue tip in the same position as that of /t/, /d/, /n/, it could not be said to belong to the apical order because the apical articulation is not distinctive in combination with laterality. In diachronic phonemic practice, it will however be found convenient to include a phoneme in a series even when it has no counterpart in the parallel series, or in an order even when it has no counterpart in parallel orders, if its general phonic behavior (allophonic deviations, distribution, etc.) is similar to that of the phonemes of that series or of that order. In the case presented above of a language with /p/, /t/, /k/, /m/, /n/, it would probably be advisable to include /k/ in the non-nasal series. But there might not exist the same reasons in our second theoretical example for placing /l/ in the apical order.

The relationships existing between phonemes of the same order are usually rather different from those between phonemes of the same series. In the former case they would seem generally to be bilateral, whereas in a series they would be multilateral. In other words, phonemes of the same order would form a binary opposition or, if there are more than two of them, a complex of binary oppositions. On the contrary, all phonemes of a series would stand in the same relation to one another. If a language has, among other phonemes, /p/, /b/, /m/, /t/, /d/, /n/, they will form three series, and an order of labials, an order of apicals, and so forth. Thence:

$$
\begin{array}{llll}
p & t & .\ .\ . \\
b & d & .\ .\ . \\
m & n & .\ .\ .
\end{array}
$$

The /m/ and /n/ phonemes are likely to be normally voiced, but occasionally unvoiced without losing their identity; /p/ will be defined as unvoiced (in opposition to /b/), non-nasal (in opposition to /m/), labial (in opposition to /t/ and others); /b/ will be defined as voiced (in opposition to /p/), non-nasal (in opposition to /m/), labial (in opposition to /d/ and others); /m/ will be defined as nasal (in opposition to /p/ and /b/) and labial (in opposition to /n/ and others). It is clear that /p/ and /b/ have two characteristics in common, non-nasality and labiality, which they are the only ones to share. They are said to form a bilateral opposition, and, as one unit, they enter into another bilateral opposition with /m/. One can also say that /p/ and /b/ stand in exclusive relation, since they are the only phonemes to share the distinctive features of labiality and non-nasality.

The relation between the different phonemes of a series (or the different pairs of a correlation) seems to be of a different nature. Theoretically at least, every one of them is opposed exactly in the same way to any one of the others.

This will explain why a correlation, the simplest coherent partial pattern, consists of an indefinite number of orders but of only two series of phonemes standing in a one-to-one exclusive relation, the same for all pairs.

Two or more parallel correlations form what is called a "bundle." A bundle can be made up of three series, as in the case of

```
p   t   .  .  .
b   d   .  .  .
m   n   .  .  .
```

presented above; of four series grouped in various ways, as for instance in a language combining phonemically voice and aspiration and presenting e.g. the four labials /p/, /b/, /ph/, /bh/; of five series or more.

In practice however, there would seem to be exceptions to this clear-cut opposition between bilaterality inside orders, and mutilaterality characteristic of series: a labial order consisting of /p'/, /p/, and /p'/ might be more naturally conceived of as a triad than as a combination of two binary oppositions. In many languages two orders of hissing and hushing sibilants seem to stand in particularly close relation since they appear in partial complementary distribution.[12] In the case of vocalic patterns, three vowels of the same order such as /i/, /ü/, /u/ form a triad, and to present them in the frame of two binary oppositions would certainly distort reality. On the other hand, phonemes of the same series such as /i/ and /e/ or /e/ and /ε/ are found in certain languages to be in partial complementary distribution.

These facts and a number of theoretical considerations have induced some scholars to attempt a reduction of all phonemic oppositions to the type we have seen to prevail inside orders.[13] It has for instance been suggested that the phonemes of consonantal series actually form a more closely knit pattern than the one which is suggested by a linear presentation. The oppositions in such a series should result from combinations of acute or grave quality with two different degrees of "compactness." Thereby a close parallelism could be established with vocalic patterns, and a considerable reduction in the number of distinctive features would be achieved.

We can not enter here into a discussion of the advantages or disadvantages of such a method in synchronic studies. In diachronic matters it would seem so far that not too much is gained by departing from a linear conception of the relations between the consonantal phonemes of varying degrees of articulatory depth. In a pattern with the four phonemes /p/, /t/, /c/, and /k/, /p/ would share with /k/ the distinctive feature of graveness, and /p/–/k/ would be parallel to /t/–/c/. Yet it is found that, diachronically, passages from the /c/

---

[12] As for instance in German.

[13] Roman Jakobson was the first scholar to advocate such a reduction: see *Proceedings of the Third Intern. Congress of Phon. Sciences*, Ghent 1939, 34–41, and *Kindersprache, Aphasie und allgemeine Lautgesetze, Språkvetenskapliga sällskapets förhandlingar* 1940–1942, Uppsala 1941, 52–77. It was applied by J. P. Soffietti in his *Phonemic Analysis of the Word in Turinese*, New York 1949, and by Roman Jakobson and J. Lotz in Notes on the French Phonemic Pattern, *Word* 5.151–158. The latest exposition of the procedure is to be found in *Preliminaries to Speech Analysis, The Distinctive Features and their Correlates*, Technical Report No. 13, January 1952, Acoustics Laboratory, Massachusetts Institute of Technology, by Roman Jakobson, C. G. M. Fant, and M. Halle.

type to the /t/ type are quite frequent, and so are shifts from /k/ to /c/, but /p/
and /k/ are kept well apart. The frequent shift of [kʷ] to [p] can not be
adduced to support a close kinship of /p/ and /k/, because [kʷ] combines a
dorsal and a labial articulation and [p] can only result from a hardening of
the latter and a release of the former. Generally, a diachronic approach
requires a greater concern with phonetic reality than is possible when we are
bent upon reducing the number of distinctive features to a minimum. Even in
a language like French where /k/ has no exact fricative counterpart /x/, and /š/
no occlusive partner /č/, /š/ can not be said to be the fricative or continuant
counterpart of /k/ because it can not be maintained that a velar fricative
normally tends toward a hushing articulation as a result of its fricative
nature.[14] Two phonemes can only be said to belong to the same order if
they both present the local characteristic articulation in exactly the same
form or in forms which deviate from each other only through features which
can be fully accounted for as due to the synchronic influence of a concomitant
articulation: in Arabic the tongue-tip articulation of "emphatic" /t/ takes place
much farther back than that of "non-emphatic" /t/, but the two phonemes still
belong to the same order, because the retracted articulation of /t/ is readily
accounted for as resulting from the concomitant velar or pharyngeal articulation which is the permanent characteristic of modern Arabic "emphasis." On
the contrary, in a language where /t/ has the normal apical articulation, and
/s/ is predorsal, we have no right to include the two of them in the same
"dental" order, because we do not see why a tense fricative counterpart of /t/
should have a predorsal and not the same apical articulation. It may, in
certain cases, be difficult to decide whether two phonemes belong to the same
order or not, and we have in practice to reckon with borderline cases, but
phonologists should be warned against identifying orders as defined above
with the traditional loose grouping of the phonemes of a language into the
ready-made classes of labials, labiodentals, dentals, palatals, and velars.

All this does not mean that a componential analysis of phonemes that
strives at maximal reduction of the number of distinctive features and
eventually reveals unheeded connections between the seemingly most remote
sections of the pattern, may not have to play a role in diachronic considerations: /k/ and /a/, for instance—which are described as "compact" as opposed
to /t/ and /p/, /i/ and /u/—will often evince parallel evolutionary trends, as
when they tend toward [e] and [æ] i.e. a more "acute" pronunciation, a

---

[14]In such a case, it would of course be redundant to state that such an opposition as
/š/–/k/ is one of hush-friction vs. velarity-plosion, and descriptive economy is achieved by
reducing it to friction vs. plosion (or continuant vs. interrupted; cf. *Preliminaries to
Speech Analysis*, 6 and 21) because the hush-velarity opposition can thus be eliminated.
But it should be clear that descriptive economy is achieved here through blurring the
actual synchronic relationship between two phonemic units. Descriptive economy does
not necessarily do full justice to functional and structural reality.

phenomenon which we find for instance in Anglo-Frisian and Old French. This might mean that, in such cases, the palatalization of dorsals before front vowels is not entirely conditioned by the quality of the following vowel as usually assumed, but also by a general fronting of all dorsal consonantal articulations whereby post-velars become velars, velars become post-palatals, and so forth. This "acutization" would of course still have to be explained, but it is scientifically preferable to operate with one unknown cause than with several, one for each of the individual changes. It is a fact however that a presentation of the pattern in terms of orders, series, correlations, and bundles, with its concomitant insistance on the details of phonetic reality, is as a rule more revealing of evolutionary probabilities.

Since most phonemes actually result from combinations of distinctive articulations, we may expect that in many cases a change in the performance of a phoneme will result from a modification of only one of these articulations. If a /t/, characterized by a certain apical and a certain glottal articulation, is found to change, it may be that only the nature of its apical articulation is affected, or only that of its glottal distinctive feature. A change in the apical articulation, as for instance a retraction of the tip of the tongue from the upper teeth toward the alveolas, if it is not in some way connected with the glottal behavior characteristic of /t/ and the other phonemes of the same series, will probably affect not only /t/, but all the other phonemes of the apical order, e.g. /d/ and /n/. Similarly, a change in the glottal articulation which characterizes /t/ as opposed to /d/ will affect not only /t/ but all the phonemes of the voiceless series, e.g. /p/ and /k/. In other words, it may be expected that every distinctive articulation will change irrespective of the other articulations with which it may combine in order to form individual phonemes. This is what we actually find in the most varied languages: as a rule, when in a given language /t/ is being "aspirated," it is found that other phonemes of the voiceless stop series are also being "aspirated," which means that the glottal articulation is shifted irrespective of the oral articulations with which it combines. If /d/ is being unvoiced, /b/ and /g/ will probably be unvoiced too. If /k/ is palatalized in certain conditions, /g/ is likely to be palatalized in the same conditions, and the difference in glottal articulation between /k/ and /g/ will not determine a different treatment. All this is of course well-known and it is felt that what would need investigation are the cases in which one phoneme of a given series shows a specific treatment of its glottal articulation, or one phoneme of a given order presents a shift of its local oral articulation which is not being shared by the other phonemes of the order.

All this has obviously an important bearing upon our present research. If, as we have assumed, the functional yield of an opposition is one of the factors in its preservation or elimination, it is clear that the opposition of two articulatory features which serve to keep distinct not merely two isolated phonemes, but two large series or orders will, everything else being equal, be far more resistant. We have seen that the actual yield of the English /θ/–/ð/ opposition is extremely low. But this is not what really counts: the feature of voice supplemented by concomitant differences in articulatory strength, which distinguishes /ð/ from /θ/ is also the one which distinguishes /v/ from /f/, /z/ from /s/, /ž/ from /š/, /č/ from /ǰ/ and helps to keep /b/ apart from /p/, /d/ apart from /t/, /g/ apart from /k/. The functional yield of the opposition of voice to its absence is in English tremendous, and contributes to the stability of a large section of the consonantal pattern. All this does not mean of course that the phonetic nature of such an opposition is not likely to change in the course of time, but that if a change takes place, it is less likely to result in a merger than if the opposition were limited to a single pair.

Apart from the stabilizing influence exerted by the high functional yield of correlated oppositions, we probably have to reckon with a further factor of stability resulting from the mere frequency of the articulations characteristic of series and orders. Linguistic features which recur frequently in the chain are likely to be learned earlier and remembered better than those which appear less often. This is obvious in the case of morphological and lexical elements and syntactic patterns, and should apply to phonemic items as well. Although we still lack a large body of scientifically observed data relating to the acquisition by children of the most varied phonemic patterns, it would seem that in general correlated oppositions are acquired earlier than non-correlated ones. Here again, stability does not mean resistance to change, since perfect imitation on the part of the child should not prevent sound change from taking place, and should only prevent mergers.

If it is true that such oppositions as are integrated in a correlation or a bundle of correlations are *ipso facto* more stable than the ones between non-correlated phonemes or between a correlated phoneme and a non-correlated one, it will mean that phonemes outside of the integrated pattern will vary much more freely. If for simplicity's sake we assume complete fixity for correlated phonemes, and incessant erratic wanderings for non-correlated ones, we shall come to the conclusion that, at some time or other, every one of the latter will, just by mere chance, assume a phonetic shape which will make it the correlative partner of some other. Let us, for instance, assume the following correlation:

$$f \quad s \quad š$$
$$v \quad z \quad ž$$

plus a /x/, theoretically no part of the correlation since it has no voiced partner, but behaving exactly like /f/, /s/, and /š/. There is in the same language a trilled phoneme /r/, normally voiced, which is not integrated because it has no voiceless counterpart, whose articulation has been shifting around, and whose range of dispersion includes some non-trilled perform-ances. A day may come when it will assume a post-velar fricative articulation which will make it the voiced partner of /x/. It will be integrated in the correlation which will henceforward appear as

f	s	š	x
v	z	ž	γ

and that will be the end of its erratic wanderings. As a matter of fact, there certainly is more to this than pure chance, and we have to reckon with some amount of attraction on the part of the integrated pattern. Let us assume that the /r/ phoneme was at some time a uvular trill. Pure least effort would probably result in weakening certain of its performances to sheer friction. But friction at the uvular level would not be so very different, both articulato-rily and acoustically, from the post-velar friction characteristic of /x/. Since the performances of /r/ are normally voiced, there is no functional resistance against a merger of the two fricative articulations. The oral articulation of /x/ will exert an attraction on that of /r/ or maybe the reverse. This means that, at a certain point of time, speakers will no longer take the trouble to keep apart two minimally distinct articulations whose distinction does not serve any useful purpose. Attraction thus amounts to confusion of two neighboring articulations that have been allowed to drift closer and closer because their difference is never distinctive, since they characterize only such phonemes as are sufficiently distinguished by means of other features.

This attraction exerted by a closely knit pattern on marginal phonemes has been referred to as the filling of "holes in the pattern"[15] (Fr. "cases vides,"[16] Sp. "casillas vacías"[17]). This phrase is undoubtedly picturesque, but it is apt to deter linguists from a painstaking analysis of the successive pro-cesses involved. "Paper phonetics" has been severely and justly criticized. Juggling with the symbols of phonemic charts would be equally dangerous and reprehensible. Isolated phonemes do not rush into structural gaps unless they are close enough to be attracted, and whether they are attracted depends on a variety of factors which always deserve careful investigation. Further-more, we shall see below that what looks like a hole on the chart does not necessarily correspond to a linguistically favorable combination of articula-

[15]The term is found in K.L. Pike's *Phonemics*, Ann Arbor 1947, 117b.

[16]Probably used for the first time by this author in La phonologie synchronique et diachronique, *Conférences de l'Institut de linguistique de l'Université de Paris* (1938) 6.53.

[17]See Alarcos Llorach, *Fonología española*, Madrid 1950, 80–81.

tions. Yet it can not be denied that phonemes in groups tend to impose their articulatory types upon isolated phonemes.[18]

In dealing with pattern attraction, it is often tempting to oppose integrated to non-integrated phonemes, but it is more accurate to work with various degrees of structural integration. We have first of all to take into consideration phonemes whose phonic make-up and general behavior are that of an existing series, but which lack the partners that would integrate them in a correlation, e.g. /k/ in a language with /p/, /t/, /k/, /m/, /n/, but no /ŋ/. In such a case we might say that /k/ is ready for integration through the filling of the [ŋ] gap. In a pattern like

p	t	k
b	d	
m	n	ŋ

/k/ is undoubtedly integrated, but less so than /p/ or /t/. It is clear of course that we could not speak of "holes in the pattern" unless we reckoned with /k/, in the two preceding examples, as somehow integrated. In a language where an apical /l/ is the only lateral, it may be both theoretically and practically advisable not to place it in the same order as /t/, /d/, or /n/, and to consider it as non-integrated. But that language may present geminate consonants whose frequency is comparable to that of their simple partners in intervocalic position. Although, in a descriptive study, these geminates would still be analyzed as successions of two single consonants—so that geminated *t* would be /tt/, geminated *l* /ll/, and so forth—they would, on account of their frequency, play a functional role similar to that of single phonemes. We would be justified in speaking of a correlation opposing a series of single and one of geminated consonants; /l/ and /ll/ would thus be integrated into a correlation just as /t/ and /tt/ and /n/ and /nn/. But of course /t/ and /n/ would remain more fully integrated than /l/ because they would belong to other correlations than only that of gemination.

The theory of pattern attraction could accordingly be summarized by stating that the phonemes of a pattern tend to be as fully integrated as conflicting factors make it possible. This means that filling of holes may involve phonemes which already had some degree of integration, but which, through the process, will emerge as more fully integrated. Let us revert to the above-sketched Hauteville shift as a good illustration of this kind of process.

Both before and after the shift, the normal length vocalic phonemes of

[18]For a detailed analysis of a clear case of pattern attraction, see A. Martinet, "The Unvoicing of Old Spanish Sibilants," *Romance Philology* 5.139. In his pioneering article Phonetic and Phonemic Change, Language 12.15–22, A. A. Hill uses the term "phonemic attraction" for a different phenomenon resulting in partial or total phonemic confusion; cf. 21.

Hauteville can be ordered into three series characterized as front-retracted (/i/ type), front-rounded (/ü/ type), back-rounded (/u/ type), with four orders (or degrees of aperture) which we can designate as 1, 2, 3, and 4. The fourth order presents only one phoneme, /a/, in which front-back and retracted-rounded oppositions are neutralized. All these phonemes further enter a correlation composed of one nasalized and one non-nasalized series. The phonemes of the nasalized series are fewer than those of the non-nasalized one, which is frequently the case in similar patterns. Only the more open orders present nasal phonemes. This results from the fact that nasal articulation is detrimental to the clarity of the concomitant oral articulation since it implies that part of the air escapes through the nose and is thus lost for the oral cavity proper. Yet the wider the oral aperture, the more air will flow through it, so that open nasal vowels are likely to be more distinct than close ones. This may account for a frequently observed tendency for nasal vowel phonemes to become more and more open.

Before the shift, the two patterns, oral and nasal, must have been

1	i		ü		u		
2		e	ö		o	ẽ	
3			ε			ɛ̃	ɔ̃
4			a			ã	

There are two gaps in oral order no. 3, to wit [œ] and [ɔ]. The [œ] gap is not rare in such patterns and may be easily accounted for: for a relatively large degree of aperture, it is more difficult to distinguish between retraction and protrusion of the lips. The comparative rarity of /œ/ as a distinct phoneme is thus due to the same articulatory and acoustic factors as those that determine the frequency of a single phoneme for order no. 4. There are thus only two oral phonemes for the whole of the two most open orders. Since the opposition of /ε/ to /a/ is one not only of aperture but also of depth, it is understandable that speakers should have tended to neglect the difference between apertures 3 and 4, which was irrelevant in the rest of the oral pattern, and to stress the difference between front and back articulation, which was largely supported elsewhere. In the process /a/ passed from middle to back. The result was first an oral pattern with only three degrees of aperture

1	i		ü		u
2		e	ö		o
3			æ	a	

where the margin of security was wider between 2 and 3 than between 1 and 2.

The original nasal pattern had one more phoneme at the front than at the back; among nasal phonemes, /ẽ/ was less fully integrated than /ɛ̃/ or /ɔ̃/ since it was the only unit to combine nasality with aperture no. 2. We have seen that speakers would tend to open nasal vowels, and therefore /ẽ/ was exerting a pressure downward. In the frame of the nasal pattern, /ɛ̃/ could not become more open without threatening to impinge upon the domain of /ã/, which in its turn could hardly shift toward the back because of the proximity of /ɔ̃/; /ɛ̃/ was thus squeezed between the gradually opening /ẽ/ and the resistance of its more open and back congeners. Random weakly nasalized deviations of /ɛ̃/ were apt to be favored since there no longer was any /ẽ/ in the pattern. Eventually /ɛ̃/ was totally denasalized, and /ẽ/ could occupy its former position. The resulting situation is actually attested in dialects spoken a few miles from Hauteville where the pattern may be represented as follows:

```
1        i              ü              u
2             e         ö         o
3    (ɛ̃>)    ɛ              [ɔ]         (ẽ>)  ɛ̃        ɔ̃
4                   æ    a                          ã
```

Here, a fourth degree of aperture has reassumed phonemic relevance, but only in the front series; at the back, aperture no. 3 is only represented by contextual variants of the /a/ phoneme. At Hauteville, all the allophones of /a/ have passed to [ɔ], and /æ/ has shifted back to middle position, hence:

```
1        i              ü              u
2             e         ö    o
3                  ɛ         ɔ                ɛ̃        ɔ̃
4                       a                          ã
```

a pattern which shows much more complete integration than the original one.

A few very natural objections to the structural approach could be raised at this point: How is it that after so many millennia of uninterrupted speech practice, patterns should still be in need of structural integration? What has been called the original Hauteville pattern was of course "original" only in the sense that we chose to make it the starting point of our research. But, just like any other Romance pattern, it was nothing but one of the numerous avatars of the Latin vocalic pattern, a pattern which may have enjoyed at some period a fair degree of integration. We have of course to assume that the trend toward structural integration is at work all the time. But how can we explain that there should always be grist for its mill? Why could phonemic patterns not reach perfect stability? Or do we mean that the beautifully balanced modern Hauteville pattern has reached such a stage of perfection that it would last forever if the dialect itself were not doomed to disappear in the course of the next sixty years?

These are many questions which require separate answers. First, what we have presented of the modern Hauteville pattern looks perfectly harmonious, but so much harmony may actually involve some strain on the physiological latitudes: the usage of certain speakers would seem to indicate that the back series, with its four phonemes, is somewhat too crowded, and this could be a germ of instability.[19] Second, we have left out the short vowel phonemes whose pattern shows clear signs of disintegration,[20] and if the dialect were to live, we or our successors might probably witness a total reshuffling of the vocalic pattern which might be necessitated by a dephonemicization of quantitative differences. Completely harmonious patterns are probably never reached, and even if one were found which would seem to stand close to structural perfection, it would be at the service of a language which, like all languages, would be used for the expression of changing needs. These needs, acting through syntax, lexicon, morphology, tempo, intonation, and others, would ultimately manage to destroy the beautiful phonological balance. Third, languages do not evolve in ivory towers. The Hauteville dialect for instance has, for centuries, been spoken by an increasing number of bilinguals whose medium of inter-regional communication and intellectual expression is French. Before that time, it was a local variety of a larger dialectal unit whose most prominent and prestige-endowed users were bilinguals, also with French as a medium of wider communication. Even before French was actually spoken in the region by the leaders of the community, a number of linguistic features of all sorts, phonological as well as others, must have seeped through chains of contiguous forms of speech all the way from Northern France, politically dominant since the rise of the Frankish empire. Dominant cultural languages do not necessarily preserve the integrity of their patterns better than local patois when they spread over large heterogeneous areas and become the linguistic mediums of whole nations.

All this accounts for the never-ceasing phonological fermentation that can be observed practically everywhere. There will always be holes in patterns and phonemes moving in to fill them. New series and new orders will appear, resulting either from general reshufflings or from the coalescence of successive phonemes of the spoken chain, the result of new accentual conditions, articulatory imitations, etc. These new series and orders will not always be complete from the start; for some time there will remain gaps which ensuing generations may fill through either sound change or borrowings.

The creation of a hushing order in early Castilian affords an interesting

---

[19]Description phonologique . . . 36 and 38.

[20]Cf., *ibid.*, what is said, pp. 44 and 56, about a tendency toward making ĕ the phonemic equivalent of zero.

illustration of the ways through which a new phonemic type can expand by convergence of the most varied elements[21]: the first hushing units must have resulted from the coalescence of apical articulations with neighboring newly evolved Romance [i̯], hence word-medial /č/ and /š/; the corresponding holes in the word-initial pattern must have been filled mainly by borrowings from neighboring dialects. Word-initially the voiced hushing phoneme (probably [ǧ]) was normally a reflex of Vulgar Latin *yod*, but intervocalic *yod* was never modified, and the corresponding hole in the word-medial pattern was filled by early Romance /l^y/ passing to [ž]. This rather startling treatment can be understood only if we keep in mind that geminated (at that time probably just strong) *l* was tending toward its modern [l^y] reflex, and was exerting a pressure upon earlier /l^y/.

This Castilian process further affords a welcome illustration of what we might call the action of a phonemic catalyst. We have so far assumed that functional yield, even if it were practically nil, would act as a deterrent against merger. But if the opposition in question is between a fully integrated phoneme and one that is not, or upon which some phonemic pressure is being exerted, a minimal functional yield will not act as a deterrent and, on the contrary, an articulatory attraction is likely to take place. In simpler, less technical terms, if a well-integrated phoneme is extremely rare, it may attract a not so well integrated neighboring unit. In the case of early Castilian there must have been a few words in which the [zi̯] cluster was preserved, having escaped the metathesis whereby BASIUM became *beso;* these rare [zi̯] clusters naturally yielded [ž] as in *frijuelo* from PHASEOLUM.[22] This new /ž/ phoneme occurring word medially was well integrated in an order which presented, further, word medial /č/ and /š/. But the instances of this phoneme were so few as to exclude any homonymic conflict if what had been /l^y/ merged with it; /l^y/, which was being unintegrated by the pressure of a former /ll/, must have been attracted by /ž/. Attraction, as we have presented it before, results from the confusion of two articulations when concomitant articulations suffice to preserve phonemic identity. In the case of a catalyst we have the confusion of two characteristic articulations when this does not actually result in confusion of words and forms. Functionally the two phenomena are quite parallel. They both result in articulatory economy without any impairing of communication.

IV. Inertia and Asymmetry

The most serious resistance to phonemic integration stems from the limitations set up by human physiology to the combination of the most varied

---

[21]See "The Unvoicing of Old Spanish Sibilants," 135–136, 140–141.

[22]See Vicente García de Diego, *Gramática histórica española*, Madrid 1951, 103.

articulations. The articulations themselves may conflict if they involve neighboring organs. But, more often, the incompatibility will be acoustic, i.e. hearers will find it difficult to perceive a difference between various combinations of the same type, at least in ordinary speech conditions.

We have, in what precedes, indicated in several occasions how some physiological necessities may counteract phonemic integration. We have pointed out that vocalic correlations are quite generally much better represented in the higher than in the lower orders: /œ/ as a phoneme is probably rarer than /ö/ or /ü/; patterns with three series (e.g. of the /i/, /ü/, and /u/ types) practically never keep these three series distinct for the lower order, which is easily accounted for by pointing out that, with maximally open jaws, the lips will be automatically retracted, and that it will become difficult to distinguish between a front and a back oral cavity. The difference of aperture between [o] and [u] will be smaller than that between [e] and [i], although it corresponds to the same maxillary angle. From the point of view of the speaker who has to control the play of his muscles, the proportion [o]:[u] = [e]:[i] will be correct; but acoustically the distinction between [e] and [i] will be clearer than that between [o] and [u]. For the same number of phonemes in the front and in the back series the margins of security will be narrower at the back than at the front, and this may partially account for diverging comportments of the two series. We have also seen that concomitant nasalization affects the clarity of vocalic articulations, which means that there are articulatory combinations which are acoustically good, and others which are not so good.

If phonemes were not of phonic nature but resulted e.g. from combinations of flags, if /p/ for instance, instead of being, say, voiceless and bilabial, was performed by stringing the Stars and Stripes and the Union Jack along the same line, /t/ by combining the Stars and Stripes with the French Tricolor, /d/ by adding to the latter the Danish Dannebrog, and so forth, any combination of two flags would be just as good as any other. We can not combine voiced and voiceless articulation, but we could combine the Stars and Stripes with the Dannebrog. Furthermore, if in order to make morphemes or words, we should produce a succession of different flag combinations, any combination could follow any other, so that a word could easily be composed of /ptd/ if the respective units involved were performed as described above. Not so of course with distinctive units performed as sounds. The vowel-consonant dichotomy, with its syllabic corollary is imposed upon us by the nature of the so-called speech organs. The vocalic and consonantal patterns may overlap in certain languages, but they are always organized according to two different models. Even if we should agree with Jakobson that, in human speech generally, the coordinates are the same for vowels and consonants, we would find, in individual languages, no constant parallelism between the two patterns: Czech would have a quadrangular consonantal system and a triangular vocalic one:

$$t \quad p \qquad i \qquad\qquad u$$
$$c \quad k \qquad\qquad a$$

and Finnish just the reverse:

$$t \qquad\quad p \quad i \quad u$$
$$k \qquad\quad æ \quad ɑ$$

The necessity of alternating, in the spoken chain, between closed and open articulatory complexes, which naturally result from the combination of different types of articulation, opposes the integration of all the phonemes of a language into one closely-knit pattern: the opposition of voice to its absence plays a great role in consonantal matters; with vowels, on the contrary, voice is almost indispensable and therefore phonemically irrelevant. Some distinctive features can be found to characterize both vowels and consonants, but not too easily in the same language. Palatalization of consonants and front vowel articulation may be conceived as the same feature, with whatever actual difference that may exist being determined by concomitant vocalic or consonantal features; but where, as in Russian, we might believe that the two coexist, more careful observation will often show that if consonants enter a correlation of palatalization, the vowel series will actually be distinguished by the play of the lips: Russian i' is frequently pronounced far back in the mouth, and /u/ may, in certain contexts, be performed as [ü].

The case of nasality is interesting since it will combine with both consonantal and vocalic articulations, but not equally favorably with all consonants and all vowels: most languages distinguish /b/ and/or /p/ from /m/, /d/ and/or /t/ from /n/; /ñ/ is probably about as frequent as its non-nasal counterparts /ɟ/ and /c/, but /ŋ/ as a distinct phoneme is rarer than /g/ and /k/, which may be due to a tendency of the two velar articulations to conflict. Nasal fricatives as distinct phonemes are extremely rare since friction requires a pressure which can not be obtained if the air is allowed to flow unhindered through the nose. The rarity of liquid nasals can be accounted for in very much the same way. We have already seen that, for similar reasons, nasality combines better with open than with closed vocalic articulations; but, in any case, nasal vowels are never so clear as oral ones, and this should account for their relative infrequency and instability as phonemic units. With stop articulations, experience shows that nasalization as such is easily perceived, but, unless [m] and [n] are clearly exploded, the place of oral occlusion can be identified only with difficulty, as shown by the frequent neutralization of nasal consonants in syllable final position where they are assimilated to the following consonant and, if word final, merged into [n] or [ŋ].[23]

All this means of course that there will be gaps in patterns which are not likely ever to be filled, or if they are, only as a result of a fairly exceptional concurrence of circumstances. The phonemes characterized by acoustically or articulatorily unfavorable combinations will, everything else being equal, be less stable than others combining features with a high degree of compatibility. Orders and correlations will tend to expand as far as human physiology, and certain conditions inherent to the specific language, will permit. To an original /m, n/ nasal series a /ñ/ is added in Vulgar Latin when a palatal order is formed. In Germanic a tendency to simplify the clusters of nasal and homorganic oral stop (cf. the discrepancy between the spelling and the pronunciation of Eng. *lamb, comb;* Danish has gone farthest with its mute *d* in *land*) has resulted in the phonemicization of the dorsal nasal [ŋ] ; the same phenomenon is found in Sanskrit as a result of the reduction of all final consonant clusters to one phoneme, hence /n/ + dorsal > /ŋ/. A general weakening of implosion is likely to yield a whole pattern of nasal vowels. In all these cases, we can hardly speak of filling of holes since the appearance of the new phoneme or phonemes is obviously determined by trends which have nothing to do with pattern attraction. In most of these shifts the main factor probably was least effort, which was allowed to play in certain domains where communicative needs offered little resistance and in the frame of certain prosodic situations involving a specific nature of accent and a given pattern of syllabification.

Linguistic evolution in general can be conceived of as regulated by the permanent antinomy between the expressive needs of man and his tendency to reduce his mental and physical exertions to a minimum. On the plane of words and signs, every language community will have to strike a balance between an expressive trend toward more numerous, more specific, and less frequent units, and natural inertia which favors fewer, more general, and frequent ones. Inertia will be there all the time, but expressive needs will change, and the nature of the balance will vary in the course of time. Uneconomical expansion, i.e. one which would entail more exertion than the community would deem worth while, will be checked. Inertia, when felt to be excessive, i.e. detrimental to what is felt to be the legitimate interests of the community, will be censored and punished. Linguistic behavior will thus be regulated by what Zipf has called the "Principle of least effort,"[24] a phrase

[23]For a general survey of the restrictions imposed upon the expansion of correlations by the inertia and assymetry of speech organs, see A. Martinet, Rôle de la corrélation dans la phonologie diachronique, *TCLP* 8.273–288.

[24]*Human Behavior and the Principle of Least Effort*, Cambridge, Mass., 1949, 56–133.

which we would rather replace by the simple word "economy"[25].

Linguistic economy is ultimately responsible for the very existence of phonemic articulation: the inertia of the organs involved in the production and reception of speech phenomena makes it impossible for any normal human vocal language to afford a specific homogeneous and distinctive phonic product for every linguistic sign. Yet communication requires distinct expression for each. A satisfactory balance is reached by limiting to a few dozens the number of specific and distinctive expressive units, the phonemes, and by combining them successively into distinct signifiers. Economy is further achieved by making these units result from combinations of non-successive phonic features, but of course only such combinations as will best serve communicative purposes. We find here an antinomy between what we have called the trend toward phonemic integration and the inertia and asymmetry of the organs opposing the inclusion of all phonemes into a theoretically perfect, immutable pattern. When a vocalic pattern presents four phonemically relevant degrees of aperture in the front series, phonemic integration will tend to preserve or produce four relevant degrees of aperture in the back series. When the vocalic structure of Classical Latin with its three relevant degrees of aperture eked out by a quantitative distinction was, by elimination of the latter, reorganized into a four order pattern, in most of the Romania the reshuffling followed the same procedure in the front and at the back. But for the same number of phonemes in the two series the asymmetry of the organs entailed narrower margins of security in the back series. The mutual pressure could be relieved by diphthongization of the phonemes of one order or more. But in such a case diphthongization resulting from a gradual increase or decrease of the maxillary angle in the course of the articulation of the vowel would not be restricted to the back series but would extend to all the vowels of the same order: where ϱ became *uo*, *ẹ* would become *ie*, and pattern symmetry would be preserved. A tendency to merge orders 2 and 3 might also affect equally the front and back series. If on the contrary the pressure was relieved by gradual fronting of /u/, the back series would from then on only distinguish between three orders and the pattern remain asymmetrical.[26]

The effect of the asymmetry of speech organs is also clear in the case of consonant patterns, not only when we think of the obvious restrictions to the spread of various correlations, but also in the course of certain wholesale mutations when it is found that some orders proceed more rapidly than others. An articulatory weakening will as a rule decisively affect bilabials before the other orders: /p/ is frequently weakened to [h] or zero where /t/ and /k/ are preserved. A shift affecting strongly articulated consonants is

[25]La double articulation linguistique, *TCLC* 5.34
[26]See Haudricourt–Juilland, 17–58, 98–113.

likely to act more rapidly on the phonemes of the apical order, as seen for instance in Modern Danish where, of the three energetically articulated aspirates, /t/ is the first to show unmistakable signs of affrication.[27]

A full awareness of the existence of this asymmetry will, in many cases, help to account for such changes as seen only to affect a single phoneme. It will make clear that this seemingly isolated change is, in fact, the outcome of a general trend, variously warped by specific conditions, hastened if these are favorable, delayed if they are not: a general articulatory strengthening acting upon a series of spirants may change a [þ] into [t], but will never change an [f] into a stop, and will simply make the articulation of [s] more energetic; [ɣ] may remain a spirant when [ð] is made an occlusive, whereas [ƀ] becomes a stop in strong (e.g. initial) positions but remains a spirant elsewhere.[28]

In combination with the various factors considered above, asymmetry should go a long way toward accounting for most of the phenomena which could be described as local modifications or reorganizations of phonemic patterns. When, in such matters, we find two sections of the same language community striking out into different phonological paths, we shall find, as a rule, that both courses had their functional, structural, and physiological justifications, and that the factors responsible for the divergence must have been such imponderables as will always escape scientific scrutiny when human behavior is involved.

V. Prosody and Non-Phonemic Pressure

Still largely unexplained remain such changes as affect whole orders, series, correlations, bundles, and even the system, both vocalic and consonantal, in its entirety. When investigating these, all the previously discussed factors should be kept in mind. It will be found that the direction and amplitude of every one of them is, as a rule, largely dependent on the nature and diachronic comportment of the structural environment. The behavior of orders and series will be reminiscent of the one we have ascertained above in the case of our three phonemes A, B, and C, and this is easily understandable since the whole of an order or of a series differs from the whole of another order or series in exactly the same way as we assumed A differed from B or from C. Orders and series will merge, just like phonemes, but in most well-documented cases we shall find that, for classes as well as for individual phonemes, a relatively low functional yield may have played a role. But if we can thus account for some of the modalities of these changes, we have so far no way of telling what started them.

---

[27]Cf. Henrik Abraham, *Etudes phonétiques sur les tendances évolutives des occlusives germaniques*, Aarhus 1949, 108.

[28]Cf., e.g. A. Martinet, Some Problems of Italic Consonantism, *Word* 6.35–41.

Among the possible factors in such changes we shall distinguish between internal and external ones. By internal factors, we mean here the
influences exerted upon the pattern of phonemes by those sections of the
linguistic structure we have not so far considered, namely the complex of
prosodic, "suprasegmental," features, and the system or systems of meaningful elements. Among external factors, we should distinguish between the
influences exerted by other linguistic structures, those of other dialects of the
same language or of other languages, and the fairly mysterious non-linguistic
factors whose importance may well have been grossly exaggerated by our
predecessors. We can not deal here with the influence of other linguistic
structures.[29] Let it suffice to say that they would deserve to be taken into
consideration far more than has generally been done so far.

One would have a right to object to our separating, in the present
survey, prosodic from phonematic features. It can indeed not be denied that,
at least in some languages, suprasegmental features can be arranged into
patterns very similar to those we have established for phonemes. For instance, the tones of many south-eastern Asiatic languages could be grouped
into orders and series just like the phonemes of the same languages. Most of
what we have said above about the comportment of phoneme patterns would
apply just as well to such tone patterns. The function of these tones is
distinctive like that of phonemes, and the mutual diachronic relations they
entertain with the phoneme patterns must be of the same type as those
between different sections of such patterns. Accent, which can be defined as
prominence given to one syllable in the word, or whatever meaningful unit
has prosodic relevance, may at times assume some distinctive function,
particularly when it is found to appear in two or more phonemically distinct
types. These two or more distinct types may pattern in very much the same
way as tones proper, their difference being generally one of pitch or melody.
In so far as they exert distinctive function, prosodic features have, from a
diachronic standpoint, to be considered together with the purely distinctive
features we find combined into phonemes. They form with vowels and
consonants three natural classes of distinctive units. We have, in what
precedes, pointed to a definite tendency to avoid the use, in the same
language, of certain features for both consonants and vowels. In a similar
way, it is found that, for instance, prosodic intensity, if distinctive, usually
excludes phonemically relevant vocalic intensity manifested under the form
of quantity.[30]

Yet the basic function of accent as such is not distinctive. When its

---

[29]Cf. "The Unvoicing of Old Spanish Sibilants," generally, and 152–156 in particular.
[30]See, e.g. N. S. Trubetzkoy, *Grundzüge der Phonologie*, Prague 1939, 180, or
Principes de phonologie, Paris 1949, 215.

place in the unit it characterizes is not predetermined by the phonematic make-up of that unit, it may occasionally evince some sort of distinctive power (cf., e.g. Sp. *córtes–cortés*). But this is normally a by-product. Accent is really there to characterize and localize the word (or a certain type of morpheme or phrase) in the spoken context. If the localization is approximate, its function has been called culminative. If it is accurate, its function is demarcative. The true function of accent is less clear in languages where it is a traditional feature than where a new accentual pattern is being developed at the expense of tradition. In contemporary French, for instance, the weak traditional phrase-final accent seems to be increasingly overshadowed by what has been called the accent of insistence. This accent has two concurrent forms, an emotional and an intellectual one. The former is usually characterized by stressing and lengthening of the first consonant of the word, the latter by some prominence given to the first syllable. Formally, the two varieties are clearly distinct only in words beginning with a vowel (*im'possible* vs. *'impossible*), and, even then, emotional accent can be heard on the first syllable (*c'est 'impossible*).[31] In what could be dubbed "didactic style," first syllable prominence is widely prevalent and its function is clearly demarcative; by setting individual words apart from the context, it gives a bolder relief to the successive articulations of thought. The functional difference between phonemes and such an accent is obvious: phonemes contribute only indirectly to the expression of the semantic contents of language, and therefore the expressive needs of man will as a rule affect phonemes only through devious channels; this still optional accent is an immediate reflex of these expressive needs; its intensity will vary from one utterance to another and mirror exactly the communicative purposes of the speaker. Such an accent is linguistic in the narrow sense of the word because its existence is determined by an inherited convention, but its arbitrariness is highly limited in the sense that, once it has been accepted in principle by a community, the details of its actual use will be regulated by what we may call psychological factors. Even when such an accent has been stabilized and has ceased to be optional, it will be liable to various degrees of intensity whereby meaning will be conveyed directly from speaker to hearer.

What has just been said about accent applies largely to all the prosodic features grouped under the heading of intonation. In many languages, an utterance final melodic rise is the functional equivalent of an interrogative morpheme such as Fr. *est-ce que*, Russian *li*, Lat. *-ne*. Once tone, as automatic accompaniment of every syllable or mora, and occasional phonemically distinctive uses of accents have been discounted, prosodic features may be said to belong to the same linguistic plane as meaningful units, and,

---

[31] See J. Marouzeau, Quelques aspect du relief dans l'énoncé, *Le français moderne* 13.165–168, with references to former contributions by the same author.

just like them, to be liable to be directly affected by communicative needs. But the physical nature of their performances is such as to exert a deep influence on those of the phonematic units of the spoken chain.

This is of course clear in the case of stress accent, which, when particularly strong, is known to play havoc with inflexional endings[32] if it does not happen to bear on them, and which must also be ultimately responsible for the most revolutionary reshufflings of phoneme patterns. The umlaut phenomenon illustrates most clearly how processes that originally affect phonemic units in the spoken chain, lead eventually to a reorganization of the phoneme pattern. The prominence of a syllable can only be achieved at the expense of the other syllables of the word; as stress increases in one part of the word, the other parts become more weakly articulated, hence blurring of vocalic distinction and, frequently, syncope. This, in itself, does not affect the inventory of the phonemes, only their distribution. In many cases, this would be expected to result in the elimination of a large number of useful distinctions; OHG *scóno* and *scóni* would have merged into **scōn*, if speakers had not unconsciously favored in the second form such deviations of /ō/ as were determined by a tendency to anticipate the front articulation of /i/; hence, of course, the eventual split of /ō/ into /ō/ and /ō̄/ attested in German *schon* and *schön*. This shows how the phoneme pattern can be made to expand when the average number of phonemes per word is diminishing, and how, more generally, demarcative needs can enlarge the phoneme inventory and lead to a reshaping of the system.

But of course the well-known umlaut process is only one way, among many others, whereby prosodic non-distinctive features can affect the phoneme pattern. This, a central problem of diachronic linguistics, should receive far more attention than has been granted to it so far, since prosodic features are the most normal channel through which the varying communica-

---

[32] It is clear of course that the energy with which stressed syllables are pronounced varies greatly from one language to another. Stress is, for instance, decidedly weaker in Spanish than in Italian, and probably weaker in standard Italian than in standard German. Some languages, like German, show close contact of stressed short vowels and following consonants; others have loose contact in such cases. When Bloomfield writes, *Language*, 385: "many languages with strong word stress do not weaken the unstressed vowels" and cites among them Italian, Spanish, Czech, and Polish, he obviously wants to convince his readers that stress as such can not be held entirely responsible for vowel blurring. But his examples do not carry conviction: neither Czech nor Polish accent can be said to be particularly energetic; in standard Castilian, accent is uncommonly weak. In such matters, it is particularly important to distinguish between the successive stages of the same language. It is commonly assumed that "Germanic accent" is vowel-blurring. But it remains to be proved that, e.g. in contemporary English and German, absence of stress is actually conducive to the blurring of vocalic distinctions. For Standard German, at least, this seems highly doubtful.

tive needs of speech communities can influence the pattern of distinctive features. As factors of phonological changes, prosodic features are extremely powerful precisely because they are immediate responses to the needs of expression. The speaker of Modern French who makes an extensive use of optional initial accent is prompted to do so by a desire to make his statements as clear and convincing as possible. How could he imagine that he may be paving the way toward the establishment of initial stress as an automatic feature of the language, which may eventually result in blurrings, mergers, and syncopes? We do not mean hereby that the phonetic trends launched by, say, a strong stress accent will develop blindly, ruthlessly destroying any piece of linguistic machinery that happens to be in their way. If the vocalism of unstressed endings plays in the economy of the language too important a role to be wiped out, speakers may be induced to save some of their articulatory energy for the final syllable of every word. When, as it seems, prehistoric Latin developed a word initial stress, wide-spread blurring of vocalic timbres took place in medial syllables, but final syllables, in which lay the expression of most morphological categories, were hardly affected. At a much later period, when the language had extensively weakened its adverbs into mere grammatical tools, a new onslaught of prosodic intensity resulted in the wholesale massacre of a declensional pattern which by that time must have become a burden rather than a real help.

In this rapid survey of the ways through which communicative needs may influence the phoneme pattern, we should of course mention again the assumed role of the functional yield of oppositions. But, by the side of this conservative action, it would remain to be seen whether the necessities of expression could not, in some cases, be directly instrumental in enlarging some sections of the phoneme pattern. If some phonemically relevant feature, say, glottalization, happened to be the frequent mark of a morphological or lexical category, could it not be imagined that speakers would be tempted to combine it with new articulations and extend it beyond those sections of the phoneme pattern where we would normally expect to find it? The example we have to offer does not illustrate exactly this type of action, but rather the extension of a correlation beyond its expected range under the pressure of an all-pervading pattern of morphophonemic alternations; most Breton consonants may be grouped into two series of strong and weak units; weak stops are voiced and their strong counterparts are generally voiceless; the strong member of phonetically voiced pairs often evinces a tendency to devoicing, a tendency fully developed in Welsh. This strong-weak opposition frequently coincides with the morphophonemic pattern of "lenited" versus "non-lenited" consonants; /b/ for instance is the phonemic weak counterpart of /p/ and also, in the morphology, the "lenited" equivalent of it. Since, however, [b] could also be the "non-lenited" counterpart of /v/, a tendency has been at work to distinguish phonemically between morphologically "strong" [b] alternating with /v/ and morphologically weak [b] alternating with /p/. As a result, we have today to reckon with two *b* phonemes: a strong *b* transcribed /bb/ which Breton speakers tend to unvoice and which they have in consequence some difficulty in keeping apart from /p/, and a weak fully voiced /b/. The distinction is widely neutralized, or rather it has only got a foothold in a very specific position, namely word initially within an utterance if the last phoneme of the preceding word is a vowel.[33]

This last illustration and the preceding suggestions should by no means be conceived of as exhausting all possibilities of direct diachronic influence of one of the linguistic planes upon the other. Neither in this final section nor in the previous parts of this study has there been any attempt at being exhaustive. A complete functional and structural theory of phonological evolution will have to be based upon a much larger body of structurally sifted material than is available to date. The justification for the sketchy and tentative outline which has been presented here is that it may incite diachronically inclined linguists to utilize in their investigations some of the conclusions arrived at after two decades of phonemic research.

[33]See F. Falc'hun, *Le système consonantique du breton*, Rennes 1951, 63–65.

10

AN ISSUE IN THE THEORY OF SOUND CHANGE: THE NEOGRAMMARIAN POSITION AND ITS DISCONFIRMATION*

Paul M. Postal

1. The Problem

Fundamentals. This second part of the present monograph[1] is concerned principally with sound change. But it must be understood as part of the controversy between autonomous and systematic phonemics which was primarily at issue in Part I. Even more deeply, however, the second part of the present inquiry must be considered against the background of an older and more basic dispute, namely, that between those who hold that linguistics must necessarily be antimentalistic, positivistic, behavioristic, etc., and those who, like the present author and workers within generative grammar generally, hold that linguistics is inherently a mentalistic discipline.

There are a number of ways to attempt to justify the view that linguistics must be mentalistic. One might, for example, attack the common but seldom defended claim that antimentalism has some justification in terms of the philosophy of science. That is, one could attempt to show that no valid reconstruction of the principles of scientific inquiry generally excludes mentalism. Or one might argue that mentalistic assumptions define a natural, significant field of inquiry in which claims can be justified or overthrown as in other fields, a domain which is in large part explicitly recognized and investigated within the ancient disciplines of traditional grammar and rationalistic philosophy. Similarly, one might argue that various antimentalist, behaviorist, and/or extreme positivistic positions lead to empirically absurd

*Pg. 231–260 (chapters 10 and 11) in *Aspects of Phonological Theory* by Paul M. Postal. Copyright © 1968 by Paul M. Postal. Reprinted by permission of Harper & Row, Publishers, Inc., and of the author.

[1]Part II is a greatly expanded version of a paper "Taxonomic Phonemics and Sound Change" which was read before the summer meeting of the Linguistic Society of America, Bloomington, Ind., August 1964. The present version owes a great deal to criticism and suggestion by R. P. Kiparsky, E. Garcia, E. Hamp, S. J. Keyser, and D. Perlmutter, to all of whom I am very grateful.

and untenable results. All of these modes of argument have in fact been attempted. This has in effect been the burden of much work on the foundations of generative grammar. Cf. especially Chomsky (1964b), (1959), (1965), (1966); Katz (1964), (to appear); Postal (to appear a), (to appear b). More substantively, one might try to show that some well-established domain of linguistic fact and data can only be understood in mentalistic terms. This is the approach which will basically be followed here.

I shall argue that the domain of so-called "sound change" can only be understood against the background assumption that a linguistic description describes a mentalistic domain, namely, the internalized linguistic knowledge of a native. Involved in this discussion are the claims that: (1) only the conception of systematic phonemics makes it possible to understand sound change; (2) the facts of sound change support systematic phonemics vis-à-vis autonomous phonemics.

Sound change, it is claimed, can only be understood against the background of a valid conception of language. Too briefly put, one must at the very least assume that a language is an infinite set of <u>sentences,</u> which are triples of phonetic, syntactic, and semantic properties generated by a finite abstract object, or <u>grammar,</u> which consists of a set of partially independent elements called <u>rules</u> and a <u>lexicon,</u> or dictionary. Such grammars are represented in human neural systems and provide implicit knowledge of the languages they define. A grammar is thus in certain ways analogous to a computer program in that it is a formal system partially determining the behavior of a physical system, a formal system which can be represented in hardware of various types but which is in no way identical to any such representation.

Incidentally, it is perhaps worth explaining the emphasis here on the discussion of American positions on sound change in view of the obviously secondary role which American linguists have played in the development of historical linguistics. This emphasis is based on a certain judgement; namely, that in spite of the predominance of European work in the substantial area of diachronic linguistics, it has been American writings which are in the forefront of the attempt to provide a theoretical analysis of the nature of phonological change and to relate the character of this change to theories of synchronic linguistics, to modern developments in phonology, and to methodological assumptions about the proper nature of linguistic inquiry. And these matters are ultimately those on which it is hoped the present discussion may shed some light. It is thus my impression that, although the historical views to be critically discussed here are generally accepted by the majority of historical linguists regardless of nationality, it has been American linguists who have made the theoretical assumptions most explicit and who have tried most strenuously to relate them to assumptions about the nature of language generally, about the character of phonemic representation, and about the nature of phonetics, etc., which are the issues in which we are most interested.

An Issue in the Theory of Sound Change. The present section is concerned with a straightforward question of linguistic fact which has, however, very deep and far-reaching consequences for any theory of phonological change and for phonology generally. The question is this. Are there quite regular and generally characterizable "sound changes," which describe the successive states of the linguistic history of any languages, that are not describable in purely phonetic terms? That is, are there systematic changes in the phonetic output whose positions of occurrence are unstatable in terms of any set of phonetic environments although the positions of occurrence are stable if reference is made to the morphophonemic and/or superficial grammatical structure of the relevant strings? This question is of interest for the following reasons.

Within modern linguistics, there is a widely accepted position on the nature of phonological change (I refer here to change which is independent of language contact) which claims that there are basically two subtypes; one, regular phonetic change which is describable in purely phonetic terms, or in phonological terms (autonomous phonemic) based only on phonetics and contrast;[2] and another kind, sporadic, unsystematic, etc. called analogy.[3] The position is that changes which are regular and systematic, i.e. which operate throughout the lexicon in generally specifiable conditions (where by "generally specifiable" one means statable without giving a list of relevant morphemes), are necessarily purely phonetic, that is, phonetic changes which occur in phonetically specifiable environments. Although, as we shall see

---

[2]For purposes of this discussion, there is no need to distinguish phonetic environments from autonomous phonemic environments, since autonomous phonemes are either uniquely defined as, or equivalent to, sets of phonetic segments in sets of phonetic environments. Hence any environment stated in terms of autonomous phonemes can be replaced by a normally more complex but equivalent environment in terms of a set of phonetic segment sequences.

[3]"Analogy" is really an unfortunate term. There is reason to believe that rather than being some sharply defined process, analogy actually is a residual category into which is put every kind of linguistic change which does not meet some set of a priori notions about the nature of change. In particular, I think that the term "analogy" has been used very misleadingly to refer to cases of perfectly regular phonological change in which part of the conditioning environment involves Surface Constituent Structure; i.e. changes which happen only in nouns, or only in verb stems, etc. I suspect that an analytic survey of cases which have been referred to as "analogy" would yield many instances of regular phonological change with nonphonetic environments, that is, many cases bearing on the issues raised in the present section. For some further discussion cf. the references to work of Kuryłowicz and related comments in Chapter 12.

presently, this position is widely accepted in modern linguistics, indeed is essentially coextensive with the view that modern autonomous phonemics is the key to understanding phonological change,[4] the clearest and most extensive statements are probably still those of Leonard Bloomfield, especially in his *Language* (1933) (the following quotes are from pages 353, 353–354, 354, 363, 364, and 369 respectively):

> Historically interpreted, the statement means that sound change is merely a change in the speakers' manner of producing phonemes and accordingly affects a phoneme at every occurrence, <u>regardless of the nature of any particular linguistic form in which the phoneme happens to occur.</u> (Emphasis mine: PMP)

> The limitations of these <u>conditioned sound changes</u> are, of course, purely phonetic, since the change concerns only a habit of articulatory movement; phonetic change is independent of non-phonetic factors such as the meaning, frequency, homonymy, or what not, of any particular linguistic form.

> A great part of this dispute was due merely to bad terminology. In the 1870's, when technical terms were less precise than today, the assumption of uniform sound change received the obscure and metaphorical wording "phonetic laws have no exceptions." It is evident that the term "law" here has no precise meaning, for a sound-change is not in any sense a law, but only a historical occurrence. The phrase "have no exceptions" is a very inexact way of saying that non-phonetic factors, such as the frequency or meaning of particular linguistic forms, do not interfere with the change of phonemes.

> The neo-grammarian[5] hypothesis implies that sound-change is unaffected by semantic features and concerns merely the habits of articulating speech-sounds.

> The neo-grammarians define sound-change as a purely phonetic process; it affects a phoneme or type or phonemes either universally or under certain strictly phonetic conditions, and is neither favored nor impeded by the semantic character of the forms which contain the phoneme.

> Phonetic change, as defined in the last chapter, is a change in the habits of performing sound-producing movements.

An excellent selection of similar statements by Bloomfield from less well-known publications of the period before 1933 has been provided by C. F. Fries (1962a:199–202).

The whole of Bloomfield's discussion of sound change makes it clear,

---

[4]I ignore here and throughout the distinction often drawn between phonetic change and phonemic change, that is, between phonetic changes which affect the system of autonomous contrasts and phonetic changes which do not and thus affect only the allophonic pattern.

[5]It is not at all clear that the position maintained by Bloomfield is really equivalent to that of the 19th-century Neogrammarians, as is now widely assumed. This depends very much on how the older concept of "regular analogy" is to be interpreted.

as do the statements of others who hold similar positions, that "semantic character" in statements like these is to be interpreted to include not only semantic features in the strict sense, but also grammatical and morphophonemic properties of the forms, i.e., to exclude every possible type of environmental factor but phonetic.

More modern statements of this position of the <u>purely phonetic</u> character of regular sound change are not hard to find. Hoenigswald, for example, puts it as follows(1960:76):

> In the case of phonemes there are no such bifurcations; the set of all discourse-long environments in which a phoneme occurs splits up into subsets such that the replacement for the phoneme in each subset is a different phoneme at the later stage and such that the subsets do not overlap: at the time when some of the instances of E k go to k (*clip* > *clip*) and others go to ϕ (*knot* > (*k*)*not*), there are no environments whatever in which the outcome is, at the given time and place, ambiguous; sound change is, in this sense, entirely REGULAR. In a somewhat different way this has already been said above . . . , where it was pointed out that phonemic split affects positional allophones; synchronically (here with reference to the earlier stage of a change), any environment, even if minimal, determines a definite positional allophone or range of positional allophones.

And for a restricted type of change[6] the case is put thus by W. Chafe (1959:482):

> Zero is an acceptable reconstruction only if epenthesis is plausible as a historical explanation. Epenthesis is plausible whenever the environments in which it might have taken place are definable in strictly phonological (read <u>autonomous phonemic</u>, i.e. by footnote[2] phonetic: PMP) terms.

Gleason (1961:395) states it as follows:

> There are two important characteristics of such a change that require comment. In the first place, what is shifting is not the pronunciation of a specific sound in a specific place, say a certain word. If it were, we might expect the same sound to change in a different way in some other place. Instead, the shift affects the statistical norm based on all occurrences of the given phoneme in a given environment—that is, on all occurrences of a certain allophone. In turn this norm controls the pronunciation of this allophone whenever it occurs. Phonetic change, therefore, affects allophones as wholes. Within the understanding that the effect is statistical, phonetic change affects any given allophone consistently. This is commonly expressed by saying that PHONETIC CHANGE IS REGULAR. This means that any phonetic change will affect all instances of the sound concerned in the positions in which it is operative. The same phonetic change may affect all the allophones of a given phoneme, or only a single allophone.

---

[6]This restriction is unimportant, especially so because one of our counterexamples to the position advocated is a case of epenthesis.

Martinet (1952:3) accepts basically the same view:

> We shall, in what follows, center our attention on "regular" sound changes, the type whereby all the performances of a given phoneme, everywhere or in a well defined context, are eventually affected. . . . In the frame of the present exposition, it is completely immaterial whether a change affects a phoneme in all contexts or only in phonemically well defined ones, whether what is eventually merged or kept distinct is two phonemes or two combinatory variants of different phonemes.

And again (1953:1):

> It should be clear that diachronic phonemic theory is based upon the assumption that, apart from well defined cases, the meaning, function, or use of a given word cannot influence the phonetic evolution of its phonemic components. It is clear that if, in synchronic descriptions, we are able to ascribe all the sounds of a language to a definite number of phonemes, it is because all the realizations of a given phoneme in a given context are, as a rule, found to shift in the same direction and at the same rate of velocity.

And Waterman (1963:54) states it:

> A more acceptable phrasing might be: "Within certain limits of time and space, the same sounds, given the same conditions (read phonetic conditions: PMP) behave in the same way."

And Fries (1962:51) asserts:

> The following statement attempts to summarize briefly the chief features of what is meant by the heading of this section—'Phonetic Laws Without Exceptions' . . . we infer that there was a change in the native speaker's manner of pronouncing a particular 'sound,' and that this change
> (1) affected every occurrence of that 'sound' in essentially the same phonetic surroundings,
> (2) operated within a particular span of time and within a particular dialect or group of dialects,
> (3) was not interfered with by any nonphonetic factors such as meaning, homonymy, etc.

And this position is also strongly maintained by C. F. Hockett in his well-known text (1958). We shall not, however, quote any statement from there because Hockett has extended and reformulated his position in his recent Presidential Address to the Linguistic Society of America.[7] This work is the most extensive recent statement and attempt at justification of the

---

[7]"Sound Change," paper read before the meeting of the Linguistic Society of America, New York, December 1964. I am indebted to Professor Hockett for providing me with a copy of this paper.

position we are discussing here. We feel it deserves separate attention and have devoted an entire chapter (14) to its analysis.

The view under consideration is also strongly advocated by R. A. Hall, although a really good illustrative quote is difficult to find (1964:295):

> Phonological development is to be divided into two aspects: phonetic change and phonemic change. The former involves simply change in speakers' habits of making sounds; . . .

A similar remark holds for I. Dyen (1963:631), whose position is as follows:

> Now we can usefully describe what is ordinarily meant by *regular* phonetic change among comparative linguists in the following way. Let us take the words of the earlier stage and construct a set of rules by which the words are to be transformed into the words of the later stage. The rules permit that (1) for a phoneme sequence of the earlier stage there is one and only one phonemic transform everywhere, or that (2) for a phoneme sequence of the prior stage there are various transforms, but for each transform each set of environments of the phoneme sequence of the prior stage is mutually exclusive with the set of environments for each other transform of that phoneme sequence.

Dyen's discussion makes it quite clear that "environment" must be understood here in terms of autonomous phonemics (i.e. phonetically). More than seven decades ago Hermann Paul (1891:58) wrote:

> If we, therefore, speak of the uniform operation of sound-laws, this can only mean that in the case of sound-change occurring within the same dialect, all the separate cases, in which the same sound-conditions occur, are treated uniformly. It must either happen, therefore, that where the same sound existed previously, the same sound always remains in the later stages of development as well; or where a separation into different sounds has occurred, there must be a special reason to be assigned; and, further, a reason of a kind affecting sound alone—such as the effect of neighboring sounds, accent, place of syllable, etc.—for the fact that in one case one sound has arisen and in another a different one. No doubt we must take into account in this all the different factors in the production of sound.

We thus see that modern linguistics is in general dominated by this traditional Neogrammarian conception of sound change. This view can be taken as the generally accepted view of the nature of sound change today, a view enshrined in our textbooks and manuals and underlying actual historical work undertaken within the framework of modern phonemics. The determination of the truth value of this conception is thus a matter of the greatest importance. If, for example, it could be shown to be false, a reconsideration of the mass of work in historical phonology for almost a century would be required, work which is often considered among the most solid and unimpeachable results of linguistic science.

In recent years, those working within the framework of generative grammar have claimed that correct synchronic phonological descriptions of natural languages are incompatible with the autonomous phonemic view of phonology which has developed in modern (post-1933) linguistics, both European and American. As we have seen in Part I, the chief property of autonomous phonemic descriptions is that phonological representations must be arrived at solely on the basis of phonetic facts plus knowledge of which utterance pairs contrast (i.e. are not free variants or repetitions) and hence independently of considerations having to do with grammatical structure and morphophonemic alternations. There is obviously a striking similarity between the principles which define modern autonomous phonemics and those which characterize the Neogrammarian position on sound change. Indeed the former can be looked upon as simply the result of making the claims of the latter synchronic. Whereas the Neogrammarian position asserts in effect that all the regular systematic statements or rules, the so-called *Lautgesetze*, which describe the change of phonological structure, must be purely phonetic in both operation and environment, modern autonomous phonemics asserts that all the rules which describe the relation between phonemic and phonetic representation must be determined purely on phonetic grounds, given knowledge of contrast. This contrasts with the phonological position of generative grammar, which recognizes many rules with nonphonetic environments in synchronic phonological descriptions and likewise claims that such rules may therefore be added over time and thus play a role in describing sound changes.

We can now see the importance of the simple factual question raised at the outset. Upon the answer to this question hinges the correctness of crucial aspects of the view of sound change which dominates modern linguistics of the pre-generative type. We may distinguish three distinct views of regular sound change with respect to the kinds of environments in which these occur:

(PI)   Autonomy[8]—the view that *no* regular sound changes require reference to morphophonemic or superficial grammatical environments.

(PII) Non-Autonomy—the view that *some* regular phonetic changes take place in environments whose specification requires reference to nonphonetic morphophonemic and/or superficial grammatical structure.

(PIII) Inseparability—the view that *all* regular phonetic changes take place in environments whose specification requires nonphonetic information.

[8]For this three-way distinction and similar criticisms of the position developed in this regard by Ferguson, cf. Chomsky (1964b: 110–111).

(PI) is, as we have seen, the dominant modern view. (PII) is the view suggested by phonological work done within the framework of generative grammar. (PIII) is a position which has never been held by anyone past or present. It is defined and discussed here briefly only because a failure to distinguish between (PII) and (PIII) has led to recent confusions about the evidence which could bear upon the relative merits of (PI) and (PII), the basic question to which the present investigation is addressed.

In his review of Halle's *The Sound Pattern of Russian*, the first modern study to reject explicitly the autonomous framework of phonology, C. F. Ferguson (1962:284–297) rightly assumed that the conflict between the view of Halle and others working within the generative framework (that phonology is not independent of grammar, and that phonological representation is determined in part by grammatical and morphophonemic facts as well as phonetic ones) and the dominant autonomous position which he maintains is properly argued in terms of historical as well as synchronic phonology. Ferguson argued that historical evidence refutes the position Halle maintained (exclusively on synchronic grounds). His remarks require full quoting:

> The effect of Condition (3a)[9] is to set a careful line between phonology and grammar, and it is the abandonment of this condition and erasure of its dividing line which constitute the greatest break between the current approaches to phonological analysis and that of Chomsky and Halle. It may seem plausible, as they suggest, that the sound system of a language is so intimately tied up with its grammar, and functions so completely as a tool of the grammar, that any attempt to treat it separately from the grammar is fundamentally mistaken. The autonomy of phonology, however, is a concept arrived at as the result of over a century of linguistic research, and the concept is not to be discarded lightly: to discard it would surrender some of the most striking achievements of linguistic science.

Ferguson then attempts to document this latter claim with the following remarks:

> First, the autonomy of phonology was forced upon investigators in historical linguistics in the nineteenth century by the facts of language change. The discovery of Verner's Law made clear that, in general, phonological change takes place under conditions and within limitations which are in phonological terms and not in grammatical or semantic terms. The conditions under which these particular changes took place involved features such as voicing or voicelessness of neighboring sounds and the position of accent with regard to the sound in question, and the changes took place not only not in terms of grammatical conditions but in many cases in direct opposition to "natural" grammatical parallels and analogies.

[9]Condition (3a) is the requirement that, given a phonemic description, the phonemic representation of a form is uniquely determined by its phonetic representation.

On the basis of this factual summary Ferguson then concluded with the following summary dismissal of the position he was criticizing:

> A synchronic analysis which ties phonology and grammar up in a neat bundle not only falsifies the current situation but makes it impossible to understand the diachrony. One area of flux which is of importance diachronically is the borderline between phonology and grammar, where the fit of the two segmentations shifts and structural change takes place.

Although Ferguson is certainly correct in assuming that historical evidence bears on the question of the truth values of the incompatible theories of autonomous phonemics and generative phonology, his argument against the latter is thoroughly vitiated by its failure to distinguish position (PII), the position implied by generative phonology, and (PIII). Let us note that (PI) is consistent only with the existence of regular sound changes with purely phonetic environments. (PII) is consistent with the existence of regular sound changes with both purely phonetic and with more abstract environments. The existence of a single sound change of the latter variety is not only consistent with (PII) but supports (PII) vis-à-vis (PI) with which any such change is incompatible. (PIII) is consistent only with the existence of changes whose environments are not fully phonetic. Hence the existence of a single purely phonetic sound change refutes (PIII) vis-à-vis (PI) and (PII).

Consider now Ferguson's criticism of Halle's position. The evidence which Ferguson brings forth is the existence of purely phonetic sound changes, in particular Verner's Law. Such sound changes, which obviously exist and whose existence has surely not been denied by any reputable linguist for decades, thoroughly refute position (PIII), a matter of limited interest since no one maintains (PIII). However, such evidence has no bearing whatever on the relative correctness of (PI), which Ferguson believes, and (PII), the position implied in the phonological theory he was criticizing, since both (PI) and (PII) are consistent with the existence of purely phonetic sound changes. Hence by failing to distinguish (PII) from (PIII) through an appeal to the metaphor of "tying up phonology and grammar in a neat bundle" Ferguson fails to deal with the problem he raised, and his rejection of the position of generative phonology on historical grounds is without basis. This is a good illustration of the fact that in serious discussion of rival linguistic theories, imprecise and metaphorical statements of the opposing positions cannot be tolerated.

The real problem for linguistics at the moment is not to evaluate position (PIII), an artifact no one does or could maintain, but to decide between (PI) and (PII). It is to this real question that the next chapters of this study are addressed by way of the factual matter alluded to at the beginning. Ferguson has argued that generative phonology "makes it impossible to understand the diachrony." I shall argue that the reverse is the case, and that on the contrary, it is autonomous phonemics with its historical corollary, position (PI), which has this property, for the quite simple reason that there exist sound changes inconsistent with (PI). I shall argue this chiefly on the basis of some examples from the Northern Iroquoian languages. This will extend the counterevidence to the principles of autonomous phonemics (cf. Part I) strongly into the area of diachronic linguistics, and will provide grounds for the assertion that the version of the Neogrammarian position on sound change so strongly advocated by Bloomfield and generally accepted thereafter is mistaken; i.e. it will provide grounds for the assertion that the theory of sound change must be formulated around position (PII), not around position (PI) as is the case today. I shall try to accomplish this principally by showing that there are quite regular and easily characterized sound changes which relate contemporary Mohawk and Oneida to proto-Mohawk-Oneida which are indescribable in purely phonetic terms, although they have quite elementary descriptions in terms of representations which would now most likely be called "morphophonemic."

Empirical Disconfirmation of the Neogrammarian Position

2. Some Iroquoian Sound Changes

Mohawk. Proto-Mohawk-Oneida[1] had consonant-resonant consonant clusters which included the following types [wr, nr, sr, tr, kr, tn, sn, kn, tw, sw, kw, sy].[2] With certain minor exceptions irrelevant to the present discus-

---

[1] I should like to indicate here my indebtedness to F. G. Lounsbury for my knowledge of much of the following factual material, a large proportion of which was originally uncovered by him. I am also grateful to him for providing all of the Oneida forms quoted below. This is not to say, however, that he necessarily endorses the arguments given here or agrees with any particular assertions made in this study.

[2] This class of clusters also included [sy], [ty], [ky], [ny], [ry]. These were, however, later eliminated from the narrow phonetic level in Mohawk by rules which turned the initial consonant palatal and dropped the following glide. In discussing protosequences I enclose the elements in phonetic brackets "[ ]". This is not necessarily to indicate a claim about the most detailed phonetic form which these had in the protolanguage, but only to indicate their phonetically crucial properties. That is, such representations are used where most contemporary linguists would quote protoforms or sequences in autonomous phonemic writing. In quoting phonetic sequences, I give no more detail than is necessary to illustrate the point under discussion. In quoting full forms, however, narrower representations are given. Unlike the examples in Part I,

sion (for example, proto [nr] is, in contemporary Oneida, pronounced [ndl]), these clusters still exist in Oneida. In Mohawk, however, these have, with one particular type of exception, been eliminated *on the phonetic level* by the introduction of the epenthetic vowel [e], identical in quality to other distinctive, nonepenthetic [e] vowels which derive from those which existed in the parent language. Hence any autonomous phonemic description of Mohawk must consider these epenthetic [e] vowels to be phonemic although they are easily predicted in systematic terms and are thus not part of the dictionary representations of forms. For instance, an item like [o'nerahte$^{?}$] 'leaf' has a systematic representation which can be abbreviated $\#$wa + o + nraht + $^{?}\#$. The effects of the epenthesis sound change on Mohawk are illustrated by the Mohawk-Oneida cognates in the following list:

	Mohawk			*Oneida*
(11.1)	[onuta'keri$^{?}$]	Mo. 'beer,' On. 'sugar'	(11.10)	[onuta'kli$^{?}$]
(11.2)	[kâ':sereh]	'vehicle'	(11.11)	[kâ':slet]
(11.3)	[yê':teru$^{?}$]	'she, someone resides'	(11.12)	[yê':tlu$^{?}$]
(11.4)	[teninû':we$^{?}$s]	'we 2 inclusive like it'	(11.13)	[tninû':wehse$^{?}$]
(11.5)	[seninû':we$^{?}$s]	'you 2 like it'	(11.14)	[sninû':wehse$^{?}$]
(11.6)	[yakeninû':we$^{?}$s]	'we 2 exclusive like it'	(11.15)	[yakninû':wehse$^{?}$]
(11.7)	[tewanû':we$^{?}$s]	'we several like it'	(11.16)	[twanû':wehse$^{?}$]
(11.8)	[sewanû':we$^{?}$s]	'you several like it'	(11.17)	[swanû':wehse$^{?}$]
(11.9)	[sata'weya$^{?}$t]	'come in'	(11.19)	[sata'wyaht]

Consider now proto [kw]. No examples of epenthetic [e] from [kw] are given above. But these are the crucial cases for our discussion. For in fact, the rule of [e] epenthesis which Mohawk has added is indescribable in purely phonetic terms, just because of the behavior of proto [kw] under this addition. This follows since these vowels were introduced only between *some* but not *all* [kw]. Furthermore, and most significantly, those proto [kw] which were split by epenthetic vowels were in no way distinguishable in *phonetic* terms from those which were not, although, with one exception, they are *automatically* distinguished in morphophonemic terms. It can easily be shown that whether or not epenthesis took place in such cases was determined by two different sorts of factors: in some cases, the Surface

---

voicing and tenseness in consonants are not marked except in affricates, the latter only for reasons having to do with my personal transcription habits. Like previous examples, aspiration is not marked. The accent mark of course indicates stress, the colon length, and a circumflex 'ʌ' over a vowel falling tone.

Syntactic Structure was relevant, but more generally, the underlying phonological structure which differentiated phonetically like elements was a determining factor.

If we investigate the following Mohawk-Oneida cognate forms we find
that we must distinguish four different types of [kw] sequence:

Mohawk		*Oneida*	
(11.19) [kewi′stos]	'I am cold'	(11.26) [kwi′stos]	
(11.20) [rawi′stos]	'he is cold'	(11.27) [lawi′stos]	
(11.21) [yakwanû′:weʔs]	'we several exclusive like it'	(11.28) [yakwanû′:wehseʔ]	
(11.22) [ya′kwaks]	'we several exclusive eat it'	(11.29) [ya′kwaks]	
(11.23) [ra′kwas]	'he picks it'	(11.30) [la′kwas]	
(11.24) [ru′:kweh]	'man'	(11.31) [lukwe′]	
(11.25) [o′:kwireʔ]	'branch'	(11.32) [o:kwi′leʔ]	

In forms (11.21) and (11.22), we find [kw] sequences in contemporary
Mohawk not broken by epenthesis and for the same reason. Irregularly, and
for reasons which are inexplicable, [kw] simply did not undergo epenthesis
when the [k] was the first person morpheme and the [w] the first element of
the plural morpheme, despite the fact that this same [k] element plus *stems*
beginning with w did yield epenthesis, as can be seen in form (11.19), and
despite the fact that when the w which begins the plural morpheme was
preceded by s of the second person morpheme or the t of the inclusive person
sequence, epenthesis also occurred. (Compare forms (11.7) and (11.8) with
form (11.21).) Hence the irregularity in (11.21) and (11.22) is wholly a
function of the sequence first person + plural. It should be emphasized that
this irregularity is 'regular' in the sense that it happens throughout the
language in both noun and verb prefixes regardless of stem or inflection
whenever this sequence of morphemes is juxtaposed. Here then we have a
case of a regular sound change being impeded in a particular grammatical
environment, a situation definitely not countenanced by position (PI). Although significant, this case of failure of epenthesis with first person and
plural is not the most essential argument which can be given against (PI).[3]

A second type of [kw] sequence is shown in the perfectly regular forms
like (11.19), in which epenthesis occurs as expected, i.e. as in tw, sw, etc.,
sequences. Next take form (11.23), which also does not undergo epenthesis.
The epenthesis rule does not operate in this case because the underlying
representation of this [kw] is ko. Compare Mohawk forms like:

(11.33) [wahá′:koʔ] 'he picked it'

[3]Another case of grammatically conditioned sound change within the history of
Mohawk and Oneida is known to me. I have not discussed it in the text because certain of

Given the fact that [ko] and [kw] alternate in Mohawk morphemes, it is not self-evident that the underlying or basic representation is ko. The arguments for this are, however, strong. First of all, there is a general rule in the language that within morphemes, no sequences of the type consonant + w are allowed. Choice of the representation kw for stems like 'to pick' would force a partial rejection of this regularity. On the other hand, ko occurs within morphemes regardless of how the class of stems involving [kw]-[ko] alternations are treated. Second, choice of kw would complicate the rule of [e] epenthesis which operates in the environment: Any Consonant—Resonant Consonant,[4] but not in these cases. Finally, the rule which turns o to [w] is the quite general one which operates in the environment —Vowel (and is needed not only for stem final vowel plus aspectual suffix, but also for other cases, for example, those involving the objective

---

the facts in Oneida, which I have not studied personally, are unclear. Mohawk has a rule which deletes word final [+Abrupt Onset] segments in *nouns* only (actually only nouns which are not reduplicating animal names). Thus compare the Mohawk noun-verb pairs:

Nouns		Verbs	
[kâ':sereh]	'vehicle'	[keˀserchtanû':weˀs]	'I like vehicles'
[odzi'stoh]	'star'	[kdzistohkwanû':weˀs]	'I like stars'
[o'shes]	'syrup, honey'	[keshestanû':weˀs]	'I like honey'
[ka'tsheˀ]	'bottle, can'	[ketsheˀtanû':weˀs]	'I like cans'
[o'hšdžʌˀ]	'bone'	[kšdžʌˀtanû':weˀs]	'I like bones'

with the verbs:

[i':sek]	'eat it'
[rakâ':rut]	'let him make a hole'
[tke'htak]	'let me believe it'
[keˀnikû':rarak]	'let me be careful'

Oneida has a similar rule whose domain is, however, more limited in ways that are not completely clear to me. Thus compare Oneida noun forms like:

[o'shes]
[odzi'sto]
[oˀšdyʌˀ]

in which word final [+Abrupt Onset] segments drop, with Oneida noun forms like:

[kấ:slet]̚
[kaná:talok]̚

in which they do not. We can see then that, regardless of details, Mohawk has in fact extended the rule of dropping in nouns to a further set of cases. But since this extra deletion is grammatically conditioned (only in nouns), is it another case of nonphonetic sound change whose environment is partially determined by Surface Syntactic Structure.

[4]One of the facts which leads to a [+Consonantal] systematic representation for phonetically [−Consonantal] [w] and [y] in Mohawk, as discussed in footnote 18 of Chapter 8, is their behavior as resonant or liquid consonants in this rule. Cf. footnote 6 of this chapter.

morpheme). However, if w̲ is chosen as basic, the rule to turn this to [o] is not nearly as simple. For this rule would have to operate in terms of both preceding the following environments, since w̲ normally drops instead of going to [o] in __Consonant:

(11.34) [waho':taʔweʔ]   'he slept'   waʔ+hra+o+itaʔw+ʔ

(11.35) [ro':taʔs]   'he sleeps'   hra+o+itaʔw+s

Hence the environment for this putative rule cannot be simply

$$\underline{\hspace{1cm}} \begin{cases} \text{Consonant} \\ \text{Glide} \end{cases},$$

which is more complicated than the environment of the o̲ to [w] rule anyway, but would have to involve preceding structure as well. There are thus very strong reasons for considering the underlying representation of the [kw] sequence in forms like (11.23) to be ko.[5] And it is simply a fact that [kw] sequences which derive from ko̲ never permit epenthesis.[6]

Finally, in forms (11.24) and (11.25) there is no epenthesis because the [kw] sequence here must be considered the representative of the single morphophoneme p *h*,[7] which also existed in the proto-language, although the

---

[5]The treatment of stem final [o]-[w] and [i]-[y] alternations in the Northern Iroquoian languages is an interesting and difficult one which has, I think, never been adequately managed in the past. Seduced by the phonetic parallelism here, all past treatments have assumed that either the full vowels are basic in both cases or the glides are basic. Lounsbury, for example, in his unpublished Master's Thesis (1946), treated w̲, and y̲ as basic. W. L. Chafe, in all of his work on Seneca, also assumed that w̲ and y̲ are basic here. In my Doctoral Thesis (1962), I assumed that o̲ and i̲ were basic. But I am now convinced that, at least for Mohawk, it is necessary to treat o̲ as basic in the [o]-[w] cases, but y̲ as basic in the [i]-[y] cases. This follows because the [w] in the former cases does not behave like the true consonantal, systematic w̲, behaves under a variety of rules, but the [y] in the latter cases does obey the rules which hold for consontal systematic y̲. This issue is discussed at length in Postal (to appear c).

[6]One might assume that this failure of epenthesis is accounted for by order of rules, i.e. that the epenthesis rule precedes the rule which yields the [w], thus preventing epenthesis. But this is not true, and the order of rules is the opposite. What prevents the epenthesis is the fact that the 'w' element which is introduced from o̲ is not marked [+Consonantal], and hence does not define the proper environment for epenthesis. This 'w' element thus contrasts with systematic w̲ which is marked [+Consonantal] at the point at which the epenthesis rule applies. In the final, most narrow representation, these elements fall together as a [−Consonantal] glide. What may seem here simply an ad hoc solution is in fact highly motivated and general. I have justified it in some detail in Postal (to appear c). Cf. also footnote 18 of Chapter 8.

[7]As pointed out in footnote 16 of Chapter 8, the labial character, which is both implied by the notation p̲ and definitely claimed by the $\begin{bmatrix} +\text{Grave} \\ +\text{Diffuse} \end{bmatrix}$ structure this is meant to abbreviate, has not been justified in the present work. It is interesting, in this historical context, that Chafe (1964), in his recent work arguing for genetic relationship

falling together of the phonetic realizations of this single element with the [kw] which come from k + w and ko dates to a period before the separation of the Northern Iroquoian languages, i.e. to something on the order of three millennia ago. Again, the evidence which shows that in contemporary Mohawk the [kw] sequences in forms like (11.24) and (11.25) are representatives of a single systematic phonological element (morphophoneme) is overwhelming. First of all, this eliminates a set of exceptions to the rule of [e] epenthesis. Second, as was briefly discussed in Chapter 7, there is a rule in the language that stressed vowels are long before (systematically) single consonants. And there is length before these [kw] sequences but not before those in forms where the [kw] comes from k + w or ko (here absence of length is due to rule ordering). Hence recognition of a single element here also regularizes the description of length. Furthermore, although this is not obvious (Postal (to appear c)), recognition of systematic p simplifies the statement of the restrictions, briefly discussed in Chapter 8, that k and y do not occur within morphemes before i,[8] while p and w do not occur within morphemes before rounded vowels (o, u). Finally, the 'w' elements after velars behave differently in word final and prerounded vowel position than true w, which is represented by [f] in the former position and by [y] in the latter. In both of these positions p yields [k].[9]

Hence there is no doubt that in systematic phonemic terms, contemporary Mohawk has a single consonantal phoneme which is represented phonetically by [kw] and [k]. This is, on roughly similar grounds, also true of Oneida, and hence by direct inference was also the case in the proto-

---

between Siouan and Iroquoian, finds [p] - [kw] differences distinguishing cognates. He thus sets up a Proto-Siouan-Iroquoian *p which became [kw] in most Seneca environments and [p] in Siouan. Hence to the extent that Chafe's conclusions can be accepted, it is fairly clear that what I claim is systematic p in contemporary Mohawk had a labial origin *historically*. What is controversial then is the claim that this labial character has been maintained in the underlying systematic representations of Mohawk, and probably contemporary Iroquoian languages generally, even though the labial elements have essentially been lost phonetically. Notice that it is only within the framework of a systematic phonemic theory embodying the Naturalness Condition that a claim of underlying labial character makes sense. Cf. footnote 11 of Chapter 4.

[8]There are a handful of exceptions to the former generalization with k, for example [ki'tkit] 'chicken.' This should only figure as one exception, incidentally, since it is a case of reduplication.

[9]Actually, I have run across a handful of related speakers who quite exceptionally pronounce p as [kw] in word final position. Since the basence of [w] here in the standard dialects dates to proto-Iroquoian, this is another case of nonphonetic sound change; nonphonetic, because this [w] appears for these few speakers only after those [k] which come from word final systematic p and not those from word final k. I have not utilized this example in the text because it is limited to a few speakers and because I have not as yet been able to study it in detail.

language. And cognate comparisons with other Iroquoian languages, for example Seneca, show that the merging of p with ko + vowel < œ + w dates to before the split of the Northern Iroquoian languages. Compare:

A. For p

	Seneca	Mohawk
(11.36)	/tɛ:nɔhtahkwayɛɔ^ʔ/	[wahtahkwarn'kʌh]
	'they bet on a shoe'	'white shoes'
(11.37)	/hekä:hkwa:^{ʔ}ah/	[tkarahkwi'nekʌ^{ʔ}s]
	'afternoon = less sun'	'the sun rises'
(11.38)	/kɛkwitekhneh/	[kʌkwitê':neh]
	'spring'	'spring'

B. For ko + vowel

	Seneca	Mohawk
(11.39)	/yesa'e^{ʔ}tä:kwas/	[rasahe^{ʔ}ta'kwas]
	'she picks out the beans'	'he picks beans'
		[wahasahê':^{ʔ}ta ko^ʔ]
		'he picked beans'
(11.40)	/sæ:kweh/	[rara'kwas]
	'you choose it'	'he chooses'
(11.41)	/^{ʔ}ɛkæ:ko^ʔ/	[ʌhara':ko^ʔ]
	'I shall choose'	'he will choose'
(11.42)	/^{ʔ}ɛɔti:wake'skwahse:k/	[rake'tskwas]
	'they masc. pl. will get up the ceremony'	'he raises it'
(11.43)	/^{ʔ}ɛyɔtya^{ʔ}ta'kesko^ʔ/	[ʌhake'tsko^ʔ]
	'people will arise'	'he will raise it'

C. For k + w

	Seneca	Mohawk
(11.44)	/akwahsi^{ʔ}ta^ʔ/	[yakwahsi^{ʔ}tâ':keh]
	'our feet'	'our feet'
(11.45)	/wa^{ʔ}akwayɛ:^{ʔ}/	[wa^{ʔ}akwa':yʌ^ʔ]
	'we ex. pl. put down'	'we leave it, set it'

Seneca examples (11.36), (11.37), (11.38), (11.39), and (11.44) are from Chafe (1963:36, 38, 39, 35, and 12 respectively). Seneca examples (11.40) through (11.43) and (11.45) are from Chafe (1961:242, 250, 232, 246, and 168 respectively). Chafe's representations are of course autonomous phonemic rather than literally phonetic. They are, however, very close to phonetic.

Summing up, it can be seen that the sequences in Mohawk which correspond to phonetic [kw] in Oneida can be understood only in terms of at least four distinct underlying or systematic phonemic interpretations. Namely, as k + w irregularly marked as not undergoing epenthesis when representing first person + plural, as ko, as a single element p, and as perfectly regular k̲ ̲+̲ ̲w̲. One need make only two assumptions to make the facts of change automatic consequences of the addition of the following schematically stated rule (this rule is discussed and stated precisely in Postal, to appear c) to the grammar of proto-Mohawk but not proto-Oneida, that is, to the grammars of some but not all speakers of proto-Mohawk-Oneida:

(11.46) null → [e] in the environment: [Consonant]_____[Resonant Consonant]

The first assumption is that the three-way systematic contrast between k̲ ̲+̲ ̲w̲, k̲o̲, and p̲ existed in proto-Mohawk-Oneida, which is hardly questionable. The second is that the added rule of epenthesis operated *not* on phonetic or autonomous phonemic representation, but on the much more abstract systematic phonemic representation, a structure which is independently motivated by a host of other phenomena. Actually, this latter statement is something of a simplification. For the rule of epenthesis would operate on the systematic representation of forms directly only if it were added as the first phonological rule, which was certainly not the case. More precisely then, this added rule operated on sub-representations which were derived from the systematic structure by previous rules, but which were not identical to phonetic or autonomous phonemic representations. In this way the rule was able to distinguish the identical phonetic sequences which ultimately resulted from the grammar of proto-Mohawk-Oneida prior to the rule addition, despite the fact that *phonetic contexts* provided no unique specification of whether a proto-Mohawk-Oneida [kw] would or would not be affected by the new rule.

Oneida. As striking support of the claim that the Mohawk data just discussed concerning [e] epenthesis is not some kind of peripheral or accidental occurrence, or due to some overlooked or misinterpreted facts, there is the crucial evidence of a parallel development in Oneida. Just as one must postulate that Mohawk has added to the proto-grammar a rule which is unstatable in autonomous phonemic terms because of the varying structural characterizations of the phonetic sequence [kw], so also Oneida has added a quite different rule which is indescribable in such limited terms for exactly the same reasons.

In both languages the ancient rule of stress assignment still functions. The penultimate vowel in a multivowel word is stressed. This rule must, of course, be stated on a relatively abstract representation; one, for example, which does not include epenthetic vowels of various types, only one of which is that discussed earlier. This representation is hence neither phonetic nor autonomous phonemic. Oneida has, however, added a rule which Lounsbury (1946:58–59) refers to as the Oneida Accent Shift. The full details of this rule need not concern us, but one of its effects is to move the stress from the penultimate to the final nonepenthetic vowel of a word provided that only a *single consonant* intervenes. Thus compare the following Mohawk and Oneida forms:

Mohawk		Oneida	
(11.47) [waha':koˀ]	'he picked it'	(11.50) [waha:kô']	
(11.48) [wakhuri':yoʰ]	'I have a good gun'	(11.51) [wakhuliyo']	
(11.49) [waha':kʌˀ]	'he saw her'	(11.52) [waha:kʌ̂']	

But the striking thing is that those [kw] sequences in Oneida which represent systematic phonological or morphophonemic p̲, i.e. exactly those which correspond with those morpheme internal [kw] in Mohawk that are not derived from k̲o̲, permit the accent shift to take place, *but no others do.* This has in fact already been illustrated by the Oneida forms (11.29) through (11.32). In (11.29) the accent has not shifted because the [kw] represents k̲ + w̲; in (11.30) it has not shifted because the [kw] represents k̲o̲ where the o̲ yields a [w] in the representation before the shift rule applies. But in (11.31) and (11.32) the accent does shift because in these forms there is underlying p̲, still a single consonant in the abstract representation at the point when the accent shift rule applies. Note that the final [e] in (11.32) is epenthetic and hence the penultimate rule places the stress originally on the initial [o].

The same fundamental and independently motivated analysis of morphophonemic structure accounts for the facts of accent shift with respect to [kw] in Oneida as accounts for the epenthesis facts with respect to [kw] in Mohawk. Surely nothing could show more clearly the depth and reality of the underlying structural differentiation in the proto-system of what were unquestionably phonetically identical [kw] sequences, or show more clearly the fundamental role that morphophonemic structure plays in perfectly regular and systematic phonological change.

Alternatives. Of course, at least for those not familiar with Iroquoian, it is reasonable at this point to suggest the possibility that, at the time when the antecedents of contemporary Mohawk and Oneida [kw] and [k(e)w] were differentiated by the epenthesis and accent shift sound changes, they were in fact phonetically distinct. However, comparison of the languages with each other and with other Iroquoian languages makes it clear that this is quite out of the question. The sound changes we are discussing are quite recent. Lounsbury (1946:58) dates the Oneida Accent Shift to the beginning of the 19th century at the earliest. The Mohawk epenthesis rule is perhaps a few hundred years older.

The exact age of this rule is difficult to determine. The oldest relevant material would seem to be the materials recorded in *The Voyages of Jacques*

Cartier, dating to the 1530's. These contain several hundred recordings of Iroquoian words and expressions. Unfortunately, it is unclear exactly what languages are represented in these materials. It appears that they contain items from more than one Iroquoian dialect. Some of the forms do appear to be Mohawk, and in epenthesis positions one does not find the epenthetic [e] recorded. Thus one finds <u>tigneny</u> 'two' where contemporary Mohawk has [té kenih]. If, therefore, these forms in the Cartier *Voyages* are in fact recordings of 16th century Mohawk, this places an upper bound of four hundred years as the maximum age of the Mohawk rule of [e] epenthesis between consonant and resonant consonant. For discussion and analysis of these forms, cf. Barbeau (1959).

On the other hand, a glance at the other Iroquoian languages shows that <u>ko</u> before a vowel and the single systematic element <u>p</u> have been phonetically [kw] for at least several millennia. This follows, for example, from the fact illustrated above that Seneca has cognate forms with [kw] in all the positions of Mohawk <u>k + w</u>, <u>ko</u>, and <u>p</u> and from the fact that the Seneca-Mohawk-Oneida split has been estimated by Lounsbury (1961:2) to have taken place approximately twelve to fifteen hundred years ago. Therefore, in order to postulate phonetic differences in Mohawk and Oneida during the present millennium, it would be necessary to say that <u>ko</u>, <u>p</u>, and <u>k + w</u> fell together in proto-Iroquoian, then redivided in Oneida and Mohawk, and then separately in both languages largely fell together again, obviously an inconceivable set of occurrences. Even worse for the view of purely phonetic sound change is the fact, pointed out to me by Eric Hamp, that if one compares form (11.22) in Mohawk with form (11.29) in Oneida, one finds that the postulation of phonetic differences leads to inconsistent assertions about the proto-language. For in Mohawk, in order to prevent epenthesis, one would like to say that the antecedent of the [kw] in (11.22) was a single phoneme in say 1400 to 1800, but in Oneida in order to prevent the accent shift one would have to say that the antecedent of (11.29) was a consonant sequence. But the antecedents of (11.22) and (11.29) are the same. Clearly any hypothetical phonetic differences between [kw] sequences in Mohawk and Oneida during this millennium are completely untenable.

My colleague R. P. Kiparsky has pointed out that in view of the apparent role played by relative chronology in these arguments about Mohawk [e] epenthesis and Oneida Accent Shift, it is advisable not to leave the impression that the chronologies are based purely on Stammbaum considerations. That is, the chronologies are not based simply on assuming that within a set of related languages the more widespread rule is necessarily older and that all instances of some rule within a family must have the same unique origin with only genetic transmission. While one cannot assume that wider distribution necessarily means greater age, and while one must admit that the same rule may arise within the same family independently, of course in general the probability of these happenings is smaller than that of the contrary assumption. This is especially the case when the rules in question are not of the type which commonly arise again and again. Nonetheless, one must allow for the existence both of "drift," i.e. independent origin of the same rule within separated members of a family, and for the possibility of rule borrowing. And it might be claimed, for example, that a rule of the form o̲ to [w] before vowels, which plays an important role in our arguments above, is sufficiently common as not to rule out the possibility of multiple origin.[10]

It should therefore be pointed out that anyone who disputes the relative chronologies assumed in the arguments above must face the following kinds of difficulties. I shall consider only the assumed chronology: o̲ to [w] before vowels, penultimate accent, Mohawk [c] epenthesis. In Mohawk, Oneida, and Seneca, the basic stress rule accents the penultimate vowel within a word. But each language has developed subsidiary accent rules which affect at least some stress positions. Seneca, in particular, has developed a highly complex system of rules which are such that phonetic stress is only in the most indirect way related to the original penultimate accent. However, in all cases the vowel count for penultimate accent placement does not count the vowel of the [o] - [w] alternations which motivate the o̲ to [w] rule. Hence in Mohawk hra̲ + ko̲ + as̲ is [ra′kwas]. This then argues strongly that the accent rule is later in each of these languages than the o̲ to [w] rule. Further, the Mohawk epenthetic [e] rule in no case adds vowels which are counted in the accent placement. Therefore straightforward considerations show that [e] epenthesis is later than the o̲ to [w] rule.

In order to object to this argument it would be necessary to deny that

---

[10]What is really common is the shift of high back rounded vowels to [w] before other vowels. This fact is one of several arguing that the *phonetically* mid back rounded vowels [o] of Mohawk are actually *systematically* high ([+ Diffuse]) vowels. Other evidence for this derives from the fact that o̲ falls into a set with other diffuse vowels i̲, u̲ with respect to relevance for the gravity dissimilation of w̲ and p̲ discussed in Chapter 8. It seems then that these three vowels are divided from the other three Mohawk vowels a̲, ʌ, e̲ by being [+ Diffuse], that i̲ differs from o̲ and u̲ in terms of Grave, and that o̲ and u̲ are distinguished, as are a̲ ʌ, by nasality. Both ʌ and u̲ have phonetic manifestations which are [+ Nasal]. If this analysis is correct, it provides a rare instance where the nasality of nasal vowels is not predictable in systematic terms. The analysis is not entirely secure because there are rules which introduce both. [ʌ] and [u] in certain positions as a function of non-Nasal vowels. I have not, however, been able to justify any use of these rules to predict instances of lexical [ʌ] and [u]. For further discussion cf. Postal (to appear c).

the fact that the accent rule ignores the o̲ which switches to [w] means that the accent rule is later, or to deny that the fact that the accent rule ignores the vowels of the [e] epenthesis rule means that the epenthesis rule is later. But this can be done only at the cost of asserting that these rules were nonphonetic sound changes.[11] It thus appears that on grounds independent of Stammbaum considerations, any quarrel with the relative chronologies assumed above is poorly founded and in any event irrelevant to the deeper point. For any change of the chronologies of the rules for o̲ to [w], accent placement, and [e] epenthesis in Mohawk yields other nonphonetic sound changes. An analogous argument for Oneida yields the same conclusion for the rules of o̲ to [w], accent placement, and Oneida Accent Shift. Similar arguments can be given for the other cases involving p̲ and k̲ + w̲. It is thus evident that the relative chronologies are supported not only by Stammbaum considerations, but also by internal arguments which can be disputed at best only by positing nonphonetic sound changes of exactly the sort whose existence is supported by the argument with the originally assumed chronology. Thus the situation is as follows: the chronologies assumed in our arguments are supported by Stammbaum considerations, internal arguments, and limited textual evidence, all of which dovetail to support the same conclusions, which have never been questioned by students of Iroquoian (i.e. my chronological claims are completely uncontroversial). But more significantly, even if one should choose to deny the chronology, one would be led to the recognition of other nonphonetic sound changes so that the deeper point is maintained in any event.

It is also possible, I suppose, that someone will at this point wish to speak of analogy. It should be clear that all talk of this type is completely pointless and without foundation in these cases. As ordinarily understood, analogy only makes sense, if at all, to explain correspondences or lack of

---

[11]This ignores the logical possibility of setting up a large number of ad hoc changes which have no independent justification. For example, it might be hypothetically suggested that in fact [e] epenthesis addition is historically earlier than penultimate accent, but that these vowels are irrelevant for the stress count for the following reason. When first introduced they were rising-tone vowels, the subsequently added accent rule stressed only level-tone vowels. After a while, the rising-tone [e] fell together with other [e] as level-tone vowels. Such hypothetical accounts deserve no consideration whatever. For as noted earlier, if historical accounts are not constrained to pick the simplest solution and to accord with linguistic universals (which, for example, will specify rising-tone as Marked and thus highly unlikely to appear in an epenthesis rule), the claim that all rules are purely phonetic is empty. One can always construct a sufficiently long, ad hoc, chain of happenings which will reduce any set of changes to purely phonetic environments. The example given here is, of course, a straw man. But no other analysis conceivable to me really has any more justification. Epenthesis is clearly a unitary phenomenon which must be accounted for by a single rule. This means that it was either added to the grammar after the accent rule or was a nonphonetic sound change; etc.

them which cannot be brought under general rules (that is, rules operating for the lexicon as a whole.)[12] But in the cases we have considered, the correspondences *are* a result of general rules, although they are ones which violate the constraints imposed by the Neogrammarian view of sound change, which is thereby shown to be false. Notice further that in these cases there is nothing to analogize *to*, and indeed the force of analogy, had it operated, would have shifted the forms which violate the Neogrammarian constraint in such a way that they would not violate it. Especially in the case of the lack of epenthesis between first person and plural in Mohawk, all the force of analogy would be expected to have yielded epenthesis to bring the first person plural exclusive paradigm into line with the second person and inclusive paradigms. Clearly analogy can be invoked in these Iroquoian cases only as a kind of terminological magic wand.

[12]In his Doctoral Thesis, Kiparsky (1965) argues convincingly for the inadequacy of the proportional, allomorph-regularizing view of analogy. He proposes instead that analogy is actually a perfectly regular type of sound change involving the simplification and reordering of phonological rules.

Part III
DIACHRONIC SYNTAX

11

DIACHRONIC SYNTAX AND GENERATIVE GRAMMAR*

Elizabeth Closs Traugott

1. The Problem.[1] The objectives of diachronic linguistics have always been to reconstruct the particular steps by which a language changes, and also to hypothesize about processes of language change in general. Recent discussion of the latter problem has frequently involved five closely related proposals.[2] First, language changes by means of a series of individual innovations. These innovations consist primarily in the addition of single rules to the grammar of the adult speaker. Second, these innovations usually occur at some point of break in a grammar; for example, "before the first morphophonemic rule involving immediate constituent structure of the utterance . . . before the phonological rules that eliminate boundary markers from the representation."[3] Third, these innovations are passed on to the next generation when the child imitates the adult. A child may internalize the adult's grammar; or, more probably, he will simplify it. This is because children have an ability, not shared by most adults, to construct by induction from the utterances to which they have been exposed, the simplest grammar capable of generating sentences. The simplification will give rise to a discontinuity in transmission from generation to generation. In the interests of preserving intelligibility, this discontinuity will be minimal. Fourth, when-

*From *Language* 41. 402–415 (1965). Reprinted by permission of the author and the Linguistic Society of America.

[1]I am deeply indebted to Morris Halle and Edward S. Klima for valuable criticism of an earlier draft of this paper. My thanks are also due to Sheldon Sacks, James Sledd, and Robert P. Stockwell for many helpful suggestions.

[2]For these proposals and their corollary, see especially Morris Halle, "Phonology in generative grammar," *Word* 18.64–8 (1962), and the revised version in Jerry A. Fodor and Jerrold J. Katz, eds., *The Structure of Language: Readings in the Philosophy of Language*, 344–9 (Englewood Cliffs, N. J., 1964).

[3]*Word* 18.66, ft. 12; *Structure* 346, ft. 13.

ever the discontinuity results in radical changes such as restructuring, a mutation occurs. Finally, these mutations, which affect the overall simplicity of the grammar, are rare.

The significance of the intelligibility criterion is summarized by Halle as follows:[4]

> Linguistic change is normally subject to the constraint that it must not result in the destruction of mutual intelligibility between the innovators—i.e. the carriers of the change—and the rest of the speech community ... This restriction clearly affects the content of the rules to be added ... the number of rules to be added must also be restricted, for very serious effects on intelligibility can result from the simultaneous addition of even two or three otherwise innocuous rules.
>
> It may be somewhat less obvious that the requirement to preserve intelligibility also restricts the place in the order where rules may be added. All other things being equal, a rule will affect intelligibility less if it is added at a lower point in the order than if it is added higher up.

A corollary of these various proposals is that the simplest rules in a synchronic grammar will mirror the relative chronology of those additions which do not affect the overall simplicity of the grammar. In other words, synchronic grammars reflect INNOVATIONS. They do not, however, reflect MUTATIONS.

These arguments have been presented mainly in connexion with phonological change. Ramification in all other areas of the grammar has been taken for granted, but has not been investigated in detail. Klima hints at the validity of the general claim that a synchronic syntax reflects historical change when he remarks in his article, "Relatedness between grammatical systems,"[5]

> Although motivated by a purely synchronic principle of simplicity (shortness of rules), the order in which the styles are considered does, in fact, recapitulate comparable aspects in the historical development of the pronouns.

No systematic attempt has, however, been made to investigate the five hypotheses cited above in the light of syntactic change. It is the purpose of this paper to make such an attempt, and to draw some minimal conclusions which any theory of language change must include.

2. Representative Data. The investigation will be based on the history of the verbal auxiliary *Aux* in English. The relationship between one period of the language and another will be presented in terms of the relationships

---

[4]*Word* 18.66; *Structure* 346.
[5]*Lg.* 40.2 (1964).

between transformational generative[6] grammars of ninth-century Old English, mid-fifteenth-century Middle English, late-sixteenth-century Early Modern English,[7] and Modern English. By *Aux* I mean the tense marker, modals, the perfect and progressive helping verbs, and a few other helping verbs which will be specified in the course of this paper.

Attempts will be made to reconstruct the intermediate steps that account for the *Aux* structures and so to account for the types of innovations that can reasonably be assumed to underlie the observed mutations.

3. *Modern English.* Consider first Modern English *Aux* constructions as a type of control, since they are well known and have been accounted for in grammars that fulfill the strongest requirements of transformational generative theory.[8]

---

[6]The notion of grammar is developed by Noam Chomsky, *Syntactic structures* ('s-Gravenhage, 1957).

Questions have frequently been raised concerning the feasibility of using this notion of grammar in historical analysis, in particular concerning the appeal to intuition. A linguist theorizing about a living language ideally has as a control his own native intuition and that of the speakers around him, or at worst the native intuition of speakers of a language foreign to him. Against such intuition he can test, among other things, degrees of grammaticality and types of ambiguity. With dead languages, however, the linguist can rely only on the limited data available to him, and at best on a secondary "native intuition" which can arise only after several years of close association with the language. He can find very few, if any, syntactically minimal pairs from which to set up paradigms of grammatical versus ungrammatical sentences. Deviation and ambiguity are even more elusive. If we take in its strongest terms the requirement placed on linguistic theory that it should characterize and predict all and only the sentences of the language and also account for the native speaker's competence in producing and understanding utterances of the language, we might ultimately conclude that a grammar can be written only by a native speaker, not a foreigner, and that grammars of dead languages cannot be written at all. The degree of accuracy will naturally vary according to the degree of acquaintance with the language. But this does not mean that all investigation of language not native to the linguist must de facto be abandoned, any more than any theory of history, whether cultural or geological, must be rejected because we cannot recapture all and only the characteristics of previous eras. We may quite legitimately put forward a theory of a dead language, in terms of a grammar which fulfills the requirements of descriptive adequacy and explanatory power. This theory will be based on all observable data, and also on unobservable data when necessary, i.e. when the logical consequences of the model would not match the observable data without this hypothesis. As in analysis of a living language, that model will be the simplest which will characterize the sentences of the corpus, and so the infinite set of unobserved sentences which pattern with them. Within such a framework, deviance as well as grammaticality can tentatively be made explicit.

[7]For fuller versions of these grammars, see Closs, *Syllabus for English 110, History of English* 11–6, 24–9, 34–7 (mim., University of California, Berkeley, 1964); *Deep and surface structure in Old English* (in preparation).

[8]See especially Chomsky, "A transformational approach to syntax" in Archibald A. Hill, ed., *Third Texas conference on problems of linguistic analysis in English* 131–2,

The set of optional Modern English auxiliary verbs is established according to the following criteria: position relative to other verbs, especially in passives, negatives, emphatics, interrogatives; use in tag questions and other reduced sentences; occurrence with *n't*; and possibility of occurrence under weak stress. These verbs include (1) the subset of modals *M* (*can, may, must, shall, will*), which all require a following verb in its base form, as in *I will go, I will have gone* where *go* and *have* are base forms; (2) the nonmodal operators: *have* requiring a past participle marker *PP*, and *be* requiring a present participle marker *PrP*. Any one or more of these subsets of auxiliary verbs may occur optionally, but only in the order described: *M—have—PP —be—PrP.*

In addition to these optional formatives, every verbal construction obligatorily carries one tense marker *T*, whether the helping verbs are present or not. *T* always occurs with the first member of the construction: *He would have come,* **He will has come,* **He will have comes.* For this reason, *T* is generated to precede the helping verbs and *MV* and every *Aux* is said to contain at least *T*. The formants can all be generated by the following rules. Only those elements relevant to *Aux* constructions are included here.

3.1 S→NP—VP

3.2 VP→Aux—MV

3.3 MV→ $\left\{ \begin{array}{l} V_t\text{—}NP \\ V_iNP \\ \vdots \end{array} \right\}$

3.4 Aux→T (M) (have—PP) (be—PrP)

3.5 M→can, may, must, shall, will

A low-level affix switch rule assigns *T* to its correct position after the verbal base immediately following it.

Verbal constructions with *do* can all be accounted for by blocking the minimal auxiliary formant *T* from the main verb base in negatives, emphatics, interrogatives, tag questions, and imperatives, as in

(1) *He does not go*

(2) *He does go*

(3) *Does he go?*

(4) *What does she see?*

(5) *She went home, did she?*

(6) *Do be good*

144–7 (Austin, 1962); Klima, "Negation in English" in Fodor and Katz, eds., *The structure of language: Readings in the philosophy of language* 251–3 et passim; Robert B. Lees, *A grammar of English nominalizations* 19–20 et passim (Bloomington, 1960). For a discussion of the criteria by which the set of auxiliary verbs is set up, see James Sledd, *A short introduction to English grammar* 106–9 (Chicago, 1959).

In other words, *do* is automatically and obiligatorily generated as a dummy carrier wherever *T* is blocked from a main verb base *MV*.

4. *Old English*.[9] The shape of the optional part of *Aux* was considerably different at other stages of the language, and this one factor to a very large extent accounts for the differences in structure of active statements, and also of passives, negatives, and interrogatives.

As at all other periods, *T* was obligatory in Old English. There is a subset of the optional helping verbs which functions very largely like the subset of modern modals, and whose members are actually their cognates: *cunn-, mag-, mot-, scul-, will-,* all requiring an infinitive marker *Inf*. These may be exemplified by

(7) *Or.214.5: Ac þær hie hit georne ongitan cuþen* 'But when they could readily understand it'

(8) *Or.100.19 Ic mæg eac on urum agnum tidum gelic anginn þæm gesecgan* 'I can also tell of a beginning similar to that in our own times'

(9) *Or.30.33: For ðon þe hio hyre firenluste fulgan ne moste* 'Because she could not satisfy her desires'

(10) *Or.218.20: Ic sceal eac niede þara monegena gewinna geswigian þe on eastlondum gewurdon* 'I shall also by necessity be silent about those many battles that took place in the East'

(11) *Or.140.30: Þa he & þa consulas hie attellan ne mehton* 'When he and the consuls could not count them'

In addition there is the cognate of the Modern English perfect helping verb, *habban* 'to have' which requires *PP*, provided that *MV* is transitive (V_t):

(12) *Or.172.18: Ac him hæfdon Pene þone weg forseten* 'But the Carthaginians had blocked his way'

Occasionally *MV* may be one of a small set of intransitives (V_i), largely a set of verbs of movement, here classified as $V_{i_{move}}$, as in

(13) *Or.196.22: Þa Scipia hæfde gefaren* 'When Scipio had gone'

The perfect auxiliary of intransitives is regularly, however, formed by the verb *wesan* 'to be'—*PP*, as in

(14) *Or.4.17: Hu Orosius sæde þæt he wære cumen* 'How Orosius said that he had come'

(15) *Or.236.19: Þider hi þa mid firde gefaren wæron* 'To the place where they had then marched with the army'

---

[9]Quotations for Old English are derived from Henry Sweet, ed., *King Alfred's Orosius*, EETS 79 (London, 1883), abbreviated *Or.*; and from Henry Sweet, ed., *King Alfred's West-Saxon version of Gregory's Pastoral Care*, EETS 45, 50 (London, 1871), abbreviated *CP*. References are to page and line numbers.

There are also three progressive auxiliary verbs requiring *PrP* (realized in Old English as *-ende*). They are *wesan* 'to be', *beon* 'to be', and *weorðan* 'to become', here classified as the subset *BE*. Examples of each of these progressives are

(16) *Or.*236.29: *& him æfterfylgende wæs* 'And was following him'

(17) *Or.*12.35: *Þæt seo ea bið flowende ofer eal Ægypta land* 'So that this river floods all the land of Egypt'

(18) *CP.*405.25: *Ð in eagan weorðað gesionde ðinne bebiodend* 'Your eyes shall see your master'

Progressive auxiliary verbs may occur with *M*, but apparently not with perfect auxiliary verbs. In (19), for example, we find *M* and progressive. Sentences like (20) with *M* and progressive would be possible, but not (21) with *M* and perfect auxiliary nor (22) with *M*—perfect—progressive:

(19) *Or.*110.10: *Nu ic wille eac þæs maran Alexandres gemunende beon* 'Now I shall also consider Alexander the Great'

(20) *Ic sceal feohtende beon* 'I shall be fighting'

(21) **Ic sceal gefuhten habban* 'I shall have fought'

(22) **Ic sceal feohtende gebeon habban* 'I shall have been fighting'

A further restriction is placed on the nonmodal operators: they do not occur in passive formations. Although we find (23) with the passive auxiliary formant (*BE* requiring *PP*) in the environment of *M*, (24) and (25) with passive formants in the environment of perfect and progressive auxiliary verbs respectively are ungrammatical:

(23) *Or.*128.5: *Þa Darius geseah þæt he oferwunnen beon wolde* 'When Darius saw that he would be conquered'

(24) **Þæt he oferwunnen geworden hæfde* 'That he had been overcome'

(25) **Þæt he oferwunnen wesende wæs* 'That he was being overcome'

The examples above demonstrate that the word order is very different from that in Modern English. At the end of the ninth century the following patterns are favored, but are by no means exclusive:[10]

(a) In coordinate *and* clauses and in subordinate clauses, especially temporal clauses with time adverbs, the finite verb (*MV* carrying *T*) often

---

[10]Recent detailed discussion of word-order problems include S. O. Andrew, *Syntax and style in Old English* (Cambridge, 1940); Paul Bacquet, *La structure de la phrase verbale à l'époque Alfrédienne* (Paris, 1962); C. R. Barrett, *Studies in the word-order of Aelfric's Catholic Homilies and Lives of the Saints* (Cambridge, 1953); Charles R. Carlton, *Syntax of the Old English Charters* 170–256 (unpub. doctoral diss., Michigan, 1958); David P. Harris, "The development of word-order patterns in twelfth-century English" in Albert H. Marckwardt, ed., *Studies in languages and linguistics in honor of Charles C. Fries* 187–98 (University of Michigan, 1964); Bruce Mitchell, "Syntax and word-order in 'The Peterborough Chronicle' 1122–1154," *Neuphilologische Mitteilungen* 65.113–44 (1964).

occurs at the end. If there are helping verbs, *MV* will usually be followed by the nonmodal operators and *M*. The last helping verb will carry *T*. For coordinates see (16), for subordinates (7), (9), (11), (15), (23).[11]

(b) In independent clauses,[12] the finite verb occurs nonfinally except in simple intransitive sentences. If a helping verb is present, *MV* will usually be preceded by *M* or a nonmodal operator, as in (8), (10), (12), (18). When there are two helping verbs, *M* will usually precede *MV*, and the perfect or progressive will follow, as in (19).

Most linguists consider that the order subject (*SU*)—object (*O*)—main verb (*MV*) + auxiliary (*Aux*) which is typical of coordinate and dependent clauses is a "reversal" of the normal order *SU—Aux—MV—O*. In terms of simplicity of description and explanatory power, however, it is by far the simplest to set up the Old English verb phrase in the order *SU (O) MV* + *Aux*. This will automatically account for most coordinate and subordinate clauses. A rule will then specify that in independent clauses the last helping verb is moved to position before *MV*; in this way just one rule will account for the fact that if there is one helping verb, it precedes *MV*, but if there are two, only *M* precedes *MV*. Other orders will be accounted for by a stylistic variant rule. Independent motivation for such an analysis is provided by negative constructions formed with *ne*. If the verb is finite, *ne* precedes *MV*:

(26) *Or*.19.10: *He cwæð þæt nan man ne bude be norðan him* 'He said that no man lived north of him'

If there is a helping verb in type-(a) sentences, *ne* precedes the last helping verb, as in (9), (11); in type-(b) sentences it precedes whichever helping verb precedes *MV*. The negative of (19) would therefore be

(27) *Nu ic nille eac þæs maran Alexandres gemunende beon* 'Now I shall also not consider Alexander the Great'

Furthermore, this analysis obviates the necessity of an affix switch rule, a rule which has no independent motivation, especially as *T* never has to be blocked from *MV* in Old English to generate a dummy carrier.

The *Aux* will therefore be optimally generated by [13]

4.1   S → NP—VP

---

[11](13), (14), (17) are examples of deviation from this rule.

[12]"Independent clauses" here include "demonstrative clauses" introduced by demonstrative adverbs *þa* 'then', *þonne* 'then', *þær* 'there' in which the finite verb or one helping verb usually precedes the subject (cf. Andrew, *Syntax and style in Old English* 3). Both independent clauses with demonstrative adverbs and those without share the main features of verb order under discussion.

[13]The rules are particularly interesting in that they are basically similar to those suggested by Emmon Bach for German, "The order of elements in a transformational grammar of German," *Lg*. 38.263–9 (1962).

V_{ix} in Rule 4.4 stands for the class of all V_1 that are not $V_{i\ move}$. It includes verbs homonymous with the members of $V_{i\ move}$.

4.2 $VP \rightarrow MV + Aux$

4.3 $MV \rightarrow \begin{Bmatrix} NP{-}V_t \\ V_i \\ \vdots \end{Bmatrix}$

4.4 $V_i \rightarrow \begin{Bmatrix} V_{i_{move}} \\ V_{i_x} \end{Bmatrix}$

4.5 $Aux \rightarrow \left(\begin{Bmatrix} PP{-}habb, \text{ in env. } V_t\_\_, V_{i_{move}}\_\_ \\ PP{-}wes, \text{ in env. } V_i\_\_ \\ (PrP{-}BE)\,(Inf{-}M) \end{Bmatrix} \right) \quad T$

4.6 $M \rightarrow$ cunn, mag, mot, scul, will

4.7 $BE \rightarrow$ beo, wes, weorþ

5. *Middle English.*[14] By the thirteenth century, the normal word order is similar to that in Modern English. That is, we find *Aux—MV (O)* favored in both independent and dependent clauses. The simplicity criterion therefore requires that this order be generated as basic for Middle English. Such analysis furthermore provides just the kind of information we need to account for the fundamental differences in verb-phrase order between Old and Middle English. Although there is not the independent motivation that *do* provides in Modern English for setting up the members of *Aux* in the order *T (M)* . . . , since no dummy carrier is generable in Middle English, this analysis is simplest, as all other orders can then be derived easily from the basic form. Other constructions can also be neatly accounted for. The negative, for example, is formed during the earlier part of the Middle English period by *ne* preceding *T*—first base as in (28); or by *nat* following *T*—first base as in (29); or by both *ne* and *nat* as in (30). By the fifteenth century, negatives are more generally formed by *not ~ nat* after *T*—first base, as in (31), (32):

   (28) Ch.*Mel.*2266: *He ne foond neuere womman good* 'He never found a good woman'

   (29) Ch.*Mel.*2170: *It aperteneth nat to a wys man* 'It is not suitable for a wise man'

   (30) Ch.*Mel.*2220: *Yet ne wolde he nat answere sodeynly* 'Yet he did not want to answer immediately'

   (31) PL.III.104.22 (1456): *And yff the maters went not to my maister entent* 'And if the matters did not go according to what my master had planned'

[14]Quotations for Middle English are taken from Hans Kurath, Sherman Kuhn, John Reidy, eds., *Middle English dictionary* (Ann Arbor, 1954—); James Gairdner, ed., *The Paston letters 1422–1509* (London, 1904), abbreviated *PL.*, with references to volume, page, and line numbers; and Geoffrey Chaucer, *The text of the Canterbury Tales*, ed. John M. Manly and Edith Rickert (Chicago, 1940).

(32) *PL.*III.87.1 (1456): *And of suche as I will not write* 'And of such things as I will not write about'

As far as the shape of *Aux* is concerned, there has been considerable increase in the complexity of membership, but there is already greater environmental generalization for the perfect participle constructions. The modals are the cognates of the Old English forms and need not concern us here. As in Old English, Early Middle English modals require *Inf*, but owing to a regular late-fourteenth- and early-fifteenth-century rule, this marker is lost and is usually not overtly marked by the mid-fifteenth century. The perfect auxiliary has undergone partial reversal of context restriction: *have—PP* is used for both transitives and intransitives:

(33) *PL.*III.103.24 (1456): *Which Fenn hath promised* (V_t) *to doo* 'Which Fenn has promised to do'

(34) *PL.*IV.1710: *Wherfore the people was greved be cauce they had labored* (V_i) *so often* 'For this reason the people were grieved because they had labored so often'

(35) Ch.*Mel.*3000: *For ye han entred* (V_i) *in to myn hous by violence* 'For you have entered my house by violence'

A subset of V_i may also occur with *be—PP*; its members, interestingly enough, are mainly the cognates of exactly those same verbs of movement which in Old English were the only ones that could occur with *habb—PP*:

(36) *PL.*IV.68.13: *But I undrestande ther is comen an other writte to the undrescheryff* 'But I understand that another writ has come to the undersheriff'

(37) Ch.*Mel.*2160: *And by wyndowes ben entred* 'And have entered through the windows'

There is only one progressive formant: the verb *be* requiring *PrP*. More significant for the history of *Aux* is that the perfect occasionally follows the modal and the progressive occasionally appears after the perfect helping verb, instead of being mutually exclusive with it. When this is the case, only *have—PP*, not *be—PP*, precedes the progressive formant. Examples of this complex construction occur mainly in poetry, as in Chaucer's *Knight's Tale*:

(38) Ch.*Kt.T.*929: *We have been waytynge al this fortenyght* 'We have been waiting all this fortnight'

(39) **We been been waytynge al this fortenyght*

Of special interest is the additional use from Early Middle English times of *do* and *gin* as auxiliaries, both requiring *Inf* at their first introduction.[15] Both were originally used only as main verbs; throughout the period

---

[15]Clear loss of identity as *MV* is indicated by the occasional interchange in different MSS of *gin—Inf* and *do—Inf*; cf. *Cursor Mundi*, Göt. 2009 (c. 1400): *A neu liuelad gan he bigin* 'He began a new kind of life', with MS variants *con, cun* (reduced forms of *gan*) and

homonymous verbs *do* 'to cause to' and *gin* 'to begin to' persist as main verbs taking infinitive complement nominalizations; another homonymous verb *do* was a member from Old English times of a small class of substitutive verbs. The auxiliary verbs in question originated in poetry; *do* spread to prose by the late fourteenth century, cf.

> (40)   *Appeal Usk in Bk.Lond.E.26/101 (1384): So they diden pursuwe thynges a-yeins the Franchise of london for euer* 'So they pursued matters opposing the franchise of London for ever'

Gin, however, never became established in prose. Only *do* is generated as a formant in the mid-fifteenth-century grammar; a complete version of this grammar would generate *gin* as a deviant member of *Aux*, restricted to poetry. A grammar of Middle English prior to c.1380 would, however, specify restriction to poetry of both *do—Inf* and *gin—Inf* (*Inf* is still marked at this time).[16]

Among examples of auxiliary *do* in the *Paston Letters* are

> (41)   *PL.III.2.26 (1454): As for the prist that dede areste me* 'As for the priest who arrested me'
>
> (42)   *PL.IV.149.37 (1465) More plainly than I may do wryte at thys tyme* 'More plainly than I may write at this time'
>
> (43)   *PL.IV.143.14 (1465) Yf they wold do pay such dewts* 'If they would pay such debts'

From (42), (43) and several other passages, it is clear that *do* may occur after *M* and *have—PP*. There is independent motivation for analysing *do* as a second position nonmodal operator mutually exclusive with *be—PrP*: both, for example, fail to occur in passive formation.

The grammar must therefore specify at least the following phrase markers:

5.1 $S \rightarrow NP$—VP

5.2 $VP \rightarrow Aux$—MV

5.3 $MV \rightarrow \begin{Bmatrix} V_t\text{---}NP \\ V_i \\ \vdots \end{Bmatrix}$

5.4 $V_i \rightarrow \begin{Bmatrix} V_{i_{move}} \\ V_{i_x} \end{Bmatrix}$

5.4 $V_i \rightarrow$

5.5 $Aux \rightarrow T (M) \left(\begin{Bmatrix} (have\text{---}PP & \begin{pmatrix} be\text{---}Prp \\ do \end{pmatrix} \\ be\text{---}PP, \text{ in env.} & \text{---}V_{i_{move}} \end{Bmatrix} \right)$

5.6 $M \rightarrow$ conn, mow, moot, shal, wol

---

also *dud*. A summary and bibliography of studies on *do* and *gin* is provided in Tauno F. Mustanoja, *A Middle English syntax I: Parts of speech* 600–15 (Helsinki, 1960).

[16]On some of the problems in accounting for specifically poetic deviance, cf. Samuel R. Levin, "Poetry and grammaticalness," in Horace Lunt, ed., *Proceedings of the ninth international congress of linguists* 308–15 ('s-Gravenhage, 1964).

6. *Early Modern English.*[17] By the late sixteenth century we find further changes. The chief of these are further development of *have—PP* in the environment of V_i; the spread of *do* as an auxiliary verb; and the appearance of the progressive in passive constructions.

As in Middle English, *do* is not a dummy carrier, but a regular optional member of *Aux*; do constructions occur side by side with finite verb constructions in unemphatic assertion, negative, and interrogative sentence types. In one particular, however, the behavior of *do* differs from that of its cognate in middle English: it invariably occurs without other helping verbs:

(44) *N.I.191.21–5: Alledging many examples . . . how studie dooth effeminate a man* 'Alleging there were many examples . . . of how study makes a man effeminate'

(45) **Alledging many examples how study may do effeminate a man.*

(46) *N.I.158.17: Thereby I grew to consider how many base men . . . enjoyed content at will* 'From this I came to consider how many base men . . . enjoyed contentment at will'

(47) *N.I.185.16: I do not doubt (Doctor Diuell) but you were present* 'I do not doubt (Dr. Devil) that you were present'

(48) *N.I.208.12: That loue not to goe in greasie dublets* 'That do not like to walk about in greasy doublets'

(49) *N.II.314.1: Why did I enter into anie mention of my owne misusage?* 'Why did I make any mention of the way I myself was misused?'

(50) *N.II.302.5: Why iest I in such a necessarie perswasiue discourse?* 'Why do I jest in such a necessary persuasive discourse?'

A few Early Modern Northern manuscripts still show use of *do* after other operators, both in prose and in poetry:

(51) *Reg.Manor Scawby Lincolnsh.* (1597): *That the Carrgraues shall doe execute theire office truely* 'That the Cargraves shall execute their duties properly'

(52) *Scot.poems 16th C.II.189* (1578): *And many other false abusion The Paip hes done invent* 'And the Pope has invented many other false abuses'

Since *do* as a second-position nonmodal operator is restricted to Northern dialects, we may assume that by the sixteenth century in England at least *do* had become an independent helping verb, mutually exclusive with modals, perfect and progressive auxiliaries; it is still incompatible with the passive formant.

---

[17]Data for Early Modern English are derived from the *Oxford English dictionary*; and Ronald B. McKerrow, ed., *The works of Thomas Nashe* (Oxford, 1958), abbreviated *N.*, with references to volume, line, and page numbers.

In the light of the considerations given above, *Aux* may be set up for Early Modern English by the following rules:

6.1 $S \rightarrow NP—VP$

6.2 $VP \rightarrow Aux—MV$

6.3 $MV \rightarrow \left\{ \begin{array}{l} V_t—NP \\ V_i \\ \vdots \end{array} \right\}$

6.4 $V_i \rightarrow \left\{ \begin{array}{l} V_{i_{move}} \\ V_{i_x} \end{array} \right\}$

6.5 $Aux \rightarrow T \left(\left\{ \begin{array}{l} (M) \\ \\ do \end{array} \right\} \left(\left\{ \begin{array}{l} (\text{have}—PP)\ (\text{be}—PrP) \\ \text{be}—PP, \text{ in env.}\underline{\quad\quad}V_{i_{move}} \end{array} \right\} \right) \right)$

6.6 $M \rightarrow$ can, may, must, shall, will

Of particular interest is the sporadic appearance of the progressive in passive formations. Unlike passive constructions with other members of *Aux*, these passives are not formed with *be—PP*. We find patterns of the kind *The man is seeing by X*, not *The man is being seen by X*.[18]

(53)   Deloney, *Gentle Craft* 132.45:[19] *While meat was bringing in* 'While food was being brought in'

The final stages in the development to Modern English consist in the loss of *be—PP* in the environment of most intransitive verbs, the restriction of *do* during the eighteenth and nineteenth centuries to certain explicitly determined environments, and the requirement of *be—PP* in passive constructions, whatever the membership of *Aux*. At the present stage of the language, *Aux* provides the least choices, but is also maximally generalized.

7. *Types of Change.* These then are the major mutations in the history of *Aux*. Comparison of the different grammars reveals several types of change, all of which have far-reaching effects on sentence structure. The changes may be summarized as follows:

(a)   reversal of order;

(b)   loss of class-context restriction;

(c)   realignments of existing structures, without radical system change, as when the Old English maximal *Aux* was extended to *T (M)* and two successive optional nonmodal operators;

---

[18]The latter is a modern construction which did not come into general use until the nineteenth century. The first clear instance of a passive of this type cited by Fernand Mossé, *Histoire de la forme périphrastique être + participe présent II: Moyen-anglais et anglais moderne* par. 263 (Paris, 1938), is from a letter by Robert Southey: *A fellow whose uppermost upper grinder is being torn out by a mutton-fisted barber.* For detailed discussion of the history of the passive progressive, see Mossé, ibid., pars. 231–81.

[19]Thomas Deloney, *Works*, ed. Francis O. Mann (Oxford, 1912).

(d) addition or loss of formants, as when *do* was added, and later when *be—PP* (perfect auxiliary verb) was lost;

(e) and finally, closely related with this, really radical changes of system membership, e.g. when *do*, which was a member of the lexical system, gave rise to an operator in the syntactic system; or later when *do*, which was an optional member of *Aux*, became an obligatory, predictable element, generable as a formative in the transformational component.

8. Innovations Accounting for Changes. It remains to be seen how these changes came about and how they may be considered a paradigm of language change in general.

The minimal change that must be postulated to account for reversal of word order is the growing tendency to favor *SU—Aux—MV (O)* order in all clauses. This tendency, which is amply attested by twelfth-century data, must have developed in two stages: first, preponderance of constructions with a finite verb or one helping verb preceding *O*, as in (19); and second, attraction of a second optional member of *Aux*, if present, to pre-*O* position. The word "tendency" is used advisedly. All through Old English, both *Aux—MV* and *MV + Aux* patterns existed. What must be accounted for is the fact that the optimal grammar for Old English specifies *MV + Aux* and a rule allowing for certain stylistic switches of auxiliary verbs, but no affix-switch rule. The optimal grammar for Middle English, on the other hand, specifies *Aux—MV*, a rule allowing for certain stylistic switches of auxiliary verbs, and an affix-switch rule. Any synchronic Old English grammar will mirror the two orders for auxiliary verbs. For Middle English we need a new grammar. In other words, the mutations can only be reflected by a different set of rules.[20]

---

[20] A synchronic grammar cannot account for these changes, except so far as it treats different dialects, or different reflexes of different changes. When Klima says the order in which he describes the rules for pronouns in different dialects reflects the historic order of change, he is actually referring to the order of mutations, not innovations. Each set of rules for each dialect requires different ordering of basically the same rules. Each set has its own unique relationship to the rest in the structure of the language, and cannot be collapsed under the same grammar except as a discrete subset of the grammar. It has been suggested that grammars should provide rules accounting for synchronic relatedness between grammatical systems, such that different systems may be regarded as modifications or extensions of a given basic system. This is essentially what Klima's grammar does for pronouns. In addition, it has been suggested that grammars should provide rules accounting for diachronic relatedness between grammatical systems, also such that the different systems may be regarded as modifications or extensions of a given basic system. Such grammars would reveal with great clarity the similarities and differences between stages of the language, and would provide in simpler, i.e. more compact, form the same information

The same is true of changes in context restriction of the perfect auxiliary. As OE *habb—PP* came to predominate, it took over the function of *BE—PP*. We might postulate that since those intransitive verbs that were most frequently used (verbs of movement) could occur with both *habb—PP* and *BE—PP*, $V_{i_{move}}$ became a model for other intransitive verbs which, although more numerous, were less frequently used. It is also noteworthy that Middle English was a time when word formation by changes of class membership or extension to new class membership was becoming particularly common; in particular, many new transitives were being formed from intransitives.[21] This meant that class-context restriction was no longer clear, and that ambiguity between the perfect auxiliary formant *be—PP* and the homonymous passive formant could arise.[22]

A further innovation was the extension of the mutually exclusive set of perfect and progressive auxiliaries to two compatible nonmodal operators. Throughout the history of English up to the nineteenth century, and still today in the case of most sentences in which the main verb is the copula *be*, the structure "base *be* followed by base *be*" has been ungrammatical or at least deviant. Although Modern English sentences of the type *The students are being attacked* are grammatical, *The students are being hungry* is ungrammatical. Strong pressure against such structures must account for the lack of passive progressives with the passive formant in Early Modern English. It also seems to account for the lack of progressives following perfect auxiliaries of the type *be—PP* in Middle English. Unless we are to assume that perfects followed by progressive helping verbs were possible only in transitive verb constructions, we are led to conclude that the two nonmodal operators became compatible AFTER both intransitives and transitives could take *have—PP* as the perfect auxiliary. Once the two became compatible, a mutation arose.

Although I have attempted so far to cover only those changes that took place within the *Aux* rule alone, I have had to mention far-reaching repercussions on the whole system. Change in word order requires, for simplicity of description and explanatory power, the introduction of an affix-switch rule. Behavior of progressive auxiliaries raises the question of the cooccurrence of two *be* bases. Other changes in the *Aux* further demonstrate clear cases of

---

that separate grammars of different stages of the language provide. They cannot, however, specify actual change or provide historical perspective. A grammar of the actual changes would be a kind of algebra accounting in the simplest way possible for all relevant changes, in their chronological order.

[21]See F. Th. Visser, *An historical syntax of the English language* 93–138 (Leiden, 1963).

[22]Visser, ibid. 131, suggests that this ambiguity was one of the factors leading to the transitivization of intransitives.

overall system changes. *Do*, which was a main verb requiring infinitive nominalizations, came to be reinterpreted as an auxiliary, presumably because it was followed by an unmarked infinitive. Perhaps pressure of continued association with the main verb *do* (which, as a main verb, could be preceded by auxiliary verbs) countered the tendency to use *do* in modal position; instead it came to fill the same slot as the progressive. This slot was in itself somewhat variable since it was an innovation. The very character of this third position may account for the fact that *do* came to be used more and more as an independent unit which could not tolerate other auxiliary verbs in its environment. Its failure to pattern with other members of *Aux* then further favored the eventual mutation, by Modern English, to nonmembership in the regular *Aux* construction, and to restriction to certain predictable environments.

9. *Theory of Language Change.* Given a knowledge of mutations, such as those in the development of *Aux*, and of the innovations that account for those mutations, can we say that the five proposals for a theory of language change outlined at the beginning of this paper account for syntactic change?

The proposition that language changes by means of a series of individual innovations seems to be fully supported by the history of the *Aux*, in which we can see each step develop individually. The second proposal is that the innovations usually occur at the end of some natural division of the grammar. This must give us pause. Within the syntactic component there are three main points of break: the point where the phrase structure ends and the lexicon begins; the point where the lexicon ends and the transformational subcomponent begins; and finally the point where the syntactic component ends and the morphophonemic begins.[23] Of the changes discussed, the only one that enters at such a break is the affix-switch rule, and this is the result of a mutation, not an innovation giving rise to a mutation; besides, it is largely motivated by simplicity of description rather than by actual language data when it is introduced for Middle English. Changes in context restriction of

---

[23]Further subdivisions may or may not be made according to the particular model of grammar adopted. Grammars like Lees's *Grammar of English nominalizations* allow for certain groupings in the phrase structure according to sets of subcategorizations; Charles Fillmore's study "The position of embedding transformations in a grammar," *Word* 19.208–31 (1963), specifies groupings for two-string vs. one-string transformations. In the latest models, however, such as Chomsky's blocking grammar and Klima's nonblocking grammar (cf. Klima, "Current developments in generative grammar," forthcoming in *Kybernetika* I, Prague), the phrase-structure component is minimal and cannot be subject to groupings. Context restrictions and subcategorizations are largely specified in a lexicon in which the only significant groupings are the overall categories *N*, *V*, *Adj*, etc.; only in the filter transformations do we find areas in which the concept "point of break" is significant for syntax.

the perfect and progressive verbs occur within the high-level *Aux* rule, and do not enter at the end of the phrase structure. *Do* extends lexical membership of the category of infinitive complement taking transitives to nonlexical membership of this same high-level *Aux* rule; again, it is not possible to hypothesize that it entered as a low-level phrase-structure subcategory and was then reinterpreted as part of the *Aux*. The third proposal, that innovations are passed on to generation after generation, and the fourth, that mutations occur when the new generation reinterprets a grammar so as to effect radical changes such as restructuring, seem to be well borne out by syntactic evidence. The viability of the fifth proposal, however, that mutations are rare, is doubtful as far as syntactic change is concerned. The *Aux*, which is such a small part of the grammar, demonstrates at least six types of mutation. The four different types of pronominal usage which Klima discusses support in a totally unrelated area the observation that mutation in syntax is not rare, although it seems to be relatively infrequent in phonological change.

In view of the factors discussed above it appears that any theory of language change must include the proposals that language changes by means of the addition of single innovations to an adult's grammar, by transmission of these innovations to new generations, and by the reinterpretation of grammars such that mutations occur. Restriction of innovations to points of break seems not to be viable as a generalization for language change, nor does the statement that mutations are rare. Both these proposals must be limited to the area of phonological change.

12

DIACHRONIC CHANGE IN THE COMPLEMENT SYSTEM*

Robin Lakoff

A comparison of the superficial syntax of the complement systems of Latin and Spanish might surprise the linguist who expects that two closely related languages will look alike in all respects. He is already aware from comparing lexical entries in the two languages that there is a very high correlation between words found in Latin and words found, with the almost same form and the same or virtually the same meaning, in Spanish. If he were to inspect the phonology of the two languages, he would find that Spanish shared a great many of the rules of Latin, though perhaps differently ordered, and that the superficial form of the phonological component of Spanish is easily identified as derived from Latin. Even in the morphology, where more change is discernible, the relationship is apparent: each of the tense-endings in Spanish can be shown to be derived from a readily identifiable Latin form.[1] Even though the classical Latin grammar did not, for example, make use of *habeo* to form auxiliaries, as Spanish uses *haber*, still *habeo* exists in Latin, and is occasionally found as a sort of auxiliary even in the classical language.[2] But when one comes to inspect the syntax of Spanish, one finds that, on the surface, it resembles that of Latin very little. The complement system is a case in point.

---

*Reprinted from *Abstract Syntax and Latin Complementation* by Robin Lakoff by permission of the M.I.T. Press, Cambridge, Massachusetts, and of the author. Copyright © 1968.

[1]The reader is referred for discussion to the following works: J. Foley, *Spanish Morphology*, doctoral dissertation (unpublished), Cambridge, Mass.: M.I.T., 1965. P. Kiparsky, *Phonological Change*, doctoral dissertation (unpublished), Cambridge, Mass.: M.I.T., 1965.

[2]For example, as early as Plautus *habeo factum* is used with the meaning 'I have (something) done,' a meaning very close to 'I have done (something).' *Fidem quam habent spectatam iam et diu cognitam.* (Cic. Caec. 11) 'The faith that they have already seen and long known.'

6.1 Previous Work on Syntactic Change

A cursory inspection of complement sentences in Spanish will convince the examiner that the grammar of Spanish has little to do with the grammar of Latin. The distribution of the various complementizers in Spanish is very different from that of Latin, and the complementizers themselves are different in form. Complement rules, such as equi-NP-deletion and *it*-substitution, occur in Spanish where they do not in Latin, and vice versa. For these and other reasons, it is easy to understand why most traditional grammarians who have dealt with the subject have concluded that there is a drastic change between Latin and Spanish and that there is little relationship between Latin constructions and most of their equivalents in Spanish. If this is true, then syntactic change is different from phonological change, where there is no wholesale changing of rules.

Historical linguists tracing the changes in syntax between Latin and Spanish have had surprisingly little to say of substantive value. All that is usually done is to document changes in constructions, note when the first indications of each change were observed, and give subjective explanations of how each change might have been induced. The changes in one construction—for example, in the purpose clause—were felt not to be related to the changes in any other construction—for example, in the types of complementizers that could follow verbs of wanting—because there was no mechanism at the disposal of Romance philologists to account for any relationship between superficially different constructions.

In the preceding chapters, we have proposed and discussed a theory in which the superficial forms of sentences may be very different from their underlying forms. The idea that the same abstract representation might produce very different superficial representations, with different sets of rules, enables serious work in syntactic change to begin. The first serious and detailed study of syntactic change in a generative grammar was done by Klima. He showed that, for English, changes in the syntax could be produced by changes in the ordering of rules, rather than by the rules themselves.[3] In this chapter, we shall consider changes of a different sort.

We shall restrict ourselves to an examination of a few of the rules that have been discussed in the second and third chapters in order to see whether and how each occurs in the grammar of modern Spanish and, if there are changes from Latin, how these changes may be described and whether the resultant complement system of Spanish differs from that of Latin. Where it differs, we shall attempt to pinpoint the location of the difference and see in what part of the grammar these differences occur.

[3]For example, in "Relatedness between Grammatical Systems," *Language*, Vol. 40, No. 1 (January–March 1964), pp. 1–20.

6.2 The Location in the Grammar of Governed-Rule Change

In our inspection of the changes in the complement system between Latin and Spanish, we shall be dealing almost exclusively with governed rules. Some of the changes that will be examined are the following:

1. The complementizers that occur with various classes of verbs in Latin are usually different from the ones that occur with corresponding words in Spanish. In some cases we shall find a situation that occurs nowhere in Latin: that the choice of complementizer in certain classes of words is dependent on whether the noun of the lower sentence is identical to that of the higher sentence.
2. The complementizers themselves look different from their Latin counterparts, even when they appear to be performing identical functions in the grammar. Thus, *que*-subjunctive does not look like *ut*-subjunctive, but it is used in much the same way.
3. Equi-NP-deletion applies in more classes of verbs in Spanish than it does in Latin. It is also obligatory in Spanish: in Latin the rule is frequently optional (as in verbs of wishing) or nonapplicable (as in verbs of saying and thinking).
4. *It*-substitution occurs in Spanish optionally in subject complements where it does not occur in Latin. (In Latin it occurs in underlying subject complements only if it obligatorily applies in a given class of verbs; it is never optional. In Spanish it is optional for some classes of subject complements.)
5. Sentence types that in the last chapter we suggested were produced through the presence of abstract verbs sometimes behave differently in Spanish. We shall ask whether the change follows any pattern.

Upon inspection of the types of changes just summarized, it will be seen that there is no need to change any of the transformational rules that have been given in order to describe the changes from Latin to Spanish. The changes all come about because of changes in the properties of the verbs themselves. In the second chapter the operation of redundancy rules in the grammar of English was discussed, and in the third chapter their operation in the grammar of Latin. These redundancy rules specified which of the governed rules each meaning-class of verbs underwent. For example, a redundancy rule states that in Latin *for-to* complementizer-change is obligatory for verbs of saying and thinking, and *ut*-subjunctive complementizer-change for verbs of ordering. For a verb of saying or thinking, if it takes *for-to*, it is unmarked, and if it takes anything else, it is marked. But a verb of ordering taking *for-to* is marked, while such a verb taking *ut*-subjunctive is unmarked. For verbs of wanting and wishing, the choice is optional between *for-to* and *ut*-subjunctive. It is stated nowhere in the transformational component that *impero* undergoes *ut*-subjunctive complementizer-change and that *iubeo* undergoes *for-to*. Nor is it stated in any way in any of the transformational rules that *impero* is regular and *iubeo* irregular. The fact that *impero* takes *ut*-subjunctive and *iuneo* takes *for-to* is indicated in the representation of each verb in the lexicon, along with its phonological specifications. This is true for every verb in the language and for every governed rule. Thus, the redundancy rule for verbs of saying in classical Latin states that equi-NP-deletion is nonapplicable even if the structural description for that rule is met. For verbs of wishing, the redundancy rule will state that equi-NP-deletion is optional. For verbs of trying or of being able, on the other hand, equi-NP-deletion will be obligatory. All of these facts are represented in the lexicon and the redundancy rules; hence, if any of them change in time, the change will take place, not in the transformational component, but in the lexicon and in the redundancy rules; the latter will state what is regular and what is not for a given meaning-class, as well as what rules can apply at all. Hence, although complementizer-placement and change, equi-NP-deletion, and *it*-substitution, all governed, act in Spanish to produce very different structures superficially from their counterparts in Latin, this is not to be ascribed to a difference or change in these rules themselves; it is a change in the redundancy rules instead. Since these define regularities in the lexicon, it is not surprising that they change readily, since the lexicon is the most flexible part of a grammar.

What we have found and shall document in succeeding sections of this chapter is that redundancy rules can change in the following ways: they can extend to new classes of verbs rules that formerly did not apply to them; they can make rules that did apply to a class cease to apply, thus restricting the domain of a rule; and they can make rules optional in a class that were obligatory, and make obligatory rules that were optional.

Can anything be said about what causes the redundancy rules to change? In some cases, yes. Several of the cases we are about to discuss changed in a way to make the superficial structure of Latin more closely resemble that of Greek. These "borrowings" from Greek appear, in many cases, to have remained in Latin and to be at present part of the synchronic grammar of Spanish. Other changes appear to have arisen spontaneously within Latin itself, and were not influenced by Greek. (It is, of course, conceivable that the Latin spoken in Spain was influenced by the indigenous languages of Iberia and that these encouraged the apparently spontaneous changes. But there is no reason to believe this, and it is easier merely to assume these changes occurred spontaneously.) We shall discuss the changes that are found in the complement rules under two categories: first, changes influenced by Greek models, or Hellenisms; second, changes that arose spontaneously in Latin.

6.3. Hellenisms

It is well known that there are found in some Latin writings departures from the norm of Latin influenced by Greek constructions that resemble the aberrant Latin forms; these departures are usually called "Hellenisms" or "Grecisms." Two different types of borrowings are illustrated in the outline in the next paragraph. Brenous and other writers have discussed these borrowings at length. Their intuitive conclusions do not differ materially from ours; we are attempting here to explain formally, and within the framework of transformational grammar, why certain changes, and not others, are found and how these changes may be accounted for in terms of the synchronic grammar of Latin.

In dealing with this topic, one must be careful to distinguish between two types of aberrant sentences, both of which might be called "Hellenisms."

Type 1.   Found in the writings of non-native speakers of Latin:
   A.   Use of rules that are found in Greek, but not found at all in Latin. Example (*Bellum Hispaniense* 14, 1): *Eius praeteriti temporis*, for *Eo praeterito tempore*, 'That time being past', where genitive absolute (Greek construction) is substituted for the ablative absolute. This should be distinguished from B.
   B.   Nonapplication of a rule that ought to apply in Latin without any discernible influence on the writer of the grammar of Greek. Example (same work): *Quod factum licet necopinantibus nostris esset gestum*, 'A deed which it was allowed to our unfortunate men to do'. Violation of sequence-of-tenses rules, which apply in Greek as well as Latin.

Type 2.   Found in the writings of native speakers of Latin, for literary effect:
   Example: *Phasellus ille quem videtis, hospites, ait fuisse navium celerrimus.* (Cat. 4, 1) 'The vessel that you see, guests, says that it was the swiftest of ships.'

Type 1 is not considered true Hellenism. Type 2 is what we are speaking of, and what most grammarians restrict themselves to, when they discuss Hellenism.

In the example given for Type 2, the writer was conscious that he was adapting a Greek rule of grammar into Latin, and was doing it for literary effect. In Example A of Type 1, the writer may well have been Hellenizing unconsciously. The writer is a native speaker of Latin and knows the language well enough to be aware that he is deviating from the norm. It must be remembered that Greek was a prestige language in Rome, and imitating it consciously was an indication that the imitator was a cultured and highly educated man. Type 1 is probably due more to ignorance of Latin than to a desire to transfer a Greek rule into Latin grammar. It was not used by any native speaker of Latin, as Type 2 would have been.

Keeping to this definition of Hellenism, we find that not every rule in Greek was borrowed, or could have been borrowed, into Latin. For example, there is an equivalent in Greek to the *for-to* complementizer: it appears as accusative-infinitive, just as in Latin. A Roman wishing to Hellenize might borrow this complementizer-changing rule by using it in a class of verbs where it was not normally used in Latin, but where it was normal in Greek. He could do this because the rule itself existed in Latin and was not altogether foreign to it. But there is another complementizer in Greek (which makes use of a larger number of complementizers than Latin), *hos*-indicative. *Hos* is roughly equivalent to *ut* in Latin, but *ut* never occurs with the indicative. Therefore, it is evident that there is no rule corresponding to the Greek *hos*-indicative complementizer-changing rule in Latin. For this reason, this rule was never borrowed, and one never sees examples of *ut*-indicative anywhere in Latin. It appears that a language does not borrow rules outright: it is merely able to borrow the constraints on their applicability.[4]

6.4 Hellenisms and Synchronic Spanish

As an example of the influence of Greek models on Latin grammar, let us examine an instance where Greek may well have influenced Latin, and where the effect is present in Spanish: the operation of the rules of complementizer-change and equi-NP-deletion, in the verbs of saying and thinking.

In Latin these verbs had to undergo *for-to* complementizer-change, but although the sentence might then meet the structural description of equi-NP-deletion, it could not undergo it. Thus, *Dico me venire*, 'I say that I am coming', is grammatical in Latin, but **Dico venire* was not. But a similar situation does not exist in Spanish.

In Spanish the most common complementizer for the class of verbs of saying and thinking is *que*-indicative, the descendant of *quod*-indicative in Latin. Later in the chapter the change from *for-to* to *quod*-indicative in these

---

[4]This idea has been expressed before, for example, by Brugmann ("Die mit dem Suffix -to- gebildeten Partizipia im Verbalsystem des Lateinischen und des Umbrisch-Oskischen, "*Indogermanische Forschungen*, Vol. V (1894), pp. 89–152):

> Das hat man hier, sonst gewöhnlich, unter Grazismus nicht zu verstehen, dass der lateinischen Sprache etwas ihr von Haus aus völlig Fremdes aufgepfropft wurde, sondern es wurde nur ein seinem Ursprung nach echt einheimischer Anwendungstypus, weil er im Griechischen ein von den Römern empfundenes Analogon hatte, nach diesen ausländischen Muster weiter ausgebildet.

verbs will be discussed. *Que*-indicative is always grammatical in this class of verbs.

(1a) Yo digo que Juan ha venido. 'I say that John has come.'
(1b) Yo digo que yo he venido. 'I say that I have come.'

Thus far, the situation is easily described: there has been a curtailment in the applicability of *for-to* complementizer-change. It does not apply to verbs of saying and thinking in Spanish. But this is not true. It does apply, but only if the structural description of equi-NP-deletion is met: the subjects of the higher and lower sentences must be identical. Otherwise, *for-to* complementizer-change cannot occur. Even where it can occur, it is optional (cf. sentence (1b)).

(2a) Yo digo haber venido. 'I say that I have come.'
(2b) *Yo digo (a) Juán haber venido. 'I say that John has come.'

The relationship between the Latin sentences and the Spanish ones is not immediately obvious. On inspection, it appears that two significant changes have taken place: (1) there are two possible complements (*for-to* and *que*-indicative) rather than only one (*for-to*) for verbs of this class; and (2) if *for-to* applies, equi-NP-deletion must apply, while in Latin, equi-NP-deletion could not apply. For the second to occur in Spanish, the first must also have taken place; there must be a means in the language for expressing sentences like (1a). If *for-to* were the only complementizer possible for this class, and *for-to* complementizer-change could occur only if the SD for equi-NP-deletion had been met, it would be impossible to express sentence (1a) in Spanish. Therefore, the two changes are in some way connected, although this connection cannot be described formally.

The first change is probably not the result of Greek influence on Latin but rather a spontaneous development in Vulgar Latin. It would be rather tempting to think that this is not the case and that the use of *hoti*-indicative with verbs like *lego*, 'say', in Greek influenced verbs of saying in Latin. But if this were really the way it happened, *quod*-indicative undoubtedly would not be found with verbs of thinking and perceiving, which in Greek occur with accusative-infinitive or with poss.-*ing* (accusative plus supplementary participle, in Greek, where *it*-substitution applies to the subject of the lower sentence regularly in these verbs), never *hoti*-indicative. In Latin, verbs of saying and verbs of thinking act alike with respect to complementizer-change. We find in Petronius (45, 10) sentences like *Sed subolfacio, quia nobis epulum daturus est Mammea*, 'I have a feeling that Mammea is going to throw a party for us'. Here the verb is a verb of perception, and if the use of *quod* (*quia*) were a Hellenism, it could not be used with a verb of this class. The use of *quod* in object complements is probably a spontaneous change on the part of Latin.

The second change, however, appears definitely to have occurred under the influence of Greek. In Greek, there is a division between verbs of saying and verbs of thinking, with respect to which complementizer-changing rules they undergo. Most verbs of thinking must undergo accusative-infinitive complementizer-change. But most verbs of saying do not normally undergo any of the rules of complementizer-change; they take *hoti*-indicative as a complementizer, which is equivalent to *quod*-indicative in Latin. There is one notable exception: a common verb of saying in Greek, *phemi*, always takes accusative-infinitive. When it does this, it will undergo equi-NP-deletion if the structural description of this rule is met, otherwise not. Therefore, if one wants to say in Greek, *I say that Cyrus is good*, one has the option of using *lego* (or another verb of its class) with *hoti* and the indicative, or *phemi*, with the accusative-infinitive.

(3a) Lego hoti Kuros agathos estin.

(3b) Phemi Kuron agathon einai.

If one wants to say, *Cyrus says that he is good* (where *he* refers to Cyrus) he also has two choices. He can use *lego*, just as in (3a), or he can use *phemi*, with an infinitive alone. In this case, *agathos*, 'good', will be in the nominative, because the subject of the lower sentence will have been deleted (and its accusative case marking with it) before agreement across copula takes place.

(4a) Kuros legei hoti agathos estin.⎫
(4b) Kuros phesi agathos einai.　　⎬ 'Cyrus says that he is good.'
　　　　　　　　　　　　　　　　　 ⎭

We find numerous examples of Latin writers adopting the Greek *phemi*-construction in Latin and allowing sentences embedded in verbs of saying and thinking to undergo equi-NP-deletion. The sentence given under Type 2 of the outline in Section 6.3, *Phasellus ille quem videtis, hospites, ait fuisse navium celerrimus*, is identical in construction to a sentence like (4b). In this way, a rule is borrowed by a native speaker of Latin into a meaning-class in which it usually does not apply. But equi-NP-deletion applies elsewhere in Latin, of course. This borrowing eventually became a part of the grammar of Vulgar Latin: sentences analogous to (2a) occur in all the Romance languages. The change between the behavior of verbs of saying and thinking, with respect to complementizer-change and equi-NP-deletion, in Latin and in Spanish may be traced through classical to Vulgar Latin and into Spanish as follows:

Redundancy Rule F
Classical Latin: $V_{\text{saying/thinking}}$
　　　　　　　　　　u *for-to* $\supset$ + *for-to*
　　　　　　　　　　Other complementizer-changing rules are not applicable; equi-NP-deletion is not applicable.

Redundancy Rule G

Vulgar Latin: $V_{saying/thinking}$
u *for-to* ⊃ *opt. for-to*
Other complementizer-changing rules are not applicable; equi-NP-deletion is probably optional if SD is met for this class for at least some speakers.

Redundancy Rule H

Spanish: $V_{saying/thinking}$
u *for-to* ⊃ opt. *for-to*: SD equi-NP-deletion is met.
Other complementizer-changing rules are not applicable; equi-NP-deletion is obligatory if *for-to* complementizer-change has applied, but not applicable otherwise.

These rules may be compared with the situation in Greek:

Redundancy Rule I [a]

Phemi: u *for-to* ⊃ + *for-to*
Other complementizer-changing rules are not applicable; equi-NP-deletion is obligatory.

Redundancy Rule I [b]

Lego: *For-to* is not applicable unless passivization SD is met; u *hos*-indic. complementizer-change ⊃ opt. *hos*-indic. complementizer-change, equi-NP-deletion is not applicable.

Neither of the possibilities in Greek corresponds exactly to the situation in Latin, nor does the Greek correspond exactly to the Spanish, but it appears that the way Latin changed was in the direction of the Greek, by borrowing part of the Greek set of redundancy rules.

There is another example of Hellenism-inspired change. In Latin, *it*-substitution applies only when it applies obligatorily, in subject complements—principally, with verbs like *begin, end, tend, continue*. Thus, **Marcus aequus est ire* and **Marcus veri similis est ire* are both ungrammatical, even when *for-to* complementizer-change has applied.

In Spanish, on the other hand, we find sentences like the following:

(5a) Hacerlo él sería imposible. 'For him to do it would be impossible.' (Lit., 'He would be impossible to do it.')

The following is also grammatical:

(5b) Hacerlo le sería imposible. 'It would be impossible for him to do it.'

In (5a), *it*-substitution has applied. The rule is optional for this verb and for many verbs of this class; native speakers are divided over which are acceptable and which are not. But it is certainly acceptable for some subject-complement-taking verbs for most speakers of Spanish. This is a clear departure from Latin. But we have shown that *it*-substitution must operate somewhere in the grammar of Latin: perhaps in object complements and certainly in flips and passives. Therefore, the rule could be extended, either spontaneously or through borrowing, into the class of subject complements where it is optional.

If we look at Greek, we notice that in this language, *it*-substitution is very frequent in these environments.

(6a) Sokrates dunatos estin ienai. 'Socrates is possible to go' = 'It is possible for Socrates to go.'

(6b) Sokrates axios estin ienai. 'Socrates is right to go.'

These occur alongside of sentences without *it*-substitution, though the latter are less frequent.

(7a) Dunaton esti Sokrate ienai. 'It is possible for Socrates to go.'

(7b) Axion esti Sokrate ienai. 'It is right for Socrates to go.'

What appears to be happening here is that through the influence of Greek the domain of applicability of *it*-substitution has been extended, so that it can apply in subject complements optionally, instead of applying only in those cases where it was obligatory.

6.5 Spontaneous Governed-Rule Change

Where change in governed rules occurs spontaneously, the same restrictions on what can change apply as in those cases where the change was influenced by the grammar of Greek. Here, too, the data we have looked at are insufficient as a source from which to draw conclusions. If it should actually turn out to be true that governed-rule change occurs only when it is an extension or restriction of rules already in the grammar of a language, and that therefore a governed rule was never added to a language, this would be a startling conclusion and one that is not anticipated in any theory of linguistic change. Obviously, the whole subject of syntactic change and, within it, the subject of governed-rule change warrant serious study.

We shall discuss here one particularly interesting case of spontaneous governed-rule change between Latin and Romance. It is interesting not only in itself but in its power to explain other facts about Spanish that have previously been treated as unrelated.

In Latin, verbs of wanting and wishing could undergo either *for-to* or *ut*-subjunctive complementizer-change. The two were about equally common. If *for-to* was chosen, equi-NP-deletion was optional. Thus, all the following were found:

(8a) Volo ut sim consul. 'I want to be consul.'

(8b) Volo me esse consulem. 'I want to be consul.'

(8c) Volo esse consul. 'I want to be consul.'

If the subjects are different, both *for-to* and *ut*-subjunctive are still possible.

(9a) Volo ut Marcus sit consul. 'I want Marcus to be consul.'

(9b) Volo Marcum esse consulem. 'I want Marcus to be consul.'

In Spanish, not all these possibilities exist. If the SD of equi-NP-deletion is met, *for-to* is the only possibility for verbs of this class. If the SD of equi-NP-deletion is not met, *que*-subjunctive (developed from *ut*-subjunctive) is the only complementizer found.[5]

(10a) Quiero ir a Madrid. 'I want to go to Madrid.'

(10b) Quiero que Juan vaya a Madrid. 'I want John to go to Madrid.'

(10c) *Quiero que vaya a Madrid. 'I want to go to Madrid.'

(10d) *Quiero (a) Juan ir a Madrid. 'I want John to go to Madrid.'

These facts can be described in terms of changes in redundancy rules alone. There is no change in the rules themselves. Thus, verbs of wanting and wishing in Latin are described in the following redundancy rule:

Redundancy Rule J. For verbs of wanting and wishing:

Complementizer-change (must undergo one of these rules):

u R (*for-to*) $\supset$ opt. R (*for-to*)

u R (*ut*-subj.) $\supset$ opt. R (*ut*-subj.)

u R (. . .) $\supset$ R (. . .)

u R (equi-NP-deletion) $\supset$ opt. R (equi-NP-deletion)

In Spanish, the redundancy rule is more complicated:

Redundancy Rule K. For verbs of wanting and wishing.

Complementizer-change (must undergo one of these rules):

If SD of equi-NP-deletion is met:

u R (*for-to*) $\supset$ + R (*for-to*)

u other complementizer-changing rules $\supset$—other complementizer-changing rules

Equi-NP-deletion is obligatory.

---

[5]The beginnings of this change can be seen as early as late Vulgar Latin: *Per nos ipsos non volumus emendare, sed quod ante nos veniat* (*Formulae Salicae Merkelianae* 259, 33), 'We do not wish to change by ourselves, but [we wish] that it may come before us.' It is not clear how to interpret this example; we do not know whether the writer was familiar enough with Latin not to make mistakes in complementizer-change. If he was familiar with Latin to that degree, this sentence may reflect the fact that the Spanish redundancy rule had its origin in Vulgar Latin. If, on the other hand, he was a speaker of a proto-Romance language that contained this rule, he might merely have been applying a rule of his own language to Latin, much as the author of the *Bellum Hispaniense*, cited in the text earlier, did with Greek. This sentence and numerous others like it also indicate that the change from *ut* to *quod* occurred in Latin itself, rather than separately in the individual Romance languages. *Quod* (both the complementizer and the relative pronoun), then changed to *quid*, the interrogative form; but this was purely morphological and did not affect the meaning. *Quod* was apparently first extended into object complements, with the indicative, at least as early as Petronius, and probably earlier. After this, *ut* was replaced everywhere by *quod*, leaving the subjunctive complementizer on the verb. All cases of *quod* then changed to *quid*.

If SD of equi-NP-deletion is not met:

u R (*for-to*) ⊃—R (*for-to*)

u R (*que*-subj.) ⊃ + R (*que*-subj.)

u other complementizer-changing rules ⊃—other complementizer-changing rules

This change in the redundancy rule will give the correct structures in Spanish. Thus, in this case, where the superficial structure of sentences in Spanish appears very different from that of Latin, we can show that this is merely a change in the redundancy rule, rather than a change in the syntactic component. This is a very different claim from the one made by most Romance philologists: that the construction itself changed between Latin and Spanish. To say that the construction changed is to imply that the rule which produced the construction changed, rather than that the meaning-class itself changed its properties. In all of these cases, too, the change is one that takes place throughout a whole meaning-class, rather than in individual verbs. When *dico* becomes able to take *quod*, for example, *aio* and *puto* presumably can also do so, as can all the other verbs of this class. It is not that any verb becomes irregular but rather that the regular situation for a meaning-class shifts. Calling this a change in redundancy rule expresses this fact precisely. So, for example, when verbs of ordering change their redundancy rule between Latin and Spanish, it is changed so that both *que*-subjunctive and *for-to* are optional, rather than *ut*-subjunctive being unmarked and *for-to* being marked, as it was in classical Latin. For all verbs of ordering in Spanish this is the situation. It would be interesting, if we had cases of irregular verbs that kept their phonological shape and meaning between Latin and Spanish—if *iubeo*, for example, were retained in the grammar of Spanish—to see whether all the marked and unmarked features were erased on all verbs of ordering, when the rule changed, so that the Spanish form of *iubeo* was regular like the others of its class, taking either *for-to* or *que*-subjunctive. Alternatively, it might keep its markedness, and undergo only *for-to*. There are few cases, however, of irregular verbs being retained. They seem much more liable to be lost than do regular verbs.

6.6 Abstract Verbs and Syntactic Change

Finally, we should ask how changes in governed rules affect the abstract verbs we spoke of in the preceding chapter. If it can be shown that changes in the redundancy rules for real verbs had, in at least some cases, the same effect on abstract verbs of the same classes, it will strengthen the argument that abstract verbs exist. It is difficult to explain how an independent subjunctive changes its properties or becomes an independent infinitive in the course of time—and why it changes in a manner similar to verbs that have the same meaning as the independent construction—unless one can assume that there are real verbs in the underlying structure, governing the application of rules, and that the changes in the redundancy rules affect these verbs as well as the ones present in the superficial structure. There is some evidence for changes in the properties of several of the abstract verbs that were discussed in the preceding chapter.

In Latin, verbs of ordering, if unmarked, underwent *ut*-subjunctive complementizer-change. The abstract verb [*imper*], as well as the other abstract verbs of ordering, such as [*hort*] and [*insist*], had the same property. In Spanish, on the other hand, unmarked verbs of ordering undergo either *for-to* or *que*-subjunctive. The following sentences are both equally grammatical, and synonymous:

(11a) Le mandé a Juan irse. 'I ordered John to go away.'
(11b) Le mandé a Juan que se fuese. 'I ordered John to go away.'

In Spanish, there are two imperative types found. One is a form derived from [*imper*] and *que*-subjunctive. The other is derived from [*imper*] and *for-to*. They are interchangeable, although the second is much commoner, just as (11b) is commoner than (11a).

(12a) Callarse. 'Be quiet.'
(12b) Cállese. 'Be quiet.'

The abstract verb [*imper*] remains regular in Spanish and changes its properties along with the other verbs of its class.

Another example of this type can be seen in subject complements. In Latin, as we have said, these cannot undergo *it*-substitution in most cases. The abstract verbs of these classes sometimes take *for-to* complementizers. When they do, they cannot undergo *it*-substitution, like other members of their meaning-class.

In Spanish, verbs in which *it*-substitution is inapplicable in Latin can undergo this rule optionally (cf. sentence (5a)). Then it might be expected that abstract verbs of these classes might undergo *it*-substitution if they occurred with *for-to* complementizers. We find sentences in Spanish such as the following:

(13a) ¿Casarme yo? 'I get married?' = 'Is it likely that I would get married?'
(13b) ¿Ir él a Madrid? 'He go to Madrid?'

These cases are identical in meaning to sentences in Latin containing the abstract verb [*veri simile*]. In Latin, these occurred either with *ut*-subjunctive or with *for-to*. In the latter case, the superficial structure contained an accusative and an infinitive. In Spanish, *it*-substitution has taken place: the pronouns *yo* and *él* are unambiguously nominative case. This can be accounted for only if we assume that *it*-substitution has operated. Here, then, is another example of a regular abstract verb retaining its regularity with respect to a rule and changing along with its meaning-class. In these cases, it should be pointed out again, the transformational rules have not been changed at all, although the superficial constructions have changed considerably.

In Latin, the abstract verb of wishing, [*vel*], was irregular, Other verbs of its class could optionally undergo either *for-to* or *ut*-subjunctive complementizer-change, but [*vel*] could undergo only the latter. In Spanish, it retains its irregularity and behaves just as it did in Latin, although the regular verbs of its class have changed their properties.

(14a)   ¡Que vaya yo a Madrid! 'Would that I might go to Madrid!'
(14b)   ¡Que vaya Juan a Madrid! 'Would that John might go to Madrid!'
(14c)   *Ir me a Madrid! 'Oh, to go to Madrid!'
(14d)   *Ir (a) Juan a Madrid! 'Oh for John to go to Madrid!'

In Latin, [*vel*] was marked as m *for-to*, indicating that it could not undergo it. It must retain this marking in Spanish.

Finally, we have an example of an abstract verb that was irregular in Latin changing its properties to become regular in Spanish. This kind of lexical change is not unheard-of in real verbs: there is a tendency for marked forms to lose their markings—that is, for irregular verbs (or nouns) to become regular. This fact is well known in relation to morphological irregularity. So, for example, *facio* in Latin has an irregular method of forming the passive: it employs a suppletive form *fio*. But in Spanish the passive of *hacer* is regularly formed, *hacerse*. The case presented here is an example of a syntactic property of a verb becoming more regular. The case is that of the abstract verb of wanting or meaning, [*vol*], found in purpose clauses.

In Latin, [*vol*] was irregular in the same way that [*vel*] was: it could undergo only *ut*-subjunctive complementizer-change. In Spanish, on the other hand, purpose clauses behave precisely as verbs of wanting and wishing behave.

(15a)   Fuí a Madrid para ver a mi amigo. 'I went to Madrid to see my friend.'
(15b)   Fuí a Madrid para que Juan hablase conmigo. 'I went to Madrid so that John might speak with me.'

In (15a), the subject of [*vol*], which must be identical to that of the main verb, is identical to that of *ver*. According to Redundancy Rule 5, when there is identity between the subject of a verb of wanting and the subject of the embedded sentence, *for-to* complementizer-change is obligatory. Normally, the only way to say (15a) in Spanish is by using the infinitive, although very rare exceptions are found (and are found equally rarely after verbs of wanting), and native speakers recognize these sentences as exceptional. Likewise, (15b) is the only possibility if the subjects are not identical, again with rare exceptions. Thus, purpose clauses in Spanish behave just like verbs of wanting and wishing and unlike any other class of verbs. The only way to account for the behavior of these sentences in Spanish is to assume an abstract verb [*vol*], which behaves like a regular verb of wanting.

6.7 Changes in Other Complementation Rules

The changes occurring in the other rules that we have discussed can be considered briefly. Passivization must operate in Spanish, but we do not know whether its form has changed: we do not know what its form is in Latin, or in English, for that matter.

Flip must operate in Spanish to produce sentences like (16). In the first, only flip has operated; in the second, *it*-substitution operates as well.

(16a) Me parece que Juan esta enfermo. 'It seems to me that John is sick.'

(16b) Juan me parece estar enfermo. 'John seems to me to be sick.'

In Spanish, as in Latin, we have no clear evidence for extraposition, but the evidence is lacking for slightly different reasons. We commonly find sentences like the following:

(17) Es probable que Juan fué a Madrid ayer. 'It's probable that John went to Madrid yesterday.'

If sentence (17) were *Lo es probable* . . . , this sentence would be evidence for extraposition. But *lo*-deletion is apparently obligatory in Spanish except under special circumstances, and **Lo es probable que* . . . is not grammatical. This sentence could still be considered evidence for extraposition on the strength of the fact that the subject noun phrase with *que* follows the verb. But Spanish, although it is not a free-word-order language and therefore has no scrambling rule, nonetheless does have an optional rule that changes the order of subject and verb. Thus we have *Yo quiero ir a Madrid* and *Quiero yo ir a Madrid*. Sentence (17) may be an example of interchange of the subject (*lo que Juan . . . ayer*) and the verb (*es probable*), followed by obligatory *lo*-deletion, rather than a case of extraposition.

That-deletion, found in both Latin and English, does not operate in Spanish. Thus, *Digo Juan viene is not grammatical; *Digo que Juan viene* is the only possibility. This appears to be true both with *que*-indicative and *que*-subjunctive.

Preposition-deletion does not operate at all in Spanish:

(18a) Consintimos en el plan. 'We consented to the plan.'

(18b) Consintimos en que Juan fuese. 'We consented to it that John should go.'

In these sentences, *consentir en*, 'agree to', is like the verbs in English that take prepositions other than *of*. But even these prepositions are deleted before *that* and *for-to* in English. They are never deleted in Spanish. *It*-deletion, as we pointed out earlier, is obligatory. *For*-deletion seems also to be obligatory, since there is no evidence in Spanish of this complementizer at all: either the subject noun phrase undergoes equi-NP-deletion, or it undergoes *it*-substitution. In either of these cases, the preposition is deleted obligatorily.[6]

6.8 Conclusions

In this chapter, we have discussed at length the changes that took place between Latin and Spanish in several of the governed rules of the complement system. In these cases, the superficial syntax of Spanish appears very different from that of Latin. The first assumption one might make in these cases is that changes had taken place in the transformational component of the grammar, either adding, deleting, or reordering rules, or changing the form of these rules. But in none of the cases examined is this the way to interpret the change. What seems to have happened, instead, is that the redundancy rules governing the application of these rules in specific meaning-classes of verbs have undergone change, and these redundancy rules alone have been changed. This is not presented as a well-established theoretical position, that governed rules do not change their form, for lack of sufficient evidence. More research on this question must be done. If it turns out that we have been dealing here with special cases and that there exist in language examples of governed rules that have changed in time, this is not to be considered surprising but, rather, the expected conclusion. We know of cases where ungoverned rules change, and we know of nothing that differentiates governed from ungoverned rules in such a way as to cause them to differ with respect to their diachronic behavior. If, however, the conclusion presented here for these few cases should prove to be true, it will show that there is more difference between governed and ungoverned rules than there is now thought to be, and this will be a starting point for a great deal of crucial work on syntax and syntactic change.

[6]It is possible that there is one case of the preposition being retained, but this is very speculative. It is probable that, if the preposition were to appear, it would appear as the preposition *a*, which means 'for-to,' as well as functioning as the direct object marker with animate nouns. Because it functions as direct object marker, it appears to be the replacement in Spanish of the accusative case ending and is therefore a likely candidate for the equivalent of Accusative in the accusative-infinitive complementizer. In the infinitive of ordering described previously, we sometimes find sentences like *¡ A callar!* with the same meaning as *¡ Callar!* It is perhaps possible to hypothesize that *a* is retained here, alone in Spanish as far as I know, after the noun phrase has been deleted. (The noun is always the second person pronoun and is always deleted in this situation. Thus, this noun phrase-deletion is not like equi-NP-deletion or preposition-deletion that results from *it*-substitution but may be ordered later than preposition-deletion, and hence preposition-deletion will not apply here.) This occurrence of *a* is not to be confused with its use after certain verbs, such as *esforzarse a*, 'strive to,' in *Yo me esfuerzo a acabar este capitulo*, 'I am striving to finish this chapter,' where *a* is a preposition that is part of the verb itself, rather than one introduced as a complementizer, and is parallel to *for* in *hope for*.

Part IV
DIALECTOLOGY

Part IV
DIRECTORY

13

FAMILY TREE, WAVE THEORY, AND DIALECTOLOGY*

Ernst Pulgram

At one time or another, practically all linguists, including those whom no one could accuse of holding antiquated views, employ such terms as "parent language," "daughter languages," "*Ursprache*," "*langue-mère*," "related languages," "language families," "inherited (as opposed to borrowed) features," and similar ones. They generally give explicit warning, or consider it implicitly understood, that these kinship terms are used metaphorically; that in calling the Romance languages "descendants" or "daughter languages" of Latin, one must not forget that they still are Latin, albeit in a modern, much altered form. Yet to say that French, Italian, Spanish, etc. *are* Latin, or neo-Latin, amounts to an equally metaphorical figure of speech, or else reflects such an overextension of the term "language" as to make it inoperative: for if a language proposes, by definition, to facilitate cooperation among its speakers, then Latin and French cannot lightly be called one and the same language, since Cicero and Voltaire would not be able to communicate successfully with one another if each used his native tongue. True, it is impossible to say at what point exactly between 500 A.D. and 1000 A.D. Latin ceases and French begins. Yet such philosophical considerations of classification must not deter us from pragmatically classifying languages.

The idea of "kinship" is as old as William Jones' discovery, in the eighties of the eighteenth century, that certain languages which he knew and compared and whose resemblances could not to such a degree be fortuitous, must have sprung from some common origin. Jones' successors, Bopp, Rask, Grimm, and Pott continued on this assumption of kinship and descendance, and considered the reconstruction of the mother-language their principal task. When Schleicher finally devised his genealogical tree, he was not at all promulgating any new theory of Indo-European relationships, but he simply

*From *Orbis* 2.67–72 (1953). Reprinted by permission of the author and *Orbis* (bulletin international de documentation linguistique [Louvain]).

presented schematically the method of comparative philology as practiced by his predecessors, himself, and, indeed, largely though not exclusively, by ourselves.[1] For if we list, or seek, an etymon in an etymological dictionary, our aim is in effect to determine the older form of which the later or present form is a development. (This does not mean, by the way, at least nowadays, that the reconstruction of so-called Indo-European etyma necessarily constitutes an endorsement of the theory of a single Indo-European uniform proto-language, rather than several dialects which had a number of isoglosses in common). Yet since we established that, barring an overextension of the term "language," the older and the newer form ought to be referred to as belonging to two different languages, the indication of a relationship of these two languages in metaphorical terms of kinship is, it seems to me, quite appropriate and useful. The statement that ". . . if Sanskrit, Greek, Latin and Germanic are sister languages, Hittite is only a cousin . . ."[2] is picturesquely intelligible, whether you think it factually true or not.

It must be conceded to those who today refute completely the validity of the family tree scheme, that Schleicher himself, unlike ourselves, did not think of his *Stammbaum* and *Ursprache* and *Tochtersprachen* as metaphorical terms but as natural facts. Departing from the view that languages are natural organisms independent of their speakers, he concluded, as did his contemporaries in the natural sciences, that each specimen is derived by progenation from some predecessors, and ultimately all from some prototype. Here Schleicher was wrong, because language is no such organism. If he furthermore ever thought that his genealogical tree could furnish evidence on the relative location of the various dialects and on their subsequent geographic spread, if he ever meant to indicate any local or chronological measurements by the length of the branches of his tree, he was also wrong. The Stammbaum shows schematically the lines of descent and a relative chronology of languages: Sanskrit was spoken before Serbian, and the two languages, no matter how dissimilar, are provedly—and there is no better way of putting it—related. But to show that much, the tree is a good schematic device, though no more. Schleicher and his followers were equally wrong if they ever claimed that the genealogical tree in any manner represented any physical realities of the peoples and tribes which spoke these languages, such as their origins, their migrations, their blood relationship, and their racial history and peculiarities. It has often enough been said that "language" may, but need not necessarily, coincide with "nation" or "race,"

[1]Cf. Leonard Bloomfield, *Language* (New York, 1933), 311: "The earlier students of Indo-European did not realize that the family-tree diagram was merely a statement of their method. . . ."

[2]E. H. Sturtevant, "The Prehistory of Indo-European: A Summary," *Language*, 28 (1952), 177–181, 177.

and that no extra-linguistic statement can be correctly made on the basis of linguistic evidence alone, or vice versa.

To remedy these shortcomings Schmidt devised his wave scheme which turned out to be remarkably illuminating and successful. But in their enthusiasm over this memorable restatement of Indo-European developments, scholars proceeded too ruthlessly in chopping down the family tree: the old trunk was still solid in the core, and a radical pruning would have preserved its usefulness. In their eagerness to correct and forestall various historical, geographical, ethnological, and indeed linguistic pseudo-corrolaries emanating from the genealogical tree, many linguists also denied its purely schematic and metaphoric value for indicating linguistic relationships. Since the tree, stripped of all other pretensions, visualized, as I said, the very method of contemporary comparative philology, the Schmidt-reformers should also have felt obligated, for the sake of consistency, to swear off comparative philology as a method of research. This, inconsistently though luckily, they did not do. But it remains a pity that the family tree has ever since been in ill repute, so that students nowadays are taught to shun it in favor of the wave theory.

Yet Schmidt's protests against, and his rejection of, Schleicher's Stammbaum had really deeper roots, I believe, though Schmidt himself might not have immediately realized this. While his quarrel was ostensibly with the family tree and especially its overreaching implications, the true source of trouble lay in fact with the comparative method as until then commonly practiced. For the truth was that the pure, unadulterated comparative philology had reached an impasse, since it did not "allow for varieties within the parent language or for common change in the related languages."[3] It could no longer persist in its attempts to explain all linguistic facts in purely diachronic comparative terms of historic sequence and descent, but it had to learn to answer satisfactorily such questions as these: When linguistic agreements in two families cannot be accounted for through inheritance from a parent speech, how can they be explained? Why is common-Indo-European not necessarily equivalent with proto-Indo-European? How can one explain such resemblances as are inconsistent with those upon which a hypothesis of closer relationship between two language families has been founded?

Wherever two Indo-European linguistic families, say, Italic and Keltic, are shown by virtue of their position on the family tree to be more closely related to one another than each is to the other families, the implication according to the family tree is that they together continue a trait or traits of the Indo-European mother language. However, we know now that this can be factually true only with the proviso that they have not passed together,

[3]Bloomfield, 314.

separate from the others, through a period of common development. For if they have passed through such a period of common development, the agreements between them cannot furnish any evidence as to the state of proto-Indo-European. If, therefore, a family tree is faultily designed, one will of necessity infer from it the wrong answers to questions on linguistic relationships.

Here Schmidt's wave theory provided appropriate theoretic and visual corrections by showing that linguistic areas may overlap, and that in these overlaps dialect features may spread as waves do on a quiet pool, so that linguistic agreements may be not inherited but acquired. The pure comparative method, and with it the family tree simile, presupposes a "clear-cut splitting off of successive branches, but the inconsistent partial similarities show us that later changes may spread across the isoglosses left by earlier changes."[4] It was the great merit of Schmidt's wave theory to provide a visual scheme, entirely different from the family tree, which could plainly and correctly account for the overlapping of isoglosses and explain inconsistent partial similarities.

Now if the family tree device corresponds to one aspect of the modern comparative method, the wave theory presents the other principal aspect of linguistic investigation, namely dialectology, dialect geography. Schmidt perhaps never thought of himself as a dialectologist; the term was not fashionable in his day. But it may be significant that the beginnings of scientific linguistic geography and the incorporation of its methods and results into comparative linguistics fall in the same period.[5] Thus it was Schmidt's wave theory which supplemented and completed Schleicher's genealogical tree, even as dialect geography opened new paths in Indo-European linguistics and provided a method for clearing up the residue of problems which a theory committed to the definite, clean cleavage of daughter languages from an ideally uniform parent language could not successfully handle.[6]

[4]Bloomfield, 318.

[5]Schmidt's wave theory was published in 1872. In 1876 Georg Wenker began an investigation of the dialects of the Düsseldorf area; in 1881 he published the first of six maps of what was to become a dialect atlas of Germany. He was followed by H. Fischer with an atlas for Swabia in 1895, then by Gilliéron and Edmont who started publishing their French atlas in 1896.

[6]Cf. Bloomfield, 321: "The conflicting large-scale isoglosses in the Indo-European area . . . show us that the branches of the Indo-European family did not arise by the sudden breaking up of an absolute uniform parent community. We may say that the parent community was dialectally differentiated before the break-up, or that after the break-up various sets of daughter communities remained in communication; both statements amount to saying that areas or parts of areas which already differ in some respects may still make changes in common. The result of successive changes, therefore, is a network of isoglosses over the total area. Accordingly, the study of local differentiations in a speech area, *dialect geography*, supplements the use of the comparative method."

There is no question but that the designs of the spreading waves and of the spreading branches are nothing but visual devices, schematic sketches, with all the shortcomings and advantages of such pictures. The misleading implications of the family tree have already been pointed out. The wave picture is of course not innocent of pitfalls either. It can only be used to show graphically how at any given moment (and that is important!) the relative geographic position of various dialects is responsible for the fact that contiguous dialects may possess in common linguistic features which only one of them inherited directly from the parent speech. No single map of intersecting and overlapping linguistic areas (i.e. isoglosses) can furnish evidence, beyond directional clues for a forecast, as to the historical linguistic developments; these can only be gleaned from a series of sketches in which the successive dislocations and the shifting of areas become apparent.[7]

Both the wave and the tree diagram have their limitations. No scholar could divine the existence of Hittite and Tocharish before their discovery merely by contemplating a family tree or a wave picture, for no such design can of and by itself suggest the existence of a hitherto unknown tongue: there is in them no structural force, no *Systemzwang*, of the kind which, in a correctly devised and mathematically unobjectionable celestial map will lead an astronomer to postulate the existence and fix the location of a hitherto unseen heavenly body. (The planet Pluto was thus theoretically discovered before it was actually seen). Not even today, long after the discovery of Hittite and Tocharish, scholars can quite agree on the place of the two dialects on either the family tree or the wave diagram. In terms of the genealogical tree, there is no agreement whether Hittite is a branch of proto-Indo-European like Sanskrit, Germanic, Keltic, etc., or a descendant of an earlier Indo-European form of speech, that is, a sister language of proto-Indo-European.[8] And in terms of the wave scheme the question arises how one should on a map accommodate Tocharish which is a western, a *centum* dialect, although its known documents of the 7th and 8th centuries of our era were found in eastern Turkestan. We shall in fact have to resign

---

[7]Cf. Hermann Hirt, *Die Indogermanen* (Strassburg, 1905), 1.95: "Die Wellentheorie ist also im Hinblick auf die historischen Tatsachen wenig glaublich, sie ermöglicht uns nur, soweit sie zu Recht besteht, die ursprünglichen Lageverhältnisse der indogermanischen Sprachen einigermassen zu bestimmen."

[8]Cf. the reference to footnote 1, p. 68. Vittor Pisani, La question de l'indo-hittite et le concept de parenté linguistique, *Archiv Orientálni* 17, part 2 (1949), 251–264, thinks, however, that Forrer and Sturtevant, in dealing with the classification of Hittite, " . . . ont eu recours à l'expédient le plus usé et le plus suranné de la méthodologie Schleicherienne, c'est-à-dire à l'arbre généalogique, et ils ont enrichi la mythologie linguistique d'une nouvelle 'langue-mère' dont on n'avait pas le moindre besoin." (257) It is interesting to note that Pisani has since suggested another simile or schematic design to visualize linguistic relationship, namely that of a river-system with its various sources and tributaries, in an article entitled Parenté linguistique, *Lingua* 3 (1952) 3–16.

ourselves to more than one family tree and more than one wave diagram for the moment, at least until these questions have found irrefutable answers, unless our partisanship or our convictions are strong enough to reject all but one right now.

If it is true, as I hope to have shown, that the family tree and the wave diagram are usable not for the illumination of uncharted areas but merely for the illustration of the known or what is believed to be true, that they are representations of our two primary methods of investigation in accord with the principal types of linguistic differentiation, that they are complementary and no more exclude one another than do comparative linguistics and dialect geography, then it may be agreeable to use both types of visualization of linguistic processes as legitimate didactic devices, though always with due warning as to their figurative nature and their impermanence in the face of new discoveries and insights.

14

ON THE THEORY OF PHONOLOGICAL ASSOCIATIONS AMONG LANGUAGES*

Roman Jakobson

Is it still necessary to recall that linguistics belongs to the social sciences and not to natural history? This is certainly an evident truism; yet, as so often happens in the history of science, even though an antiquated theory is abolished, there are numerous residual aspects that remain that have escaped the control of critical thought.

The doctrine of Schleicher, the great naturalist in the domain of linguistics, has been shaken for some time, but one still finds many survivals of it. It is because of his thesis—that the physiology of sounds is the "basis of all of grammar"—that the place of honor in the science of language is still reserved for this auxiliary, strictly speaking, extrinsic discipline. In giving way to a more integrated conception, linguistic tradition renounces only with difficulty the rule that the author of the *Compendium* had sustained and that since his time has taken root: "One must above all devote oneself to the most exact study of a single object, without even thinking about the systematic construction of the whole system." But it is the tendency to explain the grammatical and phonological similarities of two languages by their descent from a common ancestor, and to envisage similarities susceptible of being explained only in this manner, that remains without doubt the most stable element of the doctrine in question.

For those, however, who no longer take seriously the simplistic genealogy of languages, the image of the Stammbaum (that is, of genealogical tree, according to the apt label of Schuchardt) nevertheless retains its vigor. The problem of common patronymity due to a single stock still persists in being

*From *Proceedings of the Fourth International Congress of Linguists* (Copenhagen, 1938), pp. 45–58. A slightly different version appeared as a supplement to N.S. Trubetzkoy, *Principes de Phonologie* (Paris, 1949), tr. by J. Cantineau. Reprinted in Jakobson, *Selected Writings*, I (Mouton, 1962), 234–246. (Original title: "Sur la théorie des affinités phonologiques," tr. by A.R.K.) Reprinted here by permission of the author.

the essential preoccupation of the comparative study of languages. Nevertheless, this tendency is in disagreement with the sociological orientation of modern linguistics. In effect, the exploration of inherited resemblances from a common prehistoric stage is, in the comparative social sciences (for example, in the study of art, habits, or customs), only one of the questions to be treated, and the problem of the development of innovating tendencies prevails over the problem of linguistic residues.

Moreover, this liking for puzzles and strictly genealogical solutions no longer corresponds to the actual state of natural history, and linguistics runs the danger of remaining even more naturalistic than the natural sciences themselves. We will permit ourselves to refer to several eminent specialists such as L. Berg, A. Meyer, M. Novikoff, M. Osborn, and L. Plate.[1] To the atomism of yesterday, one opposes a conception of the whole determining all of its parts. If orthodox evolutionism taught that "one must only take into consideration similarities of structure of the speech organs if they show that the carriers of these organs descend from one and the same ancestor," the researchers of our day, on the contrary, point out the importance of secondarily acquired similarities, either by means of related organisms that did not descend from the same common ancestors or through organisms with absolutely different origins at the end of a convergent development. Thus "the resemblances shared by two forms can be a secondary fact recently acquired, and on the contrary, the differences can be an inherited primary fact." Under these conditions, the distinction of organisms related to each other and not related to each other loses its decisive character. Convergent development, taking in immense masses of individuals over a vast territory, is to be considered a predominant rule.

It is one of the great merits of one of the founders of modern linguistics, Antoine Meillet, that he brought to our attention a fact too often unnoticed, in spite of its great scope: agreements between two or more languages frequently arise after the breaking up of the mother tongue and result, much more so than one thinks at first, from parallel developments. To the traditional idea of two successive stages, unity and plurality, the doctrine of Meillet opposes, on the one hand, the idea of unity within plurality, and on the other hand, that of plurality within unity. From its beginning he teaches, a community "does not have complete linguistic homogeneity." Thus arises, beside the traditional concept of initial identity, the important notion of identical development. N. S. Trubetzkoy has tried to delimit these two notions and accordingly proposed at the First Congress of Linguists that two

---

[1]See especially L. Berg, *Nomogenesis* (London, 1926) and M. Novikoff, *L'homomorphie comme base methodologique d'une morphologie comparée* (Prague, 1936).

types of language grouping should be distinguished: associations (*Sprach-bünde*), which possess remarkable resemblances in their syntactic, morpho-logical, and phonological structure, and families (*Sprachfamilien*), character-ized above all by a common foundation of grammatical morphemes and common words. (Let us note, furthermore, that according to Meillet, "It is never by differences or agreements in vocabulary that one can establish linguistic parentage.")[2] Thus a family of languages can possess, and ordinar-ily does, besides these material details, similarities of grammatical and phonological structure. This amounts to saying that similarity of structure is independent of the genetic relationship of the languages in question and can relate in different ways languages of the same origin or different descent. Similarity of structure is not opposed, therefore, but is superimposed on the notion of the linguistic parentage of languages. This fact requires the concept of linguistic affinity. According to the apt definition of P. van Ginneken, presented at the Second Congress of Linguists, an affinity does not exclude original parentage, but is only an abstraction from it.

An affinity, or in other words a similarity of structure unifying contig-uous languages, unites them into an association. The notion of association of languages is larger than that of family, which is only a particular case of association. Meillet observes that "in the case where evolution has been to a large extent identical, the result is the same as if there had been unity from the beginning." The convergence of developments (*Wahlverwandschaft*, ac-cording to the term of Goethe) manifests itself as much in the modifications that a system undergoes as in its conservative tendencies, and notably in the sorting out of constructive principles destined to remain intact. Initial iden-tity, which comparative grammar uncovers, is only itself a stage of conver-gent development and does not exclude in any way simultaneous or earlier divergences.

One is acquainted with the tendency of a great many phonological facts to spread out in waves, and one has more than once pointed out that contiguous languages of different origin contain a great many resemblances in their phonological as well as their grammatical structure (for example, Jespersen, Sandfeld, Schmidt, Vendryes, and in particular Boas and Sapir[3]). Frequently these affinities, although uniting contiguous but nonrelated lan-

---

[2]It is the distinction between original parentage or consanguinity and acquired parentage or affinity that corresponds to this classification in Italian linguistic thinking, inspired by the work of d'Ascoli (Bartoli, Pisani). P. Schmidt unites contiguous languages that show structural resemblances into *Sprachkreise*, but he sees in such a grouping only the residue of a stage earlier than the one revealed by the study of a family of languages. Thus the problem of acquired similarities threatens to disappear again before the problem of genetic similarities.

[3]Cf. R. Jakobson, *Int. Journal of Amer. Ling.*, X, pp. 192 ff.

guages, divide linguistic families as well. Thus the domain of Russian (including that of White Russian and of Ukrainian) and of Polish is opposed to the Czechoslovak region by the lack of a quantitative opposition of vowels, and it forms in this way a group with most of the Finno-Ugric languages and Turkic languages of European or Cisuralian Russia,[4] whereas several other languages of the Finno-Ugric and Turkic family possess this opposition: for example, Hungarian belongs, from this point of view, to the same group as Czech and Slovak. The isophones of an affinity cross not only the limits of a family of languages but often even those of a single language. Thus the western dialects of Slovak are grouped according to the lack of a quantitative opposition alongside the neighboring languages of the northeast, that is, of Russian and Polish.

Linguists, however, by looking only superficially at the disturbing question of phonological affinities, are wrong to leave it on the periphery of their research. The facts wait to be analyzed and clarified.

It is known that a language differs even between two speakers of the same language. The great revelator of linguistic paradoxes, Ferdinand de Saussure, has enabled us to appreciate these two antithetical aspects: *la langue*, purposeful identity, an indispensible condition of comprehension, and *la parole*, personal manifestation that individualizes the role of every speaker. He reduces the reciprocal relation of regional speakers of a dialect to a similar dualism. Here also "two forces continually act simultaneously and in a contrary direction": on the one hand, it is the particularist spirit, or parochial spirit; on the other hand, the spirit of community or the unifying force, whose "intercourse" (to use the expression borrowed by the author from English) is only a typical manifestation. But the play of these two opposing forces does not confine itself only to the limits of one language: innovating as well as conservative convergences in the structure of two or more contiguous languages arise as a result of the unifying force, whereas divergences are a result of the particularist spirit.

There is no difference in principle between the manifestation of the unifying force within the framework of one language and within a group of contiguous languages. Where contact is heaviest (for example, at a frontier, in a mixed region, or at an exchange center), one observes a tendency toward establishing means of mutual communication, toward a common language. Many traits of this common language often show a particular facility to extend themselves beyond the boundary of intercourse. In short, it is unimportant whether the common language under examination is an interdialectal language trying to unite the dialects of one nation or a mixed language to be used for international exchanges. The tendency to speak like somebody else is not confined to the mother tongue alone. One wants to be understood by a

---

[4]Cf. V. Skalicka, *Archiv Orientálni*, VI, pp. 272 ff.

stranger and tries to speak like him. Thus the Russians and the Norwegians, talking with each other in their commercial relations in Russenorsk, a mixed language, beautifully analyzed by M. Broch, were careful to speak the language of their interlocutor, a fact that is made clear, moreover, by the term that Russenorsk has for itself: *"mga pá tvoya"* ('I like you'). The Russians of the extreme west, in speaking their mother tongue with Chinese, deform it à la Chinese to such an extent that certain of their yellow speakers, according to M. Georgievskij, often protest. The phonological particularities of mixed formations, whatever they may be, have the exotic attraction of something foreign. Expressive language and fashion take possession of these elements, give them new functions, and contribute to their spread.

Consequently, neither the birth of a mixed language nor the spread of the results of such a mixture necessarily presuppose a biological crossing, and moreover biological crossing does not lead necessarily to a blending of languages. Otherwise, we would be obliged to admit that the language of Alexander Pushkin, a typical half-caste and creator of the modern Russian literary language, is only an "alien language."[5] Hugo Schuchardt, one of the great minds of German science, is led to deny not only a relationship of causality between biological and linguistic hybridizations, but even the possibility of such a relationship: "When a mixture of languages occurs in conjunction with a mixture of peoples, the latter does not depend on the former, but both depend rather on something else. The cause of language hybridization is social rather than psychological in nature." Even though the change of the affricate *c* to *s* in the Greek pronunciation of Russian implanted itself in the language of Russian peasants on the coastline of Lake Azov, the Greeks themselves finding a welcome among the Russians, this linguistic fact only accompanies the crossbreeding and should not be understood as the biological effect of it.

Imitation is certainly a powerful factor in the formation of linguistic waves, whatever the medium of their propogation: either a language or a group of contiguous languages. Nevertheless, it is wrong to view imitation as the only factor or even the decisive and indispensable one. According to the penetrating thesis of Meillet, it is the existence of a collective tendency that dominates everything, whereas the role of imitation, whether large or small, is only an accessory factor in the realization of changes, so that the linguist can easily afford not to be aware of it. A change of linguistic structure could not take place in a local dialect if there were not an identical collective tendency for this change. It is, then, convergence that is the essential phenomenon. The facultative role of the individual who takes the initiative for a convergence consists uniquely in anticipating and in hastening its development. Both within the limits of a single language or an association of

[5]Cf. *Muttersprache* (1933), pp. 420 ff.

languages, an innovation in structure can spread, as we have already pointed out, by contagion, according to the term of de Saussure (*Course*, p. 283) or simply by parallel tendencies. This last case is that of independent parallel evolution. Contagion could not occur if a parallelism of tendencies did not exist. But contagion itself is not necessary, even though a center of radiation is a favorable auxiliary for the extension of a change; and convergent evolution is made easier and accelerated when it can be supported by some model. The action of contagion is therefore neither necessary nor sufficient in order for a linguistic affinity, especially a phonological one, to occur.

Under the influence of the initial stress of Karelian, several Russian dialects of Olonetz have moved the stress on the last syllable to the first syllable of the word, whereas the stress on the other syllables has remained intact. In spite of this imitative change, the accent of the word has retained, in these dialects, its significative function, which is foreign to the Karelian accent (*posýpali*, plural of the preterit of the perfective aspect of the verb "recover"—*posypáli*, the same form of the corresponding imperfect verb), whereas the demarcative function of the Karelian accent (which marks the beginning of a word) has received in the dialects in question only a partial and negative equivalent, that is, the accented syllable cannot be the final one of a polysyllabic word.[6] The dialects of the southeast of Macedonia can serve as a contrary example. In these dialects the free accent has been modified, and it is probably the three syllable rule of Greek that has provided the model for it. But whereas in Greek the accent has a significative function, its demarcative function being purely negative (the third syllable after the accent cannot belong to the same word), in a part of the Macedonian dialects the third (or, in other dialects, the second) syllable before the end of the word has been generalized as the place of the accent, so that in Macedonian the accent has changed its function from significative to demarcative. The change has therefore been more radical than that suggested by the model. In neither of these two examples has contagion led to a clear affinity.

But there exist some cases where the result of imitation lacks even a partial resemblance to the model. According to the observations of Sergievskij, the language of the Russian gypsies ordinarily accents the last syllable of the word; but in words borrowed from Russian, including oxytones, the accent falls always on the second-to-last syllable (Russian: *zimá, sud'bá, vesná*; Gypsy: *zýma, súd'ba, vásna*). From the point of view of Gypsy, the principle of a free accent is inadmissible, and the accent must continue to depend on the end of the word. But the Gypsies had noticed that in Russian, contrary to their mother tongue, the accent is not attached to the final syllable. This is why they fixed the accent on the penultimate syllable,

[6]On the difference between these two categories of phonological means, see N. Trubetzkoy, *Proceedings of the Second Intern. Congr. of Phonetic Sciences*, pp. 45 ff.

rather than because it is where the accent falls on the relative majority of Russian words.[7] The class of words felt as autochthonous and those felt as foreign form in language, as Mathesius has pointed out in his studies on the structure of borrowings, two different stylistic levels. In the above case, these two levels are opposed to each other by the different place of the fixed accent. If the feeling for the foreign origin of borrowings from Russian into Gypsy was to become erased and if the two levels fused, there would result either a unification of the place of the accent or an opposition of the two accents, final and penultimate, as a means of differentiating the meanings of words. Thus we see that borrowings themselves do not modify the phonological structure of a language: it is only their assimilation that is capable of introducing into a language new elements. Even in this last case, a languages does not necessarily appropriate unusual elements. The simplest solution, and apparently the one most used, is that which consists of adopting words of foreign origin to the laws of the indigenous structure. As much as we are able to reproduce foreign words with our own habits of pronunciation, so are we able, on the other hand, to imitate and reproduce a foreign pronunciation of our own lexicon. The celebrated Czech reformer of the fifteenth century, Jan Hus, reproached his compatriots for pronouncing *more Teutonicorum* ordinary *l* instead of hard *l*. It is the spread of Czech among the German population of the cities of Bohemia that influenced urban Czech—and because of this influence, rural Czech—in causing it to lose the distinction of the two lateral phonemes. Borrowings of vocabulary are neither a sufficient nor indispensable condition for phonological contagion. Consequently, there is no necessary connection between a phonological or grammatical affinity and a common linguistic stock. A language accepts elements of foreign structures only when they correspond to its own developmental tendencies. Consequently, the importation of elements of vocabulary cannot be a mother force for phonological development, but at the most, one of the sources at the disposal of such developments.

In examining cases of phonological contagion, one would not be able to explain, by appealing to the intermediary of external factors, either those facts that are the result of imitation or even the direction of contagion. If the "Russian common language" (see the definition of Sommerfelt[8]) sanctioned and propogated the essential phonological feature of the southern dialect of Great Russian, that is, the fusion of unstressed *o* and *a* into a single phoneme,

---

[7]For similar reasons, in Czech, the people are persuaded when listening to Russian that there is a fixed accent on the penultimate syllable. From the point of view of Czech, where there is an initial accent, the accent is necessarily tied to the limits of the word; and as is shown by the study of the emphatic Czech accent (secondary or dialectal), it is the accent on the penultimate that is the admissible variant.

[8]*Actes du Quatrième Congrès de Linguistes*, Copenhagen, 1938, p. 42 ff.

one would not be able to explain this preference by any kind of economical or political condition. The internal reason for the phenomenon in question, however, is very clear: the suppression of a phonological distinction is more likely to be imposed on speakers who already possess it, than a supplementary distinction can be introduced where it is lacking.

External circumstances admit of the two opposed directions of phonological contagion. Contrary to the current opinion, the action that a language exercises on the phonological structure of another language does not presuppose necessarily any political, social, or cultural preponderance on the part of the former. If it is true that the dialect of those dominated is influenced by the dialect of the dominating, the latter, on the other hand, trying to extend itself, adapts itself to the linguistic usages of the dominated. The Poles occupied from the fifteenth to the sixteenth centuries a predominant position with respect to their immediate neighbors to the east, and it is in this period that White Russian was formed, whose essential phonological characteristics result from Russian pronounced by Poles. It is also true, as Polish linguistic studies reveal, that common Polish adapted itself to the phonological structure of White Russian and of Ukrainian. At present, the substratum theory,[9] in fact, is based on the principle that the dominated speakers are able to pass on certain of their linguistic features to the language of the dominating speakers.

In addition to the phonological characteristics that tend to go beyond the limits of one language and to extend themselves across vast continuous domains, there are others that only rarely go beyond the limits of a single language or even dialect. Thus, these are the first that are ordinarily found to be clearly felt as a distinctive trait separating those languages that possess them from surrounding languages. The opposition of palatal and nonpalatal consonants, for example, is felt as the dominant phonological characteristic of Russian and of the neighboring languages. It is this opposition and the concomitant facts that a poet and Russian linguist, A. Aksakov, declares to be "the emblem and the crown" of the phonological system of the Russian language. Other Russian poets find a Turanian character there (Barjuskov, A. Belyj), which is foreign to the Europeans (Trediakovskij, Mandel'stam). Regional scholars search out with passion the real essence of the phenomenon in question precisely in its local variation: the Ukrainian Puskar brags about the "neutralizable opposition" found in his mother tongue, whereas the Votyak Bausev, on the other hand, sets off the sharpness of the "constant opposition"[10] found in Votyak and in Zyrian. It is equally curious that those languages that do not have the phonological palatalization of consonants

[9]Cf. J. Pokorny, *Mitteilungen d. Anthropol. Ges. in Wien*, LXVI, p. 70 ff.
[10]On these terms see N. Trubetzkoy, *Journal de Psychologie*, XXXIII, p. 18.

sometimes experience a veritable aversion for it. As Chlumsky notes in this respect, "it is a fairly common point of view to see an articulatory weakness in palatalized sounds. And not only that: one is led to attribute a part of this weakness to those people who possess palatalized sounds, notably, for example, the Russians. Oh! these poor Russians, with them everything is palatalized!"[11] In the languages of Europe confined to "palatalized languages," one observes frequent cases of palatalization used in the formation of pejorative words.[12] These pronounced attitudes of adherence and repulsion show the force of contagion and the persistence of the phenomenon in question.

Languages possessing the systematic opposition of palatalized and nonpalatalized consonants form a vast continuous domain. This affinity disaggragates many families of languages. Thus among the Slavic languages it is only Russian, including White Russian and Ukrainian,[13] the majority of Polish dialects, and the Bulgarian dialects of the east that are included in the palatalizing languages; among the Romance and Germanic languages, only the Rumanian dialects on the one hand, and the Yiddish of White Russia on the other, are a part of this group; among the Indo-Iranian languages, only the dialects of the Polish and Russian Gypsies; within the Finno-Ugric family, only Mordvinian, Cheremis, Votyak, Zyrian, the western dialects of Lappish, Finnish, and Estonian, and the southern dialects of Karelian and Vepsian belong to the association in question. Apart from these, several peripheral cases (like Iranized Uzbek) and the Turkic languages of the USSR, Poland, and Bessarabia are also part of it. However, in the majority of Turkic languages in this domain, the opposition of palatalized and nonpalatalized consonants has a demarcative function, whereas in the majority of Finno-Ugric languages cited and in the rest of the languages of the same geographical area, this opposition has a significative function.[14] The affinity examined here, moreover, comprises, to the east, the Samoyed group, the majority of the Mongol languages, the Dungan dialect of Chinese, Korean, and Japanese; to the south, the Northern Caucasian languages; and to the west, Lithuanian and to some extent Lettish. It gains in relief, if one notices that beyond this continuous domain that we have just traced, the continent

---

[11] *Recueil des travaux de Premier Congrès des philologues slaves*, II, p. 542.

[12] Cf. Machek, *Fac. Phil. Univ. Carolinae Pragensis, Práce*, XXII, pp. 10 ff.

[13] Only the Old Russian enclave within Estonian territory *(poluvercy)* has lost the palatalization of consonants.

[14] Among the Finnish languages, it is Cheremis that, in some of its dialects, makes use of the opposition in question in a demarcative way (V. Vasil'ev, *Elementarnaja grammatica maripkogo jazyka*, 1927), and on the other hand it is certain Turkish dialects of the Kipchak group such as (1) Karaite in the Northeast, (2) Armeno-Kipchak, extinct (both studied by Kowalski), and (3) the dialects of the Central Crimea (reported by Polivanov) that have by similar means transformed the above opposition from its demarcative function to a significative one.

that one calls *Eurasia sensu latiore* does not have (with the exception of Irish and the Basque languages) palatalization of consonants as a phonological fact.

A language can at the same time be a part of different phonological affinities that do not overlap, in the same way that a language can have peculiarities that link it to different dialects. While the nucleus of the association just mentioned contains only monotonic languages (devoid of polytony), its two peripheries, the one on the east (Japanese and the Dungan dialect of Chinese) and the one on the west (Lithuanian and Lettish dialects, Estonian), belong to two large associations of polytonic languages (that is, languages capable of distinguishing the meanings of words by means of two different pitches). Polytony tends ordinarily to embrace a considerable number of languages. This is true, for example, for central Africa and America. The association of polytonic languages of the Pacific contains, besides Japanese and Korean, also Ainu, the Sino-Tibetan languages, the Annamite and Malayan languages, and several coastal languages of North America. In Europe the area of polytony embraces the languages bordering the Baltic: besides the languages mentioned above on the west coast of the Baltic, most of the Scandinavian languages, the northern Kashoubian dialects, and several seaboard German dialects. It juts out to the south by embracing, as especially Frings has pointed out, German and Dutch dialects of the Rhine Basin.[15] The question of the geographical limits of German polytony still remains open.[16] I learned from N. S. Trubetzkoy that Eberhard Kranzmayer has discovered phonological oppositions of word pitch in many Alpine dialects of German. More to the south, we find a closed polytonic area embracing the majority of Serbo-Croatian and Slovenian dialects, as well as northern Albanian. This deep southern enclave of the Baltic association of European polytonic languages forms only one branch of an even greater association, that is, the languages that contain two distinct varieties of word accent. This duality is realized either in the form of two opposed pitches (polytony in the proper sense of the word), or in the form of a vocalic pronunciation of a glottal stop opposed to a vocalic pronunciation without glottal stop (to this type belong, in addition to Livian, those Danish, Lithuanian, and Lettish dialects that are not of the first type. There are those that combine both distinctions), or finally in the form of a strong syllabic juncture, which is opposed to a weak syllabic juncture (a fact spread over the domain of Germany and Holland). The passage of one of these types to the other is easy and vacillating.

Thus the study of the geographic distribution of phonological facts makes it clear that many of these facts usually go beyond the limits of one

[15]*Braunes Beiträge*, LVIII, pp. 110 ff.
[16]Cf. P. Menzerath, *Teuthonista*, V, pp. 208 ff.

language and tend to embrace several contiguous languages, independent of their genetic relationships or of the absence of any of these relationships. Besides the affinities mentioned,[17] let us point out, as examples, the phonological association taking in the vast territory between southern Alaska and central California, populated by numerous languages that belong to different families, but all possessing a series of glottalized consonants;[18] the association of languages of the Caucasus, whose consonantal system presents the same character and that takes in the northern and southern Caucasian languages, Armenian, Ossetic, as well as the Turkic and Gypsy languages of Trans-Caucasia;[19] the Balkan association[20] and the one that includes various languages of the region of Samarkand (different Iranian dialects, a part of Uzbek and some residues of Arabic).[21] But these are only the first isolated attempts within a vast domain that is still to be explored. Since in linguistic geography, it seems that isophones that cross the limits of languages are frequent and almost the norm, and since presumably the phonological typology of languages is not unrelated to their distribution in space, it would be important for linguistics (historical as well as synchronic) to use some collective activity to establish an atlas of the phonological isoglosses of the languages of the whole world, or at least of entire continents.[22]

The examination of phonological facts that is confined to the limits of a given language runs the risk of cutting up and disfiguring the problem. Thus the facts considered within the limits of a single language or family of languages appears to us simply as the effect of a particularist attitude; but as soon as one looks at them from a larger point of view, one discovers there are effects of a communal spirit. For example, the polytony of the northern Kashoubian dialects opposes them to the rest of the Polish Kashoubian area as well as marks their participation in the Baltic association of polytonic languages; the dialects of those languages that border the western frontier of Russia possess for the most part the phonological palatalization of consonants; and it is precisely the belonging of these dialects to the great association of palatalizing languages, and not their simple divergence to the interior dialects of Finnish, Lettish, and Polish, and so forth, that is to be noted. The dislocation, during the Middle Ages, of the Slavic world into polytonic dialects (Serbo-Croatian and Slovenian), monotonic ones with free quantity

---

[17]Cf. R. Jakobson, *K charakteristike evrazijskogo jazykovogo sojuza* (Paris, 1931).

[18]E. Sapir, *Language*, XX, Chap. IX.

[19]N. Trubetzkoy, *TCLP*, IV, p. 233.

[20]B. Havranek, *Proceedings of the First Intern, Congr. of Phonet. Sciences*, pp. 28 ff.

[21]E. Polivanov, *Uzbekskaja dialektologija i uzbeksky literaturmyj jazyk* (Taskent, 1933), pp. 10 ff.

[22]The International Association for Phonological Studies, in its meeting of 29 August 1936, decided to prepare a phonological atlas of Europe.

(western Slavic), and monotonic ones with free accent (Bulgarian and western Slavic) cannot be completely elucidated, if one does not take into consideration the three distinct associations of which the Slavic dialects have become a part.

The complete analysis of a phonological phenomenon cannot confine itself either to the limits of a single language or even to the limits of an entire association of languages that has such a phenomenon. The mutual distribution of different phonological associations is not arbitrary. One observes that phonological facts tend to form adjacent areas; the area of polytony, for example, is for the most part contiguous to that of the vocalic pronunciation of the glottal stop. A given vicinity favors the birth or the persistence of closely related phonological phenomena, and this vicinity includes languages that, in addition to their pecularities, have certain common traits: thus the association of polytonic languages in Europe is part of a much greater association of languages with two kinds of accent. We have pointed out that the association of palatalizing languages is combined in the west as well as in the east with an association of polytonic languages. It is not very probable that this symmetry of two frontiers of the same association is due simply to chance. In confronting the different isophones forming linguistic affinities on the one hand and the distribution of grammatical facts on the other, one sees appear bundles of isoglosses; and one is also struck by the regularities between the limits of the associations on the one hand and geographical limits that are political and physical in nature on the other. Thus the area of palatalizing monotonic languages coincides with the geographical area known as *Eurasia sensu stricto*, a whole that detaches itself from the European and Asiatic domain by many peculiarities of its physical and political geography. Certainly, the correspondences of different isoglosses are, in general, only approximative: thus to the west, the limit of phonological palatalization of consonants goes beyond the western frontier of Eurasia, as it is traced by geographers, but this takes in only one percent of the surface of the area of palatalizing monotonic languages, and the convergence still remains very convincing.

The important problem is not to deduce linguistic affinities from any extrinsic factor. What is relevant today is to describe them and to put into relief their correspondences in terms of geographical unities of a different kind, without bias and without premature generalizations, such as the explanation of phonological affinity by parentage, or by the mixture or expansion of languages or of linguistic communities.

15

IS A STRUCTURAL
DIALECTOLOGY POSSIBLE? *

Uriel Weinreich

1. In linguistics today the abyss between structural and dialectological studies appears greater than it ever was. The state of disunity is not repaired if "phoneme" and "isogloss" occasionally do turn up in the same piece of research. Students continue to be trained in one domain at the expense of the other. Field work is inspired by one, and only rarely by both, interests. The stauncher adherents of each discipline claim priority for their own method and charge the others with "impressionsim" and "metaphysics," as the case may be; the more pliant are prepared to concede that they are simply studying different aspects of the same reality.

This might seem like a welcome truce in an old controversy, but is it an honorable truce? A compromise induced by fatigue cannot in the long run be satisfactory to either party. The controversy could be resolved only if the structuralists as well as the dialectologists found a reasoned place for the other discipline in their theory of language. But for the disciplines to legitimate each other is tantamount to establishing a unified theory of language on which both of them could operate. This has not yet been done.

While the obstacles are formidable, the writer of this paper believes that they are far from insurmountable. The present article is designed to suggest a few of the difficulties which should be ironed out if the theories of two very much disunited varieties of linguistics, structural and dialectological, are to be brought closer together. A certain amount of oversimplification is inevitable, for the "sides" in the controversy are populous and themselves far from unified. The author would not presume to function as an arbitrator. He simply hopes, without a needless multiplication of terms, to stimulate discussion with others who have also experienced the conflict of interests —within themselves.

*From *Word* 10.388–400 (1954). Reprinted by permission of the International Linguistic Association.

If phonological problems dominate in this paper, this is the result of the fact that in the domain of sounds structural and non-structural approaches differ most;[1] semantic study has (so far, at least) not equalled sound study in precision, while in the domain of grammar, specifically structural points of view have had far less to contribute.

2. Regardless of all its heterogeneity, structural linguistics defines a language as an organized system. It was one of the liberating effects of structural linguistics that it made possible the treatment of a language as a unique and closed system whose members are defined by opposition to each other and by their functions with respect to each other, not by anything outside of the system. But since organization must have a finite scope, one of the major problems in a structural linguistic description is the delimitation of its object, the particular system described. Only in ideal cases can the linguist claim to be describing a whole "language" in the non-technical sense of the word. In practice he must delimit his object to something less. One of the steps he takes is to classify certain items in his data as intercalations from other systems, i.e. as "synchronically foreign" elements (e.g. *bon mot* in an otherwise English sentence). Another step is to make certain that only one variety of the aggregate of systems which the layman calls a "language" is described. These steps are taken in order to insure that the material described is uniform. This seems to be a fundamental requirement of structural description.

To designate the object of the description which is in fact a subdivision of the aggregate of systems which laymen call a single language, the term "dialect" is often used. But if "dialect" is defined as the speech of a community, a region, a social class, etc., the concept does not seem to fit into narrowly structural linguistics because it is endowed with spatial or temporal attributes which do not properly belong to a linguistic system as such. "Dialects" can be adjacent or distant, contemporary or non-contemporary, prestigious or lowly; linguistic systems in a strictly structural view can only be identical or different. It is proposed that the term "dialect" be held in reserve for the time being and that, for purposes of structural analysis as set forth here, it be replaced by "variety."

In deference to the non-structural sense of "dialect" as a type of speech which may itself be heterogeneous, some linguists have broken down the object of description even further to the "idiolect" level. This term has been used in the United States to denote "the total set of speech habits of a single individual at a given time." The term has been seriously criticized on two

---

[1] Some of the phonological points made here were inspired by N. S. Troubetzkoy's article on linguistic geography, "Phonologie et géographie linguistique," *TCLP* 4.228–34 (1931); reprinted in his *Principes de phonologie*, Paris, 1949, pp. 343–50.

grounds: (1) constancy of speech patterns may be more easily stated for two persons in a dialogic situation (a kind of *dialecte à deux*) than for a single individual; (2) there are differences even within an "idiolect" which require that it be broken down further (e.g. into "styles").

"Idiolect" is the homogeneous object of description reduced to its logical extreme, and, in a sense, to absurdity. If we agree with de Saussure that the task of general linguistics is to describe all the linguistic systems of the world,[2] and if description could proceed only one idiolect at a time, then the task of structural linguistics would not only be inexhaustible (which might be sad but true), but its results would be trival and hardly worth the effort.

The restriction of descriptive work to homogeneous material has led to a paradox not quite unlike that proposed by Zeno about motion. A moving arrow is located at some point at every moment of time; at intermediate moments, it is at intermediate positions. Therefore it never moves. Rigidly applied, the typical elements of structural description—"opposition" and "function of units with respect to other units of the same system"—have come close to incapacitating structural analysis for the consideration of several partly similar varieties at a time. Fortunately, the progress of research no longer requires absolute uniformity as a working hypothesis.[3]

Structural linguistic theory now needs procedures for constructing systems of a higher level out of the discrete and homogeneous systems that are derived from description and that represent each a unique formal organization of the substance of expression and content. Let us dub these constructions "diasystems," with the proviso that people allergic to such coinages might safely speak of supersystems or simply of systems of a higher level. A "diasystem" can be constructed by the linguistic analyst out of any two systems which have partial similarities (it is these similarities which make it something different from the mere sum of two systems). But this does not mean that it is always a scientist's construction only: a "diasystem" is experienced in a very real way by bilingual (including "bidialectal") speakers and corresponds to what students of language contact have called "merged system."[4] Thus, we might construct a "diasystem" out of several types of Yiddish in which a variety possessing the opposition /i~ɪ/ is itself opposed to another variety with a single /i/ phoneme. Be it noted that a Yiddish speaker in a situation of dialect contact might find information in the confusion of /i/ and /ɪ/ of his interlocutor, which is opposed, on the diasystem level, to his own corresponding distinction. It might tell him (in a "symptomatic" rather

[2]Ferdinand de Saussure, *Cours de linguistique générale*, Paris, 1949, p. 20.

[3]André Martinet, in preface to Uriel Weinreich, *Languages in Contact*, Linguistic Circle of New York, Publication no. 1, 1953, xii + 148 pages, p. vii.

[4]*Languages in Contact*, pp. 8f.

than a "symbolic" way) where, approximately, his interlocutor is from.

It may be feasible, without defining "dialect" for the time being, to set up "dialectological" as the adjective corresponding to "diasystem," and to speak of dialectological research as the study of diasystems. Dialectology would be the investigation of problems arising when different systems are treated together because of their partial similarity. A specifically structural dialectology would look for the structural consequences of partial differences within a framework of partial similarity.

It is safe to say that a good deal of dialectology is actually of this type and contains no necessary references to geography, ethnography, political and cultural history, or other extra-structural factors. In Gilliéron's classic studies, the typical (if not exclusive) interest is structural rather than "external." In the diasystem "French," we may very well contrast the fate of *gallus* in one variety where *-ll-* > *-d̦-* with its fate in another variety where this phonological change did not take place, without knowing anything about the absolute or even relative geography or chronology of these varieties. Non-geographic, structural dialectology does exist; it is legitimate and even promising. Its special concern is the study of partial similarities and differences between systems and of the structural consequences thereof. The preceding is not to say, of course, that "external' dialectology has been surpassed; this subject will be referred to below (section 7).

Dialectological studies in the structural sense are, of course, nothing new. Binomial formulas like "Yiddish *fus/fis* 'foot'," which are often condensed to *f*$\overset{u}{i}$*s* etc., have always been the mainstay of historical phonology. But it should be noted that structural dialectology need not be restricted to historical problems to the extent to which it has been in the past. Consequences of partial differences between varieties can be synchronic as well as diachronic. The following is an example of a "synchronic consequence." In one variety of Yiddish (we stick to Yiddish examples for the sake of consistency), the singular and plural of 'foot' are distinguished as (*der*) *fus* vs. (*di*) *fis*, while in another variety, both numbers are *fis*. Now, in the number-distinguishing variety, the singular, *fus*, occurs also as a feminine (with *di*); even so, the distinction between singular and plural can still be made in terms of the vowel: *di fus* "sg."—*di fis* "pl." In the other dialect, *fis* is invariably masculine, perhaps as a consequence of, or at least in relation to, the fact that there only a masculine could distinguish between sg. *der fis* and pl. *di fis*.[5]

If structuralism were carried to its logical extreme, it would not allow for the type of comparisons suggested here: it could only study relations

---

[5]For an example of synchronic consequences in phonemics, see Anton Pfalz, "Zur Phonologie der bairisch-österreichischen Mundart," *Lebendiges Erbe; Festschrift . . . Ernst Reclam*, Leipzig, 1936, pp. 1–19, which is at the same time one of the rare instances of German phonemics and of structural dialectology.

within systems; and since in a perfect system all parts are interrelated ("tout se tient"), it is hard to see how systems could even be conceived of as partially similar or different; one would think that they could only be wholly identical or different. Considerations of this nature prevented orthodox Saussureanism of the Geneva school from undertaking the study of gradually changing systems, since it was felt that languages could only be compared, if at all, at discrete "stages."[6] But a more flexible structuralism has overcome this hurdle by abandoning the illusion of a perfect system, and is producing notable results in the diachronic field.[7] We should now take the further step of asserting the possibility of a synchronic or diachronic dialectology based on a combined study of several partially similar systems.

This step in structural linguistic theory would, it seems, do much to bring it closer to dialectology as it is actually carried on.

3. We come next to dialectology's share in the proposed rapprochement. The main objection raised by structuralists against dialectology as usually practice might be formulated thus: in constructing "diasystems" it ignores the structures of the constituent varieties. In other words, existing dialectology usually compares elements belonging to different systems without sufficiently stressing their intimate membership in those systems.

In the domain of sounds, this amounts to a non-phonemic approach. A traditional dialectologist will have no scruples about listening to several dialect informants pronounce their equivalents of a certain word and proclaiming that these forms are "the same" or "different." Let us assume four speakers of a language who, when asked for the word for 'man', utter 1. [man], 2. [man], 3. [mån], and 4. [mån], respectively. On an impressionistic basis, we would adjudge 1 and 2 as "the same," 3 and 4 as "the same," but 1 and 2 as "different" from 3 and 4. Yet suppose that informant 1 speaks a variety in which vowel length is significant; phonemically his form is $_1$/mān/. Informant 2 does not distinguish vowel length, and has given us $_2$/man/. We can further visualize a variety represented by informant 3 where a vowel with maximum degree of opening has the positional variant [å] between /m/ and /n/; phonemically, then, we have $_3$/man/. In the fourth variety, no such positional variation exists; that form is perhaps $_4$/mon/. The structural analysis is thus different from the non-structural one: 2 and 3 now turn out to be possibly "the same" (but only, of course, if the systems are otherwise also identical), while 1 and 4 appear to be different. Structural linguistics requires that the forms of the constituent systems be understood

[6]Albert Sechehaye, "Les trois linguistiques saussuriennes," *Vox romanica* 5.1–48 (1940), pp. 30f.; H[enri] Frei, "Lois de passage," *Zeitschrift für romanische Philologie* 64.557–68 (1944).

[7]Cf. the bibliography of diachronic phonemics by Alphonse G. Juilland in *Word* 9.198–208 (1953).

first and foremost in terms of those systems, since the formal units of two non-identical systems are, strictly speaking, incommensurable.[8]

A similar requirement could be made about the units of content, or "semantemes." It would not do to say, for instance, that the word *taykh* in one variety of Yiddish is "the same" as *taykh* in another if, in the one, it is opposed to *ózere* 'lake', and hence means only 'river', while in the other it is not so opposed and stands for any sizable 'body of water'. Similar structural cautions would be required with respect to "synonyms" in the diasystem. In the diasystem "Yiddish," *baytn*, *shtékheven*, and *toyshn* all signify approximately 'to exchange', but they cannot be synonyms on the variety level if they do not all exist in any one variety.

A grammatical example might also be cited. In terms of function within the system, it would not be justified to identify the feminine *vaysl* 'Vistula River' of two Yiddish varieties if in the one it is opposed to a neuter *vaysl* 'eggwhite', while in the other it is completely homonymous with the (also feminine) word for 'eggwhite'. It is even doubtful whether any two feminines in these two varieties could be legitimately identified in view of the fact that one of the varieties does not possess a neuter gender altogether.

The dialectologist is used to comparing directly the "substance" of different varieties. The demand of the structural linguist that he consider the train of associations, oppositions, and functions that define linguistic forms seems to the dialectologist complicating, unreasonable, and unnecessary ("metaphysical"). To show up the disagreement most clearly, let us represent the phonic problem just discussed on a map and compare the traditional and the proposed structural treatments of it. Obviously the structural approach involves complications, but the dialectologist will become convinced of their necessity when he realizes that phonemics, like structural linguistics generally, represents not a special technique for studying certain problems, but a basic discovery about the way language functions to which structural linguists are completely committed.

Since, in the structural view, allophonic differences between sounds are in a sense less important than phonemic differences, the "substantial" isogloss (Map 2) which separates [a] from [å] in the overall /a/ area is *structurally somehow less important than the purely formal isogloss which separates pronunciations of* [mån] = /man/ *from those of* [mån] = /mon/; the latter isogloss may not reflect any difference in "substance" at all; it would not show up on the non-structural map (Map 1). The traditional dialectologist naturally wonders what he stands to gain by the drawing of such "metaphysical" lines. But if dialectological maps are considered diachronically as snapshots of change, and if it can be shown that the difference

[8] *Languages in Contact*, pp. 7f.

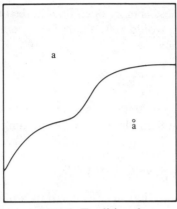

Map 1: Traditional

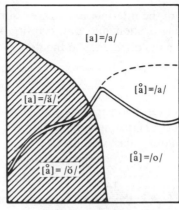

Map 2: Structural

The Vowel in 'man' in Language X

On map 2, a continuous single line divides areas with different phonemic inventories (shaded area distinguishing vowel length, unshaded area not distinguishing it). The double line separates areas using different phonemes in this word (difference of distribution). The dotted line separates allophonic differences.

between phonemes and allophones can be material in determining sound change, it may be possible to convince the dialectologist that the structural map is after all more true to the reality of functioning language. Similar arguments, perhaps, could also be persuasive insofar as they are pertinent to grammatical and lexical matters.

If dialectologists would consider the functions of the elements which they use in their comparisons, their conception of a "diasystem" would come close to that proposed here for structural linguistics and might lead to the unified theory which is so badly needed.

4. The partial differences which are proposed as the specific subject matter of dialectologic study may be of two kinds: differences of inventory and differences of distribution. While the latter are the standard material of comparative study, the former have not received their due stress.

As an example of a difference in inventory, let us take a simple phonemic case first. In the following discussion, single slashes enclose sets of phonemes and single tildes designate phonemic oppositions in a variety identified by a preceding subscript number; oppositions in the constructed diasystem are characterized by double tildes, and the formulas for the diasystems are surrounded by double slashes. Given two varieties with identical five-vowel systems, we might construct the following diasystem: $_1 _2//i \approx e \approx a \approx o \approx u//$. Now let us assume that in one of the varieties, the front vowel of the intermediate degree of openness is more open than in the other; choosing a phonemic transcription which would reflect this fact, we might indicate the difference in the diasystem thus:

$$_{1,2} \bigg/\bigg/ \; i \approx \frac{_1e}{_2\epsilon} \approx a \approx o \approx u \; \bigg/\bigg/ .$$

Given two varieties, one of which (1) distinguishes three front vowels, the other (2) distinguishing four, we might formulate the corresponding part of the vowel diasystem thus:

$$_{1,2} \bigg/\bigg/ \; \frac{_1/\,i \sim e \sim æ\,/}{_2/\,i \sim e \sim \epsilon \sim æ\,/} \; \approx a \approx o \ldots \; \bigg/\bigg/ .$$

Here is the actual vowel inventory of Yiddish considered as a diasystem of three dialects, 1. Central ("Polish"), 2. Southwestern ("Ukrainian"), and 3. Northwestern ("Lithuanian"):

$$_{1,2,3} \bigg/\bigg/ \; \frac{\dfrac{_1/\,i: \sim i\,/}{_2/\,i \sim \textsc{i}\,/}}{_3i} \approx e \approx \frac{_1/\,a: \sim a\,/}{_{2,3}a} \approx o \approx u \; \bigg/\bigg/ .$$

Similarly differences in inventory of grammatical categories might be stated, e.g. between varieties having two against three genders, three as against four conjugational types, and the like. All examples here are tentative and schematic; the possibilities of a more analytical statement of the diasystem, based e.g. on relevant features, remain to be investigated.

One thing is certain: In the study of language contact and interference (see section 5), a clear picture of differences in inventory is a prerequisite.[9]

Differences in distribution cannot be directly inferred from a comparison of the differences in inventory, although the two ordinarily stand in a definite historical relationship. For example, in the diasystem "Yiddish" described above, the phoneme $_3$/i/ in variety 3 usually corresponds to either $_2$/i/ or $_2$/ɪ/ in cognates of variety 2, and to either $_1$/i:/ in cognates of variety 1 ($_3$/sine/: $_2$/sɪne/: $_1$/sĭne/ 'enmity'). This is, as it were, a correspondence between the nearest equivalents. But many $_3$/o/'s correspond to /u/'s in variety 1 and 2, even though all three varieties today possess both /o/ and /u/ phonemes. Thus, /futer/ means 'father' in varieties 1 and 2, but 'fur' in variety 3; /meluxe/ means $_{1,2}$'craft' and $_3$'state'; /hun/ means $_{1,2}$'rooster' and $_3$'hen.' For the tens of thousands of speakers for whom the contact of these varieties is an everyday experience, these "Yiddish" sound sequences are not fully identified until the particular variety of Yiddish to which they belong is itself determined. Now no one would deny that a form like Yiddish [fĭ ˇl] ($_{1,2}$'full,' $_3$'many') is identified fully only in conjunction with its meaning in

[9] *Ibid.*; pp. 1f.

one of the varieties, i.e. when account is taken of the differences in distribution of sounds in cognates occurring in the several varieties. The less obvious point made here is that the form is not fully identified, either, if relevant differences in *inventory* are not accounted for, i.e. if it is not rendered in terms of the phonemes of one of the concrete varieties: [fil] = $_1$/fĩl/, $_2$/fɪl/, $_3$/fil/.

Recent descriptive work on American English phonemics has come close to treating the language as a "diasystem" without, however, satisfying the requirements set forth here. The widely adopted analysis of Trager and Smith[10] provides a set of symbols by which forms of all varieties of American English can be described. It makes it possible, for example, to transcribe Southeastern /pæys/ *pass* in terms of some of the same symbols used in /pæt/ *pat* of the same dialect or in /pæs/, /bəyd/ *bird*, etc., of other varieties. This violates the principle advocated here that the phonemic systems of the varieties should be fully established before the diasystem is constructed. We are not told whether in the phoneme inventory of Southeastern American English, the /æy/ of *pass* does or does not correspond as an inventory item to the /æ/ of other varieties. We cannot tell if the [o] of *home* of Coastal New England is the same phoneme, or a different phoneme, from the [ow] in *go* in the same variety. For reasons of this type, the system has been criticized as providing not a phonemic description or a set of descriptions, but a "transcriptional arsenal."[11] Yet the remaining step toward the establishment of a phonemic diasystem is not difficult to visualize.

5. We might now restate and specify the suggested position of structural dialectology in linguistics as a whole. SYNCHRONIC DIALECTOLOGY compares systems that are partially different and analyzes the "synchronic consequences" of these differences within the similarities. DIACHRONIC DIALECTOLOGY deals (a) with DIVERGENCE, i.e. it studies the growth of partial differences at the expense of similarities and possibly reconstructs earlier stages of greater similarity (traditionally, comparative linguistics); (b) with CONVERGENCE, i.e. it studies partial similarities increasing at the expense of differences (traditionally, substratum and adstratum studies, "bilingual dialectology,"[12] and the like).

The opposite of dialectology, which hardly needs a special name, is the study of languages as discrete systems, one at a time. It involves straight

---

[10]George L. Trager and Henry Lee Smith, Jr., *An Outline of English Structure* (= *Studies in Linguistics, Occasional Papers* 3), Norman (Okla.), 1951, esp. pp. 27–9.

[11]Einar Haugen, "Problems of Bilingual Description," *Report of the Fifth Annual Round Table Meeting on Linguistics and Language Teaching* (= [Georgetown University] *Monograph Series on Languages and Linguistics* no. 7), in press.

[12]For an essay in bilingual dialectology, see Uriel Weinreich, "*Sábesdiker losn* in Yiddish: a Problem of Linguistic Affinity," *Word* 8.360–77 (1952).

description of uniform systems, typological comparisons of such systems, and diachronically, the study of change in systems considered one at a time.

6. It was stated previously that diasystems can be constructed *ad hoc* out of any number of varieties for a given analytic purpose. Constructing a diasystem means placing discrete varieties in a kind of continuum determined by their partial similarities. However, in passing from a traditional to a structural dialectology, the more pressing and more troublesome problem is the opposite one, viz. how to break down a continuum into discrete varieties. What criteria should be used for divisions of various kinds? Can non-technical divisions of a "language" into "dialects," "patois," and the like be utilized for technical purposes?[13]

Before these questions can be answered, it is necessary to distinguish between standardized and non-standardized language. This set of terms is proposed to avoid the use of the ambiguous word, "standard," which among others has to serve for "socially acceptable," "average," "typical," and so on. On the contrary, STANDARDIZATION could easily be used to denote a process of more or less conscious, planned, and centralized regulation of language.[14] Many European languages have had standardized varieties for centuries; a number of formerly "colonial" tongues are undergoing the process only now. Not all leveling is equivalent to standardization. In the standardization process, there is a division of functions between regulators and followers, a constitution of more or less clearcut authorities (academies, ministries of education, *Sprachvereine*, etc.) and of channels of control (schools, special publications, etc.). For example, some dialectal leveling and a good deal of Anglicization has taken place in the immigrant languages of the United States, and we might say that a word like *plenty* has become a part of the American Norwegian koinê.[15] But in the sense proposed here, there is no "standardized" American Norwegian which is different from Old-World Norwegian, and from the point of view of the standardized language, *plenty* is nothing but a regional slang term.

Now it is part of the process of standardization itself to affirm the identity of a language, to set it off discretely from other languages and to strive continually for a reduction of differences within it. Informants of

[13]The possibility of introducing some scientific rigor into existing loose terminology has been explored by André Martinet, "Dialect," *Romance Philology* (1953/54), in press. The article by Václav Polák, "Contributions à l'étude de la notion de langue et de dialecte," *Orbis* 3.89–98 (1954), which arrived too late to be utilized here as fully as it deserves, suggests that we call "language" a diasystem whose partial similarities are grammatical while its partial differences are phonologic and lexical.

[14]Cf. *Languages in Contact*, pp. 99–103. An interesting book about standardization is Heinz Kloss, *Die Entwicklung neuer germanischer Kultursprachen von 1300 bis 1950*, Munich, 1952.

[15]Einar Haugen, *The Norwegian Language in America*, Philadelphia, 1953, p. 588.

standardized languages react in a peculiar way; moreover, it is much easier to deal with samples of a standardized language, to make generalizations about it and to know the limits of their applicability. On the level of non-standardized or FOLK LANGUAGE,[16] a discrete difference between one variety and others is NOT a part of the experience of its speakers, and is much more difficult to supply. For example, it is easy to formulate where standardized Dutch ends and standardized German begins, but it is a completely different matter to utilize for technical purposes the transition between folk Dutch and folk German.

On the whole dialectologists have avoided dealing with standardized languages and have restricted themselves to folk language.[17] Consequently, in practice as well as in theory the problem of dividing and ordering the continuum of language is especially serious with respect to the folk level and not the standardized level. Time was when the continuum of folk language used to be divided on the basis of (usually diachronic) structural features, e.g. the geographic limits of a certain phonological development. Either one isogloss which the linguist considered important was selected (e.g. *k/x* as the line between Low and High German), or a bundle of isoglosses of sufficient thickness was used as a dividing line. In either case, the resulting divisions were not, of course, all of the same degree; they were major, minor, and intermediate, depending on the thickness of the bundle or the relative importance of the key isogloss. It is evident that no unambiguous concept of dialect could emerge even from this optimistic methodology any more than a society can be exhaustively and uniquely divided into "groups."

Classificatory procedures of this type are today virtually passé. Dialectologists have generally switched to extra-structural criteria for dividing the folk-language continuum. The concept of language area (*Sprachlandschaft*) has practically replaced that of "dialect" (*Mundart*) as the central interest in most geographic work,[18] and ever more impressive results are being obtained in correlating the borders, centers, and overall dynamics of language areas with "culture areas" in a broader sense. Instead of speaking, for instance, of the *helpe/helfe* and *Lucht/Luft* isoglosses as the border between the Ripuarian and Moselle-Franconian "dialects" of the German Rhineland, linguistic

---

[16]Interesting parallels could be developed between the sociolinguistic opposition "standardized"—"folk" and the social anthropologist's opposition between the cultures of complex (industrialized) and folk societies or strata of society; cf. e.g. George M. Foster, "What Is Folk Culture?" *American Anthropologist* 55.159–73 (1953).

[17]Some people are not averse to calling modern standardized languages "Indo-European dialects," or speaking of "literary dialects." Dialectology in the sense proposed in this paper need not restrict itself to the folk level, but such usage is one more reason why the term 'dialect' ought to be held in abeyance.

[18]This is particularly evident in the methodologically most advanced German Swiss work; cf. the publications series *Beiträge zur schweizerdeutschen Mudartforschung* edited by Rudolf Hotzenköcherle.

geographers now speak of the Eifel Barrier between the Cologne and Trier areas. This Eifel mountain range happens to be the locus not only of those two random isoglosses, but, among others, also the dividing line between *kend* and *keŋk* 'child', *haus* and *hus* 'house', *grumper* and *erpel* 'potato', *heis* and *gramm* 'hoarse'; between short-bladed and long-bladed scythes, grey bread in oval loaves and black bread in rectangular loaves, New Year's twists and New Year's pretzels, St. Quirin as the patron saint of cattle and the same as the patron of horses, two different types of ditty addressed to the ladybug, etc.[19] The line is meaningful as a reflex of a medieval boundary which can in turn be accounted for by more permanent climatic, orological, hydrographic, and other geographic factors.[20]

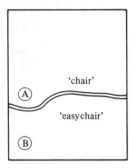

Map 3: Meaning of *shtul* in East European Yiddish (Schematized)

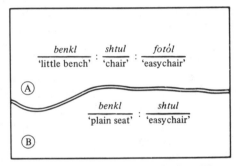

Map 4: Designations of Seats in East European Yiddish (Schematized)

The search for ways to divide the folk-language continuum has also led to statistical correlation methods.[21] Rather than plotting the border lines of single selected structural features, which may be impossible in areas of amorphous transition, the following procedure is used. Inquiries are made at various points concerning the presence or absence of a whole list of test features; then the correlation between the results at some reference point and at all other points is computed, and may be represented cartographically, points with similar correlation coefficients being surrounded by lines which have variously been called "isopleths" or "isogrades." Theoretically related

[19]Linguistic data from Adolf Bach, *Deutsche Mundartforschung*, Heidelberg, 21950, pp. 123ff.; ethnographic data from Adolf Bach, *Deutsche Volkskunde*, Leipzig, 1937, p. 228.

[20]In the United States, Hans Kurath (*A Word Geography of the Eastern United States*, Ann Arbor, 1949), has successfully combined strictly linguistic with "external" criteria in breaking down the relatively undifferentiated American folk-language area.

[21]See David W. Reed and John L. Spicer, "Correlation Methods of Comparing Idiolects in a Transition Area," *Language* 28.348–60 (1952).

to this procedure are the tests of mutual intelligibility between dialects.[22] All these procedures must depend on an arbitrary critical constant (or constants) for the drawing of a dividing line (or lines, of various degrees of importance), but they do yield an insight into the makeup of a continuously varying language area which supplements, if it does not supersede, the results derived by other methods.

In the domain of dialect sociology, where transitions are perhaps even more continuous and fluid than in dialect geography, the use of extra-linguistic correlations and statistical sampling techniques offers promising possibilities of research in an almost untrodden field.[23]

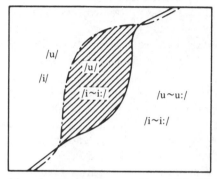

Map 5: Non-Congruent Vowel-Length Isoglosses in Language *Y*

The use of the social-science tools of "external dialectology" can do much to supplement the procedures outlined for a structural dialectology. One problem for combined structural and "external" linguistic investigation is to determine what structural and non-structural features of language have in fact helped to break up the folk-language continuum into the non-technical units of "dialects," "patois," etc. This combined research might get to the heart of the question of diasystems as empirical realities rather than as mere constructs. One of its by-products might be the formulation of a technical concept of "dialect" as a variety or diasystem with certain explicit defining features.

[22]Cf. for example C. F. Voegelin and Zellig S. Harris, "Methods for Determining Intelligibility Among Dialects of Natural Languages," *Proceedings of the American Philosophical Society* 95.322–9 (1951).

[23]See the interesting paper by Stanley M. Sapon, "A Methodology for the Study of Socio-Economic Differentials in Linguistic Phenomena," *Studies in Linguistics* 11.57–68 (1953). A scheme for the classification of varieties of a language according to their function (ecclesiastic, poetic, scientific, etc.) to replace the unsatisfactory terminology of "styles" has been proposed by Yury Šerech, "Toward a Historical Dialectology," *Orbis* 3.43–56 (1954), esp. pp. 47ff.

7. Finally a word might be said about the interrelationship of structural and "external" points of view applied to a specific dialectological problem. Given a map showing an isogloss, the "external" dialectologist's curiosity is likely to concentrate on the locus of that isogloss. Why is it where it is? What determines the details of its course? What other isoglosses bundle with it? What communication obstacle does it reflect?

The structural dialectologist has another set of questions, stemming from his interest in partial differences within a framework of partial similarity. To take up the semasiological example of Map 3 (which is schematized but based on real data), if *shtul* means 'chair' in zone A, but 'easychair' in zone B, then what is the designation of 'easychair' in A and of 'chair' in B? Every semasiological map, due to the two-faceted nature of linguistic signs, gives rise to as many onomasiological questions as the number of zones it contains, and vice versa. If we were to supply the information that in zone A, 'easychair' is *fotél'*, while in zone B 'chair' is *benkl*, a new set of questions would arise: what, then, does *fotél'* mean in B and *benkl* in A?[24] This implicational chain of questions could be continued further. The resulting answers, when entered on a map, would produce a picture of an isogloss dividing two lexical systems, rather than two isolated items (see Map 4). This would be the "structural corrective" to a traditional dialect map.

It is easy to think of dialectological field problems for the solution of which "external" and structural considerations must be combined in the most intimate manner. Such problems would arise particularly if the cartographic plotting of systems should produce a set of narrowly diverging isoglosses. Assume that an isogloss is drawn between a variety of a language which distinguishes short /u/ from long /u:/ and another variety which makes no such quantitative distinction. The structuralist's curiosity is immediately aroused about length distinctions in other vowels. Suppose now that the variety that distinguishes the length of /u/ does so also for /i/; but that the isoglosses, plotted independently, are not exactly congruent (Map 5). Some intriguing questions now arise concerning the dynamics of the vowel pattern of the discrepant zone. Nothing but an on-the-spot field study closely combining structural analysis and an examination of the "external" communication conditions in the area could deal adequately with a problem of this kind.

8. In answer to the question posed in the title of this paper, it is submitted that a structural dialectology is possible. Its results promise to be most fruitful if it is combined with "external" dialectology without its own conceptual framework being abandoned.

---

[24]The actual answer is that *fotél'* is not current in zone B, while *benkl* means 'little bench' in zone A.

16

ON THE MECHANISM
OF LINGUISTIC CHANGE*

William Labov

Introduction

This paper outlines the approaches to the explanation of linguistic change which are being followed in our current research within the context of the speech community. It is now clear that many theoretical problems of linguistic structure cannot be resolved without data from the speech community;[1] here I will focus on the converse proposition—that linguistic change cannot be explained by arguments drawn from purely internal relations within the system, even if external, sociolinguistic relations are recognized as additional conditioning factors. In the mechanism of linguistic changes which we have observed, the two sets of relations are interlocked in a systematic way.

The investigations which form the basis for the present discussion are studies of linguistic change on the island of Martha's Vineyard, and in New York City; the principal focus will be on the process of sound change. The chief techniques used in this research have been described in several previous papers and publications, along with a certain amount of the data and the findings.[2] The data to be presented here may be considered representative of a much larger set of facts and correlations derived from these studies.

*Reprinted from Georgetown University Monograph Series on Languages and Linguistics: Monograph No. 18, Report of the 16th Annual Round Table Meeting, Georgetown University Press, Washington, D.C., 1965, pp. 91–114. Reprinted by permission of the author and publisher.

[1]This point of view is developed in detail in W. Labov, "The aims of sociolinguistic research," to appear in the report of the Sociolinguistics Seminar held at Bloomington, Indiana, in the summer of 1964, under the auspices of the Social Science Research Council.

[2]"The social motivation of a sound change," *Word* 19:273–309 [1963]; *The Social Stratification of English in New York City*, Columbia University Dissertation, 1964; "Phonological correlations of social stratification," in Gumperz and Hymes [eds.], *The*

The problems of linguistic evolution. Despite the achievements of 19th century historical linguistics, many avenues to the study of linguistic change remain unexplored. In 1905, Meillet noted that all of the laws of linguistic history that had been discovered were merely possibilities:[3]

> ... it remains for us to discover the variables which permit or incite the possibilities thus recognized.

The problem as we face it today is precisely that which Meillet outlined sixty years ago, for little progress has been made in ascertaining the empirical factors which condition historical change.[4] The chief problems of linguistic evolution might be summarized as five questions:

1. Is there an over-all direction of linguistic evolution?
2. What are the universal constraints upon linguistic change?
3. What are the causes of the continual origination of new linguistic changes?
4. By what mechanism do changes proceed?
5. Is there an adaptive function to linguistic evolution?[5]

One approach to linguistic evolution is to study changes completed in the past. This has of course been the major strategy of historical linguistics, and it is the only possible approach to the first two questions—the direction of linguistic evolution, and the universal constraints upon change. On the other hand, the questions of the mechanism of change, the inciting causes of change, and the adaptive functions of change, are best analyzed by studying in detail linguistic changes in progress. The mechanism of linguistic change will be the chief topic of the discussion to follow; however, many of the

---

Ethnography of Communication, American Anthropologist, Vol. 66, No. 6, Part 2, December 1964, pp. 164–176; "The reflections of social processes in linguistic structures," in Fishman, J. [ed.], *A Reader in the Sociology of Language* [to appear, Mouton]; "Hypercorrection by the lower middle class as a factor in linguistic change," in Bright, W. [ed.] *Proceedings of the U.C.L.A. Conference on Sociolinguistics* [to appear]; "Stages in the acquisition of standard English," in Davis. A. [ed.], *Proceedings of the Conference on Urban School Dialects and Language Learning* [to appear].

[3]*Linguistique historique et linguistique générale*, [Paris, 1921], p. 16.

[4]There has actually been a retrograde movement in this respect, in the sense that treatments of linguistic change which are essentially ahistorical have become popular. Chronological detail is deliberately set aside in such articles as H. Pilch, "The rise of the American English vowel pattern," *Word* 11:57–93 [1955], and M. Halle, "Phonology in a generative grammar," *Word* 18:54–72 [1962].

[5]This question is all the more puzzling when we contrast linguistic with biological evolution. It is difficult to discuss the evolution of the plant and animal kingdoms without some reference to adaptation to various environments. But what conceivable adaptive function is served by the efflorescence of the Indo-European family? On this topic, see "The aims of sociolinguistic research," cited above, and D. Hymes, "Functions of speech: An evolutionary approach," in Gruber, F. C. [ed.], *Anthropology and Education* [Philadelphia, 1961].

conclusions will plainly be relevant to the questions of inciting causes and adaptive functions of change, and it will be apparent that more complete answers to these questions will require methods similar to those used here.

An essential presupposition of this line of research is a uniformitarian doctrine: that is, the claim that the same mechanisms which operated to produce the large scale changes of the past may be observed operating in the current changes taking place around us.

A Strategy for the Study of Linguistic Changes in Progress

Although answers to the three questions given above are the ultimate goals of our current research, they do not represent the actual strategy used. For the empirical study of changes in progress, the task can be sub-divided into three separate problems which jointly serve to answer the questions raised above.

1. The *transition* problem is to find the route by which one stage of a linguistic change has evolved from an earlier stage. We wish to trace enough of the intervening stages so that we can eliminate all but one of the major alternatives. Thus questions of the regularity of sound change, of grammatical influence on sound change, of "push chains" versus "pull chains," of steady movement versus sudden and discontinuous shifts, are all aspects of the transition problem.

2. The *embedding* problem is to find the continuous matrix of social and linguistic behavior in which the linguistic change is carried. The principal route to the solution is through the discovery of correlations between elements of the linguistic system, and between those elements and the non-linguistic system of social behavior. The correlations are established by strong proof of concomitant variation: that is, by showing that a small change in the independent variable is regularly accompanied by a change of the linguistic variable in a predictable direction.[6]

3. The *evaluation* problem is to find the subjective [or latent] correlates of the objective [or manifest] changes which have been observed. The indirect approach to this problem correlates the general attitudes and aspirations of the informants with their linguistic behavior. The more direct

---

[6]The concept of the linguistic variable is that developed in "The linguistic variable as a structural unit," paper given before the Washington, D.C. Linguistics Club in October, 1964. The definition of such a variable amounts to an empirical assertion of co-variation, within or without the linguistic system. It appears that the fundamental difference between an explanation of a linguistic change, and a description, is that a description makes no such assertion. In terms of a description of change, such as that provided by Halle, *op. cit.*, there is no greater probability of the change taking place in the observed direction, as in the reverse direction. Note that the embedding problem is presented here as a single problem, despite the fact that there are two distinct aspects: correlations within the linguistic system, and with elements outside the system. The main body of this paper provides justification for this decision.

approach is to measure the unconscious subjective reactions of the informants to values of the linguistic variable itself.

With tentative solutions to these problems in hand, it would be possible to provide an explanation of a linguistic change which answers the three questions of inciting cause, mechanism, and adaptive function. As in any other investigation, the value of an explanation rises in relation to its generality, but only to the extent that it rests upon a foundation of reliable and reproducible evidence.

The Observation of Sound Change

The simplest data that will establish the existence of a linguistic change is a set of observations of two successive generations of speakers— generations of comparable social characteristics which represent stages in the evolution of the same speech community. Hermann obtained such data at Charmey in 1929, by developing Gauchat's original observations of 1899.[7] We have such data for Martha's Vineyard, adding the 1961 observations to the 1933 data of the Linguistic Atlas.[8] For New York City, we add the current data of 1963 to the Linguistic Atlas data of 1940; in addition, we have many other reports, including the excellent observations of Babbitt in 1896 to add further time depth to our analysis.[9]

Solutions to the transition problem proposed here will depend upon close analysis of the distribution of linguistic forms in *apparent time*—that is, along the dimension formed by the age groups of the present population. Such an analysis is possible only because the original simple description of change in *real time* enables us to distinguish age-grading in the present population from the effects of linguistic change.[10]

The evidence obtained in the research reported here indicates that the regular process of sound change can be isolated and recorded by observations across two generations. This process is characterized by a rapid development of some units of a phonetic sub-system, while other units remain relatively constant. It affects word classes as a whole, rather than individual words: yet these classes may be defined by a variety of conditions, morphophonemic and

---

[7]"Lautveränderungen in der Individualsprache einer Mundart," Nachrichten der Gesellschaft der Wissenschaften zu Göttingen, *Phil.-his. Kl.* XI: 195–214 [1929]; L. Gauchat, *L'unité phonétique dans le patois d'une commune*, [Halle, 1905].

[8]H. Kurath et al., *Lingustic Atlas of New England* [Providence, 1941].

[9]Y. A. Frank, *The Speech of New York City*, University of Michigan dissertation, 1948; H. Kurath and R. A. McDavid, Jr., *The Pronunciation of English in the Atlantic States* [Ann Arbor, 1961]; A. F. Hubbell, *The Pronunciation of English in New York City* [New York, 1949]; E. H. Babbitt, "The English of the lower classes in New York City and vicinity," *Dialect Notes* 1:457–464 [1896].

[10]C. Hockett, "Age-grading and linguistic continuity," *Language* 26:449–457 [1950].

grammatical as well as phonetic. It is regular, but more in the outcome than in its inception or its development. Furthermore, it appears that the process of sound change is not an autonomous movement within the confines of a linguistic system, but rather a complex response to many aspects of human behavior.

Some comment is required on the possibility of observing regular sound change, since arguments inherited from the neogrammarian controversy have impeded the progress of empirical research in this area. The inheritors of the neogrammarian tradition, who should be most interested in the empirical study of regular change in progress, have abandoned the arena of meaningful research in favor of abstract and speculative arguments. Indeed, Bloomfield and Hockett have maintained that phonetic change cannot in principle be observed by any of the techniques currently available.[11] Hockett has proceeded to identify sound change with a level of random fluctuations in the action of the articulatory apparatus, without any inherent direction, a drift of the articulatory target which has no cognitive, expressive or social significance.[12] All of the empirical observations of change in progress which have been reported are explained as the results of a complex process of borrowing, and are relegated to a type of linguistic behavior known as the fluctuation or conflict of forms. No claims are made for the regularity of this process, and so the basic tenet of the regularity of sound change has been deprived of all empirical significance. Furthermore, the changes which actually are observed are regarded as unsystematic phenomena, to be discussed with anecdotal evidence, subject to forces "quite outside the linguist's reach," factors which "elude our grasp," fluctuations "beyond our powers" to record.[13]

The evidence of current research suggests that this retreat was premature, that the regular process of sound change can be observed by empirical

[11]*Language* [New York, 1933], p. 347, 365; *A Course in Modern Linguistics* [New York, 1958], p. 439, 444. Hockett writes: "No one has yet observed sound change: we have only been able to detect it via its consequences. We shall see later that a more nearly direct observation would be theoretically possible, if impractical, but any ostensible report of such an observation so far must be discredited." His theoretical proposal is that "over a period of fifty years we made, each month, a thousand accurate acoustic records . . . all from the members of a tight-knit community." The suggestion to multiply the data in this way is not necessarily helpful, as the experience of sociological survey analysts has shown: for relatively small numbers are needed to measure change in a population if the bias of selection is eliminated or minimized. Otherwise, we merely multiply the errors of measurement.

[12]According to Hockett, the variables responsible for sound change include "the amount of moisture in the throat, nose and mouth of the speaker, random currents in his central nervous system, muscular tics . . . the condition of the hearer's outer ear [presence of wax or dirt] . . ." *Op. cit.*, pp. 443–444.

[13]Bloomfield, *op. cit.*, pp. 343–368.

methods. The refinements in methodology called for are not the mechanical elaborations suggested by the writers cited above; for the mere multiplication of data only confounds analysis and perpetuates the bias of selection. It is rigor in the analysis of a population and in the selection of informants which is required. Furthermore, we need ingenuity in the resolution of stylistic variation, to go beyond the sterile method of endless dissection into idiolects. With such techniques, we find that regularity emerges where only confusion was seen before. Random fluctuations in articulation can certainly be found: indeed, this is the level of "noise" which prevents us from predicting the form of every utterance which our informants will make. But it would be an error to ascribe a major role to such fluctuations in the economy of linguistic change. The forces which direct the observed changes appear to be of an entirely different order of magnitude, and the changes take place much more rapidly than any process of random drift could account for.[14]

A single example of a sound change recently observed will be used to illustrate the general approach to solving the transition, embedding and evaluation problems. This example is one of the simplest cases—that of the centralization of (aw) on Martha's Vineyard. In the development of this case, some new evidence will be presented on the mechanism of sound changes which has not been published before.

The Centralization of (aw) on Martha's Vineyard

We begin with a clear-cut case for the existence of a linguistic change from observations in real time. In 1933, Guy Lowman found no more than the barest trace of centralization of /aw/; the significant variation observed was the fronting of /aw/ from [aʊ] to [æʊ]. In 1961, a comparable set of older eighth generation descendants of Yankee settlers from the same villages showed a very pronounced centralization of /aw/—now clearly the variable (aw).[15]

The *transition* problem is studied through a detailed examination of the

---

[14]Thus the following table contrasts the two points of view:

Neogrammarian:	sound change	fluctuation of forms	ultimate regularity
Present discussion:	sub-linguistic fluctuations	sound change	ultimate regularity

[15]In the notation used here, parentheses indicate the linguistic variable, while slashes indicate bi-unique phonemes and brackets phonetic notation as usual. Thus (aw) represents the variable in general; (aw-2) is a particular value of the variable; (aw)-22 is an average index score for the variable.

distribution of forms through apparent time—that is, through the various age levels in the present population.[16] The first step in the analysis is to construct a quantitative index for discrete values of the variable:[17]

aw-0	[au]
aw-1	[a⊥u]
aw-2	[ɐu]
aw-3	[əu]

The index of centralization was constructed from this scale by averaging the numerical values assigned to each variant. Thus (aw)-00 would mean no centralization at all, while (aw)-3.00 would mean consistent centralization at the level of [əu]. This index was applied to interviews with 69 informants by rating each of the words in which (aw) occurred. The first approach to the transition problem can then be made by correlating average (aw) index scores for these interviews with the age level of the speakers. The first three columns of Table 1 show a regular correlation, in which the centralization index rises regularly for four successive age levels.

TABLE 1

Centralization Indexes by Age Level

Generation	Age Level	(aw)-	(ai)-
Ia	over 75	0.22	0.25
Ib	61–75	0.37	0.35
IIa	46–60	0.44	0.62
IIb	31–45	0.88	0.81

The over-all tendency of Table 1 represents an amalgamation of many different types of speakers and many different trends in the use of (aw). Figure 1 presents a more detailed analysis of the transition problem for a critical sub-group. Here are displayed the percentage distribution of lexical items for eight individuals from 92 to 31 years of age. The horizontal axes show the four coded levels of the variable (aw). The vertical axes are the percentages of lexical items used with each variant. The vocabulary is broken into two sections that are tabulated separately: the solid line represents words in which (aw) is followed by a voiceless obstruent, as in *out*, *house*, *about*, *mouth*; the broken line represents all other words [and princi-

[16] In this case, as in many others, the original sample was too small to allow us to study differences in age levels; only four informants were chosen on Martha's Vineyard in 1933.

[17] The original impressionistic scale had six levels. Instrumental measurements of a sample of these ratings indicated that four levels could be distinguished with a high degree of conformity to formant positions. See "The social motivation of a sound change," pp. 286–287.

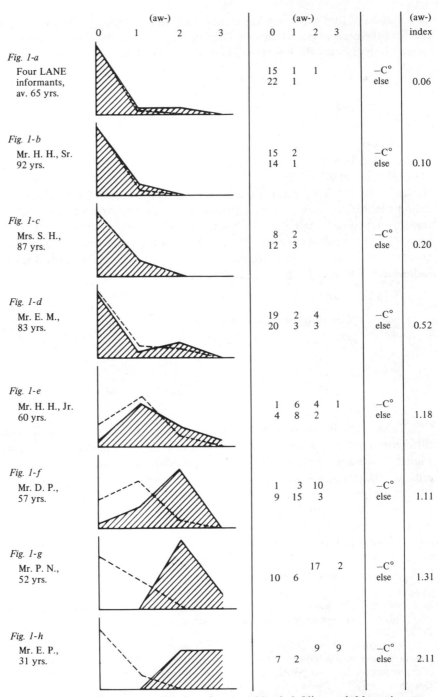

	(aw-) 0 1 2 3	(aw-) 0 1 2 3		(aw-) index

Fig. 1-a
Four LANE informants, av. 65 yrs.
15 1 1 / 22 1 — −C° else — 0.06

Fig. 1-b
Mr. H. H., Sr. 92 yrs.
15 2 / 14 1 — −C° else — 0.10

Fig. 1-c
Mrs. S. H., 87 yrs.
8 2 / 12 3 — −C° else — 0.20

Fig. 1-d
Mr. E. M., 83 yrs.
19 2 4 / 20 3 3 — −C° else — 0.52

Fig. 1-e
Mr. H. H., Jr. 60 yrs.
1 6 4 1 / 4 8 2 — −C° else — 1.18

Fig. 1-f
Mr. D. P., 57 yrs.
1 3 10 / 9 15 3 — −C° else — 1.11

Fig. 1-g
Mr. P. N., 52 yrs.
17 2 / 10 6 — −C° else — 1.31

Fig. 1-h
Mr. E. P., 31 yrs.
9 9 / 7 2 — −C° else — 2.11

Fig. 1. Stages in the centralization of (aw) on Martha's Vineyard, Massachusetts

pally those ending in a nasal, as in *town, found*, or with no consonant final, as in *now, how*, etc.] [18]

The first diagram in Figure 1 is not that of an individual, but shows the composite results for the four Linguistic Atlas informants interviewed in 1933. They show only the barest trace of centralization. The second diagram, 1-b, is that of the oldest informant of 1961, a man 92 years old. The average age of the Atlas informants was 65 years; Mr. H. H. Sr. would have been 64 years old in 1933, and so he is of the same age group. His centralization profile is quite similar to that of the Atlas informants in 1-a. In Figure 1-c, we have an 87-year-old woman who shows only a slight increase in centralization. Figure 1-d, Mr. E. M., 83 years old, indicates a small but distinct increase in the occurrence of variant (aw-2). Mr. H. H. Jr., in 1-e, is considerably younger; he is 61 years old, the first representative of the next generation, since he is the son of Mr. H. H. Sr. Here we have a marked increase in centralization, with both classes of words centered about a norm of (aw-1). In Figure 1-f, Mr. D. P., 57 years old, shows a distinct difference between words ending in voiceless obstruents and all others; the first are now centered about a norm of (aw-2), while the second group is concentrated at (aw-1). This process is carried further in the speech of Mr. P. N., 52 years old, who shows perfect complementary distribution. Before voiceless obstruents, /aw/ has an allophone which is almost always (aw-2), while before other terminals it is usually uncentralized. And at this point, there is no overlap in the distribution. Finally, in 1-h, the most extreme case of centralization, we see an even sharper separation: this is Mr. E. P., 31 years old, the son of Mr. D. P. in 1-f.

On the right hand side of Figure 1 are the figures for the actual numbers of lexical items observed, and the composite index scores for each of the eight cases. It may be noted that (aw) is only one-third as frequent as (ay), and the regularity which appears here does not require a vast corpus of observations. The regularity emerges through the controlled selection of informants, methods of elicitation, and of recording the data.

The eight diagrams of Figure 1 represent the most homogeneous type of population. All of the speakers are Yankee descendants of the original settlers of the island, all are interrelated, many from the same families, with similar attitudes towards the island. All had rural upbringing, and worked as carpenters or fishermen, with one exception. Thus the continuous development of centralization represents the very model of a neogrammarian sound change, accomplished within two generations.

The *embedding* problem was first approached by correlating the centralization of the obviously related variables (ay) and (aw)—that is, the

---

[18]The phonetic conditioning was actually much more complex than this, and both following and preceding consonants are involved. *Ibid.*, p. 290.

change of (aw) was embedded in the system of upgliding diphthongs. The Atlas records indicate a moderate degree of centralization in the 1930's, so that we know that the centralized forms of (ay) preceded the rise of (aw). The fourth column of Table 1 shows a close correlation of the two variables, with (ay) slightly in the lead at first, but (aw) becoming more dominant at the end. This pattern was repeated when the variables were correlated with a number of independent extra-linguistic factors: the occupation, education and geographic location of the speaker, and most importantly, the ethnic group to which he belonged. The significant differences in the transition rates of these various sub-groups allowed the following statement of a solution to the embedding problem:

> The centralization of (aw) was part of a more general change which began with the centralization of (ay). This initial change proceeded from a moderate level of (ay) centralization which was probably a regional and recessive trait inherited from the original settlers of the island. The increase of centralization of (ay) began in a rural community of Yankee fishermen descended directly from these original settlers. From there, it spread outward to speakers of the same ethnic group in other occupations and in other communities. The structurally symmetrical variable (aw) began to show similar tendencies early in this process. The change was also adopted by the neighboring Indian group at Gay Head, and a generation later, spread to the large Portuguese group in the more settled sections of the island. In these two ethnic groups, centralization of (aw) overtook and surpassed centralization of (ay).

Figure 1 would lead us to believe that the phonetic environment of (aw) was a powerful factor in the initiation of the sound change. Moreover, we can observe that the centralization of (ay) also showed a strong tendency towards phonetic conditioning in Generation Ib, similar to that displayed for (aw) in Generation IIb.[19] However, phonetic restriction on (ay) was overridden in the following generation, so that the Generation II shows a uniform norm for (ay) in all phonetic environments. This development would support the view that phonetic conditioning does not play a significant role as an inciting cause of the centralization of (aw), but acts rather as a conditioning factor which may be eliminated by further change.

On Martha's Vineyard, the *evaluation problem* was approached by analyzing a number of clues to the subjective attitudes towards island life which appeared in the course of the interviews. Attitudes towards summer tourists, towards unemployment insurance, towards work on the mainland, towards other occupational and ethnic groups, were correlated with data

---

[19]This phonetic conditioning is more in the nature of a continuum than that for (aw). On page 289 of "The social motivation of a sound change" is given the complete data for a speaker of the same age and background as Mr. H. H. Jr. of Figure 1.

obtained from community leaders and historical records, and then with the linguistic variables. It appeared that the rise of (aw) was correlated with the successive entry into the main stream of island life of groups that had previously been partially excluded. It was concluded that a social value had been [more or less arbitrarily] associated with the centralization of (ay) and (aw), and that social value could best be expressed as "native status as a Vineyarder." Thus to the extent that an individual felt able to claim and maintain status as a native Vineyarder, he adopted increasing centralization of (ay) and (aw). Sons who had tried to earn a living on the mainland, and afterwards returned to the island, developed an even higher degree of centralization than their fathers had used. But to the extent that a Vineyarder abandoned his claim to stay on the island and earn his living there, he also abandoned centralization and returned to the standard uncentralized forms.

The solution to the evaluation problem is a statement of the social significance of the changed form—that is, the function which is the direct equivalent on the non-cognitive level of the meaning of the form on the cognitive level. In the developments described here, the cognitive function of /ay/ and /aw/ has remained constant. It is plain that the non-cognitive functions which are carried by these phonological elements are the essential factors in the mechanism of the change. This conclusion can be generalized to many other instances of more complex changes, in which the net result is a radical change of cognitive function. The sound change observed on Martha's Vineyard did not produce phonemic change, in which units defined by cognitive function were merged or split. But many of the changes in progress that have been observed in New York City did produce such mergers and splits on the level of the bi-unique phoneme.[20] One such change is the raising of (oh), the vowel of *law*, *talk*, *off*, *more*, etc., which will serve to illustrate many aspects of the mechanism of linguistic change not relevant to the simpler example on Martha's Vineyard.

The Raising of (oh) in New York City

It was not possible to make a direct attack upon the transition problem in New York City. Although the records of the Linguistic Atlas showed sporadic raising of (oh) at a fairly low level, the Atlas informants in New York City were not selected systematically enough so that we could construct a comparable sample in 1963.[21] Furthermore, an over-all comparison of the

[20]The far-reaching shifts and mergers observed in the long and in-gliding vowel system of New York City, to be discussed below, do not affect the morphophonemic system. The detailed distribution of the variables in the process of change appear to provide evidence for the systematic status of the bi-unique phoneme. See "The aims of sociolinguistic research" cited above for discussion.

[21]Convenience was apparently a greater factor in the selection of Atlas informants in New York than on Martha's Vineyard. The great bulk of the New York population was

usage of this variable by older and younger speakers did not show the clear-cut and regular progression which we saw for (aw) on Martha's Vineyard. It was suspected that the reason for this difficulty was the greater tendency towards stylistic variation among New Yorkers, and the heterogeneity of the population in terms of socio-economic class and ethnic membership. Therefore it was necessary to attack the embedding problem first, before the transition problem.

The variable (oh) is a part of the system of long and ingliding vowels in the vernacular pattern of New York City speech which is essentially *r*-less: that is, where final and pre-consonantal /r/ does not occur as a consonantal glide. Thus (oh) occurs in the word class of *law, talk, broad, caught, off,* and *more, four, board,* etc. To establish a quantifiable index, five variants were coded as follows:[22]

(oh-1)	$[\upsilon:^{\ni}]$
(oh-2)	$[o:^{\perp}\mathfrak{d}^{\dashv\ni}]$
(oh-3)	$[\mathfrak{d}:^{\perp\ni}]$
(oh-4)	$[\mathfrak{d}:]$
(oh-5)	$[\mathfrak{v}:]$

The (oh) index score was established by taking the numerical average of the variants recorded in any given portion of speech, and multiplying by ten. Thus the consistent use of (oh-2) would give a score of (oh)-20, and a consistent use of (oh-4), a score of (oh)-40.

A method was developed in the New York City study for isolating a range of well-defined contextual styles in the speech of individual informants, and average index scores were determined for each style. A systematic approach to the sampling of a large urban population was utilized, embodying the techniques of survey methodology, and average index scores for various sub-groups of the sample population were determined for each style. The embedding problem was then attacked by correlating the five chief linguistic variables each with each other, and with other elements of the linguistic system, with the level of stylistic variation in which they were recorded, and with the independent variables of socio-economic class [occupation, education and income], sex, ethnic group and age level.[23]

Correlations of (oh) with socio-economic class revealed that the irregu-

---

poorly represented in the sample, including the working class and lower middle class. The old-family stock used for Atlas interviews represents only a very small fraction of the ethnic composition of the city, at most one or two per cent.

[22]The codification of these variants can be assisted by the use of some modal reference points. (oh-1) is at the level of the vowel of [r-less] *sure;* (oh-3) is the level of the most common Northern vowel in [r-pronouncing] *or, nor;* (oh-4) at cardinal I.P.A. [ɔ]; (oh-5) at the level of Eastern New England *cot.*

[23]The embedding problem is treated here as one problem, not two, in accordance with the general logic of this paper.

lar distribution of (oh) in the population as a whole was partly due to the fact that the change had not yet affected all social classes. Figure 2 is a style stratification diagram for (oh) in which the transition state of this variable can be seen in synchronic section. The horizontal axis represents the ten socio-economic levels used for this analysis, grouped informally into lower class, working class, lower middle class, and upper middle class. The vertical axis represents the average (oh) index scores: the lower values of (oh) are at the top, representing the higher, closer vowels, and the higher values of (oh) are at the bottom, indicating more open vowels. The index scores for each socio-economic group are entered on the diagram for each stylistic context, and values for the same style are connected along straight lines.

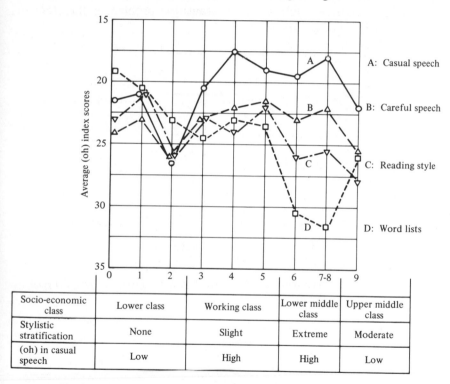

Socio-economic class	Lower class		Working class		Lower middle class	Upper middle class
Stylistic stratification	None		Slight		Extreme	Moderate
(oh) in casual speech	Low		High		High	Low

Fig. 2. Style stratification of (oh) for nine socio-economic sub-classes

Figure 2 indicates that (oh) is not a significant variable for lower class speakers, who do not use particularly high values of this vowel and show no stylistic stratification at all. Working class speakers show a recent stage in the raising of (oh): very high vowels in casual speech, but otherwise very little stratification in the more formal styles, and little tendency towards the extreme, hypercorrect (oh-4) and (oh-5). But lower middle class speakers show the most developed state of the sound change, with high values in casual speech, and extreme stylistic stratification. Finally, the upper middle class group is more moderate in all respects than the lower middle class, still retaining the pattern of stylistic stratification.

The ethnic group membership of New York City speakers is even more relevant to their use of (oh) than socio-economic class. Figure 3 shows the differences between speakers of Jewish and Italian background in the treatment of (oh) in casual speech. For all but the upper middle class, the Jewish group uses higher levels of (oh).[24] Table 2 shows that both Jewish and Italian speakers have participated in the raising of (oh), but the increase seems to have reached its maximum early for the Jewish group, and later for the Italian group. A separate solution for the transition problem is therefore required for each ethnic group.

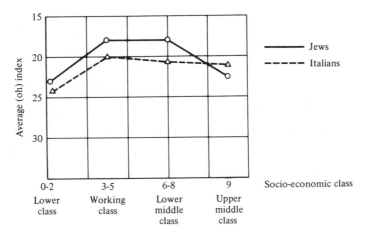

Fig. 3. Class stratification diagram for (oh) by ethnic group in casual speech

TABLE 2

Average (oh) Indexes by Age Level
and Ethnic Group in Casual Speech

Age	Jews	Italians
8–19	17	18
20–35	18	18
36–49	17	20
50–59	15	20
60–	25	30

[24]The Negro group does not show any significant response to the variable (oh), and shows a constant index of performance at a low level. As noted above, the lower class in general is similarly indifferent to (oh). Table 2 shows Jewish and Italian ethnic groups only, with the lower class excluded.

The *transition problem* for the Italian group can be seen analyzed in Figure 4. The procession of values is not absolutely regular, since socio-economic membership, sex, and other factors affect the values; nevertheless, there is a steady upward movement from the oldest speakers on the right to the youngest speakers on the left. Within the present sample of New York City speakers, this is the finest resolution of the transition problem which can be obtained.[25]

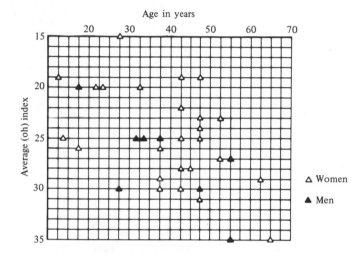

Fig. 4. Distribution of (oh) index scores for Italian subjects by age

The *embedding problem* for (oh) requires an intricate set of correlations with other elements in the linguistic system, in addition to the extralinguistic correlations exemplified above. We find that (oh) is firmly embedded within the sub-system of long and in-gliding vowels, and also related structurally to other vowel sub-systems. Quantitative studies of these relations fall into five sets:

1. There is a strong correlation between the height of (oh) and the height of the corresponding front in-gliding vowel (eh) in the word class of *bad, ask, dance,* etc. This variable originated as a raising of /æh/, but early in the evolution of New York City speech it merged with /eh/, the word class of *bare, bared, where,* etc. The relation between (eh) and (oh) is strikingly parallel to that of (ay) and (aw) on Martha's Vineyard. The front vowel was raised first, as early as the 1890's in New York, and the back vowel followed. Like (aw) on Martha's Vineyard, the variable (oh) became specialized in the

[25]Figure 4 includes Italian informants who refused the original interview, and whose speech patterns were sampled by the television interview, as described in Appendix D of *The Social Stratification of English in New York City* cited above.

usage of a particular ethnic group: to the extent that the Italian group shows higher use of (eh) in casual speech, the Jewish group shows higher values of (oh), until the difference is largely resolved in the youngest age level by merger of (eh) and /ih/, (oh) and /uh/.

2. The variable (oh) also has close relations with the higher in-gliding vowel /uh/. As we observe higher and higher variants of (oh) in the casual speech of the younger informants, it becomes apparent that a merger of (oh) and /uh/ is imminent. This merger has undoubtedly occurred in the youngest speakers in our sample from the working class and lower middle class. In fact, we have many informants who show the merger even in the most formal styles, in the reading of isolated word lists, and we can conclude *a fortiori* that the merger exists in casual speech. Close study of the variants of their casual speech shows the merger as an accomplished fact: though most listeners who are not conscious of the overlap will hear *beer* as higher than *bear*, it is in fact indistinguishable out of context.

3. There is also a close correlation between (oh) and /ah/, the long tense vowel heard in *guard*, *father*, *car*, etc. The variable (ah) represents the choice of back or center options for the subclasses of *hot*, *heart*, *hod* and *hard*. High values of (oh) are correlated with low back positions of *heart*, *hod* and *hard* [with the last two generally homonymous]; lower values of (oh) are correlated with low center positions of the vowels in these word classes. This correlation is independent of socio-economic class or ethnic group. Whereas (oh) is firmly embedded in the socio-linguistic structure of the speech community, /ah/ is not. As a linguistic variable, (ah) seems to be a function only of the height of (oh): a purely internal variable.[26]

4. (oh) is also related to the variable height of the vowel in *boy*, *coil*, etc., (oy) in the front up-gliding system. The height of the vowels in *coil* and *call* seem to vary directly together in casual speech, but only (oh) is corrected to lower values in more formal styles. (oh) carries the major burden of social significance, and is the focus of non-systematic pressure from above.

5. Finally, we find that (oh) and (oy) are jointly correlated with the variable (ay), which represents the backing or fronting of the first element of the diphthong in *my*, *why*, *side*, etc. High values of (oh) and (oy) are correlated with back values of (ay), and low values of (oh) and (oy) with low center values of (ay).

Beyond these immediate correlations, there are more indirect, diffuse relations with such variables as (aw) and /ih/, through which (oh) is con-

---

[26]The quantitative correlations are given in Chapter 12 of *The Social Stratification of English in New York City*. The relationship of (oh) and (ah) held even within a single ethnic group.

nected with all of the other vowels in the vernacular system of New York City speech. This is not the place to pursue the full details of this intricate set of structural correlations within the linguistic system: however, it should be apparent that a full solution to the embedding problem will reveal the ways in which the internal relations of linguistic elements determine the direction of sound change.[27] We can summarize the most important relations that center about (oh) in the following notation, which defines the structural units on the left hand side of the equations as linguistic variables:

$$(oh) = f_1(St, C, E, A, Sx, (eh))$$
$$(ah) = f_2((oh))$$
$$(oy) = f_3((oh))$$
$$(ay) = f_4((ah)) = f_4(f_2((oh)))$$
$$(ay) = f_5((oy)) = f_5(f_3((oh)))$$

$$St = style$$
$$C = socio\text{-}economic\ class$$
$$E = ethnic\ group$$
$$A = age\ level$$
$$Sx = sex$$

In New York City, the *evaluation problem* was approached more directly than on Martha's Vineyard. The unconscious subjective reactions of the informants to each of the variables were determined. The details of this method have been presented elsewhere;[28] in general, we can say that the reliability of the tests can be measured by the high degree of uniformity showed by New Yorkers in contrast to the scattered results from those raised outside of New York City.

The subjective reaction responses to (oh) give us a clear view of the social significance of the variable, as shown in Table 3. The majority of informants responded to the test in a way consistent with the stigmatized status of high (oh).[29] Just as the solution to the embedding problem showed no significant stylistic response to (oh) for lower class speakers, here we find that lower class speakers showed no significant (oh)-negative response. The other groups showed (oh)-negative response in proportion to the average height of (oh) used in their own casual speech, and to the degree of stylistic stratification in their speech patterns. This result illustrates a principle which holds quite generally in New York City: that those who used the highest percentage of a stigmatized form in casual speech were the most sensitive in stigmatizing it in the speech of others. Thus the lower middle class speakers

[27]In a manner which provides empirical confirmation for the view of linguistic structure expressed by A. Martinet, *Économie des changements phonétiques* [Berne, 1955].

[28]In addition to Chapter XI of the dissertation cited above, the most detailed presentation of this method is in "Subjective dimensions of a linguistic change in progress," a paper given before the Linguistic Society of America in Chicago, December, 1963.

[29]The (oh)-negative response shown here consisted of rating three speakers lower on a scale of job suitability when they pronounced sentences with high, close (oh) vowels, as compared to sentences with no significant variables. Those making the ratings were unaware that they were rating the same speakers.

between the ages of 20 and 39, who use the highest values of (oh) in their own casual speech, show 100% (oh)-negative response. Similarly, we find that the percentages of (oh)-negative response among Jewish and Italian speakers is proportionate to the height of (oh) in casual speech.

TABLE 3

Percentage of (oh)-Negative Response
by Socio-Economic Class and Age Level

Age Level	Lower Class [SEC 0–2]	Working Class [SEC 3–4]	Lower Middle Class [SEC 5–8]	Upper Middle Class [SEC 9]
20–39	25	80	100	60
40–59	18	60	62	57
60–	33	[00]	–	–

			N:			
		4	10	11	5	
		11	15	13	7	
		6	1	–	–	

This solution to the evaluation problem can hardly be called satisfactory. It is not clear why a group of speakers should adopt more and more extreme forms of a speech sound which they themselves stigmatize as bad speech.[30] Some further explanation must be given.

First of all, it has become clear that very few speakers realize that they use the stigmatized forms themselves. They hear themselves as using the prestige forms which occur sporadically in their careful speech and in their reading of isolated word lists. Secondly, the subjective responses tapped by our test are only the overt values—those which conform to the value systems of the dominant middle class group. There are surely other values, at a deeper level of consciousness, which reinforce the vernacular speech forms of New York City. We have not yet measured these more obscure forms systematically, but through anecdotal evidence we can be sure of their existence—values which cluster about the themes of group identification, masculinity, friendship ties, and so on.

In the case of the alternate preference of Jewish and Italian ethnic groups for (oh) and (eh), we can put forward a reasonable suggestion based upon the mechanism of hypercorrection.[31] The influence of the Yiddish sub-stratum leads to a loss of the distinction between low back rounded and unrounded vowels in first-generation Jewish speakers of English, so that *cup* and *coffee* have the same vowel. In second-generation speakers of Jewish

---

[30]Many subjects reacted to the test with violent and unrealistic ratings; as, for example, marking a person who used high vowels for *coffee* and *chocolate* as not even speaking well enough to hold a factory job.

[31]I am indebted to Marvin Herzog for this suggestion.

descent, the reaction against this tendency leads to a hypercorrect exaggeration of the distinction, so that (oh) becomes raised, tense and over-rounded. A parallel argument applies to Italian speakers. This suggestion is all the more plausible since hypercorrection has been demonstrated to be an important mechanism of linguistic change in a variety of circumstances.[32]

The Mechanism of Sound Change

Solutions to the transition, embedding and evaluation problems have been illustrated by two examples, drawn from Martha's Vineyard and New York City. It is possible to apply the results of our work with these and other variables to a provisional answer to the question: what is the mechanism by which sound change proceeds? The following outline is based upon analysis of twelve sound changes: three on rural Martha's Vineyard, and nine in urban New York City.[33]

1. The sound changes usually originated with a restricted subgroup of the speech community, at a time when the separate identity of this group had been weakened by internal or external pressures. The linguistic form which began to shift was often a marker of regional status with an irregular distribution within the community. At this stage, the form is an undefined linguistic variable.

2. The changes began as generalizations of the linguistic form to all members of the subgroup; we may refer to this stage as *change from below*, that is, below the level of social awareness. The variable shows no pattern of stylistic variation in the speech of those who use it, affecting all items in a given word class. The linguistic variable is an *indicator*, defined as a function of group membership.

3. Succeeding generations of speakers within the same subgroup, responding to the same social pressures, carried the linguistic variable further along the process of change, beyond the model set by their parents. We may refer to this stage as *hypercorrection from below*. The variable is now defined as a function of group membership and age level.

4. To the extent that the values of the original subgroup were adopted by other groups in the speech community, the sound change with its associated value of group membership spread to these adopting groups. The function of group membership is now re-defined in successive stages.

---

[32] *Hypercorrection* is used here not to indicate the sporadic and irregular treatment of a word class, but the movement of an entire word class beyond the target point set by the prestige model. This mechanism is evident on Martha's Vineyard, as well as New York.

[33] The stages suggested here are necessarily ordered in approximately the manner listed, but there are some re-arrangements and permutations in the data observed.

5. The limits of the spread of the sound change were the limits of the speech community, defined as a group with a common set of normative values in regard to language.

6. As the sound change with its associated values reached the limits of its expansion, the linguistic variable became one of the norms which defined the speech community, and all members of the speech community reacted in a uniform manner to its use (without necessarily being aware of it). The variable is now a *marker*, and begins to show stylistic variation.

7. The movement of the linguistic variable within the linguistic system always led to readjustments in the distribution of other elements within phonological space.

8. The structural readjustments led to further sound changes which were associated with the original change. However, other subgroups which entered the speech community in the interim adopted the older sound change as a part of the community norms, and treated the newer sound change as stage 1. This *re-cycling* stage appears to be the primary source for the continual origination of new changes. In the following development, the second sound change may be carried by the new group beyond the level of the first change.

[Stages 1–8 dealt with *change from below;* stages 9–13 concern *change from above.*]

9. If the group in which the change originated was not the highest status group in the speech community, members of the highest status group eventually stigmatized the changed form through their control of various institutions of the communication network.

10. This stigmatization initiated *change from above*, a sporadic and irregular correction of the changed forms towards the model of the highest status group—that is, the *prestige model*. This prestige model is now the pattern which speakers hear themselves using: it governs the audio-monitoring of the speech signal. The linguistic variable now shows regular stylistic stratification as well as social stratification, as the motor-controlled model of casual speech competes with the audio-monitored model of more careful styles.

11. If the prestige model of the highest status group does not corre-spond to a form used by the other groups in some word class, the other groups will show a second type of *hypercorrection:* shifting their careful speech to a form further from the changed form than the target set by the prestige group. We may call this stage *hypercorrection from above.*

12. Under extreme stigmatization, a form may become the overt topic of social comment, and may eventually disappear. It is thus a *stereotype,*

which may become increasingly divorced from the forms which are actually used in speech.

13. If the change originated in the highest status group of the community, it became a prestige model for all members of the speech community. The changed form was then adopted in more careful forms of speech by all other groups in proportion to their contact with users of the prestige model, and to a lesser extent, in casual speech.[34]

Many of the stages in the mechanism of sound change outlined here are exemplified in the two detailed examples given above. The centralization of (aw) on Martha's Vineyard appears to be a stage 4 change from below. It may indeed have reached stages 5 and 6, but the techniques used on Martha's Vineyard did not provide the evidence to decide this question. There is no doubt, however, that the centralization of (aw) is a secondary change, produced by the re-cycling process when the centralization of (ay) reached stage 8.

To place the raising of (oh) in this outline, it is necessary to consider briefly the evolution of the New York City vowel system as a whole. The first step in the historical record is the raising of (eh). We have reason to believe that the merger of /æh/ with /eh/ began in the last quarter of the 19th century.[35] The upward movement of the linguistic variable (eh) continued beyond this merger, leading to the current cumulative merger of /eh/ with /ih/ among most younger New Yorkers. For the entire community, (eh) is subject to the full force of correction from above: the change has reached stage 11, so that the linguistic variable is defined by co-variation with social class, ethnic membership, age level, and contextual style. The raising of (oh) was the first re-cycling process which began when (eh) reached stage 8. The major burden of the raising of (oh) has been carried by the Jewish ethnic group; the extreme upward social mobility of this group has led to a special sensitivity to (oh) in the lower middle class. Thus the merger of /oh/ and /uh/ has gone quite quickly, and (oh) has reached stage 11 for the lower middle class; yet it has hardly touched stage 1 for the lower class.

The third stage in the re-cycling process occurred when (oh) reached stage 8. The structural re-adjustments which took place were complex: (oy) and (ah) were closely associated with (oh), and were defined as linguistic variables only by their co-variation with (oh). Thus the raising of (oy) and the backing of (ah) were determined by internal, structural factors. Change from above is exerted upon (oh), but not upon (oy). In careful speech, a New Yorker might say [ɪts ɒːl tɪn fuːɪl], *It's all tin foil.* But the shift of (ah) and (oy) have in turn led to a shift of (ay), and this process has apparently begun a third re-cycling. Indeed, the backing of (ay) has reached

---

[34]We find some support in these observations for the idea that people do not borrow much from broadcast media or from other remote sources, but rather from those who are at the most one or two removes from them in age or social distance.

[35]See Babbitt, *op. cit.*

stage 8 itself, and produced an associated fourth re-cycling, the fronting of (aw). There are indications that (ay) has evolved to stage 9, with the beginning of overt correction from above, although (aw) has reached only stage 4 or 5.[36]

It is evident that the type of structural re-adjustments that have been considered here require a linguistic theory which preserves the geometry of phonological space. The structural relations found here are strikingly parallel to those established by Moulton in his study of co-variation of mid and low vowels in Swiss German dialects.[37] The techniques, the area, the societies studied are quite different, and the coincidence of results provides strong empirical evidence for the view of phonological structure advanced by Martinet.[38] Nevertheless, the purely internal equilibria projected by Martinet do not provide a coherent theory of the mechanism of sound change. In the scheme that has been outlined here, they are only part of a more comprehensive process, embedded in the sociolinguistic structure of the community.

Conclusion

This discussion has focused on the theme that internal, structural pressures and sociolinguistic pressures act in systematic alternation in the mechanism of lingustic change. It can no longer be seriously argued that the linguist must limit his explanations of change to the mutual influences of linguistic elements defined by cognitive function. Nor can it be argued that a changing linguistic system is autonomous in any serious sense. Here I have attempted to carry the argument beyond the mere cataloguing of possibilities by introducing a large body of evidence on sound changes observed in progress. On the basis of this evidence, we can make the stronger claim that it is not possible to complete an analysis of structural relations within a linguistic system, and then turn to external relations. The re-cycling process outlined here suggests the kind of answer we can make to the basic questions of the inciting causes of linguistic change, and the adaptive functions of change, as well as the mechanism by which change proceeds. We can expect that further investigations will modify the outline given here, but that data from the speech community will continue to form an essential part in the analysis of linguistic change.

[36]Details are provided in Chapter XII of the dissertation cited above.

[37]"Dialect geography and the concept of phonological space," *Word* 18:23–33 [1962].

[38]Both studies show strong evidence for co-variation of low vowels along the front-to-back dimension with back vowels along the dimension of height. Distinctive feature theory, in the form utilized by Halle, *op. cit.*, dissolves the geometry of phonological space into a set of independent dimensions. Even if a phonetic form of distinctive features is provided with scalar values, distinctive feature theory has no rationale for co-variation of grave and acute with compact and diffuse.

17

ORDERED RULES, DIALECT DIFFERENCES, AND HISTORICAL PROCESSES[*]

Sol Saporta

The relation between structuralism and dialectology has been the subject of occasional discussion among linguists. One extreme point of view apparently claims that since the elements of a system are defined only in terms of their relations to other elements, the systems as a whole are incommensurate. This view, which essentially legislates the problem of structural dialectology out of existence, has as a consequence the clearly untenable proposition that two dialects of English, for example, are no more similar than a dialect of English and a dialect of Chinese.

Another prevalent point of view maintains that dialect differences, at least at the phonological level but presumably on other levels as well, can be meaningfully discussed by appeal to some overall pattern, which theoretically includes all the necessary distinctions, each dialect selecting some subset of the available pool. This proposal has been objected to on the ground that it does not provide either a structural description or a set of descriptions, but merely a "transcriptional arsenal" of phonological units.[1]

Some recent studies[2] have attempted to meet this objection, insisting that structural descriptions be established independently for the varieties

*From *Language* 41.218–224 (1965). Reprinted by permission of the author and the Linguistic Society of America.

[1]A discussion of these and related points of view is found in Uriel Weinreich, "Is a structural dialectology possible?", *Word* 10.388–400 (1954). For an application of the notions presented here, see Julia Sableski, *A generative phonology of a Spanish dialect* (unpublished M.A. thesis, University of Washington).

An earlier version of this paper was delivered at the meeting of the Linguistic Society of America, summer 1964, in Bloomington, Indiana. The author's research is supported by the National Science Foundation, the National Institute of Health, and the Office of Education.

[2]For example, William G. Moulton, "The short vowel systems of Northern Switzerland," *Word* 16.155–82 (1960), and Edward Stankiewicz, "On discreteness and continuity in structural dialectology," *Word* 13.44–59 (1957).

involved before the comparisons are performed. The results are essentially typological classifications of dialects on the basis of the distinctiveness of certain features and combinations of features. One might hope that the comparison would also yield a description of the overall system (or diasystem as it has sometimes been called), although it is not clear what the nature of such a description would be.

In general, all such efforts are characterized by comparisons of the primary data. In a recent article, Morris Halle[3] suggests that a more profitable approach is the view that a speaker's linguistic behavior is best understood by an examination of the set of generative rules needed to describe the primary data, in short by the speaker's grammar. The grammars of two speakers with different dialects will differ then, in one of two ways: either the grammars will have different rules, or the grammars will have the same rules in a different order.

Halle illustrates his argument by pointing out that a comparison of the forms of American English and Pig Latin would yield differences of considerable magnitude. Pig Latin would have infixes where English has suffixes, as in /ǽtkey/ : /ǽtskey/[4] for *cat* : *cats*. Pig Latin would have no initial or final consonants but extremely complicated medial clusters; and so forth. A comparison of the set of rules, however, would reveal what most speakers agree to be the proper relationship, namely that Pig Latin has essentially the same rules as English with one additional rule for the transposition of initial consonants to word-final position and the subsequent addition of the vocalic nucleus /ey/. The two grammars then account in a reasonably straightforward way for such observations as the fact that speakers of English learn Pig Latin in a very short time. Notice incidentally the difficulties involved in trying to account for both of these dialects as parts of some overall description. It is conceivable that one could devise an inventory of affixes and state that one dialect selects suffixes where another has infixes, but there seems to be no meaningful way of saying that a particular system is characterized by the presence of initial and final consonants, and at the same time, by the obligatory absence of initial and final consonants. What Halle might have mentioned in addition is that the relationship between two dialects may be

---

[3]"Phonology in generative grammar," *Word* 18.54–72 (1962).

[4]I have retranscribed Halle's examples in a more familiar notation. The use of slant lines and square brackets is not intended to correspond to the now traditional distinction between phonemic and phonetic transcriptions. I use brackets only to make explicit when necessary the fact that a phonetic rule has been applied to yield the form in question. In a more precise presentation, slants might be used only to indicate the underlying phonological representation which serves as the input to the phonological component of the grammar. Note, however, the arguments proposed by Halle to support the view that segments have no systematic import and "are to be understood as circumlocutions introduced only to facilitate the exposition" (56, fn. 2).

irreversible. Given a form like English *street*, the Pig Latin equivalent /íytstrey/ is unambiguously derivable. But given the Pig Latin form /íytstrey/ the English form might be either *street* or *treats* unless the syllabic onset is consistently marked in Pig Latin.

To repeat, then, the grammatical description of a given dialect may be converted into an adequate description of a related dialect by the addition, deletion, or reordering of a relatively small number of rules. Indeed, it is tempting to propose that the degree of difference between dialects is nothing more than a function of the number and type of such changes. An illustration of these notions is provided by Samuel Jay Keyser[5] in his demonstration of how data from four dialects of the English of the Atlantic States can be accounted for by positing an underlying form and applying two rules.

This paper offers evidence from Spanish dialects to support the views of Halle and Keyser that comparison of the underlying rules may be more revealing than comparison of the primary data alone, and that the ordering of the rules is often a crucial consideration in such comparisons.

It should be made explicit that the choice of underlying forms and rules is motivated by the desire to account for the greatest number of facts in a manner as straightforward as possible. Nevertheless, as in the case of the additional rule needed for Pig Latin, it would not be surprising to discover that rules in a generative grammar often correspond to their historical counterparts. In other words, certain historical phenomena are often characterized precisely by the kinds of rules needed to account for related dialects, whether those dialects differ in space or in time.[6] The Spanish examples cited below illustrate dialect differences resulting from various types of historical processes, such as phonological merger, analogy, phonological split, and hypercorrection.

Consider the following singular and plural forms in three Spanish dialects.

---

[5]Review of Hans Kurath and Raven I. McDavid, *The pronunciation of English in the Atlantic states*, in *Lg.* 39.303–16 (1963). The relevant data are the pronunciations of *five, twice, down, out*, for which the underlying forms include diphthongs /ai/ and /au/. Rule 1 raises /a/ in the environment preceding a vowel plus voiceless consonant. Rule 2 is a fronting rule and applies to /a/ in the environment preceding /u/. The Charleston dialect requires rule 1, the New Bern dialect rule 2, the Winchester dialect rule 1 followed by rule 2, and the Roanoke dialect rule 2 followed by rule 1.

[6]This position is equivalent to Halle's view of ordering (64): "Since ordered rules are all but unknown in present day synchronic descriptions, the impression has spread that the imposition of order on statements in a synchronic description is always due to an oversight, to an unjustifiable confusion of synchronic and diachronic. I must therefore stress that . . . order is determined by the simplicity criterion alone and that no historical considerations have entered in establishing it." In a paper read at the meeting of the Linguistic Society of America December 1964, in New York, "Realism in historical English phonology," Robert P. Stockwell took a different view, namely that historical accuracy might be adduced as a criterion in evaluating competing sets of ordered rules.

Castilian (C)	Latin American (LA)	South Chile (SC)	
lúnes	lúnes	lúnes	'Monday'
lúnes	lúnes	lúnes	'Mondays'
lápiθ	lápis	lápis	'pencil'
lápiθes	lápises	lápis	'pencils'

For C there is a general rule for the plural expressed in (1).

$$(1) \qquad pl \rightarrow \begin{Bmatrix} s \, / \, \begin{Bmatrix} \check{V} \\ é \end{Bmatrix} — \\ \emptyset / \quad \check{V}s \; — \\ es \end{Bmatrix}$$

This rule says that the plural is represented by /s/ in the environment after all unstressed vowels and after stressed /é/, by Ø after unstressed vowels followed by /s/, and by /es/ elsewhere.[7] Thus the plural of *lunes* /lúnes/ with final /s/ is also *lunes*, but the plural of *lápiz* /lápiθ/ with final /θ/ is *lápices* /lápiθes/. In LA, however, /θ/ and /s/ have fallen together. Consequently some modification must be made in the grammar. One alternative is to list for LA all words like *lápiz* /lápis/ as exceptions to the rule—that is, to say that the plural is represented by zero after unstressed vowel plus /s/ except for a list of words, where this list corresponds exactly to words where C has /θ/. The other alternative is to keep (1) unaltered, but to add a rule like (2) for LA.

$$(2) \qquad \begin{Bmatrix} \theta \\ s \end{Bmatrix} \rightarrow [s] \; [8]$$

Linguists, presumably, whatever their persuasion, agree that rules are preferable to lists, even short lists. It is of interest to note, incidentally, that the relation between the dialects is not reversible. There is no general way of deriving C /θ/ from LA /s/.

SC has similar plurals for /lúnes/ and /lápis/. This dialect is described by reversing the order of the rules, so that (2), the falling together of /θ/ and /s/,

---

[7]The rules for Spanish are largely illustrative. In the absence of much of the relevant material, it is not clear what modifications might be required, for example, in the underlying representations. These changes would not alter the main line of the argument.

[8]This rule illustrates one of the insights which result from using features instead of the more familiar notation involving segments as the basis for phonological statements. The rule might be something like this:

$$(2') \qquad \alpha \text{ strident} \rightarrow + \text{ strident} \, \Big/ \left[\begin{array}{c} \overline{} \\ - \text{ grave} \\ + \text{ continuant} \end{array} \right]$$

where α has values plus or minus.

is applied before (1), spelling out the shape of the plural. After (2), (1) applies equally to /lúnes/ and /lápis/, yielding zero for the plural in both cases.

One might argue that it is possible, and indeed simpler, to describe SC with just (1). But this would require positing /s/ and not /θ/ in the underlying representation for *lápiz* in SC. Since there is other, independent evidence for positing /θ/ in all Spanish dialects, the saving is minimal. Furthermore, to posit different underlying forms for such intimately related dialects seems to obscure rather than elucidate their relationship.

Now, there is one difference between the reordering of rules in the example presented above and the one offered by Keyser for English. The English rules are both lower-level rules in the phonological component of the grammar, whereas one of the Spanish rules, namely (1), is a morphophonemic rule. I suggest that certain types of analogy, such as the one illustrated by the plural formation in SC, are characterized by a reordering of rules which belong to different parts of the grammar.

Other evidence for positing /θ/ among the phonological elements of LA is illustrated by the following forms.

Castilian (C)	Latin American (LA)	
kreθér	kresér	'to grow'
kréθko	krésko	'I grow'
kosér	kosér	'to sew'
kóso	kóso	'I sew'

For C, in general,[9] verbs like *crecer* /kreθér/ with /-Vθér/ or /-Vθír/ in the infinitive have a velar extension[10] in the first singular of the present indicative and all forms of the present subjunctive, i.e. before /o/ and /a/. Forms with /s/ instead of /θ/ like *coser* /kosér/ do not exhibit this alternation. In LA, then, one reasonable way of distinguishing the two classes of verbs, is to mark the [s] of [kresér] as being derived from /θ/, the [s] of [kosér] from /s/. That is, a rule for the morphophonemic alternation of verb stems must be inserted in the grammar before (2). In (3), the hyphen represents a particular kind of morpheme boundary.

(3) $\qquad$ Vθ- $\rightarrow$ Vθk- $\Big/ \quad$ — $\quad \begin{Bmatrix} o \\ a \end{Bmatrix}$

The following data illustrate a case of phonological merger.

[9]There are exceptions, e.g. *cocer* 'to cook', which do not have a velar before /o/ or /a/. These forms have to be listed in any case.

[10]Cf. Robert P. Stockwell, J. Donald Bowen, and John Martin, *The grammatical structures of English and Spanish* (to appear), who point out the parallel between the use of the velars in the verbs discussed here and in verbs like *venir* 'to come', *vengo* 'I come.' In both sets the velar occurs before /o/ and /a/, that is, the + grave, − diffuse vowels.

	Castilian (C)	Latin American (LA)	
	akél	akél	'that'
	akḗlos	akéyos	'those'
	cf.	léy	'law'
		léyes	'laws'
		papél	'paper'
		papéles	'papers'

There is a general restriction on the distribution of palatalized consonants in C. Accordingly /ĺ/ does not occur in word final position, /ĺ/ and /l/ being in morphophonemic alternation. (4) describes this alternation.

(4)   l̃ → [l] / — #[11]

In LA /ĺ/ and /y/ fall together, so that certain morphemes now exhibit an alternation between /l/ and /y/ instead of /l/ and /ĺ/. This alternation between /l/ and /y/ in LA, however, is not a general one. That is, there are medial /y/s which do not alternate with final /l/s, as in *ley : leyes*, and of course final /l/s which do not alternate with medial /y/s, as in *papel : papeles*. Exactly the appropriate forms are accounted for by adding (5), to be applied after (4).

(5) $\left\{ \begin{matrix} l̃ \\ y \end{matrix} \right\}$ → [y]

Thus, two quite general rules, appropriately ordered, account for the data in LA, obviating the otherwise necessary list of special forms like [akél] : [akéyos]. The burden of these examples is to demonstrate that in LA there remain residues of C /θ/ and /ĺ/, and that in fact, in describing LA, one is led to posit underlying forms with /θ/ and /ĺ/.[12]

---

[11]The rule is more general, applying to the palatalized nasals as well, cf. *desdeñar* 'to disdain', with palatalized nasal medially but the corresponding noun *desdén* 'disdain' with nonpalatalized nasal finally. Here too the relevance of features in such descriptions becomes clear.

[12]The proposal differs somewhat from the more traditional positing of special morphophonemes to cover different alternations. For example, the difference between /θ/ and /s/ is not that they alternate with different phonological units, but rather that they have different conditioning effects. Looked at from the point of view of internal reconstruction, if one were faced only with the data from LA, one might be tempted to suppose that in an earlier stage, the source of the final [s] in [lápis] was different from that of the final [s] in [lúnes], as indeed it was, and similarly that the medial [y] in [akéyos] was different from the medial [y] in [léyes]. This is not to claim that the methods of internal reconstruction are sufficiently developed to provide correct formulations in any systematic way. Indeed the methods are bound to fail in at least those cases where the simplest set of generative rules does not exactly correspond to the historical processes involved.

The following data illustrate a well-documented[13] dialect difference resulting from phonological split.

Castilian (C)	Uruguay (U)	
kláse	kláse	'class'
klásɛs	klásɛ	'classes'

In C, mid vowels have closed allophones in open syllables and open allophones in closed syllables, as reflected in (6), where the hyphen now indicates a syllable boundary.

(6) $\qquad$ e → ɛ / — C-

In U, final /s/ is dropped, as indicated in (7)

(7) $\qquad$ s → Ø / — #

(6) applies to both dialects, and (7), applied after (6), yields the correct forms for U. Notice, however, the consequences of the independent, so-called structural description of U. This dialect, and hence any overall pattern for Spanish, must be said to have seven vowels instead of five, with maximum contrasts only in final position and neutralization elsewhere. U will have a different consonant distribution, since /s/ does not occur in final position. The morphophonemics will be radically different, since the plural will now sometimes be expressed by vowel replacement. An ordered set of generative rules, on the other hand, requires only the addition of (7) for U with no changes for the phonetic rules or for the morphophonemic rule for the plural. In short, the layman's view that speakers of this dialect "swallow" their final /s/ is exactly right, and the argument for independent descriptions as a basis for structural dialectology loses much of its appeal.

The following data exemplify social rather than geographic dialects.

Standard (S)	Familiar (F)	Hypercorrect (H)	
soldádo	soldáo	soldádo	'soldier'
bakaláo	bakaláo	bakaládo	'cod'

The rule for deriving F from S might be something like (8), which drops certain intervocalic /d/s.

(8) $\qquad$ V́do → V́o / — #

A third dialect is characterized by hypercorrect forms like [bakaládo] with [d] alongside of [soldádo]. Application of (9) yields the forms of this dialect.

---

[13]For example, by Wáshington Vásquez, "El fonema /s/ en el español del Uruguay," *Revista de la facultad de humanidades y ciencias* 10.87–94 (1953).

(9) $\acute{V}o \rightarrow \acute{V}do \,/\,$ — #

Hypercorrection, then, is reflected in a generative grammar by a pair of rules like (8) and (9), where (9) is a mirror-image of (8), but where the input to the second rule includes more than just the output of the first.

However, the last example poses a question of some interest. As just described, H is derived from S by application of both (8) and (9). But H can be derived directly from S by merely applying (9) without (8). Such a derivation would presumbaly be descriptively simpler although historically misleading, in that it would fail to make explicit the nature of hypercorrection. In all the other cases cited, the descriptively adequate rules are also historically accurate. It would be of some interest to identify bona fide cases where historical considerations conflict with the requirements of overall simplicity. But, elaborating a suggestion made by Halle, we find that this is not such a case after all. It seems reasonable to argue that H is characterized in fact by coexistent forms, i.e. [soldádo ~ soldáo] and [bakaládo ~ bakaláo]. These data are described by making (9) optional, in which case it must apply to the output of (8) as well as to the underlying forms of S. What at first appears to be a disparity between synchronic and diachronic considerations turns out upon reexamination to be an additional case of correspondence.

Thus, when a descriptive grammar is set up to account for the greatest number of facts, it reflects certain historical processes. The converse of Roman Jakobson's view[14] that "a change is, at its beginning, a synchronic fact" is also true: synchronic facts often recapitulate historical changes. Delimiting the range of phenomena for which the claim is valid is a research question of some interest.

[14] *Results of the conference of anthropology and linguists* 18 (Indiana University publications in anthropology and linguistics, memoir 8; 1953).

Part V
UNIVERSALS AND TYPOLOGY

18

TYPOLOGICAL STUDIES AND THEIR CONTRIBUTION TO HISTORICAL COMPARATIVE LINGUISTICS*

Roman Jakobson

Alf Sommerfelt's early statement which headed my monograph on general sound laws is still vital: "Il n'y a pas de différence *de principe* entre les systèmes phonétiques du monde," or to put it more generally—*entre les systèmes linguistiques.*

1. Speakers Compare Languages. As the anthropologist reminds us, one of the most significant things about communication between men is that we have no people so primitive that they are not able to say, "Those people have a different language . . . I speak it or I don't speak it; I hear it or I don't hear it." As Margaret Mead adds, people conceive language "as the learnable aspect of other people's behavior." The interlingual code-switching can be and is practiced just because languages are isomorphic: common principles underlie their structure.

Talk in the speech community about alien languages, as any speech about speech, is labeled "metalanguage" by the logicians. As I tried to show in my 1956 address to the Linguistic Society of America, metalanguage like object-language is a part of our verbal behavior and thus a linguistic problem.

With his rare insight into simple, disregarded matters, Sapir wrote about us, as speakers: "We can . . . say that all languages differ from one another but that certain ones differ far more than others. This is tantamount to saying that it is possible to group them into morphological [one may add: phonological and syntactical] types." For us, as linguists, "it would be too easy to relieve ourselves of the burden of constructive thinking and to take the standpoint that each language has its unique history, therefore its unique structure."

*From *Proceedings of the VIII International Congress of Linguistics* (Oslo, 1958), 17–25. Reprinted in the author's *Selected Writings* I (The Hague, 1962), Mouton and Company, 523–532. Reprinted here by permission of the author.

2. Delay and Progress in Typological Studies. The failure of Friedrich Schlegel's attempt at a basic typology of language like the fallacy of his approach to the family tree of Indo-European languages does not cancel the problem but calls for its adequate solution. Premature speculations on linguistic kinship soon gave way to the first tests and achievements of the comparative historical method, whereas questions of typology retained a speculative, pre-scientific character for a long time. While genetic grouping of languages made amazing progress, the time was not yet ripe for their typological classification. The primacy of genetic problems in the scholarly framework of the past century left a peculiar imprint on the typological sketches of that age: morphological types were conceived as evolutionary stages. Marr's doctrine (*učenie o stadial' nosti*) was perhaps the last survival of this trend. But even in such a quasi-genetic aspect typology was distrusted by the neogrammarians, since any typological studies implied the descriptive technique, and any descriptive approach was banned as unscientific by the dogmatic *Prinzipien der Sprachgeschichte.*

It is quite natural that Sapir as one of the first promoters of descriptive linguistics advocated an inquiry into the types of linguistic structure. Yet the elaboration of a technique for the comprehensive description of separate languages absorbed most of the workers in the new field; any comparison was suspected of distorting the intrinsic criteria of unilingual monographs. It took time to realize that a description of systems without their taxonomy, as well as a taxonomy without description of single systems, is a flat contradiction in terms: both imply each other.

If in the inter-war period any concrete reference to typology provoked skeptical warnings, "jusqu'où la typologie peut égarer un bon linguiste," at present the need for systematic typological studies is ever more realized. A few notable examples: Bazell, as usual full of new and fruitful suggestions, drafted a program of linguistic typology in regard to syntactic relations; Milewski was the first to present a remarkable and challenging essay in the "phonological typology of American Indian languages"; Greenberg, an outstanding geneticist, effectively resumed Sapir's initiative in the typological approach to morphology (*a*) and discussed the three cardinal methods of language classification—genetic, areal, typological (*b,c*).

The genetic method operates with kinship, the areal with affinity, and the typological with isomorphism. Contrary to kinship and affinity, isomorphism does not necessarily involve either the time or space factor. Isomorphism may unite different states of one language or two states (whether simultaneous or temporally distant) of two different languages, whether contiguous or remote and whether cognate or not.

3. Not Inventory but System Is Base of Typology. The rhetorical question of Menzerath, one of the ingenious pioneers in typology, whether a given level of language "is merely a summative multitude or is bound by some structure," has obtained an unambiguous answer in modern linguistics. We speak about the grammatical and phonological system of language, about the laws of its structure, the interdependence of its parts, and of the parts and the whole. To comprehend this system, a mere listing of its components is insufficient. As the syntagmatic aspect of language presents a complex hierarchy of immediate and mediate constituents, so also the arrangement in the paradigmatic aspect is in turn characterized by a multiplex stratification. A typological comparison of various systems must take into account this hierarchy. Any intervention of arbitrariness, any deviation from the given and detectable order renders abortive the typological classification. The principle of ordered division takes ever deeper roots both in grammar and phonology, and we obtain clear evidence of the progress achieved while rereading the *Cours* of Ferdinand de Saussure, the first man who fully understood the significance of the system concept for linguistics, and who, at the same time, failed to see the compulsory order in such a distinctly hierarchic system as the pattern of grammatical cases: "C'est par un acte purement arbitraire que le grammairien les groupe d'une façon plutôt que d'une autre." Even such an obviously initial case as the nominative, the *cas zéro*, occupies, in Saussure's opinion, an arbitrary place in the case system.

Phonological typology, Greenberg is right, cannot remain "a substruction of the rather vague terminology of traditional phonetics." For a typology of phonemic systems, it has been logically imperative to submit them to a consistent analysis: "the presence of certain relationships among the attributes themselves or classes of these attributes are employed as criteria" (*c*). A typology of either grammatical or phonological systems cannot be accomplished without a logical restatement of the system which gives the maximum economy by a strict extraction of redundancies. A linguistic typology based on arbitrarily selected traits cannot yield satisfactory results, any more than the classification of the animal kingdom which instead of the productive division into vertebrates and non-vertebrates, mammals and birds, etc., would use, for instance, the criterion of skin color and on this basis group together, e.g., white people and light pigs.

The principle of immediate constituents is no less productive in the analysis of the paradigmatic aspect than in the parsing of sentences. Typology built on this principle discloses behind the diversity of phonological and grammatical patterns a series of unifying elements and substantially restricts the seemingly endless variety.

4. *Universals and Near-Universals.* Typology discloses laws of implication which underlie the phonological and apparently the morphological structure of languages: the presence of *A* implies the presence (or on the contrary the absence) of *B*. In this way we detect in the languages of the

world uniformities or near-uniformities, as the anthropologists used to say.

No doubt a more exact and exhaustive description of the languages of the world will complete, correct, and perfect the code of general laws. But it would be unsound to postpone the search for these laws until a further broadening of our factual knowledge. The question of linguistic, particularly phonemic, universals must be broached. Even if in some remote, newly recorded language we find a peculiarity challenging one of these laws, it doesn't devalue the generalization drawn from the imposing number of languages previously studied. The uniformity observed becomes a "near-uniformity," a rule of high statistical probability. Before the discovery of the duckbilled platypus in Tasmania and Southern Australia, zoologists in their general definitions of mammals did not foresee the egg-laying ones; nonetheless these obsolete definitions retain their validity for the overwhelming majority of the world's mammals and remain important statistical laws.

But even at present, the rich experience of the science of languages permits us to uncover constants which will hardly be degraded to near-constants. There are languages lacking syllables with initial vowels and/or syllables with final consonants but there are no languages devoid of syllables with initial consonants or of syllables with final vowels. There are languages devoid of fricatives but none deprived of stops. There are no languages with an opposition of stops proper and affricates (e.g. $/t/ - /\widehat{ts}/$) but without fricatives (e.g. $/s/$). There are no languages with rounded front vowels but without rounded back vowels.

Furthermore partial exceptions in cases of some near-universals call merely for a more supple formulation of the given general law. Thus in 1922, I noted that free dynamic stress and independent opposition of long and short vowels are incompatible within the same phonemic pattern. This law which satisfactorily explains the prosodic evolution in Slavic and some other Indo-European groups, is valid for an overwhelming majority of languages. Single cases of allegedly free stress and free quantity proved to be illusory: thus Wichita (in Oklahoma) was said to have both phonemic stress and quantity, but according to Paul Garvin's re-examination, Wichita is actually a pitch language with an opposition of rising and falling accent hitherto overlooked. Nonetheless this general law requires a more cautious formulation. If in a language phonemic stress co-exists with phonemic quantity, one of the two elements is subordinate to the other, and three, almost never four, distinct entities are admitted: either long and short vowels are distinguished only in the stressed syllable or only one of the two quantitative categories, length or brevity, may carry a free, distinctive stress. And apparently in such languages the marked category is not the long vowel opposed to the short, but the reduced vowel opposed to the non-reduced. I believe with Grammont that a law requiring amendment is more useful than the absence of any law.

  5. Morphic Determinism. Since the "invariant points of reference for description and comparison" are (one must agree with Kluckhohn) the focal point of typology, I venture to illustrate these relatively new problems in linguistics by a salient analogue from another science.

  The development of the science of language and particularly the transition from a primarily genetic standpoint to a predominantly descriptive approach strikingly corresponds to the contemporary shifts in other sciences, particularly to the difference between classical and quantum mechanics. This parallelism seems to me highly stimulating for the discussion of linguistic typology. I quote a paper on Quantum Mechanics and Determinism delivered by the eminent specialist, L. Tisza, at the American Academy of Arts and Sciences: quantum mechanics [and let us add: modern structural linguistics] is morphically deterministic, whereas the temporal processes, the transitions between stationary states, are governed by statistical probability laws. Both structural linguistics and quantum mechanics gain in morphic determinism what they lose in temporal determinism. "States are characterized by integers rather than by continuous variables," while "according to classical rules these systems would be characterized by continuous parameters," and "since two empirically given real numbers can never be rigorously identical it is not surprising that the classical physicist objected to the idea of definite objects of perfect identity."

  The structural laws of language are an ever nearer and clearer aim of typology and of the whole of descriptive linguistics in its newest phase, as I attempted to sum up the development in my linguistic obituary for Boas. And while one can only approve Greenberg's and Kroeber's illuminating remarks about the statistical character of "diachronic typologies" with their direction indices, the stationary typology is to operate rather with integers than with continuous variables.

  We have avoided the current label "synchronic typology." If for the modern physicist the "peculiar interplay of quasi-permanent identity and random temporal change appears to be a most fundamental feature of nature," likewise in language "statics" and "synchrony" do not coincide. Any change originally belongs to linguistic synchrony: both the old and new variety co-occur at the same time in the same speech community as more archaic and more fashionable respectively, one pertaining to the more explicit and the other to the more elliptic style, to two subcodes of the same convertible code. Each subcode in itself is for the given moment a stationary system governed by rigid structural laws, while the interplay of these partial systems exhibits the flexible dynamic laws of transition from one such system to another.

  6. Typology and Reconstruction. The corollary of the above deliberations is an answer to our pivotal question: What can typological studies contribute to historical comparative linguistics? In Greenberg's view, the typology of languages adds to "our predictive power since from a given synchronic system certain developments will be highly likely, others have less probability and still others may be practically excluded" (c). Schlegel, the anticipator of comparative linguistics and typology, described the historian as a prophet predicting backward. Our "predictive power" in reconstruction gains support from typological studies.

A conflict between the reconstructed state of a language and the general laws which typology discovers makes the reconstruction questionable. In the Linguistic Circle of New York in 1949, I brought to the attention of G. Bonfante and other Indo-Europeanists, a few such controversial items. The one-vowel picture of Proto-Indo-European finds no support in the recorded languages of the world. To my knowledge, no language adds to the pair $/t/$ – $/d/$ a voiced aspirate $/d^h/$ without having its voiceless counterpart $/t^h/$, while $/t/$, $/d/$, and $/t^h/$ frequently occur without the comparatively rare $/d^h/$, and such a stratification is easily explainable (cf. Jakobson-Halle); therefore theories operating with the three phonemes $/t/$ – $/d/$ – $/d^h/$ in Proto-Indo-European must review the question of their phonemic essence. The surmised coexistence of a phoneme "aspirated stop" and a group of two phonemes—"stop" + $/h/$ or another "laryngeal consonant"—is very doubtful in the light of phonological typology. On the other hand, views, prior or opposed to the laryngeal theory, which assign no $/h/$ to IE, disagree with the typological experience: as a rule, languages possessing the pairs voiced–voiceless, aspirate–non-aspirate, have also a phoneme $/h/$. In this connection it is significant that in those groups of Indo-European languages which lost the archaic $/h/$ without acquiring a new one, the aspirates merged with the corresponding non-aspirated stops: cf. the loss of any difference between the aspirates and non-aspirates in Slavic, Baltic, Keltic, and Tocharian, with the different treatment of the two series in Greek, Indic, Germanic, and Armenian, which all early changed some of their buccal phonemes into $/h/$. Similar help may be expected from the typological investigation of grammatical processes and concepts.

One can evade such discrepancies by practicing Saussure's approach to the reconstruction of an IE phoneme: "On pourrait, sans spécifier sa nature phonique, le cataloguer et le représenter par son numéro dans le tableau des phonèmes indo-européens." At present, however, we are equally far from the naive empiricism which dreamt about a phonographic record of IE sounds and from its opposite, an agnostic reluctance to inquire into the patterning of the IE phonemes and a timid reduction of their system to a mere numerical catalogue. If one abstains from the structural analysis of two successive states, he cannot interpret the transition from the earlier to the later state, and historical phonology is undesirably curtailed. A realistic approach to a reconstructive technique is a retrospective way from state to state and a

ish, an example of the former type, puts adjectives before the nouns they modify, places the object of the verb before the verb, the dependent genitive before the governing noun, adverbs before adjectives which they modify, etc. Such languages, moreover, tend to have postpositions for concepts expressed by prepositions in English. A language of the opposite type is Thai, in which adjectives follow the noun, the object follows the verb, the genitive follows the governing noun, and there are prepositions. The majority of languages, as for example English, are not as well marked in this respect. In English, as in Thai, there are prepositions, and the noun object follows the verb. On the other hand, English resembles Turkish in that the adjective precedes the noun. Moreover, in the genitive construction both orders exist: 'John's house' and 'the house of John'.

More detailed consideration of these and other phenomena of order soon reveals that some factors are closely related to each other while others are relatively independent. For reasons which will appear in the course of the exposition, it is convenient to set up a typology involving certain basic factors of word order. This typology will be referred to as the basic order typology. Three sets of criteria will be employed. The first of these is the existence of prepositions as against postpositions. These will be symbolized as Pr and Po, respectively. The second will be the relative order of subject, verb, and object in declarative sentences with nominal subject and object. The vast majority of languages have several variant orders but a single dominant one. Logically, there are six possible orders: SVO, SOV, VSO, VOS, OSV, and OVS. Of these six, however, only three normally occur as dominant orders. The three which do not occur at all, or at least are excessively rare, are VOS, OSV, and OVS. These all have in common that the object precedes the subject. This gives us our first universal:

> *Universal 1.* In declarative sentences with nominal subject and object, the dominant order is almost always one in which the subject precedes the object.[5]

This leaves us with three common types: VSO, SVO, and SOV. These will be symbolized as I, II, and III, respectively, reflecting the relative position of the verb.

The third basis of classification will be the position of qualifying adjectives (i.e., those designating qualities) in relation to the noun. As will be

---

with adjective-noun. This last correlation, particularly the latter half, is much weaker than the others. Schmidt gives figures based on a world sample which show good general agreement with the results from the thirty-language sample utilized here. It should be added that Schmidt's chief interest in this topic is as a vehicle for the interpretation of culture history. His results there verge on the fantastic.

[5]Siuslaw and Coos, which are Penutian languages of Oregon, and Coeur d'Alene, a Salishan language, are exceptions.

seen later, the position of demonstratives, articles, numerals, and, quantifiers (e.g., 'some', 'all') frequently differs from that of qualifying adjectives. Here again there is sometimes variation, but the vast majority of languages have a dominant order. Dominant order with adjective preceding noun will be symbolized by A and dominant order with noun preceding adjective by N. We thus arrive at a typology involving $2 \times 3 \times 2$, that is, twelve logical possibilities. The 30 languages of the sample are distributed among these twelve classes as shown in Table 1.[6]

TABLE I

	I	II	III
Po-A	0	1	6
Po-N	0	2	5
Pr-A	0	4	0
Pr-N	6	6	0

The table has been arranged so that the "extreme" types Po-A and Pr-N are in the first and fourth row, respectively. It is evident that with respect to these extremes, I and III are polar types, the former being strongly correlated with Pr-N and the latter with Po-A. Type II is more strongly correlated with Pr-N than with Po-A. It is also clear that adjective position is less closely related to types I, II, and III than is the Pr/Po contrast. The table is, I believe, a fair representation of the relative frequency of these alternatives on a world-wide basis. Type II is the most frequent; type III almost as common; type I is a definite minority. This means that the nominal subject regularly precedes the verb in a large majority of the world's languages.

Turning for a moment to genitive order, we note that this characteristic might fittingly have been utilized for typological purposes. The reason for not employing it is its extremely high correlation with Pr/Po, a fact generally known to linguists. It would thus virtually have duplicated the latter criterion. It was not chosen because Pr/Po on the whole is slightly more highly correlated with other phenomena. Of the present sample of 30 languages, 14 have postpositions, and in every one of these the genitive order is genitive followed by governing noun. Of the 14 prepositional languages, 13 have the genitive following the governing noun. The only exception is Norwegian, in which the genitive precedes. Thus, 29 of the 30 cases conform to the rule. If anything, 1/30 is an overestimation of the proportion of exceptions on a world-wide basis. We therefore have the following universal:

Universal 2. In languages with prepositions, the genitive almost always follows the governing noun, while in languages with postpositions it almost always precedes.

---

[6]The manner in which each language has been assigned can be determined from the data of Appendix I.

Turning once more to the data of Table I, we find striking evidence of lawful relationships among the variables in that of the 12 possibilities 5, or almost half, are not exemplified in the sample. All of these types are either rare or nonexistent.[7] For type I, we see that all 6 languages of the sample are Pr/N. This holds with extremely few exceptions on a world-wide basis. There are, however, a few valid examples of I/Pr/A, the mirror image, so to speak, of the fairly frequent III/Po/N. On the other hand, there are, as far as I know, no examples of either I/Po/A or I/Po/N. Hence we may formulate the following universal:

Universal 3. Languages with dominant VSO order are always prepositional.

Languages of type III are, as has been seen, the polar opposites of type I. Just as there are no postpositional languages in type I, we expect that there will be no prepositional languages in type III. This is overwhelmingly true, but I am aware of several exceptions.[8] Since, as has been seen, genitive position correlates highly with Pr/Po, we will expect that languages of type III normally have GN order. To this there are some few exceptions. However, whenever genitive order deviates, so does adjective order, whereas the corresponding statement does not hold for Pr/Po.[9] We therefore have the following universals:

Universal 4. With overwhelmingly greater than chance frequency, languages with normal SOV order are postpositional.

Universal 5. If a language has dominant SOV order and the genitive follows the governing noun, then the adjective likewise follows the noun.

An important difference may be noted between languages of types I and III. In regard to verb-modifying adverbs and phrases as well as sentence adverbs, languages of type I show no reluctance in placing them before the verb so that the verb does not necessarily begin the sentence. Further, all VSO languages apparently have alternative basic orders among which SVO always figures. On the other hand, in a substantial proportion, possibly a majority, of type III languages, the verb follows all of its modifiers, and if any other basic order is allowed, it is OSV. Thus the verb, except possibly for a few sentence modifiers (e.g., interrogative particles), is always at the end in verbal sentences. It is not logically required, of course, that languages all of whose basic orders involve the verb in the third position should also require all verb modifiers to precede the verb, but this seems to hold empirically.

---

[7]For details, see Appendix II.

[8]Iraqw, a southern Cushitic language, Khamti, a Thai language, standard Persian, and Amharic.

[9]The single case where it does not hold seems to be Amharic, which has SOV, GN, and AN, but is prepositional.

Thus, languages in which the verb is always at the end may be called the "rigid" subtype of III. In the present sample, Burushaski, Kannada, Japanese, Turkish, Hindi, and Burmese belong to this group, while Nubian, Quechua, Basque, Loritja, and Chibcha do not.[10] These considerations permit us to state the following as universals:

> *Universal 6.* All languages with dominant VSO order have SVO as an alternative or as the only alternative basic order.

> *Universal 7.* If in a language with dominant SOV order, there is no alternative basic order, or only OSV as the alternative, then all adverbial modifiers of the verb likewise precede the verb. (This is the rigid subtype of III.)

3. Syntax

Having defined the basic order typology and stated some of the universals that can be most immediately derived from the consideration of its defining properties, we turn to a number of syntactic universals, many but not all of which are associated with this typology. One set of criteria employed in this typology was the order of nominal subject, nominal object, and verb in declarative sentences. One reason for stating the criteria in this manner was that interrogative sentences tend to exhibit certain characteristic differences as compared to declarative statements. There are two main categories of questions, those of the yes-no variety and those involving specific question words. A common method of differentiating yes-no questions from the corresponding statement is by a difference of intonational pattern, as in English. Our knowledge of these patterns still leaves much to be desired. However, the following statement seems to be sufficiently documented:

> *Universal 8.* When a yes-no question is differentiated from the corresponding assertion by an intonational pattern, the distinctive intonational features of each of these patterns are reckoned from the end of the sentence rather than from the beginning.

For example, in English a yes-no question is marked by a rise in pitch in the last stressed syllable of the sentence and the corresponding statement by falling pitch. The reckoning of distinctive patterns from the end of the sentence may well hold for all intonational patterns.

Yes-no questions may likewise be signaled by a question particle or affix. Some languages use both this method and intonation as alternatives. The position of such question markers is fixed by either reference to some specific word, most frequently the verb, or the emphasized word of the

[10]However, Householder informs me that in Azerbaijani, and in most types of spoken Turkish, it is allowable to have one modifier, especially a dative or locative noun phrase after the verb.

question, or it may be fixed by position in the sentence as a whole. In languages of the rigid subtype III, it is of course impossible to distinguish between position after the verb and position at the end of the sentence. In the present sample, there are 12 languages with such initial or final particles. With reference to the basic order typology, these 12 examples are distributed as shown in Table 2.[11]

TABLE 2

	I	*II*	*III*
Initial particle	5	0	0
Final particle	0	2	5

The two examples of a final particle in group II are prepositional languages (Thai and Yoruba). The table includes only cases where there is a single such particle or affix in the language, or there are several following the same rule. In two of the languages in the samples, there is more than one such element, each with differing rules. Zapotec (I/Pr) has either an initial particle alone or this same particle in conjunction with a final particle. Songhai (II/Po) has three such particles, two of them an initial and one a final particle. These complications as well as the fact that at least one language outside of the sample belonging to (II/Po), namely, Lithuanian, has an initial particle suggest the following rather cautious statement:

Universal 9. With well more than chance frequency, when question particles or affixes are specified in position by reference to the sentence as a whole, if initial, such elements are found in prepositional languages, and, if final, in postpositional.

Where specification depends on some particular word, the particle almost always follows. Such particles are found in 13 languages of the present sample.[12] Examples of the rigid subtype III are counted in both this and the previous category. Of these 13, 12 are suffixed. They include both prepositional and postpositional languages, but none in group I. The following, therefore, probably holds:

Universal 10. Question particles or affixes, when specified in position by reference to a particular word in the sentence, almost always follow that word. Such particles do not occur in languages with dominant order VSO.

[11]Languages of type I—Berber, Hebrew, Maori, Masai, and Welsh; II—Thai, Yoruba; III—Burmese, Burushaski, Japanese, Kannada, Nubian. For Yoruba, see further note 12.

[12]In the following languages the affix or particle follows: II—Finnish, Guarani, Malay, Maya, Serbian; III—Basque, Burmese, Japanese, Kannada, Nubian, Turkish, Quechua. It precedes in Yoruba, but may be accompanied by a final particle.

The other basic kind of question, that involving an interrogative word, likewise shows a definite relationship to the basic order typology. In such sentences, many languages have a different word order than that of the corresponding declarative sentence. Characteristically, the question word comes first, except for the possible retention of normal order within smaller units (e.g., phrases). This holds in English, for example, where the question word is first in 'What did he eat?' as against the statement, 'He ate meat'. The second point is illustrated by 'With whom did he go?' as against 'He went with Henry', where the question phrase comes first but the order within the phrase itself is not disturbed. Many languages which put interrogatives first likewise invert the order of verb and subject (e.g., German 'Wen sah er?'). Such languages sometimes invert for yes-no questions, (e.g., 'Kommt er?'). It appears that only languages with interrogatives always initially invert, and only languages which invert in interrogative word questions invert for yes-no questions.[13]

In the present sample, 16 languages put the interrogative word or phrase first. They are distributed as shown in Table 3.

TABLE 3

	I	II	III
Question word first	6	10	0
Question and statement order identical	0	3	11

	Pr	Po
Question word first	14	2
Question and statement order identical	2	12

A definite relationship thus appears, and we have the following universals:

Universal 11. Inversion of statement order so that verb precedes subject occurs only in languages where the question word or phrase is normally initial. This same inversion occurs in yes-no questions only if it also occurs in interrogative word questions.

Universal 12. If a language has dominant order VSO in declarative sentences, it always puts interrogative words or phrases first in interrogative word questions; if it has dominant order SOV in declarative sentences, there is never such an invariant rule.

---

[13]The question word is first in Berber, Finnish, Fulani, Greek, Guarani, Hebrew, Italian, Malay, Maori, Masai, Maya, Norwegian, Serbian, Welsh, Yoruba, and Zapotec.

Verbal subordination to verb will be considered next. Semantically, the concepts to be considered here include time, cause, purpose, and condition. Formally, we have one or more of the following: introductory words (i.e., "conjunctions"); and verbal inflections, whether finite, involving categories of person and number (e.g., subjunctives) or nonfinite forms such as verbal nouns and gerundives. It seems probable that conjunctions are more frequent in prepositional languages, nonfinite verb forms in postpositional languages, and that finite verb forms are found in both, but this point was not investigated. In accordance with the over-all emphasis of the paper, attention was directed to the question of the relative order of subordinate and main verbal forms. Since the subordinate verb qualifies the main verb, we would expect it to precede the main verb in all languages of the rigid subtype of III. Since this subtype was defined merely in terms of the invariable precedence of noun object, the question remains for empirical verification. In fact, this turns out to be true for all the languages of this subtype in the sample and, no doubt, holds generally.[14] In languages of other types certain characteristics of individual constructions appear. The normal order everywhere is for the protasis of conditional constructions to procede the apodosis, that is, for the condition to precede the conclusion. This is true for all 30 languages of the sample. In languages of the rigid subtype of III the protasis never follows, but in other languages it will do so occasionally.

On the other hand, in expressions of purpose and volition the normal order is for these to follow the main verb except in languages of the rigid subtype of III. Here again there are no exceptions in the sample. We have therefore the following universals:

Universal 13. If the nominal object always precedes the verb, then verb forms subordinate to the main verb also precede it.

Universal 14. In conditional statements, the conditional clause precedes the conclusion as the normal order in all languages.

Universal 15. In expressions of volition and purpose, a subordinate verbal form always follows the main verb as the normal order except in those languages in which the nominal object always precedes the verb.

Another relation of verb to verb is that of inflected auxiliary to main verb. For present purposes, such a construction will be defined as one in which a closed class of verbs (the auxiliaries) inflected for both person and number is in construction with an open class of verbs not inflected for both person and number. For example, in English 'is going' is such a construction. This definition, of course, excludes the possibility of such a construction in

[14]Again, this only holds for literary Turkish, according to Householder. See note 10.

languages in which the verb has no category of person and number (e.g., Japanese). In the sample of 30 languages, 19 have such inflected auxiliaries. They are distributed among the order types as shown in Table 4.[15]

TABLE 4

	I	II	III
Auxiliary precedes verb	3	7	0
Auxiliary follows verb	0	1	8

	Pr	Po
Auxiliary precedes verb	9	1
Auxiliary follows verb	0	9

These data suggest the following universal:

Universal 16. In languages with dominant order VSO, an inflected auxiliary always precedes the main verb. In languages with dominant order SOV, an inflected auxiliary always follows the main verb.

Uninflected auxiliaries will be considered later in connection with verb inflections.

In nominal phrases, the position of attributive adjectives in relation to the noun modified is a key factor. The position of the qualifying adjective shows a definite though only statistical relation to the two other bases of the typology. A summary of these data for the languages of the sample is given in Table 5.

TABLE 5

	I	II	III
NA	6	8	5
AN	0	5	6

	Pr	Po
NA	12	7
AN	4	7

In general, then, the tendency is for adjectives to follow the noun in prepositional languages, and most strongly so in languages of type I, which are always prepositional as has been noted. There are a few rare exceptions, not in the sample, of languages of type I with adjective before the noun, as was noted earlier. Hence, we have the following *near* universal:

Universal 17. With overwhelmingly more than chance frequency, languages with dominant order VSO have the adjective after the noun.

[15]Auxiliary precedes verb in Finnish, Greek, Italian, Masai, Maya, Norwegian, Serbian, Swahili, Welsh, Zapotec. Auxiliary follows verb in Basque, Burushaski, Chibcha, Guarani, Hindi, Kannada, Nubian, Quechua, Turkish.

From the data of Table 5, it will also be noticed that there are 19 languages with adjective after the noun, as against 11 with the adjective before the noun. This is representative of a general tendency which very nearly overrides the opposite rule to be expected in languages of type III.

The position of demonstratives and numerals is related to that of descriptive adjectives in individual languages. However, these items show a marked tendency to precede even when the descriptive adjective follows. On the other hand, when the descriptive adjective precedes, then the demonstratives and numerals virtually always precede the noun likewise. The data from the sample languages are given in Table 6.

TABLE 6

	NA	*AN*
Dem. - Noun	12	7
Noun - Dem.	11	0
Num. - Noun	8	10
Noun - Num.	11	0

In one language, Guarani, numbers may either precede or follow the noun, and this case was not included in the table. In Guarani, the adjective follows the noun, as would be expected. In the case of numbers, it should be noted that for languages with numeral classifiers, it was the position of the numeral in relation to the classifier which was taken into account.[16] There seems to be no relation between the position of the numeral and the demonstrative outside of that mediated by adjective position. Languages in which the adjective follows the noun may have numeral preceding while demonstrative does not, demonstrative preceding while numeral does not, both preceding or neither preceding. Outside of the sample, however, there are a small number of instances (e.g., Efik) in which the demonstrative follows while the adjective precedes. It may be noted that other quantifiers (e.g., 'some', 'all') and interrogative and possessive adjectives show this same tendency to precede the noun, as evidenced, for example, in the Romance languages, but those cases were not studied. We have then the following universal:

Universal 18. When the descriptive adjective precedes the noun, the demonstrative and the numeral, with overwhelmingly more than chance frequency, do likewise.

An additional related observation may be noted:

Universal 19. When the general rule is that the descriptive adjective follows, there may be a minority of adjectives which usually precede, but when the general rule is that descriptive adjectives precede, there are no exceptions.

---

[16]For details, see Appendix I.

This last universal is illustrated by Welsh and Italian in the present sample.

The order within the noun phrase is subject to powerful constraints. When any or all of the three types of qualifiers precede the noun, the order among them is always the same: demonstrative, numeral, and adjective, as in English, 'these five houses'.

When any or all follow, the favorite order is the exact opposite: noun, adjective, numeral, demonstrative. A less popular alternative is the same order as that just given for the instances in which these elements precede the noun. An example of the latter is Kikuyu, a Bantu language of East Africa, with the order, 'houses these five large', instead of the more popular 'houses large five these'. We have, then, a universal:

Universal 20. When any or all of the items (demonstrative, numeral, and descriptive adjective) precede the noun, they are always found in that order. If they follow, the order is either the same or its exact opposite.

The order of adverbial qualifiers of adjectives in relation to the adjective will now be considered. This order also shows a definite relation to that between the descriptive adjective and the noun, as shown by Table 7. In the third row are cases in which certain adverbs precede and others follow.[17]

TABLE 7

	AN	NA
Adverb - Adjective	11	5
Adjective - Adverb	0	8
Adj. - Adv. and Adv. - Adj.	0	2

From Table 7 it can be seen that there is a tendency for the adverb to precede the adjective, which can be overridden only in some cases when the adjective follows the noun. The situation thus far is similar to that obtaining with regard to demonstratives and numerals. However, if we look further, we note that all of those languages in which some or all adverbs follow the adjective not only have the noun followed by the adjective, but also are all of types I and II. Thus we have a universal:

Universal 21. If some or all adverbs follow the adjective they modify,

---

[17]Languages with adjective-noun and adverb-adjective order are Burushaski, Finnish, Greek, Hindi, Japanese, Kannada, Maya, Norwegian, Quechua, Serbian, Turkish. Languages with noun-adjective and adverb-adjective order are Basque, Burmese, Chibcha, Italian, Loritja. Languages with noun-adjective and adjective-adverb order are Fulani, Guarani, Hebrew, Malay, Swahili, Thai, Yoruba, and Zapotec. Languages with noun-adjective and the rule that certain adverbs precede and certain follow the adjective are Maori and Welsh. Berber, Masai, Nubian, and Songhai—no data.

then the language is one in which the qualifying adjective follows the noun and the verb precedes its nominal object as the dominant order.

One other topic concerning the adjective to be considered is that of comparisons, specifically that of superiority as expressed, for example in English, by sentences of the type 'X is larger than Y'. A minority of the world's languages have, like English, an inflected comparative form of the adjective. More frequently a separate word modifies the adjective, as in English, 'X is more beautiful than Y', but in many languages this is optional or does not exist at all. On the other hand, there is always some element which expresses the comparison as such, whether word or affix, corresponding to English 'than', and obviously both the adjective and the item with which comparison is made must be expressed. We thus have three elements whose order can be considered, as in English *larg(er) than Y*. These will be called adjective, marker of comparison, and standard of comparison. The two common orders are: adjective, marker, standard (as in English); or the opposite order: standard, marker, adjective. These two alternatives are related to the basic order typology, as shown by Table 8.[18] A number of languages are not entered in this table because they utilize a verb with general meaning 'to surpass'. This is particularly common in Africa (e.g., Yoruba): 'X is large, surpasses Y'. Loritja, an Australian language which has 'X is large, Y is small', is likewise not entered.

TABLE 8

	I	*II*	*III*
Adjective - Marker - Standard	5	9	0
Standard - Marker - Adjective	0	1	9
Both	0	1	0
	Pr	*Po*	
Adjective - Marker - Standard	13	1	
Standard - Marker - Adjective	0	10	
Both	0	1	

Universal 22. If in comparisons of superiority the only order, or one of the alternative orders, is standard-marker-adjective, then the language is postpositional. With overwhelmingly more than chance frequency if the only order is adjective-marker-standard, the language is postpositional.

---

[18]Languages with adjective-marker-standard are Berber, Fulani, Greek, Hebrew, Italian, Malay, Maori, Norwegian, Serbian, Songhai, Swahili, Thai, Welsh, Zapotec. Languages with standard-marker-adjective are Basque, Burmese, Burushaski, Chibcha, Guarani, Hindi, Japanese, Kannada, Nubian, Turkish. Both constructions are found in Finnish.

A clear relation to the basic order typology is likewise found in constructions of nominal apposition, particularly those involving a common along with a proper noun. A number of semantic and formal subtypes are involved (e.g., titles of address, 'Mr. X,' as against appellations 'Avenue X'). The latter type is, in certain cases, assimilation to the genitive, and may therefore be expected to show a similar order (e.g., 'the city of Philadelphia'). English is somewhat ambivalent, doubtless because of adjective-noun order, as can be seen from '42nd Street' versus 'Avenue A', or 'Long Lake' versus 'Lake Michigan'. Most languages, however, have a single order (e.g., French, 'Place Vendôme', 'Lac Genève', 'Boulevard Michelet'). My data here are incomplete because grammars often make no statement on the subject, and I was dependent on text examples.[19]

In Table 9, contrary to usual practice, the genitive construction is used instead of Pr/Po since it gives more clear-cut results.

TABLE 9

	I	II	III
Common Noun - Proper Noun	2	7	0
Proper Noun - Common Noun	0	2	6

	GN	NG
Common Noun - Proper Noun	8	1
Proper Noun - Common Noun	0	8

Universal 23. If in apposition the proper noun usually precedes the common noun, then the language is one in which the governing noun precedes its dependent genitive. With much better than chance frequency, if the common noun usually precedes the proper noun, the dependent genitive precedes its governing noun.

As the concluding item in the discussion of nominal construction, we take the relative clause which modifies a noun (e.g., English, 'I saw the man who came', 'I saw the student who failed the examination'). Here again there is considerable diversity of formal means from language to language. All that will be considered here is the order as between nominal antecedent and the verb of the relative clause (e.g., 'man' and 'came' in the first sentence).

Once more the distribution of the rules of order, as set forth in Table 10, shows a clear relation to the categories of the basic order typology.[20]

[19]Languages with common noun-proper noun are Greek, Guarani, Italian, Malay, Serbian, Swahili, Thai, Welsh, Zapotec. Those with proper noun-common noun areBasque, Burmese, Burushaski, Finnish, Japanese, Norwegian, Nubian, and Turkish.

[20]The relational expression precedes the noun in Basque, Burmese, Burushaski, Chibcha, Japanese, Kannada, Turkish. The noun precedes the relational expression in

TABLE 10

	I	II	III
Relational expression precedes noun	0	0	7
Noun precedes relational expression	6	12	2
Both constructions	0	1	1

	Pr	Po
Relational expression precedes noun	0	7
Noun precedes relational expression	16	4
Both constructions	0	2

From Table 10 it is clear that if the relational expression precedes the noun either as the only construction or as alternate construction, the language is postpositional. However, outside of the sample there is at least one exception, Chinese, a prepositional language in which the relational expression precedes the noun. It is plausible to explain this deviation as connected with the fact that in Chinese the adjective precedes the noun. As with adjective-noun order there is a pronounced general tendency for the relative expression to follow the noun it qualifies. This tendency is sometimes overcome but only if (1) the language is prepositional or (2) if the qualifying adjective precedes the noun.

Universal 24. If the relative expression precedes the noun either as the only construction or as an alternate construction, either the language is postpositional, or the adjective precedes the noun or both.

Thus far nothing has been said about pronouns. In general, pronouns exhibit differences regarding order when compared with nouns. This was the reason for specifying nominal subject and nominal object in the definitions of the basic typology. One peculiarity of pronominal order is illustrated by French where we have, 'Je vois l'homme' but 'Je le vois'; that is, the pronominal object precedes, whereas the nominal object follows. Similar examples are found in a number of languages of the sample. In Italian, Greek, Guarani, and Swahili, the rule holds that the pronominal object always precedes the verb, whereas the nominal object follows. In Italian and Greek, however, the pronoun follows just as does the nominal object with imperatives. In Berber the pronoun objects, direct or indirect, precede the verb when the verb is accompanied by the negative or future particle. In

---

Berber, Fulani, Greek, Guarani, Hebrew, Hindi, Italian, Malay, Maori, Masai, Maya, Norwegian, Quechua, Serbian, Songhai, Swahili, Thai, Welsh, Yoruba, Zapotec. Both orders are found in Finnish and Nubian. In Finnish the construction with the relational expression preceding the noun is in imitation of literary Swedish (personal communication of Robert Austerlitz).

Loritja, the pronominal object may be an enclitic added to the first word of the sentence. In Nubian, the usual nominal order is SOV, but the alternative SVO is fairly frequent. For pronominal object, this alternative never occurs. In other words, the pronominal object always precedes the verb, whereas the nominal object may either precede or follow. In Welsh, in an alternative order with emphasis on the pronoun subject, the pronoun subject comes first in the sentence. In such sentences the pronominal object precedes the verb, but the nominal object follows. Finally, in Masai, whereas normal order for nominal object is VSO, a pronominal object precedes a nominal subject and immediately follows the verb.

No contrary instances occur in the sample of a pronominal object regularly following the verb while a nominal object precedes. We may therefore state the following universal:

> *Universal 25.* If the pronominal object follows the verb, so does the nominal object.

4. Morphology

Before proceeding to the question of inflectional categories, which will be the chief topic of this section, certain general considerations relating to morphology will be discussed. Morphemes within the word are conventionally divided into root, derivational and inflectional. As elsewhere in this paper, no attempt at definition of categories will be attempted. Derivational and inflectional elements are usually grouped together as affixes. On the basis of their order relation to the root, they may be classified into a number of categories. By far the most frequent are prefixes and suffixes. Infixing, by which a derivational or inflectional element is both preceded and followed by parts of the root morpheme, may be grouped with other methods involving discontinuity. Examples of such other methods are intercalation, as in Semitic, and what might be called ambifixing, where an affix has two parts, one of which precedes the entire root, while the other follows. All such discontinuous methods are relatively infrequent, and some languages do not employ any of them. The following universal on this topic is probably valid:

> *Universal 26.* If a language has discontinuous affixes, it always has either prefixing or suffixing or both.

As between prefixing and suffixing, there is a general predominance of suffixing. Exclusively suffixing languages are fairly common, while exclusively prefixing languages are quite rare. In the present sample, only Thai seems to be exclusively prefixing. Here again a relationship with the basic order typology appears.[21]

[21]The exclusively suffixing languages are Basque, Burmese, Chibcha, Finnish, Hindi, Japanese, Kannada, Loritja, Nubian, Quechua, Songhai, Turkish.

TABLE 11

	I	II	III
Exclusively prefixing	0	1	0
Exclusively suffixing	0	2	10
Both	6	10	1

	Pr	Po
Exclusively prefixing	1	0
Exclusively suffixing	0	12
Both	15	2

Universal 27. If a language is exclusively suffixing, it is postpositional; if it is exclusively prefixing, it is prepositonal.

Where both derivational and inflectional elements are found together, the derivational element is more intimately connected with the root. The following generalization appears plausible:

Universal 28. If both the derivation and inflection follow the root, or they both precede the root, the derivation is always between the root and the inflection.

There are probably no languages without either compounding, affixing, or both. In other words, there are probably no purely isolating languages. There are a considerable number of languages without inflections, perhaps none without compounding and derivation. The following probably holds:

Universal 29. If a language has inflection, it always has derivation.

Turning now to verb inflectional categories, we can state that since there are languages without inflection, there will obviously be languages in which the verb has no inflectional categories. In the far more frequent cases in which the verb has inflectional categories, a partial implicational hierarchy exists.

Universal 30. If the verb has categories of person-number or if it has categories of gender, it always has tense-mode categories.

The greater externality of gender categories in the verb can be seen from the following generalization:

Universal 31. If either the subject or object noun agrees with the verb in gender, then the adjective always agrees with the noun in gender.

Gender agreement between noun (usually noun subject) and verb is far less frequent than agreement in person and number; yet examples of the former without the latter do occur (e.g., in some Daghestan languages of the Caucasus). However, where such gender categories appear, they always seem to be associated with number also. Therefore we have the following:

Universal 32. Whenever the verb agrees with a nominal subject or nominal object in gender, it also agrees in number.

A further observation about noun-verb agreement in number may be made. There are cases in which this agreement is regularly suspended. In all such cases, if order is involved, the following seems to hold:[22]

Universal 33. When number agreement between the noun and verb is suspended and the rule is based on order, the case is always one in which the verb precedes and the verb is in the singular.

Such phenomena as the suspension of agreement are analogous to that of neutralization in phonemics. The category which does not appear in the position of neutralization, in this case the plural, may be called the marked category (as in classical Prague School phonemic theory). Similar phenomena will be encountered in the subsequent discussion.

The three most common nominal inflectional categories are number, gender, and case. Among systems of number, there is a definite hierarchy which can be stated in the following terms:

Universal 34. No language has a trial number unless it has a dual. No language has a dual unless it has a plural.

Nonsingular number categories are marked categories in relation to the singular, as indicated in the following universal:

Universal 35. There is no language in which the plural does not have some nonzero allomorphs, whereas there are languages in which the singular is expressed only by zero. The dual and the trial are almost never expressed only by zero.

The marked character of the nonsingular numbers as against the singular can also be seen when number occurs along with gender. The interrelations of these two sets of categories are stated in the following universals:

Universal 36. If a language has the category of gender, it always has the category of number.

Universal 37. A language never has more gender categories in nonsingular numbers than in the singular.

This latter statement may be illustrated from Hausa, which has a masculine and feminine gender distinction in the singular but not in the plural. The opposite phenomenon, to my knowledge, never occurs.

Case systems may occur with or without gender systems and with or without the category of number. The unmarked categories of case systems are the subject case in nonergative systems and the case which expresses the subject of intransitive and the object of transitive verbs in ergative systems. Hence we have the following universal:

---

[22]The reason for specifying order is that there are instances of neutralization of number agreement in which the order of the item is not involved. For example, in classical Greek the neuter plural goes with a singular verb without regard to order.

Universal 38. Where there is a case system, the only case which ever has only zero allomorphs is the one which includes among its meanings that of the subject of the intransitive verb.

As between number and case, where there is a distinct morpheme boundary, the following relation almost always holds:

Universal 39. Where morphemes of both number and case are present and both follow or both precede the noun base, the expression of number almost always comes between the noun base and the expression of case.

The following general statement may be made about agreement between adjectives and nouns:

Universal 40. When the adjective follows the noun, the adjective expresses all the inflectional categories of the noun. In such cases the noun may lack overt expression of one or all of these categories.

For example, in Basque, where the adjective follows the noun, the last member of the noun phrase contains overt expressions of the categories of case and number and it alone has them.

Case systems are particularly frequent in postpositional languages, particularly those of type III. In the present sample, all the languages of this type have case systems. There are a few marginal cases or possible exceptions.

Universal 41. If in a language the verb follows both the nominal subject and nominal object as the dominant order, the language almost always has a case system.

Finally, pronominal categories may be briefly considered. In general, pronominal categories tend to be more differentiated than those of the noun, but almost any specific statement in this regard will have some exceptions. As a general statement we have the following universals:

Universal 42. All languages have prenominal categories involving at least three persons and two numbers.

Universal 43. If a language has gender categories in the noun, it has gender categories in the pronoun.

Gender categories show certain relations to categories of person in pronouns, as might be expected.

Universal 44. If a language has gender distinctions in the first person, it always has gender distinctions in the second or third person, or in both.

There is likewise a relation to the category of number.

Universal 45. If there are any gender distinctions in the plural of the pronoun, there are some gender distinctions in the singular also.

5. Conclusion: Some General Principles

No attempt is made here to account for all of the universals described in the preceding sections and repeated in Appendix III. Some general principles, however, are proposed which seem to underlie a number of different universals and from which they may be deduced. Attention is first directed to those universals which are most closely connected with the basic order typology and the closely associated genitive construction. Two basic notions, that of the dominance of a particular order over its alternative and that of harmonic and disharmonic relations among distinct rules of order, are introduced. This latter concept is very obviously connected with the psychological concept of generalization.

We may illustrate the reasoning involved by reference to Universal 25, according to which, if the pronominal object follows the verb, the nominal object does so likewise. In other words, in the tetrachoric table resulting from the alternative for each of the combinations there is a single blank. Since the nominal object may follow the verb whether the pronoun object precedes or follows, while the nominal object may precede the verb only if the pronoun precedes, we will say that VO is dominant over OV since OV only occurs under specified conditions, namely when the pronominal object likewise precedes, while VO is not subject to such limitations. Further, the order noun object–verb is harmonic with pronoun object–verb but is disharmonic with verb–pronoun object since it does not occur with it. Likewise verb–noun object order is harmonic with verb–pronoun object and disharmonic with pronoun object–verb. We may restate our rule, then, in terms of these concepts as follows:

A dominant order may always occur, but its opposite, the recessive, occurs only when a harmonic construction is likewise present.

Note that the notion of dominance is not based on its more frequent occurrence but on the logical factor of a zero in the tetrachoric table. It is not difficult to construct an example in which one of the recessive alternatives is more frequent than the dominant. Dominance and harmonic relations can be derived quite mechanically from such a table with a single zero. The entry with zero is always the recessive one for each construction, and the two constructions involved are disharmonic with each other.

Harmonic and disharmonic relations, as noted earlier, are examples of generalization. In similar constructions, the corresponding members tend to be in the same order. The basis for the correspondence in the present instance is obvious, in that pronoun and noun are both objects of the verb, and the other pair verb-verb is identical. In regard to harmonic and disharmonic relations, a fair amount of freedom will be exercised based on transformational and other relations among constructions, not merely the occurrence of a zero in a tetrachoric table.

Proceeding on this basis, we now consider Universal 3. It will be noted that this universal amounts to an assertion of the nonexistence of postpositional languages of type I. Since in all of the types, I, II and III, S precedes O, this is irrelevant for the present context. This leads to the following conclusions:

> Prepositions are dominant over postpositions, and SV order is dominant over VS order. Further, prepositions are harmonic with VS and disharmonic with SV, while postpositions are harmonic with SV and disharmonic with VS.

What distinguishes type II from type III is that in type II the object follows the verb, a characteristic shared with type I. On the other hand, type III has the object before the verb. From Universal 4, which states that with overwhelmingly more than chance frequency SOV is associated with postpositions, the conclusion is drawn that OV is harmonic with postpositions while VO is harmonic with prepositions. The constructional analogies which support this are discussed later with reference to the closely associated genitive constructions. For the moment it may be noted that the relations between types I, II, and III and Pr/Po may now be recapitulated in these terms: Type I has VS which is harmonic with prepositions, and SO which is likewise harmonic with prepositions. Further, prepositions are dominant. All languages of type I, in fact, are prepositional. Type II has SV which is harmonic with postpositions and VO which is harmonic with prepositions, and prepositions are dominant. In fact, a definite majority of languages of type II have prepositions. Type III has SV and OV, both of which are harmonic with postpositions. However, prepositions are dominant. In fact, the preponderant majority of languages which have type III have postpositions, with but a handful of exceptions.

From the overwhelming association of prepositions with governing noun–genitive order and of postpositions with genitive–governing noun order but with a small number of exceptions of both types, the conclusion is drawn that prepositions are harmonic with NG and postpositions with GN.

The close connection between genitive order and Pr/Po is a simple instance of generalization. The relation of possession is assimilated to other relational notions, for example, spatial relations. In English, 'of' which marks possession is a preposition with the same order properties as 'under', 'above', etc. Further, such spatial and temporal relations are often expressed by nouns or nounlike words, for example, English 'in back of'. In many languages 'behind' = 'the back + genitive'; hence: 'X's back' = 'in back of X' parallels 'X's house'; and 'back of X' = 'in back of X' parallels 'house of X'.

The connection between these genitives and the analogous prepositional or postpositional phrases on the one hand, and subject-verb and object-verb constructions on the other, is via the so-called subjective and objective genitive. Note that in English 'Brutus' killing of Caesar started a civil war' has the same truth value as 'The fact that Brutus killed Caesar started a civil war'. The order of elements is likewise similar. In other words, in such transformations, the noun subject or object corresponds to the genitive, and the verb to the governing noun. In fact, there are languages in which the subject or the object of the verb is in the genitive. For example, in Berber *argaz* 'man' is the general form of the noun, and *urgaz* is either the dependent genitive or the subject of the verb, provided it follows immediately. Thus *iffeɣ urgaz*, 'went out the man', exactly parallels *axam urgaz*, 'the house of the man'. Berber, it will be noted, is a language of type I, and the genitive follows the noun. It likewise has prepositions rather than postpositions.

A further relationship among the variables of the basic order typology may be posited, that between genitive order and adjective order. Both the genitive and qualifying adjectives limit the meaning of the noun. There are further facts to support this. There are languages like Persian, in which both adjective and genitive dependence are marked by exactly the same formal means. Where pronominal possession is involved, some languages use a derived adjective, while others use a genitive of the pronoun. There are even instances where adjectives are used in the first and second person, while a genitive is used in the third person (e.g., Norwegian).

We may summarize these results by stating that all of the following are directly or indirectly harmonic with each other: prepositions, NG, VS, VO, NA. We have here a general tendency to put modified before modifier, and the most highly "polarized" languages in this direction are those of type I with NG and NA, a considerable group of languages. The opposite type is based on harmonic relations among postpositions, GN, SV, OV, and AN. This is also a very widespread type, as exemplified by Turkish and others in the present sample. On the other hand, the general dominance of NA order tends to make languages of the Basque type (i.e., III/Po/NA with GN order) very nearly as common as the Turkish type. It should also be pointed out that languages being highly complex structures, there are other factors at work in individual cases not included among the five factors cited at this point. One of them, demonstrative-noun order, has already been mentioned.

It is more difficult to account for the dominances than for the harmonic relations, to explain, for example, why the adjective tends to follow the noun. It may be suggested, however, that noun-adjective predominance arises from the same factor as that which makes subject-verb the dominant order. In Hockett's terminology, there is a general tendency for comment to follow topic. There is some evidence that noun-adjective does parallel subject-verb in this way. In many languages all adjectival notions are treated as intransitive verbs. The qualifying adjective is then a relative or participle of the verb. The tendency of relative clauses, it has been seen, is even stronger than that of adjectives to follow the noun. In some languages such as Arapesh in New Guinea, 'The good man came' would be literally translated 'The man is-good that-one he came'. Adjective-noun order, then, is somewhat ambivalent since analogies with other constructions involving modifiers make it indirectly harmonic with VS while the factor of topic-comment order makes it analogous with SV.

All this is far from a complete theory. Nevertheless, it does suggest that one should examine instances in which, contrary to the prevailing rules, the genitive construction is disharmonic with Pr/Po. One would reason that in such cases the genitive construction is, as it were, being attracted by the adjective-noun construction which, as has been seen, has sources of determination that are to some extent outside of the general framework of harmonic relations connected with the order of modifier and modified. For example, if, in spite of the general rule, we find genitive–governing noun order with prepositions, the reason might be the opposing pull of order adjective-noun which is harmonic with genitive–governing noun. Otherwise stated, the genitive construction should only be disharmonic with Pr/Po when Pr/Po is disharmonic with the adjective-noun order. One may include here cases in which a language has two genitive orders, indicating a probable change of type since one must, in all likelihood, be older than the other. One may further conjecture that if there are exceptions, they will be in type II, which, having both SV and VO which are disharmonic, can provide an anchor in either case for deviant genitive order.

It will be noted that Universal 5, insofar as it refers to postpositional languages of type III (the vast majority), gives a particular instance of this hypothesis; for this statement asserts that a language of type III if it has NG will also have NA. If such a language is postpositional, then NG will be disharmonic with postpositions but harmonic with NA. If we include languages with both genitive orders, then there are at least six cases, all favorable (i.e., with NA rather than AN). These are Somali and Maba with both genitive orders, and Kanuri, Galla, Teda, and Sumerian which have SOV, postpositions, NG, and NA.

This hypothesis will, however, produce some further predictions. For prepositional languages of type III, the hypothesis will be that with varying genitive order or with GN, which is disharmonic with prepositions, the adjective-noun order will be AN. I know of only two cases, Tigrinya with both genitive orders, and Amharic with GN. Both have AN in accordance with our hypothesis. For languages of type II which are prepositional and which have GN, and should therefore have AN, we have Danish, Norwegian and Swedish (possibly a single case), and English with two genitive orders.

Both fulfill the hypothesis in that they have AN. Among postpositional languages of type II, we have the Moru-Madi group in the Sudan and the fairly distantly related Mangbetu, both of which, with alternative genitive orders, have the predicted NA. We now encounter the only exceptions of which I am aware, Araucanian in Chile, with both genitive orders; and a group of Daghestan languages in the Caucasus, including some like Rutulian with NG, and others like Tabassaran with both genitive orders. Apparently all those languages of the Daghestan group which are of type III have only GN harmonizing with both postpositions and AN. If so, this is an important indication of the general validity of our hypothesis. Finally, since all languages of type I are prepositional, we have only a single case to consider, prepositional languages with GN. I know of only one example, the Milpa Alta dialect of Nahuatl described by Whorf. It has AN as expected.

Another type of relation than those that have just been considered is illustrated by Universals 20 and 29. These may be called proximity hierarchies. What we have is a rule that certain elements must be closer to some central element than some other satellite. The central element may be the root morpheme or base of a word or the head-word of an endocentric construction. Such a proximity hierarchy is likely to be related to an implicational hierarchy in the instance of inflectional categories. Just as the category of number is almost always closer to the base than expressions of case, so there are many languages with the category of number but without the category of case, and very few with case but without number. Since, by the proximity hierarchy, number is closer, it is more likely to become amalgamated with the base and so become an inflection. These hierarchies are presumably related to degrees of logical and psychological remoteness from the center, but no analysis is attempted here.

These phenomena are likewise related to those of neutralization. The more proximate category, or the implied category, tends to be more elaborate, and it is the less proximate or the implying categories which tend to be neutralized in its presence. Universals 36 and 37 are related in this manner. Number is the implied category. Gender categories are often neutralized in the marked number (i.e. nonsingular). It is much rarer for number to be neutralized in some particular gender (e.g., the neuter in Dravidian languages). With regard to number and case, number is, as has been seen, more proximate and generally present when case is present, while the opposite relation holds far more rarely. It is likewise common for certain case distinctions to be neutralized in number, while the opposite phenomenon perhaps never occurs.

Another principle is evident from Universal 34. We do not have such systems as the following: a particular grammatical category for the trial, while another embraces the dual and all numbers larger than three. In other words, disjunctiveness or lack of continuity in this respect is never tolerated.

Universals 14 and 15 possibly illustrate the same principle. The order of elements in language parallels that in physical experience or the order of knowledge. In the instance of conditionals, although the truth relations involved are timeless, logicians have always symbolized in the order implying, implied exactly as in spoken language. If *modus ponens* is used in proof, then we have a pragmatic example which follows the order of reasoning. No one thinks to write a proof backwards.

Universals 7, 8, and 40, although superficially very different, seem to be examples of the same general tendency to mark the end of units rather than the beginning. For example, in rigid subtype III, the verb marks the end of the sentence. When the inflections occur only with the final member of the noun phrase, this marks the end of the phrase. This is probably related to the fact that we always know when someone has just begun speaking, but it is our sad experience that without some marker we don't know when the speaker will finish.

The existence of a rigid subtype III, whereas there are no examples of a rigid subtype of I, is probably related to still another factor. In general the initial position is the emphatic one, and while there are other methods of emphasis (e.g., stress), the initial position always seems to be left free so that an element to which attention is directed may come first. Here Universal 12 is an example. It seems probable that in all languages expressions of time and place may appear in the initial positions in the sentence.

The discontinuity of the predicate, which commonly appears in such instances (e.g., German, 'Gestern ist mein Vater nach Berlin gefahren'), illustrates a further principle. On the whole, the higher the construction in an immediate constituent hierarchy, the freer the order of the constituent elements. It has been seen that practically all languages have some freedom of order regarding subject and predicate as a whole; whereas only a small minority have variant order in genitive constructions, and then almost always along with other differences, not merely a difference of order. Within morphological constructions, order is the most fixed of all. On the whole, then, discontinuous constituents are far less frequent than continuous ones.

As indicated in the initial section of this paper, the principles described in this section are to be viewed as no more than suggestive. It is hoped that some of them at least will prove useful for further investigation.

Acknowledgments

In addition to my indebtedness to the work of Roman Jakobson, to be mentioned in the notes, I would also like to thank Fred Householder and Charles F. Hockett for making helpful critical comments on the earlier version of this paper.

Additional note: The following facts were learned too late to be included in the paper. According to information supplied by Einar Haugen, Norwegian has both genitive orders. Note that Norwegian had been the only exception in the sample to the generalization on p. 64 [in original]. In a discussion at the International Congress of Linguistics at Cambridge in August 1962, it was pointed out that Papago, a Uto-Aztecan language, is I/Po. This is therefore an exception to Universal 3. From Mason's data it should probably be assigned to type 7 of Appendix II.

APPENDIX I

Basic Data on the 30-Language Sample

	VSO	Pr	NA	ND	N Num
Basque	III	—	x	x	—
Berber	I	x	x	x	—
Burmese	III	—	x[1]	—	—[2]
Burushaski	III	—	—	—	—
Chibcha	III	—	x	—	x
Finnish	II	—	—	—	—
Fulani	II	x	x	x	x
Greek	II	x	—	—	—
Guarani	II	—	x	—	0
Hebrew	I	x	x	x	—
Hindi	III	—	—	—	—
Italian	II	x	x[3]	—	—
Kannada	III	—	—	—	—
Japanese	III	—	—	—	—[2]
Loritja	III	—	x	x	x
Malay	II	x	x	x	—[2]
Maori	I	x	x	—	—
Masai	I	x	x	—	x
Maya	II	x	—	—	—[2]
Norwegian	II	x	—	—	—
Nubian	III	—	x	—	x
Quechua	III	—	—	—	—
Serbian	II	x	—	—	—
Songhai	II	—	x	x	x
Swahili	II	x	x	x	x
Thai	II	x	x	x	—[2]
Turkish	III	—	—	—	—
Welsh	I	x	x[3]	x	—
Yoruba	II	x	x	x	x
Zapotec	I	x	x	x	—

[1]Participle of adjective-verb, however, precedes and is probably as common as adjective following.

[2]Numeral classifiers following numerals in each case. The construction numeral + classifier precedes in Burmese and Maya, follows in Japanese and Thai, and either precedes or follows in Malay.

[3]In Welsh and Italian a small number of adjectives usually precede.

that might characterize the sentences of a language possesses psychological reality in the sense of representing the form rather than just the substance of a fluent speaker's competence. From among the pile of generalizations that might be made about the sentences of a language they select certain ones as being linguistically significant and corresponding to the generalizations that a child hearing such utterances would actually arrive at in constructing his grammar. The question, then, is how the various aspects of this hypothesis are justified.

For many features of universal grammar there is justification enough in the fact that without them it would simply not be possible to write grammars that account for the sentences of a language. Particularly in syntax, as Chomsky has pointed out, the typical problem is not choosing the right one among various theories that work but finding even one that will work at all. But with conventions which are essentially abbreviatory in nature, such as braces and parentheses, among others, real problems of empirical justification can arise. A grammar can always be replaced by another, descriptively equivalent one, in which any one of these abbreviatory notations is not made use of. There could not be a language whose sentences could be enumerated one way but not the other. Then what is the empirical force, if any, of such notational conventions?

For example, most linguists would agree that two rules of the form

$$X \to Y$$
$$Z \to Y$$

if not separated in the ordering by any other rule, should be combined by factoring out their common right hand side as follows:

$$\begin{Bmatrix} Z \\ X \end{Bmatrix} \to Y$$

We would say that the braces represent a linguistically significant generalization about these two rules. But how do we know that they do? How would we justify this convention to some linguist *A* who maintained that it was wrong and that the two rules should be kept separate? Or, to take a more likely contingency, how would we justify it to another linguist *B* who maintained that neither theory makes any verifiable truth claim as against the other, that since they are mutually convertible notational variants of each other, they represent equivalent hypotheses about the speaker's internalized grammar?

There are no conscious a priori ideas of generality that we can appeal to here in the way that we can appeal to intuitions that reflect features of structural descriptions, such as ambiguity and synonymy. The processes of normal language learning being unconscious, we have absolutely no ideas about the form of grammars, though we have clear ideas about the forms of

sentences which grammars account for. It is true that the practicing linguist soon acquires ideas about the form of grammars and such concepts as generality. **But these ideas are somehow the result of his work on languages, and we would like to know what the ideas are based on.** Nor is the fact that a generalization can be stated enough to show that it is real. All sorts of absurd notational conventions can easily be dreamed up which would express the kinds of spurious generalizations that we would want to exclude from grammars. It is necessary to justify conventions by showing that the generalizations they allow one to express do not hold accidentally. One might try to do this by arguing that a convention which can be used frequently in grammars cannot represent an accidental fact about language. But many presumably spurious conventions would come in handy very often in linguistic descriptions. For example, what about a linguist C who says that the brace notation should be extended to collapse rules of the form

$$X \leftarrow Y$$
$$Z \leftarrow X$$

into the form

$$Z \leftarrow \begin{Bmatrix} X \end{Bmatrix} \leftarrow Y$$

He will be able to show us just as many cases where such braces could be used in grammars to group rules together. Or, to cite an actual linguist, Pāṇini often makes use of an abbreviatory convention which corresponds to the following kind of use of braces, ruled out in generative grammar:[2]

$$A \leftarrow \begin{Bmatrix} B \\ E \end{Bmatrix} -|- C$$
$$D \leftarrow \begin{Bmatrix} F \end{Bmatrix} -|- G$$

What seems wrong about this is that it allows collapsing rules which represent heterogeneous processes. Of the rules combined here, two have absolutely nothing in common with each other: the top rule

[2]The reason is that abbreviatory conventions in the Indian grammatical tradition, originally an oral one, were not graphic devices such as braces, parentheses, or anything directly equivalent to them, but rather resembled the conjunction-reduction processes of natural language. In the following three sutras, for example, the bracketed words are omitted and understood as carried over from the previous sutra.

6.1.77   *iko yaṇ aci* (high vowels become glides before vowels)
6.1.78   *eco'yavāyāvaḥ* [*aci*] (e, o, ... → ay, av, ... before vowels)
6.1.79   *vānto yi pratyaye* (o, au → av, āv before y) [*eco*]

It is hardly possible to collapse these three rules into one rule by any extensions of the conventions of generative grammar.

$$A \to B/ \!-\! C$$

and the bottom rule

$$D \to F/ \!-\! C$$

But we would like the rules in a grammar to form blocks whose parts are related in some sense that goes beyond just partial identity. Ideally, the rules should be grouped into natural blocks whose parts represent different different aspects of the same basic process.

Can psycholinguistics provide experimental evidence on the form of grammars? Recent psycholinguistic experiments designed to test the psychological reality of generative grammar have been concerned mainly with two questions. One group of experiments has sought behavioral correlates to the structural descriptions postulated by generative grammar. Bever, Fodor, and Garrett have, for example, carried out a series of experiments in which they found that the location at which a burst of sound is perceived in a synchronously presented sentence differs from its objective location in a way that can be predicted from the surface constituent structure of the sentence. The goal of another group of experiments was to find evidence bearing on the claim that a system of rules such as that postulated by generative grammar is involved in producing and understanding utterances. In contrast with the successful experiments concerned with the psychological reality of structural descriptions, those concerned with the psychological reality of grammars have on the whole been a failure (Fodor and Garrett, 1967). It is true that there was an initial spate of successes in which a clear relationship seemed to emerge between the grammatical complexity of a sentence, as measured by the number of rules of the grammar that contribute to its formation, and its perceptual complexity, as measured by various experimentally obtained performance parameters. But in recent experiments with more complex linguistic material this relationship has all but disappeared. It stands to reason that the utilization of the speaker's internalized grammatical rules is a highly complex process involving elaborate ways of tracking down the relevant rules and processing sentences in such a way that parameters which tap performance directly are not going to be related at all directly to such crude grammatical properties of sentences as the number of rules involved in their derivation. The fact that grammars are not performance models presumably means that the answer to the question of whether they are correct competence models is not likely to be forthcoming by any currently known experimental techniques until the contributions of competence can be separated out from the facts about performance.

What we really need is a window on the form of linguistic competence that is not obscured by factors like performance, about which next to nothing is known. In linguistic change we have precisely such a window.

2. The Form of Linguistic Change

We can think of linguistic change in roughly the following terms. Grammars are subject to changes of two kinds: the addition of new rules to them and simplification of them. In phonology, the addition of rules corresponds roughly to the concept of "sound change" (Halle, 1962; Postal, 1968). For example, the sound change whereby final obstruents in words became voiceless in German and many other Germanic languages is the addition of the rule

1. [+obstruent] → [− voiced] / ——— #

Through alternations such as [bunt]:[bunde] (versus [bunt]:[bunt]), in which this rule is reflected, it is learned anew as part of the language by each generation of speakers, and even in modern German the underlying representations of most words retain the medially pronounced voiced segment. Yet the addition of Rule 1 does not leave the lexicon entirely unaffected. Words like *ab*, *ob*, and *weg*, which never came to stand before an inflectional ending that would cause the reappearance of an underlying voiced obstruent, are never heard after the sound change with anything but a voiceless final obstruent; in these isolated forms, succeeding generations of speakers therefore have no reason to set up underlying forms with voiced obstruents. The change thus brings about a restructuring in a tiny corner of the vocabulary.

I hope that this use of the term *generation* will not convey the absurd picture of a society horizontally segmented into a number of discrete age groups, each with its own grammar. The point is simply that a language is not some gradually and imperceptibly changing object which smoothly floats through time and space, as historical linguistics based on philological material all too easily suggests. Rather, the transmission of language is discontinuous, and a language is recreated by each child on the basis of the speech data it hears. Nor should the term *restructuring* be understood as denoting a change of some speaker's grammar into another grammar, for it refers just to a discontinuous linguistic change arising from the difference between the grammar constructed by a child and the grammar of those whose speech constituted his linguistic experience. In discussing linguistic change in these elementary terms we are, of course, missing a number of important factors which cannot in the long run be ignored. For example, as Jakobson has pointed out, metalinguistic information concerning such things as the social value of different speech forms is an important part of what a speaker knows, and Labov's recent studies (1963, 1965) show its diachronic relevance very clearly. A conception of grammar in which these broader aspects of competence are explicitly accounted for will hopefully provide a general basis for the study of their role in linguistic change.

A sound change that I will frequently refer to is umlaut in Germanic. By this rule, vowels were fronted before *i* (for example, Old High German *wurmi* > *würmi* 'worms', *tāti* > *tǣti* 'deeds', *nōti* > *nöti* 'needs'). Short *a* was not only fronted but also raised to *e* (for example, *slagi* > *slegi* 'strokes', *gasti* > *gesti* 'guests'). The original umlaut rule, then, was the following:[3]

$$2. \quad \begin{bmatrix} V \\ -\text{long} \end{bmatrix} \rightarrow \begin{bmatrix} <->\\ -\text{back} \\ <-\text{low}> \end{bmatrix} / \text{———} C_0 i$$

In modern German we encounter this rule in a somewhat different form. In the majority of dialects what we find as the productive umlaut of *a* is not *e*, as originally, but *æ*. For example, in the Low German dialect of Prignitz (Mackel, 1905–1907) we have *gasti:gesti*, *krafti:kræftig* with a low front vowel in the umlauted forms, rather than the expected *gasti:gesti*, *krafti:kreftig*. But the only *e*'s that have thus gone to *æ* are those that were productively umlauted from *a*. Phonemic *e*'s have remained unchanged. These include not only original Germanic *e* in words like *nest* but also *e* from historically umlauted *a* in words like *bet* 'bed', *net* 'net' where *e* has become phonemic since there was no reason to derive it synchronically from an underlying *a*. Analogous facts hold true in Old English as well. In terms of the grammar, this widespread change is a simplification of the umlaut rule from its original form of 2 to the form in 3:

$$3. \quad V \rightarrow [-\text{back}] / \dots$$

(I leave open here the question of what exactly the environment of umlauting in modern German is, which is irrelevant for present purposes.)

The change from 2 to 3 is an instance of the second basic type of linguistic change, simplification.[4] I shall merely illustrate this type for the moment but hope to justify it in more detail later. Simplification is a generalized and reinterpreted version of the traditional concept of analogy (Matthews, forthcoming; Kiparsky, 1965, 1967). This is particularly evident in its simplest form, namely morphological regularization as in changes of the type *brought* > *bringed*, which amount to loss of the special mark associated with lexical entries like *bring* that singles them out as morphological exceptions and specifies the nature of their exceptional behavior. Much more interesting in many respects are cases in which the simplifica-

[3] The rule must be complicated somewhat to include secondary umlaut.

[4] The term *generalization* is sometimes confusing, and I will not use it here. It is applicable in the natural sense of the word only to simplification in the structural analysis of a rule; simplification in the structural change is hardly generalization in this same sense. Even regarding the structural analysis, it is hard for some people to get used to the idea that a rule applying to stops and to *f* is less general than one applying just to stops.

tion affects the rules of the grammar rather than the lexicon. Quite commonly, such simplification leads to the loss of parts of rules from the grammar, as in the change of the umlaut rule just cited, where what is lost is
part of the rule which raises *a*. The process may even lead to the loss of
entire rules. For example, Rule 1, which devoices word-final obstruents and
once was common to all dialects of German, has been lost in some dialects
of Northern Switzerland as well as in some varieties of Yiddish. In place
of *buni:bundes* they have *bund:bundes*, with the morphophonemic distinction of voicing now again appearing phonetically in word-final position. We
know that these languages once possessed Rule 1, as it has permanently
affected the handful of isolated words like (*a*)*vek* 'away', *ap* (Yidd. *op*)
'away', which had a voiced final obstruent but lost it even morphophonemically after the phonetic devoicing took place because retention was not
motivated by any inflected forms. Hence there was also no basis for reintro-
ducing the voicing in these words once Rule 1 had dropped out of the language by simplification.

It is also evident that the *order* of rules in a grammar is subject to
historical change. Later, I will try to show that this is a special case of
simplification; right now a few examples will do. By a historically fairly old
rule of Finnish, underlying long mid vowels are diphthongized, for example,
vee > *vie*. Subsequently, the loss of certain medial voiced continuants
introduces new long mid vowels, for example, *teγe* > *tee*. In standard
Finnish, these new long mid vowels stay, and the rule introducing them
must therefore follow the diphthongization. That is, the order is

a. diphthongization
b. loss of medial voiced continuants

Yet in many dialects of Finnish the new long mid vowels have subsequently
come to join in the diphthongization, for example *teγe* > *tee* > *tie*. What this
means is that the order of the rules has changed to

a. loss of medial voiced continuants
b. diphthongization

Notice also what it does *not* mean. It does not mean what anyone coming
from traditional historical linguistics automatically tends to think it means,
namely, that in standard Finnish, where *tee* does not diphthongize,
the diphthongization rule is not ''productive.'' On the contrary, it is perfectly
productive since it must apply to underlying forms like *vee*, in which the
underlying long mid vowel must be assumed because of morphophonemic
rules such as those for past formation, for example, *vee* + *i* > *vei* like *saa*
+ *i* > *sai*, as McCawley (forthcoming *a*) has shown. The difference between
the two kinds of dialects has nothing to do with the productivity of the

diphthongization rule but simply with its order with respect to the loss of medial voiced continuants.

An example of reordering which once again involves the umlaut is the following. In the dialects of Northeastern Switzerland the back mid-vowel *o* becomes lowered to *ɔ* if it immediately precedes a dental or palatal (non-grave, or what Halle now calls a coronal) true consonant or *r*. Compare, in the Kanton of Schaffhausen (Wanner, 1941):

Retention of *o*:
before *l*: foll, holts, gold
before labials: grob, ops, holal, xnopf, doba, ofa, xopf
before velars: xoxxa, xnoxxa, rokx, kfloga, boga.
Lowering to *ɔ*:
before *r*: hɔrn, tɔrn, šɔra
before dentals and palatals: rɔss, xrɔtta, lɔsa, kšɔtta, bɔsa, pɔšt.

The distribution of allophones is given by the rule

$$
4. \quad \begin{bmatrix} V \\ -\text{high} \\ +\text{back} \end{bmatrix} \rightarrow [+\text{low}] \; / \text{———} / \; \begin{bmatrix} +\text{consonantal} \\ -\text{grave} \\ -\text{lateral} \end{bmatrix}
$$

It is necessary to restrict 4 to the back vowels. The umlauted variant *ǒ* of the vowel *o* is not lowered. The plurals of *boga* are *bǒga* and *bǒda*, both with a mid *ǒ*. Hence the relative order of 4 and umlaut must be

a. Rule 3 (umlaut)
b. Rule 4 (lowering)

This is the situation in some dialects on the northern fringe of Switzerland. Elsewhere a different state of affairs obtains.

I will take a dialect which in all other relevant respects is identical to that of the Schaffhausen area, namely that of Kesswil, in neighboring Oberthurgau (Enderlin, 1911). Rule 4 operates in unmodified form here too. All the vocabulary items cited above for the Schaffhausen dialects are found, with the same distribution of *o* and *ɔ*, in Kesswil. But the difference is that Kesswil, along with most of Northeastern Switzerland, has *ǒ* as the umlauted form of *o*, but *ɔ̌* as the umlauted form of *ɔ*. In these dialects the plural of *boga* is *bǒga*, but the plural of *bɔda* is *bɔ̌da*.

The solution which first might come to mind is that the lowering rule in 4 was simplified to apply to rounded vowels regardless of whether they are front or back. But this fails since phonemic *ǒ* does not lower to *ɔ̌* in the environment of 4. The crucial cases are such forms as *plöisli* and *fröšš* 'frog' (originally a plural form). The behavior of these isolated forms whose vowels are not lowered shows conclusively that we are in reality not dealing with a lowering of ŏ to ṓ at all, but rather with the umlauting of ɔ as well as of o. That is, the order of the rules has now become

    a. **Rule 4** (lowering)
    b. **Rule 3** (umlaut)

Applying to the same underlying forms as before, these rules now produce the segment ṓ, which did not arise under the old ordering.

3. A Criterion for Psychological Reality

Returning after this brief survey of some main types of phonological change to the initial question about the justification for assuming the psychological reality of generative grammar, suppose that we now raise this question about some aspect of generative grammar, such as the requirement that grammars contain a certain level of representation, or that they be written with the use of certain notational conventions. The conception of linguistic change sketched out above, in which linguistic structure figures crucially at several points, suggests as one test for determining the answer that we ask the question: Do the levels, the kinds of rules, and so on, which are required by this theory ever play a role in linguistic change? Taking as our example again the simple case of the brace notation, we can ask: Do blocks of rules collapsed by braces form units of a kind which can undergo systematic change? If they do, this will be a powerful argument for this notation, and if not, we will have prima facie evidence that it is a spurious notation. On such questions, evidence of the following kind can be found.

In English, underlying long vowels, which are otherwise realized as diphthongs, are shortened in two main phonological environments: before two or more consonants (for example, *keep:kept*) and in the third syllable from the end of the word (for example, *vain:vanity, severe:severity*). The rules which bring these shortenings about are the following:

$$5'. \ \ V \rightarrow [-\text{long}]/\!\!-\!\!-\!\!-\!CC$$
$$5''. \ \ V \rightarrow [-\text{long}]/\!\!-\!\!-\!\!-\!C \ldots V \ldots V$$

The theory of generative grammar requires that 5' and 5" be collapsed into a single rule as follows:

$$5. \ \ V \rightarrow [-\text{long}]/\!\!-\!\!-\!\!-\!C \left\{ \begin{array}{l} C \\ \ldots V \ldots V \end{array} \right.$$

It asserts that of the two descriptively equivalent grammars, one of which contains the two rules (5' and 5") as separate processes, and the other as a single process combined into 5 by factoring out their common part and enclosing the remainder in braces, it is the latter which is the psychologically correct one.

Rule 5 arose in Early Middle English as a generalization of a much more restricted process of shortening. In Old English, vowels were shortened before *three* or *more* consonants (for example, *gōdspell* > *godspell*, *brēmblas* > *bremblas*) and in the third syllable from the end provided they were followed by *two* consonants (for example, *blēdsian* > *bledsian*).[5] The corresponding rules were:

$$6'. \quad V \rightarrow [-\text{long}]/\text{---\!---}CCC$$
$$6''. \quad V \rightarrow [-\text{long}]/\text{---\!---}CC \cdots V \cdots V$$

Again, these rules must be collapsed as before:

$$6. \quad V \rightarrow [-\text{long}]/\text{---\!---}CC \left\{ \begin{matrix} C \\ \cdots V \cdots V \end{matrix} \right\}$$

On comparing the Old English rule in 6 and the Early Middle English (and indeed Modern English) rule in 5 we see that the only difference between them is that the later rule (5) has lost one of the required consonants in its environment. It represents a simpler, more general form of the Old English vowel-shortening process. It will apply in all cases where 6 applied but also in cases where 6 would not have applied. Evidently the change from 6 to 5 is an instance of simplification, which we have seen to be one of the basic mechanisms of linguistic change. But in a linguistic theory in which the brace notation plays no role, the relation between the Old English and the Early Middle English shortening processes is a different one. If the brace notation were not part of linguistic theory we would have two separate changes— namely, $6' > 5'$ and $6'' > 5''$—on our hands and we would be faced with the very peculiar fact that two separate, unrelated rules have undergone an identical modification at the same point in the history of English. The linguistic theory on which traditional historical grammar was based is an instance of such a theory, and traditional historical grammar has in fact failed to see the regularity here and has treated the change as two separate processes.

In the same way, we can go on to ask whether rules of the form

$$\left\{ \begin{matrix} X \\ Y \end{matrix} \right\} \rightarrow Z$$

can be added to grammars. On the assumption that sound changes are natural processes, and that the brace notation groups rules into natural blocks, we

[5]Luick (1921, pp. 204, 352–353). In isolated words the Old English shortening also applied before geminates. But in these isolated words it led to restructuring, and since there was no shortening in *derived* words in Old English, the (synchronic) phonological rule of Old English was as stated. This rule covers all cases where there was actual alternation between long and short vowels in Old English.

should predict that rules collapsed by braces should be capable of being added to grammars. There are of course numerous instances of this type of change. In fact, the addition of Rule 6 to the grammar of Old English is probably just such an instance. Similarly we should predict that rules collapsed by braces should participate in reordering as blocks.

The proposed test also has the virtue of rendering such notations eminently vulnerable to potential counterevidence from historical change. The counterclaim which would be made by the theory which excludes braces is that rules like 5′, and 5″, or 6′, and 6″, when found together in a grammar with no necessarily intervening rules forcing them apart, should be able to undergo simplification individually, in such a way that the resulting pair of rules could not subsequently be collapsed by braces. Such a change, which in this theory would be a legitimate simplification, would be neither a possible sound change nor a simplification in a theory which allows collapsing by braces, and it would therefore be excluded in the latter. If such changes could be found, they would be clear counterevidence against the brace notation and would suggest that the generalizations effected by means of braces are spurious ones. The position which excludes braces would also entail that a rule could be inserted between two rules collapsed by braces in such a way that they subsequently could no longer be so collapsed. And finally, it would also entail that the parts of rules collapsed in this way should be individually capable of reordering with other rules of the grammar. The fact that no such changes appear to exist is strong negative evidence which adds to the historical support for the essential correctness of this abbreviatory convention of generative grammar.

The aforementioned linguist C, who wanted to introduce abbreviations like

$$Y \leftarrow \left\{ X \right\} \begin{matrix} \\ \leftarrow Z \end{matrix}$$

and Pāṇini, who supported other conventions which generative grammar does not countenance, now both get a real opportunity to prove their points by showing that the blocks of rules resulting from such conventions act as units in simplification (for example, by showing cases in which the joint environment X is simplified) or by showing that they are added as units to grammars, or reordered as units with respect to other rules. There is no evidence in sight that I know of to encourage them in this search.

One answer, then, to the question concerning the empirical basis for the notational conventions of linguistic theory is that these conventions are an essential part of any attempt to characterize what is a possible linguistic change and what is not a possible linguistic change. It involves in a sense only systematically drawing the conclusions from Halle's idea (1962) that the class of possible sound changes (qua added rules) is the same as the class of possible phonological rules and bringing in the additional evidence of simplification, whose role in linguistic change Halle did not consider.

In many crucial respects this criterion for rule naturalness lends support to the assumptions which are currently made in the theory of generative grammar. But accepting the equivalence of possible sound change and possible phonological rules commits one to placing many restrictions on the notations of possible grammatical descriptions which are not at present acknowledged, and on the other hand, it suggests the need for many new conventions and new extensions of notations which should be incorporated into linguistic theory. For example, by saying that braces are needed we have only told half the story. We would like to limit the use of braces in such a way as to combine only processes which are indeed in some sense related and can jointly produce a sound change. Suppose, for example, that we found a language with three phonological processes that all applied before vowels and that did not have to be separated by other rules:

a. voiced stops become continuants
b. s becomes h
c. vowels drop

For all three processes to take place before vowels is quite natural, and examples for each of them could be cited from dozens of languages. Yet there would be something wrong about combining all three by virtue of their shared environment. It is evident that a and b are more closely related than either of them is to c, and that an adequate theory should require the combining of a and b but not c. The basis for this feeling is, I think, nothing but the fact that a and b characteristically occur together in linguistic change and thus form a natural block of phonological processes. In fact, their relatedness has really nothing to do with the fact that they share a common environment but follows from an essential kinship of the phonetic processes involved. Thus they should be grouped together in a grammar even if they both were context free. To determine the natural groupings of rules was a goal of traditional historical linguistics which has been abandoned to a large extent in structuralism, at least in America. For example, a and b would have been considered weakenings. Probably phonology would profit by attempting to develop further and to make precise such concepts, which traditional grammars use to introduce an organization into their treatments of dia-chronic phonology.

4. Diachronic Evidence Concerning Phonological Levels

The psychological reality of levels of representation which emerge in different linguistic theories is subject to verification and falsification by diachronic evidence along the same lines. A question to be asked whenever some level of representation is proposed as linguistically relevant is whether this level functions in linguistic change. For example, it would be a striking and, to my mind, conclusive piece of evidence for the reality of autonomous ("taxonomic") phonemics if it could be shown that there were sound changes whose conditioning environment could be stated naturally only at precisely this level. It should be made clear just what such a demonstration would involve. It would involve showing both that the environments of this sound change were not morphophonemic and (the crucial part) that they could not be reformulated in terms of the phonetic level without restating exactly the rules that relate the phonetic and phonemic level. Of course, it is always by definition possible to reformulate a phonemic environment in terms of phonetic representations, and what would have to be shown is therefore that such a restatement of the conditioning environment of a sound change would lose a significant generalization. A hypothetical example of what to look for would be a change in some Russian dialect which affected all voiced obstruents except [ž] and [ɣ], the two voiced obstruents in Russian which are not phonemic but always come about only by automatic voicing assimilation of /č/ and /c/. As far as I know, no one has ever presented any instance of this kind, and there is therefore no basis for the claim that the facts of sound change somehow support a level of autonomous phonemics. And as has been repeatedly argued (Halle, 1962; Chomsky and Halle, 1968; Postal, 1968, Kiparsky, 1965, 1967), the facts of sound change do provide clear evidence for a deeper level of representation in phonology.

The contention has often been made that the level of autonomous phonemics is relevant to sound change in a somewhat different way. The suggestion is that the direction of sound change is determined by tendencies toward a symmetry of phonological units. What is important for our present discussion is that these units are often held to be specifically autonomous phonemes. Much the same comments again apply: if the level in question were demonstrably the relevant one here, and the tendencies in question could really be shown to exist, then this would decisively refute those who deny its existence. But once again, the necessary proof has, to my knowledge, never been provided.

Moulton had studied the vowel systems of Swiss dialects with the purpose of testing these concepts of "phonological space." He maintained (1961) that Rule 4—the lowering of o to c before dentals, palatals, and r, whose relation to umlauting we discussed as an example of reordering——

was caused by a drive towards symmetry through "filling" the "empty slot" in the systems which Moulton supposes that these dialects possessed before the lowering took place:

$$(A)\quad
\begin{array}{ccc}
i & \ddot{u} & u \\
\vartheta & \dot{o} & o \\
 & \varepsilon & \\
 & \ae & \alpha
\end{array}
\qquad
(B)\quad
\begin{array}{ccc}
i & \ddot{u} & u \\
\vartheta & \dot{o} & o \\
 & \varepsilon & \\
 & & \alpha
\end{array}$$

But what is the justification for assuming that System B had this asymmetrical structure rather than the symmetrical structure, C, which one would have normally supposed it to have?

$$(C)\quad
\begin{array}{ccc}
i & \ddot{u} & u \\
\vartheta & \dot{o} & o \\
 & \varepsilon & \\
 & & \alpha
\end{array}$$

Why did Moulton not assign *a* to the back vowels in these dialects as he did in the *A* dialects? Moulton has discussed the reason for his choice in another article (Moulton, 1960, p. 174), where the justification given for the asymmetrical System *B* is that these dialects underwent the lowering by Rule 4: "The fact that the subsequent development of the vowel system of the North was parallel not to that of the West and Center but to that of the East confirms the belief that arrangement [*B* above] represents linguistic reality more faithfully, and suggests that arrangement [*C* above] would indeed be only a playful manipulation of symbols on paper." In other words, these dialects had an asymmetrical system because they underwent lowering of *o* to *ɔ*, and they underwent lowering of *o* to *ɔ* because they had an asymmetrical system!

In sum, one prediction to which such theories lead is that certain phonological changes should be determined by whether or not pairs of certain sounds are contrastive in some phonetic environment and hence that isoglosses formed by phonological changes should characteristically be coextensive with boundaries between different autonomous phonemic systems. Other predictions are certainly also entailed, and the cases I have mentioned by no means constitute a full or even representative illustration of the range of predictions made, nor of the kind of evidence that is available to test them. But they nevertheless show how this theory and related ones do have very specific consequences which can be tested fully on historical material. I would guess that when this is done it will turn out that real enough tendencies towards phonological symmetry exist, but that they have nothing to do with the autonomous phonemic level for which they are often claimed. Rather they are probably brought about by simplificatory phonological changes such as rule simplification and rule reordering, and the symmetry they result in is phonetic rather than phonemic symmetry. This at any rate is what the Swiss German dialect material recently investigated by Moulton suggests.

5. Diachronic Evidence Concerning Features and Underlying Representations

The particular Swiss German example that I have talked about also raises a nest of further problems unrelated to that of the reality of the autonomous phonemic level, but highly relevant to the general topic of the relevance of linguistic change to linguistic universals. It will have been noticed that phonemic System *A* above, with four distinctive vowel heights, is a clear counterexample to Jakobson's distinctive feature system, which allows only three phonemic degrees of vowel height to exist in a language. First of all, the four degrees clearly contrast in simple, underived words and cannot be predicted by any general rules from some system with only three heights in any way that would not be ad hoc. For example,

ælf 'eleven'	šelm 'rogue'	geld 'money'	bild 'picture
sæmel 'stool'	swebal 'sulphur'	šnebal 'sty (in	šwibal 'grip'
hæks 'witch'	xreps 'crayfish'	the eye)'	blits 'lightning'
hællar 'small coin'	šella 'bell'	nets 'net'	willa 'will'
	xella 'scoop'		

In addition these dialects have a phoneme *a* which is quite distinct from all of these front vowels. Evidently, then, Jakobson's features compact and diffuse (low and high) should be replaced by two other features which allow four distinctive degrees of vowel height. A natural one would be the following:

	æ	ɛ	e	i
High	−	−	+	+
Mid	−	+	+	−

Yet if we shift our point of view somewhat and regard impossible systems simply as the end points of increasing scales of markedness, the proposed change to allow four heights is a relatively minor one. In a sense, these dialects, particularly if the historical evidence is brought in, support Jakobson's thesis in the modified form that vowel systems with four heights are complex, that is, highly marked systems, in the technical sense. For historically, a four-height system of this kind had to arise in all High German dialects. However, everywhere, with the exception of some tiny Swiss areas in Appenzell and Toggenburg, the four heights have been reduced to three by mergers either of the two mid vowels or of the two low vowels. These mergers have taken place quite independently in numerous dialects and thus have the character of drift or simplification rather than of normal sound changes. What this seems to indicate is that systems of four vowel heights are unstable because of their complexity, a conclusion which is indicated in any case by the rarity of such systems in the languages of the world.

The particular way in which these four-height systems have merged to three in the various dialects is itself a small piece of historical support for the feature system which I have proposed. The other possible alternative of characterizing four vowel heights by two features would be this:

	æ	ɛ	e	i
High	−	−	+	+
Raised	−	+	−	+

There would be no natural way of formulating the merger of mid vowels here since mid vowels do not make up a natural class under these features. On the other hand, this alternative suggests mergers such as æ and ɛ or e and i which certainly do not occur. Vowel shifts of the type $i > æi$, which are common in many languages, would also be expressed more simply in the system I have proposed. However, an alternative which may be even preferable and should in any case not be counted out yet is that vowel height is not broken down into two binary dimensions at all but forms a single dimension expressed by a feature which in underlying representations can assume at most four values (and must assume at least two).

Against the analysis which posits four heights of vowels in these dialects one might try to carry the argument that this analysis is implausible because closely related dialects have only three heights, and one would expect closely related dialects to differ not in their underlying phonemic system, but only in the rules which relate phonemic representations to phonetic representations. This would be a complete non sequitur. It is an empirical observation that related dialects often have the same phonemic system, but it is not a theoretical condition on related dialects that this should be the case. To say otherwise would be to credit children with historical or dialectological knowledge which they cannot possibly possess. The fact that the children of each generation in learning their language take a fresh look at the facts means that there is reason for underlying representations to be transmitted only when the synchronic facts of the language warrant it. The argument is just as irrelevant, and for just the same reason, as it would be to maintain that language L must have rule R in its grammar because R was a sound change in L.

A more difficult objection is based on the fact that æ in these dialects is the productive umlaut of a. To account for morphological umlaut in a language like German it is necessary to set up some abstract conditioning environment which will be a property of certain endings, such as plural *-er*.

Whether this is a feature [± umlaut] as proposed by Zwicky (1967) or some phonological property of underlying representations will not matter here. Whatever this abstract environment is, generative phonology at present allows—and indeed probably requires—the trick of making it an obligatory part of isolated words like *schön, plötzlich, Tür,* which have umlaut vowels that correspond to no back vowels in any related forms. These words are then entered with underlying back vowels which undergo obligatory umlauting by virtue of this property of their underlying representations. The effect is to do away altogether with umlaut vowels in the phonemic system. In our case, then, *æ* would never be treated as phonemic and there would be only three phonemic vowel heights to worry about.

It is again the historical evidence which shows that this trick is wrong and that words like *schön, plötzlich, Tür* must have phonemic umlaut vowels. To see this let us go back to the example of reordering involving Rules 3 and 4 in Northeastern Switzerland. It will be recalled that as a result of the reordering, derived *ö* as in plural *böda* became *ǫ* but phonemic *ǫ̈* as in *plösti* was not changed. There would be no way of accounting for a change like this (by no means an atypical case) in a theory which asserted that *all* umlaut vowels are underlying back vowels, for then we would have no natural way of telling apart those that are really so derived and do undergo lowering from those which are only fictitiously so derived and do not undergo lowering. This linguistic change cannot be accounted for unless phonological theory is tightened up in some way to exclude tricks of such a kind. It is interesting to note that whatever exactly the right way to do this turns out to be, it will bring the underlying representations of generative phonology a step closer to Sapir's descriptive practice (McCawley, 1967). And once this necessary move is made, the existence of systems with four vowel heights cannot be argued away.[6]

This last conclusion has the peculiar status of at present resting entirely on historical evidence, and of a fairly indirect kind at that. Whether or not we draw it depends on what we consider the subject matter of linguistics to be. We could not draw it if we regarded a grammar simply as a theory of the sentences of a language, and a linguistic theory as a theory of grammars. For this position would entail that linguistic change is no concern of linguistic theory, although it might of course be a pleasant bonus if linguistic theory could be usefully "applied" to questions of linguistic change. But it would not cause us to demand of a linguistic theory that it must (in conjunction with a theory of linguistic change) provide an explanation of the linguistic regulari-

6 David Stampe points out to me that the naturalness condition he proposes (at this same conference) requires exactly the underlying representations which we have seen to be justified on historical grounds.

ties of diachrony. It is a very different matter if we regard a grammar as a theory of linguistic competence, and the field of linguistics as the study of universal grammar. On this view, which forms the topic of this conference and which I share, the facts of linguistic change assume a new relevance as empirical evidence on the nature of language. We must be prepared to allow them to bear on even purely synchronic questions and, for example, to let the fact that some phonological change is explainable by one linguistic theory but not by another carry weight in the choice between these two theories. The application of linguistic change to linguistic change now becomes at least as important as the converse process.

The above rather scattered observations illustrate various types of inferences that can be made about grammatical form from from the ways in which it shapes linguistic change. The reason I have dealt with phonological changes and not syntactic ones is partly that I know more about phonology, but also that the historical facts are here much easier to come by and the evidence they give is more needed in phonology than in syntax. I have been concerned not so much with establishing the virtues and faults of specific notations, levels, and so forth—much more evidence would be needed for that in almost every kind of problem dealt with above—as with making a case for the legitimacy and potential fruitfulness of certain general patterns of inference from linguistic change to the nature of grammar. In no case have the conclusions depended on very specific or controversial assumptions about linguistic change. The basic assumption from which these conclusions follow has been the very tame one that where grammar is involved in linguistic change it is involved in terms of its natural components and rules.

It is not so with another kind of inference from linguistic change to grammatical form to which I should now like to turn. This inference is based so heavily on the existence of grammatical simplification as a form of linguistic change that before proceeding to it I should like to outline the justification for assuming the existence of such a form of linguistic change.

6. Formal Justification for Simplification

The conclusion that such changes as simplification and reordering must exist does not and could not rest just on the fact that we observe related dialects to differ in the ordering of their rules, or to show minor differences in the details of essentially shared rules. That such differences are typical isoglosses is true but compatible with the position that addition of rules is the only form of phonological change. For as long as we look at dialects without knowledge of their historical origin we could explain any rule-ordering difference between them in a wave-theory fashion. For example, a spreading rule might be adopted at one position in the sequence of rules in one dialect and at some other position in another. There is another wave-theory effect which can cause pairs of rules to be differently ordered in different dialects. If Rule A spreads from West to East and Rule B spreads from East to West across some dialect area, then, if the two rules are critically ordered with respect to each other, the Western area will end up with the order A, B and the Eastern area with the order B, A. Undoubtedly these are both, in fact, quite common causes of ordering differences between dialects. Small differences in the form of rules can well occur in the course of their diffusion from one dialect to another. It has been observed that in such borrowing a narrowing down in the scope of rules often takes place. Thus the diphthongization of the long high vowels of Middle High German during its spread southward in Swiss territory was restricted to word-final position at a certain point before it stopped spreading altogether. Compare also the gradual curtailment of the High German consonant shift in the so-called Rhenish Fan.[7]

However, we find just the same types of minor differences in the form of rules and in their ordering when we compare successive stages of the same dialect rather than geographically adjacent dialects, and here the wave-theory and imperfect borrowing explanations are excluded. Furthermore, in such cases the form of rules almost always changes in the direction of greater simplicity. Can such changes be accounted for on the assumption that addition of rules is the only form of phonological change?

Consider the Finnish example cited in Section 2, in which the diphthongization rule was dialectally shifted down to follow loss of medial voiced continuants so as to apply to the long vowels which arose by this historically later rule (for example, *teye* > *tee* > *tie*). Technically, it is not impossible to account for this change by means of added rules. There are even two ways of doing it. One is to assume that a rule of loss of medial voiced continuants, identical with the original one, was entered before diphthongization, causing the original one to become vacuous and to be dropped. The other is to assume that a diphthongization rule, identical with the original diphthongization rule, was entered *after* loss of medial voiced continuants. The optimal grammar for the resulting output would once again be the desired one. The unfortunate aspect of this is the arbitrariness of the choice between the two descriptions. It is hard to see how the distinction between them could correspond to any linguistic difference. The two distinct grammars containing an identical rule at two different points which are required as virtual intermediaries seem to be mere artifacts of a theory which

[7]E. Bach has pointed out to me that these examples are not certain. If, as he suggests, rules are never narrowed down in borrowing, the case for simplification becomes ever stronger.

excludes reordering as a mechanism of change and therefore must make an
inappropriate extension of rule adding to account for a quite different kind of
process.

The difficulties become considerable in such a case as the loss of
word-final devoicing in Swiss German and Yiddish. We cannot, clearly,
simply suppose that a late rule which made final obstruents voiced was
added. Such a rule could not distinguish between morphophonemically
voiced and voiceless stops and would wrongly turn into *bund* not only the
bunt that is related to *bunde* but also the *bunt* that is related to *bunte*. In
desperation we would take recourse to an ad hoc rule which somehow would
provide morphophonemically voiced stops with a diacritic feature before
they got devoiced and later would use this diacritic feature as an environment
for revoicing, after which the diacritic feature could be deleted again. Obviously this bears not the faintest resemblance to what actually happened,
and no one would want to salvage a theory at the price of such an absurd
analysis.

Chomsky and Halle (1968) discuss a convention for handling exceptions to rules which might be used in this particular example. The idea is that
grammars can contain rules of the form

$$X \leftarrow] \; [\; - \text{next rule}]$$

where X is a specification of the special cases in which some rule must not
apply. Then it would be possible to say that a rule

$$[\quad] \leftarrow] \; [\; - \text{next rule}]$$

was placed directly before the devoicing of word-final obstruents, thus preventing everything from undergoing it. The inoperative devoicing rule would
then simply not be incorporated into the grammars of the next generation.

The difference here is not merely notational. The exception-rule solution generalizes neither to the reordering example that was just cited nor to
cases like the simplification of the umlaut rule from 2 to 3 which was
mentioned earlier. Since what was deleted here was *part* of a rule and the
Chomsky-Halle convention for handling exceptions does not allow items to
be exceptions to parts of rules, the solution which the convention made
possible in the previous case is not available here. The best we can do is to
say that the change consists of two separate but simultaneous events: first, the
rendering inapplicable of the old umlaut rule (2) by the placement of a
Chomsky-Halle exception rule before it, and second, the entering of the new
umlaut rule (3) in its stead. That is, we are forced to treat this event as a
composite product of two simultaneous changes, one of which alone would
have far more spectacular consequences than the two have together. This
leaves us completely in the dark as to why so many dialects (quite indepen-

dently of each other, as is clear from the geographical distribution) should have undergone such a complicated pair of changes.

We see that to account for such examples by added rules, we would be forced to relax the proposed restriction that a sound change is the addition of a rule to the grammar to the extent of allowing a single historical change to involve the addition of *two* rules. In that case all arguments like those in Section 3 about sound change as a criterion for rule naturalness at once go out the window. And if this is done we also prepare a welcome for innumerable absurd descriptions of other changes. For example, in the case of the Finnish reordering of diphthongization and loss of medial voiced continuants (see Section 2 above) there are now two further alternatives which add to the general arbitrariness: the change might consist of simultaneously making diphthongization inapplicable and adding an exact replica of it after the loss of medial voiced continuants, or of simultaneously making loss of medial voiced continuants inapplicable and adding an exact replica of it before diphthongization.

Also, it is now just as easy to express the reverse change, that is, a change as a result of which the order

a. loss of medial voiced continuants
b. diphthongization

changes into

a. diphthongization
b. loss of medial voiced continuants

The effect of this would be that all *ie* diphthongs derived by way of *ee* from *eye* would revert to their intermediate representation *ee*, while the *ie* the diph-thongs derived from basic *ee* would stay unchanged. There is no doubt that a theory of linguistic change should either completely exclude the possibility of such a change or at least reflect the obvious fact that that it would be a far more complex and unlikely historical event than what actually happened. But the version to which the theory that rule addition is the only form of linguistic change has been driven at this point is completely incapable of doing so. As the brute necessity of somehow accommodating one set of data has forced it to be relaxed and extended more and more, it has lost the capacity of expressing the facts about sound change that originally motivated it.

7. Simplification and Language Acquisition

To avoid this hopeless mess, the concept of simplification would be necessary even if we were concerned merely with characterizing the possible ways in which successive stages of a language could differ (which would be enough for purposes of linguistic reconstruction). But we also would like to find an explanation for why languages can change in the ways that they do. In that case, the reasons for assuming that simplification is a form of linguistic change become more compelling still. We cannot, then, close our eyes to the fact that the kind of driftlike changes which rule addition fails to handle without the special acrobatics of which samples were performed in Section 6 result in just the kind of grammars that appear spontaneously as intermediate stages in the course of the child's language-learning process.

I am not thinking just of the fact that instances of morphological analogy (*oxes*, *bringed*) are as characteristic of child language as they are of historical change, although this is perhaps the most evident instance of the correspondence. The parallelism goes deeper than that. For example, there is in many languages a drift toward multiple negation, as in substandard English 'I don't see nothing nowhere'. Such multiple negation has developed in the Romance languages and elsewhere in Europe too. Jespersen tried to attribute this drift to some vague tendency toward redundancy which he thought governed the direction of linguistic change. But this can hardly be true, for in other languages, such as Finnish, no comparable drift toward multiple negation is observed. Then it cannot be true that multiple negation is simply a general target in the direction of which all languages develop. In fact I think it is true that multiple negation appears only in those languages that have the equivalent of Klima's *neg*-incorporation rule which produces negative quantifiers such as in English *nobody*, *nothing* and French *rien*.[8] Surely this is related to the facts about the development of negation in child language found by Bellugi (cited from McNeill, 1966). She discovered that at the point at which the child's sentences like

I didn't see something.

You don't want some supper.

give way to sentences with negative quantifiers like *nobody*, *nothing*, *no supper*, a period of multiple negation at first sets in. As the child first formulates his *neg*-incorporation rule, it has not the form of standard English but of substandard English (which he very well may never have heard); and instead of producing the "normal" sentences like

I saw nothing.

Nobody likes me.

he at first comes out with

I didn't see nothing.

Nobody don't like me.

Thus some relationship between "substandard" *neg*-incorporation and "stan-

---

[8]Finnish has indefinite pronouns such as *kukaan*, *mikään*, corresponding to English *anybody*, *anything*, but a negative cannot be incorporated into them to form any equivalents of *nobody*, *nothing*.

dard" *neg*-incorporation may be responsible for the fact that the former is the natural predecessor of the latter in the development of a child's linguistic system and also the natural result of the latter by linguistic change.

These facts begin to add up when we think of language acquisition as a process in which the child arrives at adult grammar gradually by attempting to match to the speech it hears a succession of hypotheses of an increasing order of complexity (in the linguistic sense of complexity) as these increasingly complex hypotheses become available to the child through maturational change. For phonology this was clearly shown by Jakobson's spectacular discovery that the child learns phonemes in a largely fixed order, which is determined not externally by the order or frequency with which they are heard, but internally by their relative linguistic complexity, as reflected also in the rules governing the possible phonemic systems of the languages of the world (Jakobson, 1942). Thus the child first produces the maximally unmarked, unvoiced, unaspirated stops, even if these, as in English, happen not to occur (except in some special environments) and only then splits up this first stop series into two series. In phonology, then, the order in which a child incorporates a particular piece of data into his internalized grammar is determined not by frequency or order of presentation, but by the readiness of the child to assimilate the kind of structure that underlies it. If we assume that the order in which the syntactic rules of the child unfold is internally determined in the same way, we can think of the child's multiple negation as analogous to his unvoiced, unaspirated stop in the sense that both are necessary prior structures which can be discarded only after the full structure develops. This is reasonable in view of the fact that multiple negation is produced by a version of *neg*-incorporation which is in two respects simpler than the adult version of this transformation. In the first place, the adult rule not only adds a *neg* to the quantifier, but it also deletes the original *neg* after the tense; this additional operation of deletion is absent from the child's first version of the rule. Secondly, the adult rule adds a *neg* to just one single quantifier in the sentence, whereas the child spreads the *neg* over all quantifiers that appear in the sentence, producing such specimens as the following:

I can't do nothing with no string.

Normally these oversimplified intermediate grammars which the child constructs on its way to adult language eventually give way to the full complexity of the adult system. The linguistic change of simplification takes place on those relatively rare occasions when some feature of these intermediate grammars survives into adulthood and becomes adopted by the speech community as a new linguistic norm. See Jakobson's remark (p. 332 of the 1962 reprinting):

Die Sprachveränderung ist kein äusserer Beitrag, den die Kinder dem Sprachgebilde aufzwingen, sondern sie antizipieren dessen innerlich vorherbestimmte, sozusagen in der Luft schwebende Umwandlungen.

That such survival is possible is not quite so surprising when we consider the extreme imperviousness of children to adult correction of their speech, as illustrated for multiple negation by the following dialogue (McNeill, 1966, p. 69):

CHILD: Nobody don't like me.
MOTHER: No, say 'nobody likes me'.
CHILD: Nobody don't like me.
(eight repetitions of this dialogue)
MOTHER: No, now listen carefully; say *'nobody likes me'*.
CHILD: Oh! Nobody don't likes me.

Thus we can relate the concepts of rule addition and simplification to adult and child language, respectively. The typical form of rule addition is the borrowing of rules among adults; simplification typically occurs in the learning of language by children. An interesting consequence of this is that isoglosses formed by the spread of rules over a speech territory should form large, coherent dialect areas, whereas those formed by simplification should be characteristically discontinuous because of independent development of the same change in several speech communities. The historically interesting isoglosses, therefore, should be based on the presence versus absence of rules, and not on differences in the form and order of shared rules. Indeed, this is what dialectologists have always implicitly assumed. The boundaries between the major dialect areas of Germany are drawn according to the rules they have, such as the consonant shifts. The isogloss between the two forms of the umlaut rule, 2 and 3 (that is, between *e* and *æ* as the productive umlaut of *a*), would form a useless patchwork of no historical significance. Nor would anyone suppose a historical relationship between Yiddish and Swiss German on the grounds that they share the loss of the word-final devoicing rule. Very schematically, the two types of isoglosses would look like this (shaded areas are the innovating ones):

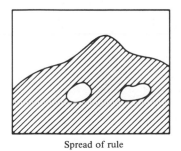

Spread of rule

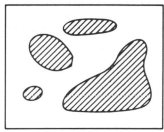

Simplification

8. Reordering as Simplification

Reordering resembles simplification both in the negative property that rule addition miserably fails to do justice to it and in the positive property of its driftlike character. I shall now claim that reordering is in fact a special case of simplification, and that the direction of reordering is predicted by general principles which assign certain types of order a higher value than others. If this can be established, then current phonological theory, which does not distinguish different kinds of linear order, is wrong and must be revised to account for this asymmetry.

To be convinced that reordering is a one-way affair, much as other simplification is, it is enough to examine the individual examples. For instance, many Swiss dialects have put the umlaut rule (3) after $o > \jmath$ (Rule 4), but none of these have made the reverse switch, and we could not easily imagine it taking place. And a dialect of Finnish in which *tie* from *teɣe > tee* becomes *tee* again but *vie* from *vee* retains the diphthong, that is, a dialect in which diphthongization reverts to its original position before the loss of medial voiced continuants (which I will now call $\gamma > \emptyset$ for short) is inconceivable. The question is how this asymmetry, intuitively evident enough in each particular case, can be given a general characterization.

Of the various functional relationships that can hold between rules, two are of relevance here. One way in which two rules, *A* and *B*, can be functionally related is that the application of *A* creates representations to which *B* is applicable. That is, the application of *A* converts forms to which *B* cannot apply into forms to which *B* can apply; schematically:

$$A. \ [\quad] > [\phi]$$
$$B. \ [\phi] > [\quad]$$

Such a relationship holds for example between $\gamma > \emptyset$ (*teɣe > tee*) and diphthongization (*tec > tie*) in our Finnish example. If the rules are applied in that order, $\gamma > \emptyset$ supplies a set of new cases (namely those derived from *eɣe*) to which diphthongization can apply. In such a situation, call *A* a *feeding rule* relative to *B* (for example, $\gamma > \emptyset$ is a feeding rule relative to diphthongization). Call this relationship between rules a *feeding relationship* (for example, $\gamma > \emptyset$ and diphthongization are in a feeding relationship) and the linear order in which the feeding rule precedes a *feeding order* (for example, 1. $\gamma > \emptyset$, 2. diphthongization is a feeding order). Then one of the principles that determine the direction of reordering is

I. Feeding order tends to be maximized.

Schematically:

$$\begin{array}{lll} A. \ [\phi] > [\quad] & & B. \ [\quad] > [\phi] \\ B. \ [\quad] > [\phi] & > & A. \ [\phi] > [\quad] \end{array}$$

A further example of I involves the several palatalizations in Slavic. By the so-called first palatalization, *k* and *g* became *č* and *ž̌*, respectively, before front vowels and *y*, for example, **kĭto > čĭto* 'what', **givŭ *ž̌ιvŭ* 'alive'.[9]

7. $\begin{bmatrix} +\text{consonantal} \\ -\text{diffuse} \end{bmatrix} \rightarrow \begin{bmatrix} -\text{grave} \\ +\text{strident} \end{bmatrix} \ / \ \rule{2cm}{0.4pt} \ \begin{bmatrix} -\text{consonantal} \\ -\text{back} \end{bmatrix}$

But the resulting voiced affricate *ž̌* has become a continuant *ž* in all Slavic languages by the rule

8. $\begin{bmatrix} +\text{voiced} \\ -\text{grave} \\ +\text{strident} \end{bmatrix} \rightarrow [\,+\text{continuant}\,]$

For example, **ž̌ivu > živŭ.*

Subsequently new front vowels came to stand after velars by the rule

9.   ai → ě

By the so-called second palatalization *k'* and *g'* (derived from *k* and *g* by an earlier rule) became *c* and *ʒ* before these new front vowels, for example, **k'ěna > cěna* 'price', **g'ělo > ʒělo* 'very':

10. $\begin{bmatrix} +\text{obstruent} \\ -\text{grave} \\ -\text{strident} \\ -\text{diffuse} \end{bmatrix} \rightarrow \begin{bmatrix} +\text{strident} \\ +\text{diffuse} \end{bmatrix}$

The resulting affricate *ʒ*, unlike the earlier *ž̌*, is retained in Old Church Slavic and in modern Polish. The grammars of these languages have Rules 7–10 as phonological rules in an order that matches their relative chronology. But elsewhere in Slavic, *ʒ* also has been replaced by its corresponding continuant, namely *z*, for example, *ʒělo > zělo*. These languages have the same four rules, but 8 must here follow 10, in order to apply to the affricate produced by the second palatalization as well. It is these two rules between which the feeding relationship obtains. Rule 10 is the feeding rule and the reordering establishes a feeding order between 10 and 8.

It should be noted that this relationship is a matter of the function and not of the form of the rules. In the Slavic example there is, as is often the case elsewhere too, a formal similarity between the related rules in that they mention some of the same features, and so on. But it would not be possible to

[9]Other aspects of the Slavic palatalizations are dealt with by Halle and Lightner in a forthcoming study. My knowledge of the rules is based entirely on their work. I state the rule here with the Jakobsonian features rather than any of the recent alternative proposals which have greatly improved the system.

define the correct relationship on the basis of the form of the rules. The two Finnish rules previously cited have very little in common, and the relationship is simply based on properties of the derivations the language has.

Another possible functional relationship between two rules is that *A* removes representations to which *B* would otherwise apply:

$$A. \ [\ \ ] \ > \ [\sim\!\phi]$$
$$B. \ [\phi] \ > \ [\ \ ]$$

Such a relationship holds for example between umlaut (*A*) and *o* > *ɔ* (*B*) in the example of Section 2. Thus the application of umlaut turns *o* into *ö*, a front vowel to which the lowering rule is no longer applicable. If the lowering rule comes first in the ordering, it applies, turning *o* to *ɔ*, and umlaut can then still apply. In the terms of the Indian grammatical tradition, umlaut is here the *nitya* or "constant" rule. Call *A* a *bleeding rule* relative to *B*, the relationship between *A* and *B* a *bleeding relationship*, and the ordering in which *A* precedes *B* a *bleeding order*. The principle which underlies the asymmetry of order in this case is the following:

II. Bleeding order tends to be minimized.

$$\begin{matrix} A. \ [\ \ ] \ > \ [\sim\!\phi] \\ B. \ [\phi] \ > \ [\ \ ] \end{matrix} \quad > \quad \begin{matrix} B. \ [\phi] \ > \ [\ \ ] \\ A. \ [\ \ ] \ > \ [\sim\!\phi] \end{matrix}$$

In this way the original order, in which umlaut preceded lowering, became switched around into the new order, in which the bleeding did not take place.

As another illustration of the effect of II, consider the relation of two rules pertaining to voiced obstruents in German. One of them, which is historically the older, is the devoicing of obstruents in word-final position (for example, *bund* > *bunt*, *tāg* > *tāk*). This is Rule 1, which has come up in the discussion several times already. The other, found only in a certain group of dialects (Schirmunski, 1962, p. 302), is the spirantization of postvocalic voiced stops, for example, *tāgə* > *tāɣə*, *sāgt* > *sāɣt* (> *sāxt*). Originally, devoicing preceded postvocalic spirantization. Since, with this order, morphophonemic final voiced stops lost their voicing before spirantization applied, they remained stops and the contrast of *tāk:tāɣə* resulted. This bleeding order, in which word-final devoicing deprives spirantization of some of the voiced stops to which it would otherwise apply, is still retained in some Alsatian, Bavarian, and Middle German dialects. More frequently the reverse ordering is found, with final voiced stops undergoing first spirantization (*tāg* > *tāɣ*) and then devoicing (*tāɣ* > *tāx*.) This order is widespread and especially common in the Low German dialects. We know that this order is a secondary development because some words like (*a*)*wek* (Standard German *weg*), where the voicing of the stop had no morphophonemic support, failed to spirantize even in the reordering dialects. This would be inexplicable unless we suppose that the devoicing was historically earlier even in these dialects in spite of the fact that it is synchronically later.

Another example can be cited from this same familiar area. A very widespread sound change in German dialects (Schirmunski, 1962, p. 212) is the rounding of *ā* to *ɔ̄*. As *ǣ*, the umlaut of *ā*, is unaffected by this change, it brings about alternations between *ɔ̄* and *ǣ* such as *šwɔ̄n* 'swan'. *šwǣn* 'Pl.', *špɔ̄t* 'late':*špǣtər* 'later'. Hence there is a bleeding order between the rules

    a. umlaut
    b. ā > ɔ̄

Many modern German dialects have just this system (see Rabeler, 1911, and Hotzenköcherle, 1934, for a Low German and Swiss German dialect, respectively). In others (for example, Wanner, 1941) the system has changed in that the umlauted form of *ɔ̄* is *ō̄*, for example, *šwōn*, *špōter*. The grammatical difference is that umlaut now applies after rather than before the rounding of *ā*. As phonemic *ǣ* in words like *tsǣ* 'tough' and *lær̄* 'empty' stays unrounded (more proof of the correctness of the argument is in Section 5) it is clear that the possibility of a simplification of the rounding rule to all long compact vowels is excluded and we are again faced with a case of reordering, which conforms perfectly to Principle II.

There is a more general principle underlying the two reordering tendencies (I and II) which combines them under a single wider concept of fuller utilization and makes their nature intuitively much clearer:

    III. Rules tend to shift into the order which allows their fullest utilization in the grammar.

If I am right that such a principle determines the direction in which reordering proceeds, then it follows that the order toward which rules gravitate in this way is linguistically simpler than its opposite. It is hard to see what other explanation there could be for such a consistent tendency toward a specific kind of order in linguistic change. As a convenient designation for the order types which are shunned and preferred according to Principles I–III, I suggest *marked* and *unmarked* order, respectively. It may well be that marking conventions analogous to those which assign the unmarked feature values in segmental phonology are the appropriate device for reflecting the asymmetry of ordering relations as well.

9. Leveling and Extension

As further justification for my assertion that unidirectional reordering tendencies exist and that they obey Principles I–III, I want to adduce an unexpected parallelism which obtains between reordering, if so constrained, and rule simplification. We can begin with a distinction drawn in traditional and structural historical grammar between two types of analogy, one called *leveling* and the other called *polarization* or *extension*. By leveling was meant roughly that existing alternations are either curtailed or eliminated altogether, with the result that allomorphs of some morphemes become more similar to each other or merge completely. Thus the change of *bunt:bunde* to *bund:bunde* would have been regarded as a leveling of the alternation of voiced and voiceless stops in word-final position. The simplification of the umlaut rule (2) to its other version (3), which replaced *kraft:kreftig* by *kraft:kræftig* would have been regarded as a leveling of the height alternation in favor of the low vowel throughout the paradigm.

Polarization, or extension, on the other hand, refers to a type of analogical change in which existing alternations spread to new instances. Here linguistic contrasts come to be more fully implemented than before, whereas leveling has precisely the opposite effect. We would presumably be dealing with extension if, for example, the alternation of medial voicing and final voicelessness in obstruents as in *tāge:tāk, bunde:bunt*, instead of being eliminated altogether, had become extended beyond its original domain to the sonorants, as has in fact happened in Icelandic. The change of the limited Old English vowel shortening rule (6) to its present more general form (5) is another instance of extension.

This distinction, implicit in traditional historical studies, though rarely drawn systematically (but see Hoenigswald, 1960, pp. 63, 108), is a useful one, partly for reasons that have to do with linguistic reconstruction. Leveling will often be recoverable by historical reconstruction, because of the relic forms which reflect older linguistic stages that leveling leaves behind. Extension, however, will in general not be so recoverable because, with certain very interesting exceptions, it cannot leave relic forms behind. The difference between these two types of analogy can be defined in terms of the formal differences of two kinds of rule simplification in a very straightforward manner. Rules consist of two parts, a structural analysis, which specifies to what forms the rule applies, and a structural change, which says what happens to these forms. In the customary notation for phonological rules, the structural change is the part between the arrow and the slash and the structural analysis is everything else. Then any rule simplification which modifies the structural change of a rule (whether or not it also modifies the structural analysis) is a *leveling*, and any rule simplification which does not modify the structural change of a rule is an *extension*. Thus the loss of final devoicing (Rule 1) and the simplification of Rule 2 to Rule 3 affect the structural change of the rule and are hence levelings, but the change of the shortening rule in English did not affect its structural change and is hence an extension.

It is a fairly surprising fact that the two kinds of reorderings we have found, namely those governed by I and II, correspond pairwise to these two kinds of rule simplifications and in turn to the traditional distinction between extension and leveling. Reordering by II results in leveling and thus corresponds to simplification in the structural change of a rule. For example, the effect of placing umlaut after $o > ɔ$ is that the height alternation in *bɔd ə:böd ə* and innumerable similar cases is leveled and the resulting forms, *bɔdə:bɔ̈də*, retain the low vowel throughout the paradigm. So, too, the reordering of spirantization and word-final devoicing results in the dropping of a two-feature alternation, *tak:taɣə* (with change of both voicing and continuance), in favor of a simpler one-feature alternation, *tax:taɣ ə* (with a continuant throughout the paradigm), that is, again in leveling. In their effect on surface forms and on the relation of surface forms, leveling by simplification in the structural change of rules and leveling by reordering in accordance with Principle II have similar effects in that they make more alike the different shapes in which morphemes appear. But they bring this effect about in different ways because leveling by rule simplification brings the forms closer to the base forms, whereas leveling by reordering takes forms farther away from their base forms. But both types share the property that they can leave behind relic forms which make the recovery of these processes by linguistic reconstruction a possibility. What guarantees us the earlier grammar in each of these cases are the forms like *weg* (in the case where the devoicing rule is lost and in the case in which it is reordered with spirantization), *plötsli* (in reordering of umlaut and $o > ɔ$), and so on.

On the other hand, reordering by I results in extension (polarization) and so corresponds to simplification which affects only the structural analysis of rules. In the case of the Slavic palatalizations (see Section 8), for example, the voiced stop:voiced affricate alternation is polarized into a voiced stop:voiced continuant alternation. It is clear that in this case any forms which undergo the old form of the rules are also going to undergo them after the reordering, so that relic forms which would allow reconstruction of the change could not be created.

These relationships are summarized in the following table.

Reordering	Corresponds to simplification of	Reconstructible by relic forms?	Surface effect
by I	Structural analysis only	No	Extension (polarization)
by II	Structural change	Yes	Leveling